Computer Communications and Networks

For further volumes:
http://www.springer.com/series/4198

The Computer Communications and Networks series is a range of textbooks, monographs and handbooks. It sets out to provide students, researchers and non-specialists alike with a sure grounding in current knowledge, together with comprehensible access to the latest developments in computer communications and networking.

Emphasis is placed on clear and explanatory styles that support a tutorial approach, so that even the most complex of topics is presented in a lucid and intelligible manner.

Siani Pearson • George Yee
Editors

Privacy and Security for Cloud Computing

 Springer

Editors
Siani Pearson
Cloud and Security Laboratory
HP Labs
Filton, Bristol, UK

George Yee
Department of Systems
  and Computer Engineering
Carleton University
Ottawa, ON, Canada

Series Editor
Professor A.J. Sammes, BSc, MPhil, PhD,
  FBCS, CEng
Centre for Forensic Computing
Cranfield University
DCMT, Shrivenham
Swindon
UK

ISSN 1617-7975
ISBN 978-1-4471-5793-9   ISBN 978-1-4471-4189-1 (eBook)
DOI 10.1007/978-1-4471-4189-1
Springer London Heidelberg New York Dordrecht

Foreword

We live in a period where almost every member of the IT community argues about cloud computing and its security and trustworthiness, and very often does this in generic terms or, worse still, with statements based on false myths and a FUD (fear, uncertainty and doubt) approach. I was therefore very pleased to read through the pages of this book, with its excellent collection of ideas, concepts and criticisms of the current state of the art, as well as cutting-edge solutions to safe provision of cloud computing, performance of informed risk-based decision-making and architecting secure, reliable and legally compliant cloud services. The book comes with a perfect timing, as it supports the cloud-computing community during a period of crucial business and policy decision-making and action (e.g., with activities including the European Cloud Strategy, Governmental Clouds and the revision of the Privacy and Data Protection legislation in the EU, the USA and New Zealand).

In my view, this is a book written by thought leaders for thought leaders, critical minds and forward looking cloud strategists.

Managing Director, Cloud Security Alliance Europe   Daniele Catteddu

Preface

... many still hesitate before the Cloud. They worry: how do I know what service
I am buying? Will my data be protected? Which providers can I trust? If I don't like what
I am getting, can I switch providers easily? Or, if I really don't like what I'm getting, can I
easily enforce the contract through legal action?

EU Commissioner Neelie Kroes – Setting up the European Cloud Partnership, World
Economic Forum, Davos, Switzerland, 26th January 2012

Overview and Goals

Cloud computing has emerged to address an explosive growth of web-connected
devices and to handle massive amounts of data. It is defined and characterized by
massive scalability and new Internet-driven economics. Despite the enormous
potential and rapid growth, privacy, security and trust for cloud remain areas of
concern and uncertainty, and the risks need to be better understood. This is a major
barrier to the switch to cloud models, due largely to lack of consumer trust and to
regulatory complexity. New solutions need to be developed urgently. Of course,
there is a strong business pull for this from regulators, governmental initiatives and
companies. For example:

> The government will push ahead with ... the shift towards cloud computing. It will mandate
> the reuse of proven, common application solutions and policies. These solutions must
> balance the need to be open, accessible and usable with the growing cyber-security threat
> and the need to handle sensitive information with due care.

from UK Government ICT Cloud Strategy, http://www.cabinetoffice.gov.uk/sites/
default/files/resources/government-cloud-strategy_0.pdf

This book analyses privacy and security issues related to cloud computing and
provides a range of in-depth cutting-edge chapters describing proposed solutions
from researchers specializing in this area. It is a collection of papers on privacy, security, risk and trust in cloud computing that is loosely based upon selected papers from
the International Workshop on Cloud Privacy, Security, Risk & Trust (CPSRT 2010)

at the IEEE 2nd International Conference on Cloud Computing Technology and Science, as well as some additional invited chapters from PC and steering committee members.

Addressing privacy issues in cloud computing is not a straightforward issue. Privacy laws both at the location of processing and at the location of data origin may need to be taken into account. Cloud computing can exacerbate this requirement, since the geographic location of processing can be extremely difficult to determine due to cloud computing's dynamic nature. Another issue is user-centric control, which can be a legal requirement and also something consumers want. However, in cloud computing, the consumers' data is processed in the cloud, on machines they do not own or control, and there is a threat of theft, misuse or unauthorized resale. Thus, the build-up of adequate trust for consumers to switch to cloud services can in some cases become an important necessity.

In the case of security, some cloud-computing applications simply lack adequate security protection such as fine-grained access control and user authentication. Since enterprises are attracted to cloud computing due to potential savings in IT outlay and management, it is necessary to understand the business risks involved. If cloud computing is to be successful, it must be trusted by its users. Therefore, we need to clarify what the components of such trust are and how trust can be achieved for security as well as for privacy.

Cloud business models can magnify privacy and security issues faced in subcontracting and offshoring. The cloud's dynamism renders inappropriate many traditional mechanisms for establishing trust and regulatory control. The cloud's autonomic and virtualized aspects can bring new threats, such as cross-virtual machine side-channel attacks, or vulnerabilities due to data proliferation, dynamic provisioning, the difficulty in identifying physical servers' locations or a lack of standardization. Furthermore, although service composition is easier in cloud computing, some services might have a malicious source. In general in the cloud, establishing risks and obligations, implementing appropriate operational responses and dealing with regulatory requirements are more challenging than with traditional server architectures.

As shown in the Trust Domains project,[1] business customers value high transparency, remediation and assurance, and if organizations can provide these, the customers will trust the organizations more and their brand image will be improved. If an organization is a cloud service provider or operator, this trust translates to a greater willingness for its customers to make the switch to cloud. This is particularly the case where business confidential or sensitive information is involved. Moreover, as customers shift to cloud models, they shift their focus from systems (which they used to control) to data and how that will be treated by other entities on their behalf. They require assurance that their data will be treated properly. This requires mechanisms to provide both adequate security for all data and also protection of

---

[1] Crane, S., Gill, M.: Framework and Usage Scenarios for Data Sharing. D1.3, Trust Domain Guide, March (2012). http://www.hpl.hp.com/research/cloud_security/ TDoms_WP1_D1_3_-_Trust%20Domain%20Guide_-_Rel_1_0.pdf

personal data. By using these mechanisms, risk is reduced both for organizations and their customers. These risks are a top concern when moving to cloud computing. For example, the European Network and Information Security Agency (ENISA)'s cloud-computing risk assessment report states "loss of governance" as a top risk of cloud computing, especially for infrastructure as a service (IaaS). "Data loss or leakages" is also one of the top seven threats the Cloud Security Alliance (CSA) lists in its *Top Threats to Cloud Computing* report.

Organization of This Book

This book reports on the latest advances in privacy, security and risk technologies within cloud environments. It is organized into eight chapters across four headings. References are included at the end of each chapter, and a Glossary of terms is given at the end of the book.

A brief description of each chapter follows.

Part I: Introduction to the Issues

Chapter 1: "Privacy, Security and Trust in Cloud Computing"
This chapter begins by providing background information on cloud computing and on the relationship between privacy, security and trust. It then assesses how security, trust and privacy issues occur in the context of cloud computing and briefly discusses ways in which they may be addressed.

Part II: Law Enforcement and Audits

Chapter 2: "Accessing Data in the Cloud: The Long Arm of the Law Enforcement Agent"
This chapter considers various forensic challenges for legal access to data in a cloud-computing environment and discusses questions of power raised by the exercise of legal access enforcement.

Chapter 3: "A Privacy Impact Assessment Tool for Cloud Computing"
This chapter discusses requirements for Privacy Impact Assessments (PIAs) for the cloud and explains how a PIA decision support tool may be constructed.

Chapter 4: "Understanding Cloud Audits"
This chapter discusses the use of cloud audits to attenuate cloud security problems, including an agent-based "Security Audit as a Service" architecture.

Part III: Security and Integrity

Chapter 5: "Security Infrastructure for Dynamically Provisioned Cloud Infrastructure Services"
This chapter discusses conceptual issues, basic requirements and practical suggestions for provisioning dynamically configured access control services in the cloud.

Chapter 6: "Modeling the Runtime Integrity of Cloud Servers: A Scoped Invariant Perspective"
This chapter proposes scoped invariants as a primitive for analyzing a cloud server for its integrity properties. A key benefit of this approach is that the confirmation of integrity can increase trust in the cloud server, and its capacity to properly handle customers' data.

Part IV: Risk Considerations

Chapter 7: "Inadequacies of Current Risk Controls for the Cloud"
This chapter examines the applicability (with respect to various service interfaces) to cloud-computing environments of controls that are currently deployed according to standards and best practices for mitigating information-security risks within an enterprise.

Chapter 8: "Enterprise Information Risk Management: Dealing with Cloud Computing"
This chapter discusses risk management for cloud computing from an enterprise perspective. The discussion includes decision-making and developments in trusted infrastructures, using examples and case studies.

Target Audiences

The target audience for this book is composed of business professionals, students and researchers interested in (or already working in) the field of privacy and security protection for the cloud and/or complex service provisioning.

This book would be of interest to an audience spanning a variety of disciplines. The broad range of topics addressed centres around privacy and security issues and approaches related to cloud computing including trust, risk and legal aspects. For newcomers to these areas, the book provides a solid overview of privacy, security and trust issues in the cloud. For experts, it provides details of novel cutting-edge research in inter-related areas as carried out by the various authors.

Acknowledgements

We would like to thank the authors for their excellent contributions to this book. In addition, we are grateful to Springer UK – and in particular Simon Rees – for helpful guidance throughout the book production process.

Our thanks are also due to our management within our respective institutions for supporting us in producing this material.

Siani Pearson
and George Yee

Contents

Part IV   Risk Considerations

Contributors

Adrian Baldwin HP Labs, Bristol, UK

Andrew Charlesworth Centre for IT and Law, University of Bristol, Bristol, UK

Nathan Clarke Centre for Security, Communications and Network Research, University of Plymouth, Plymouth, Germany

School of Computing and Security, Edith Cowan University, Perth, WA, Australia

Sadie Creese Cyber Security Centre, Department of Computer Science, University of Oxford, Oxford, UK

Yuri Demchenko University of Amsterdam, Amsterdam, The Netherlands

Cees de Laat University of Amsterdam, Amsterdam, The Netherlands

Frank Doelitzscher Cloud Research Lab, Furtwangen University, Furtwangen im Schwarzwald, Germany

Joan A. García-Espín I2CAT Foundation, Barcelona, Spain

Michael Goldsmith Cyber Security Centre, Department of Computer Science, University of Oxford, Oxford, UK

Paul Hopkins Security and Identity Management Department, Logica, Reading, UK

Martin Knahl Cloud Research Lab, Furtwangen University, Furtwangen im Schwarzwald, Germany

Diego R. Lopez Telefonica I+D, Madrid, Spain

Antonio Morales RedIRIS, Madrid, Spain

Canh Ngo University of Amsterdam, Amsterdam, The Netherlands

Siani Pearson Cloud and Security Lab, HP Labs, Bristol, UK

Calton Pu College of Computing, Georgia Institute of Technology, Atlanta, GA, USA

David Pym University of Aberdeen, Aberdeen, UK

Anand Rajan Corporate Technology Group, Intel Corporation, Hillsboro, OR, USA

Christoph Reich Cloud Research Lab, Furtwangen University, Furtwangen im Schwarzwald, Germany

Carlos V. Rozas Corporate Technology Group, Intel Corporation, Hillsboro, OR, USA

Simon Shiu HP Labs, Bristol, UK

David Tancock Department of Computer Science, University of Bristol, Bristol, UK

Ian Walden Centre for Commercial Law Studies, Queen Mary, University of London, London, UK

Jinpeng Wei School of Computing and Information Sciences, Florida International University, Miami, FL, USA

George Yee Carleton University, Ottawa, ON, Canada

Feng Zhu School of Computing and Information Sciences, Florida International University, Miami, FL, USA

Part I
Introduction to the Issues

Chapter 1
Privacy, Security and Trust
in Cloud Computing

Siani Pearson

Abstract Cloud computing refers to the underlying infrastructure for an emerging model of service provision that has the advantage of reducing cost by sharing computing and storage resources, combined with an on-demand provisioning mechanism relying on a pay-per-use business model. These new features have a direct impact on information technology (IT) budgeting but also affect traditional security, trust and privacy mechanisms. The advantages of cloud computing—its ability to scale rapidly, store data remotely and share services in a dynamic environment—can become disadvantages in maintaining a level of assurance sufficient to sustain confidence in potential customers. Some core traditional mechanisms for addressing privacy (such as model contracts) are no longer flexible or dynamic enough, so new approaches need to be developed to fit this new paradigm. In this chapter, we assess how security, trust and privacy issues occur in the context of cloud computing and discuss ways in which they may be addressed.

Keywords Cloud computing • Privacy • Security • Risk • Trust

1.1 Introduction

Although there is no definitive definition for cloud computing, a definition that is commonly accepted is provided by the United States National Institute of Standards and Technologies (NIST):

> Cloud computing is a model for enabling ubiquitous, convenient, on-demand network access to a shared pool of configurable computing resources (e.g., networks, servers, storage, applications, and services) that can be rapidly provisioned and released with minimal management effort or service provider interaction. [1]

S. Pearson (✉)
Cloud and Security Lab, HP Labs, Bristol, UK
e-mail: Siani.Pearson@hp.com

S. Pearson and G. Yee (eds.), *Privacy and Security for Cloud Computing*,
Computer Communications and Networks, DOI 10.1007/978-1-4471-4189-1_1,
© Springer-Verlag London 2013

This shared pool of resources is unified through virtualization or job scheduling techniques. Virtualization is the creation of a set of logical resources (whether it be a hardware platform, operating system, network resource or other resource) usually implemented by software components that act like physical resources. In particular, software called a 'hypervisor' emulates physical computer hardware and thus allows the operating system software running on the virtual platform—a virtual machine (VM)—to be separated from the underlying hardware resources.

The resources made available through cloud computing include hardware and systems software on remote data centres, as well as services based upon these that are accessed through the Internet; these resources can be managed to dynamically scale up to match the load, using a pay-per-resources business model. Key features advertised are elasticity, multi-tenancy, maximal resource utilization and pay per use. These new features provide the means to leverage large infrastructures like data centres through virtualization or job management and resource management.

Cloud computing (or, more simply, 'cloud') provides a market opportunity with a huge potential both for efficiency and new business opportunities (especially in service composition) and is almost certain to deeply transform our information technology infrastructures, models and services. Not only are there cost savings due to economies of scale on the service provider side and pay-as-you-go models, but business risk is decreased because there is less need to borrow money for upfront investment in infrastructure.

The adoption of cloud computing may move quite quickly depending on local requirements, business context and market specificities. We are still in the early stages, but cloud technologies are becoming adopted widely in all parts of the world. The economic potential of cloud computing and its capacity to accelerate innovation are putting business and governments under increased pressure to adopt cloud computing-based solutions.

Although the hype around cloud tends to encourage people to think that it is a universal panacea, this is not the case and quite often promoters ignore the inherent complexities added by the cloud. There are a number of challenges to providing cloud computing services: the need to comply with local and regional regulations; obtaining the necessary approvals when data is accessed from another jurisdiction; some additional complexity in terms of governance, maintenance and liability inherent to cloud; and a perceived lack of trust in cloud services. Many chief information officers (CIOs) in large enterprises identify security concerns as the top reason for not embracing the public cloud more aggressively and not benefitting from associated cost optimizations [2, 3]. Added to this rather common concern from technical audiences is a growing concern from data subjects, consumer advocates and regulators about the potentially significant impact on personal data protection and the required compliance to local regulations [4, 5]. The Patriot Act—a US federal law that can compel the legal request of customer and employee privacy information—in particular causes fears about transferring information to the USA [6]. Cloud can exacerbate the strain on traditional frameworks for privacy that globalization has already started. For example, location matters from a legal point of view, but in the cloud, information might be in multiple places, might be managed by different entities and it may be difficult to know the geographic location and which specific servers or storage devices are being used. It is currently difficult to ascertain and meet compliance requirements, as existing global legislation is complex and includes export restrictions, data retention restrictions, sector-specific restrictions and legislation at state and/or national levels. Legal advice is required, transborder data flow restrictions need to be taken into account, and care must be taken to delete data and virtual storage devices when appropriate. Although often there is a focus on security, in fact the most complex issue to address is privacy.

Context is an important aspect, as different information can have different privacy, security and confidentiality requirements. Privacy needs to be taken into account only if the cloud service handles personal information (in the sense of collecting, transferring, processing, sharing, accessing or storing it). Moreover, privacy threats differ according to the type of cloud scenario. There is a low privacy threat if the cloud services are to process information that is (or is very shortly to be) public. That is why the *New York Times* mass conversion of scanned images to PDF in the early stages of the cloud, which was at the time often highlighted as a classic demonstration of the benefits of a cloud approach, was a good scenario for cloud computing. On the other hand, there is a high privacy threat for cloud services that are dynamically personalized, based on people's location, preferences, calendar, social networks, etc. Even if the same information is involved, there may be different data protection requirements in different contexts due to factors including location and trust in the entities collecting and processing it. In addition, it should be borne in mind that there may be confidentiality issues in the cloud even if there is no 'personal data' involved: in particular, intellectual property and trade secrets may require protection that is similar to personal data and in some cases may benefit from practices and technologies developed specifically for ensuring appropriate personal data handling within the network of cloud service providers (which in this chapter we will refer to as a 'cloud ecosystem').

Opportunities are being created for some service providers to offer cloud services that have greater assurance and that employ mechanisms to reduce risk. These services might be more expensive than ones with minimal guarantees in terms of security and privacy, but in certain contexts and especially where sensitive information is involved, it is what is needed to foster trust in using such services while still allowing economic savings and other benefits of cloud computing. The potential can be very good: for small- and medium-sized enterprises (SMEs) in particular, greater security can actually be achieved via the use of cloud services than they have the expertise or budget to provide in-house. On the other hand, there are a number of potential pitfalls and complications, especially due to the global nature of business and the associated potential for increased data exposure and non-compliance with a matrix of different regulations, and these need to be addressed.

Overall, there is a paradigm change with cloud that can increase security concerns (especially loss of control, data integrity, data confidentiality and access by governments due to US Patriot Act and other legislation), resulting in complexity increasing along organizational, technical and regulatory dimensions. We shall consider these aspects further in this chapter.

The structure of the chapter is as follows:

- Section 1.2 gives an overview of cloud computing deployment and service models.
- Section 1.3 discusses the sometimes complex relationship between privacy, security and trust.
- Section 1.4 describes privacy issues for cloud computing.
- Section 1.5 describes security issues for cloud computing.
- Section 1.6 describes trust issues for cloud computing.
- Section 1.7 briefly discusses a number of approaches to addressing privacy, security and trust issues in cloud computing.
- Section 1.8 provides a summary and conclusions.

1.2 Cloud Deployment and Service Models

Building on the explanation given in the previous section, cloud computing refers to the underlying infrastructure (which may be very complex) that provides services to customers via defined interfaces. There are different layers of cloud services that refer to different types of *service model,* each offering discrete capabilities. Apart from management and administration, the major layers are:

Infrastructure as a Service (IaaS): the delivery of computing resources as a service, including virtual machines and other abstracted hardware and operating systems. The resources may be managed through a service Application Programming Interface (API). The customer rents these resources rather than buying and installing them in its data centre, and often, the resources are dynamically scalable, paid for on a usage basis. Examples include Amazon EC2 and S3.

Platform as a Service (PaaS): the delivery of a solution stack for software development including a runtime environment and lifecycle management software. This allows customers to develop new applications using APIs deployed and configurable remotely. Examples include Google App Engine, Force.com and Microsoft Azure.

Software as a Service (SaaS): the delivery of applications as a service, available on demand and paid for on a per-use basis. In simple multi-tenancy, each customer has its own resources that are segregated from those of other customers. A more efficient form is fine-grained multi-tenancy, where all resources are shared, except that customer data and access capabilities are segregated within the application. Examples include online word processing and spreadsheet tools, customer relationship management (CRM) services and web content delivery services (Salesforce CRM, Google Docs, etc.)

These three are the main layers, although there can also be other forms of service provided, such as business process as a service, data as a service, security as a service, storage as a service, etc.

Fig. 1.1 Cloud service models

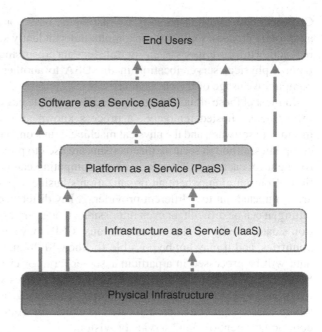

These layers form a kind of stack, as illustrated in Fig. 1.1. For example, in IaaS, consumers can deploy and run software, with a cloud service provider (CSP) controlling the underlying cloud infrastructure. In PaaS, consumers deploy (onto a cloud infrastructure run by a CSP) applications that have been created using programming languages and tools supported by that provider. In SaaS, consumers use CSPs' applications running on a cloud infrastructure that is typically provided by another CSP. In practice, IT vendors providing cloud services often include elements from several layers.

Cloud computing has several *deployment models*, of which the main ones are:

Private: a cloud infrastructure operated solely for an organization, being accessible only within a private network and being managed by the organization or a third party (potentially off premise)

Public: a publicly accessible cloud infrastructure

Community: a cloud infrastructure shared by several organizations with shared concerns

Hybrid: a composition of two or more clouds that remain separate but between which there can be data and application portability

Partner: cloud services offered by a provider to a limited and well-defined number of parties

Cloud computing services use 'autonomic' or self-regulating technologies which allow services to react and make decisions on their own, independently of

CSP operators and transparently to customers, based on preset policies or rules; autonomic processes might, for example, independently scale up service provision in reaction to a customer's usage, or transfer data processing within a virtual machine from a physical server location in the USA to another in Japan, based on the comparative usage of the physical servers.

In most of these cloud computing models, multiple customers share software and infrastructure hosted remotely—a process known as *multi-tenancy*. Hence, one instance of software, and the physical machine it runs on, serves clients from different companies, although security mechanisms are used to provide a protected VM environment for each user. Therefore, cloud computing can be thought of as an evolution of outsourcing, where an organization's business processes or infrastructures are contracted out to a different provider. A key difference is that with cloud computing, it can be difficult, or even impossible, to identify exactly where the organization's data actually is. This is partly because CSPs may have server farms in several countries, and it may not be possible for the CSP to guarantee to a customer that data will be processed in a particular server farm, or even country. Amazon Web Services (AWS) and Google have multiple data centres worldwide, details of the locations of which are often confidential. Offshoring, a term traditionally used where business processes are relocated to a different country, is thus also seen as a common element of cloud service provision.

In addition, it is the case that just as their customers use cloud services to obtain variable amounts of service provision according to their needs over time (usually referred to as 'scalability'), CSPs may themselves lease processing and storage capacity from other service providers to meet their own requirements. Thus, when a customer processes data using a CSP, that data may simultaneously reside in a jurisdiction outside that of both the customer and CSP, and on a third party's computer systems.

From a legal and regulatory compliance perspective, several of the key characteristics of cloud computing services including outsourcing, offshoring, virtualization and autonomic technologies may be problematic, for reasons ranging from software licensing, and the content of service-level agreements (SLAs), to determining which jurisdiction's laws apply to data hosted 'in the cloud' and the ability to comply with data privacy laws [7, 8]. For example, the autonomic aspect of cloud computing can pose new risks, namely, self-optimization and self-healing. Self-optimization grants a degree of autonomy in decision making, for example, automatically adapting services to meet the changing needs of customers and service providers; this challenges enterprises' abilities to maintain consistent security standards. Self-healing allows CSPs to provide appropriate business continuity, recovery and backup, but it may not be possible to determine with any specificity where data processing takes place within the cloud infrastructure [9]. Autonomic aspects of cloud computing—like many of the other aspects mentioned above—are one of its assets but need to be tailored to be compliant with privacy and legal issues.

Before considering the privacy, security and trust issues associated with cloud computing in more detail, we analyse in the next section what these terms mean and how they interrelate.

1.3   The Relationship Between Privacy, Security and Trust

Privacy and trust are both complex notions for which there is no standard, universally accepted definition. Consequently, the relationship between privacy, security and trust is necessarily intricate. In this section, we explain some of the main elements of this relationship.

1.3.1   Privacy

At the broadest level (and particularly from a European standpoint), privacy is a fundamental human right, enshrined in the United Nations Universal Declaration of Human Rights (1948) and subsequently in the European Convention on Human Rights and national constitutions and charters of rights such as the UK Human Rights Act 1998. Since at least the 1970s, the primary focus of privacy has been personal information, and particularly concerned with protecting individuals from government surveillance and potential mandatory disclosure of private information in databases. A decade later, concerns were raised related to direct marketing and telemarketing, and, later still, consideration was given to the increasing threat of online identity theft and spamming. There are various forms of privacy, ranging from 'the right to be left alone' [10], 'control of information about ourselves' [11], 'the rights and obligations of individuals and organizations with respect to the collection, use, disclosure, and retention of personally identifiable information' [12] and focus on the harms that arise from privacy violations [13]. Another influence is Nissenbaum's idea of privacy as 'contextual integrity', whereby the nature of challenges posed by information technologies may be measured. Contextual integrity binds adequate protection for privacy to norms of specific contexts that are essentially constraints on information flows, so that information gathering and dissemination should be made appropriate to the particular context [14, 15].

In the commercial, consumer context, privacy entails the protection and appropriate use of the personal information of customers and the meeting of expectations of customers about its use. For organizations, privacy entails the application of laws, policies, standards and processes by which personal information is managed. What is appropriate will depend on the applicable laws, individuals' expectations about the collection, use and disclosure of their personal information and other contextual information; hence, one way of thinking about privacy is just as 'the appropriate use of personal information under the circumstances' [16]. *Data protection* is the management of personal information and is often used within the European Union in relation to privacy-related laws and regulations (although in the USA the usage of this term is focussed more on security).

In broad terms, personal information describes facts, communications or opinions which relate to the individual and which it would be reasonable to expect him or her to regard as intimate or sensitive and therefore about which he or she might want to restrict collection, use or sharing. The terms 'personal information' and 'personal data' are commonly used within Europe and Asia, whereas in the USA, the term 'Personally Identifiable Information' (PII) is normally used, but they are generally used to refer to the same (or a very similar) concept. This can be defined as information that can be traced to a particular individual and include such things as name, address, phone number, social security or national identity number, credit card number, email address, passwords and date of birth. There are a number of types of information that could be personal data but are not necessarily so in all circumstances, such as usage data collected from computer devices such as printers; location data; behavioural information such as viewing habits for digital content; users' recently visited websites or product usage history and online identifiers such as IP addresses, radio-frequency identity (RFID) tags, cookie identifiers and unique hardware identities.

The current European Union (EU) definition of *personal data* is that

'personal' data shall mean any information relating to an identified or identifiable natural person ('data subject'); an identifable person is one who can be identified, directly or indirectly, in particular by reference to an identification number or to one or more factors specific to his physical, physiological, mental, economic, cultural or social identity; [17, p. 8]

Some personal data elements are considered more sensitive than others, although the definition of what is considered *sensitive personal information* may vary depending upon jurisdiction and even on particular regulations. In Europe, sensitive personal information is called *special categories of data*, which refers to information on religion or race, political opinions, health, sexual orientation, trade-union membership and data relating to offences or criminal convictions, and its handling is specially regulated. In the USA, social security and driver's licence numbers, personal financial information and medical records are commonly treated as sensitive. Health information is considered sensitive by all data protection laws that define this category. Other information that may be considered sensitive includes job performance information, biometric information and collections of surveillance camera images in public places. In general, sensitive information requires additional privacy and security limitations or safeguards because it can be considered as a subset of personal information with an especially sensitive nature.

Key privacy terminology includes the notion of data controller, data processor and data subject. Their meaning is as follows:

Data controller: An entity (whether a natural or legal person, public authority, agency or other body) which alone, jointly or in common with others determines the purposes for which and the manner in which any item of personal information is processed

Data processor: An entity (whether a natural or legal person, public authority, agency or any other body) which processes personal information on behalf and upon instructions of the data controller

Data subject: An identified or identifiable individual to whom personal information relates, whether such identification is direct or indirect (e.g. by reference to an identification number or to one or more factors specific to physical, physiological, mental, economic, cultural or social identity)

The fair information practices developed in the USA in the 1970s [18] and later adopted and declared as principles by the Organisation for Economic Co-operation and Development (OECD) and the Council of Europe [19] form the basis for most data protection and privacy laws around the world. These principles can be broadly described as follows:

1. *Data collection limitation*: data should be collected legally with the consent of the data subject where appropriate and should be limited to the data that is needed.
2. *Data quality*: data should be relevant and kept accurate.
3. *Purpose specification*: the purpose should be stated at the time of data collection.
4. *Use limitation*: personal data should not be used for other purposes unless with the consent of the individual.
5. *Security*: personal data should be protected by a reasonable degree of security.
6. *Openness*: individuals should be able to find out what personal data is held and how it is used by an organization.
7. *Individual participation*: an individual should be able to obtain details of all information about them held by a data controller and challenge it if incorrect.
8. *Accountability*: the data controller should be accountable for complying with these principles.

This framework can enable the sharing of personal information across participating jurisdictions without the need for individual contracts. Furthermore, the legislation supports the observation and enforcement of the protection of personal information as a fundamental right.

In Europe, the European Data Protection Directive 95/46/EC (and its supporting country legislation) implements these Fair Information Principles, along with some additional requirements including transborder data flow restrictions. Legislation similar to the European Data Protection Directive has been, and continues to be, enacted in many other countries, including Australia, New Zealand, Hong Kong, Japan and APEC. Notably, legislation in Canada, Argentina, Israel, Switzerland, Guernsey, Iceland, Lichtenstein, Norway, Jersey and the Isle of Man is considered strong enough to be 'adequate' by EC. (*Adequacy* defines how a specific country is considered to have an adequate or inadequate level of protection for processing personal data of subjects from within the European Union countries.) In contrast, the USA does not have a comprehensive regime of data protection but instead has a variety of laws—such as the Health Insurance Portability and Accountability Act (HIPAA)—which are targeted at the protection of particularly sensitive types of information. This US approach to privacy legislation is historically sector-based or enacted at the state level (e.g. the State of Massachusetts has set out appropriate security standards for protecting the personal information of residents of that state) and places few if any restrictions on transborder data flow. The USA is considered adequate for data transfer only under the limitation of the Safe Harbor agreement [20].

At the time of writing, regulations, enforcement activities and sanctions are currently increasing the world over. The USA is introducing a Consumer Privacy Bill of Rights [21], and the EU is revising their Data Protection Directive and regulation [22], with the result that FTC enforcement will be strengthened within the USA and current plans are that European DPAs will be able to impose fines of up to 2 % of worldwide annual turnover to companies that do not have mechanisms in place to underpin regulatory data protection compliance [22]. Other consequences of privacy failure for data controllers include civil liability (whereby data subjects enforce their rights), criminal liability (fines and imprisonment), investment risk, business continuity impact and reputational damage.

To summarize, privacy is regarded as a human right in Europe, whereas in America, it has been traditionally viewed more in terms of avoiding harm to people in specific contexts. It is a complex but important notion, and correspondingly, the collection and processing of personal information is subject to regulation in many countries across the world. Hence, cloud business scenarios need to take this into account.

1.3.2 Security

For the purposes of this book, by security, we mean information security. In this sense, *security* may be defined as:

Preservation of confidentiality, integrity and availability of information; in addition, other properties such as authenticity, accountability, non-repudiation and reliability can also be involved. [23]

Confidentiality is commonly but erroneously equated with privacy by some security practitioners and is:

The property that information is not made available or disclosed to unauthorized individuals, entities or processes. [23]

Security is a necessary but not a sufficient condition for privacy. Security is actually one of the core privacy principles, as considered in the previous subsection. Correspondingly, it is a common requirement under the law that if a company outsources the handling of personal information or confidential data to another company, it has some responsibility to make sure the outsourcer uses 'reasonable security' to protect those data. This means that any organization creating, maintaining, using or disseminating records of PII must ensure that the records have not been tampered with and must take precautions to prevent misuse of the information. Specifically, to ensure the security of the processing of such information, data controllers must implement appropriate technical and organizational measures to protect it against:

- *Unauthorized access or disclosure*: in particular where the processing involves the transmission of data over a network
- *Destruction*: accidental or unlawful destruction or loss
- *Modification*: inappropriate alteration
- *Unauthorized use*: all other unlawful forms of processing

Mechanisms to do this include risk assessment, implementing an information security program and putting in place effective, reasonable and adequate safeguards that cover physical, administrative and technical aspects of security. In the case of cloud computing, the CSP needs to implement 'reasonable security' when handling personal information.

Privacy differs from security in that it relates to handling mechanisms for personal information, dealing with individual rights and aspects like fairness of use, notice, choice, access, accountability and security. Many privacy laws also restrict the transborder data flow of personal information. Security mechanisms, on the other hand, focus on provision of protection mechanisms that include authentication, access controls, availability, confidentiality, integrity, retention, storage, backup, incident response and recovery. Privacy relates to personal information only, whereas security and confidentiality can relate to all information.

1.3.3 Trust

Here, we give a brief analysis of online trust. Further consideration of key aspects related to trust in the cloud and an assessment of consumer and corporate IT concerns about the cloud is given in Sect. 1.6.

Trust is a complex concept for which there is no universally accepted scholarly definition. Evidence from a contemporary, cross-disciplinary collection of scholarly writing suggests that a widely held definition of trust is as follows:

> Trust is a psychological state comprising the intention to accept vulnerability based upon positive expectations of the intentions or behaviour of another. [24]

Yet this definition does not fully capture the dynamic and varied subtleties involved. For example: letting the trustees take care of something the trustor cares about [25]; the subjective probability with which the trustor assesses that the trustee will perform a particular action [26]; the expectation that the trustee will not engage in opportunistic behaviour [27]; and a belief, attitude or expectation concerning the likelihood that the actions or outcomes of the trustee will be acceptable or will serve the trustor's interests [28].

Trust is a broader notion than security as it includes subjective criteria and experience. Correspondingly, there exist both hard (security-oriented) and soft trust (i.e. non-security-oriented trust) solutions [29]. 'Hard' trust involves aspects like authenticity, encryption and security in transactions, whereas 'soft' trust involves human psychology, brand loyalty and user-friendliness [30]. Some soft issues are involved in security, nevertheless. An example of soft trust is reputation, which is a component of online trust that is perhaps a company's most valuable asset [31] (although of course a CSP's reputation may not be justified). Brand image is associated with trust and suffers if there is a breach of trust or privacy.

People often find it harder to trust online services than offline services [32] because in the digital world there is an absence of physical cues and there may not be established centralized authorities [33]. The distrust of online services can even negatively affect the level of trust accorded to organizations that may have been long respected as trustworthy [34].

There are many different ways in which online trust can be established: security may be one of these (although security, on its own, does not necessarily imply trust [31]). Some would argue that security is not even a component of trust: Nissenbaum argues that the level of security does not affect trust [35]. On the other hand, an example of increasing security resulting in increased trust comes from people being more willing to engage in e-commerce if they are assured that their credit card numbers and personal data are cryptographically protected [36].

There can be differing phases in a relationship such as building trust, a stable trust relationship and declining trust. Trust can be lost quickly: as Nielsen states [37], 'It [trust] is hard to build and easy to lose: a single violation of trust can destroy years of slowly accumulated credibility'. Various approaches have targeted the measurement of factors that influence trust and the analysis of related causal relationships [38]. Many trust metrics have traditionally relied on a graph and have dealt with trust propagation [39, 40]; other techniques used to measure trust include fuzzy cognitive maps [41].

When assessing trust in relation to cloud computing, it may be useful to distinguish between social and technological means of providing persistent and dynamic trust, as all of these aspects of trust can be necessary [42]. *Persistent trust* is trust in long-term underlying properties or infrastructure; this arises through relatively static social and technological mechanisms. *Dynamic trust* is trust specific to certain states, contexts or short-term or variable information; this can arise through context-based social and technological mechanisms.

Persistent social-based trust in a hardware or software component or system is an expression of confidence in technological-based trust because it is assurance about implementation and operation of that component or system. In particular, there are links between social-based trust and technological-based trust through the vouching mechanism because it is important to know who is vouching for something as well as what they are vouching; hence, social-based trust should always be considered.

As considered further within Sect. 1.6, there is a complex relationship between security and trust, but in CSP models, security can be a key element in perceived lack of consumer trust.

1.4 Privacy Issues for Cloud Computing

Current cloud services pose an inherent challenge to data privacy because they typically result in data being exposed in an unencrypted form on a machine owned and operated by a different organization from the data owner. The major privacy issues relate to trust (e.g. whether there is unauthorized secondary usage of PII), uncertainty (ensuring that data has been properly destroyed, who controls retention of data, how to know that privacy breaches have occurred and how to determine fault in such cases) and compliance (in environments with data prolif-eration and global, dynamic flows and addressing the difficulty in complying with transborder data flow requirements). When considering privacy risks in the cloud, as considered already within the introduction, context is very important as privacy threats differ according to the type of cloud scenario. For example, there are special laws concerning treatment of sensitive data, and data leakage and loss of privacy are of particular concern to users when sensitive data is processed in the cloud. Currently, this is so much of an issue that the public cloud model would not normally be adopted for this type of information. More generally, public cloud is the most dominant architecture when cost reduction is concerned, but relying on a CSP to manage and hold one's data in such an environment raises a great many privacy concerns.

In the remainder of this section, we consider a number of aspects that illustrate best these privacy issues: lack of user control, lack of expertise, potential unau-thorized secondary usage, regulatory complexity (especially due to the global nature of cloud, complex service ecosystems, data proliferation and dynamic provi-sioning and related difficulties meeting transborder data flow restrictions), litigation and legal uncertainty.

1.4.1 Lack of User Control

User-centric control seems incompatible with the cloud: as soon as a SaaS envi-ronment is used, the service provider becomes responsible for storage of data, in a way in which visibility and control is limited. So how can a consumer retain control over their data when it is stored and processed in the cloud? This can be a legal requirement and also something users/consumers want—it may even be necessary in some cases to provide adequate trust for consumers to switch to cloud services.

Key aspects of this lack of user control include:

1. *Ownership of and control over the infrastructure*: In cloud computing, consumers' data is processed in 'the cloud' on machines they do not own or control, and there is a threat of theft, misuse (especially for different purposes from those originally notified to and agreed with the consumer) or unauthorized resale. See further discussion in Sect. 1.4.3.
2. *Access and transparency*: It is not clear that it will be possible for a CSP to ensure that a data subject can get access to all his/her PII. There can be lack of transparency about where data is, who owns it and what is being done with it. Furthermore, it is difficult to control (and even know) the exposure of the data transferred to the cloud because information passing through some countries (including the USA, as permitted by the US Patriot Act) can be accessed by law enforcement agencies.

3. *Control over data lifecycle*: A CSP may not comply with a request for deletion of data. Further detail is given in Sect. 1.5.4. Similarly, it is not necessarily clear who controls retention of data (or indeed what the regulatory requirements are in that respect as there can be a range of different data retention requirements, some of which may even be in conflict).
4. *Changing provider*: It can also be difficult to get data back from the cloud and avoid vendor lock-in, as considered further in Sect. 1.5.3.
5. *Notification and redress*: Uncertainties about notification, including of privacy breaches, and ability to obtain redress. It can be difficult to know that privacy breaches have occurred and to determine who is at fault in such cases.
6. *Transfer of data rights*: It is unclear what rights in the data will be acquired by data processors and their subcontractors and whether these are transferable to other third parties upon bankruptcy, takeover or merger [43].

1.4.2 Lack of Training and Expertise

Deploying and running cloud services may necessitate many jobs requiring high skills, but lack of STEM (science, technology, engineering, and mathematics) graduates in Europe and other parts of the world could make it difficult to recruit suitably qualified people. In particular, lack of trained personnel can be an issue from a security point of view.

In addition, people may lack understanding about the privacy impact of decisions they make. Technology in general exacerbates this problem as more employees are able to trigger privacy consequences, and these can be further-reaching: instead of protecting data on a server to which very few people have access, employees can now leave sensitive information unencrypted on a laptop, or expose confidential information at a flick of a switch. In the case of cloud, it is relatively quick and easy to go to a portal to request a service that is instantly provided, and it only takes a credit card if public cloud services are used like those from Salesforce and Google. Hence, unless proper management procedures are in place, there is a danger that employees could switch to using cloud computing services without adequately considering the consequences and risks for that particular situation.

1.4.3 Unauthorized Secondary Usage

There is a risk (and perhaps even an expectation!) that data stored or processed in the cloud may be put to unauthorized uses. It is part of the standard business model of cloud computing that the service provider may gain revenue from authorized secondary uses of users' data, most commonly the targeting of advertisements. However, some secondary data uses would be very unwelcome to the data owner (such as, e.g. the resale of detailed sales data to their competitors). Therefore, it may be necessary for consumers and CSPs to make legally binding agreements as to how data provided to CSPs may be used. At present, there are no technological barriers to such secondary uses, although as we consider further in various chapters in this book, it is likely that in future such agreements might be enforceable in a techno- logical sense. This will help enhance trust and mitigate the effects of the blurring of security boundaries.

1.4.4   Complexity of Regulatory Compliance

Due to the global nature of cloud computing and the many legislations in place around the world, it can be complex and difficult to ensure compliance with all the legislation that may apply in a given case.

Putting data in the cloud may impact privacy rights, obligations and status: for example, it may make it impossible to comply with some laws such as the Canadian Privacy Act or health laws. Legal protection can be reduced, and trade secrets may be impacted.

Location matters from a legal point of view as different laws may apply depend- ing on where information exists, but in cloud computing, the information might sometimes be in multiple places simultaneously; it may be difficult to know exactly where it is or it may be in transit. A complicating factor is that there are multiple copies of data located in the cloud. Furthermore, these copies can be managed by different entities: a backup SP, a provider used to respond to peak capacity needs, specialized services, etc.

Correspondingly, central properties of cloud that can make regulatory compli- ance difficult are data proliferation and dynamic provisioning. We consider these in turn. In addition, it can also be possible to violate local laws when transferring data stored in the cloud: cloud computing exacerbates the transborder data flow issue because it can be extremely difficult to ascertain which specific server or storage device will be used, due to the dynamic nature of cloud computing. These transborder data flow restrictions are a special case that we consider subsequently.

1.4.4.1   Data Proliferation

Data proliferation is a feature of cloud, and this happens in a way that may involve multiple parties and is not controlled by the data owners. CSPs ensure availability by replicating data in multiple data centres. It is difficult to guarantee that a copy of the data or its backups are not stored or processed in a certain jurisdiction, or that all these copies of data are deleted if such a request is made. This issue is considered further in Sect. 1.5.4.

Movement of data onto the cloud and potentially across and between legal jurisdictions, including offshoring of data processing, increases risk factors and legal complexity [43, 44]. Governance and accountability measures also become more complex as processes are outsourced and data crosses organizational boundaries [45]. The risks that can arise from choosing the wrong business partner can be daunting and very difficult to assess, especially in cloud-based environments, where even knowing the jurisdictions involved can be quite difficult [46]. Issues of jurisdiction (i.e. about whose courts would hear a case), which law applies and about whether a legal remedy can be effectively enforced need to be considered [47]. A cloud computing service which combines outsourcing and offshoring may raise very complex issues [48]. Hence, it can be difficult to ascertain privacy compliance requirements in the cloud.

1.4.4.2 Dynamic Provisioning

Cloud computing faces many of the same problems as traditional outsourcing, yet the dynamic nature of cloud makes many existing provisions to address this in more static environments obsolete or impractical to set up in such a short timescale. Model contracts are one example of this that is considered further in the following section. It is not clear which party is responsible (statutorily or contractually) for ensuring legal requirements for personal information are observed, or appropriate data-handling standards are set and followed [49], or whether they can effectively audit third-party compliance with such laws and standards. Neither is it yet clear to what extent cloud subcontractors involved in processing can be properly identified, checked and ascertained as being trustworthy, particularly in a dynamic environment.

1.4.5 Addressing Transborder Data Flow Restrictions

Privacy and data protection regulations restrict transfer of personal information across national borders, which includes restricting both the physical transfer of data and remote access to the data. Transfers from all countries with national legislation are restricted, so this includes EU and European Economic Area (EEA) countries, Argentina, Australia, Canada, Hong Kong and New Zealand. From EU/EEA countries, personal information can be transferred to countries that have 'adequate protection', namely, all other EU/EEA member states and also Switzerland, Canada, Argentina and Israel (since all have regulations deemed adequate by the EU). Note that no other countries have privacy regulations that are deemed adequate, so if information is to be sent to these countries, then other approaches need to be used.

One such mechanism is that information can be transferred from an EU country to the USA if the receiving entity has joined the US Safe Harbor agreement [20].

Personal information can however be transferred from any EU/EEA country to any non-EU/EEA country, other than Canada and Argentina, if model contracts have been signed and in many instances approved by the country regulator, or Binding Corporate Rules (BCRs) have been approved, or the individual has 'freely given' consent. Model contracts are contractual agreements that contain data protection commitments, company liability requirements and liabilities to the individuals concerned. Transfers from other countries with national privacy legislation (e.g. Canada, Argentina) also require contractual agreement. BCRs are binding internal agreements/contracts that obligate all legal entities within a corporate group that will have access to EU personal information to adhere to all obligations of the EU Data Protection Directive.

The problem is that these techniques (and especially model contracts as currently used) are not well suited to cloud environments. The first reason is due to regulatory complexity and uncertainty in cloud environments, especially due to divergences between the individual European member states' national laws implementing the European Data Protection Directive, 1995. The second reason is that these techniques are not flexible enough for cloud, because administering and obtaining regulatory approval for model contracts can result in lengthy delays: the notification and prior approval requirements for EU model contracts vary significantly across the EU but are burdensome and can take from 1 to 6 months to set up. BCRs are suitable for dynamic environments, but their scope is limited: they only apply to data movement within a company group, it may be difficult for SMEs to invest in setting these up and there are only a few BCRs to date, although it is a relatively new technique.

It is not just transborder data flow requirements that restrict the flow of information across borders: there may also be trade sanctions and other export restrictions, for example, restriction of cryptography and confidential data from the USA.

Not knowing which routes transnational traffic will take makes it very difficult to understand the particular laws which will apply. However, one interpretation of Section 4 of the Directive 95/46/EC is that transit of data through the territories is not relevant from the legal point of view: for example, if data are transferred from France to the USA, whether the data flows through network links that run via UK and Canada seems to be irrelevant from the legal point of view [7: P103].

Even if transit of data is not relevant to consider, it is still difficult to enforce transborder data flow regulations within the cloud. Cloud computing can exacerbate the problem of knowledge of geographic location of where cloud computing activities are occurring, as due to its dynamic nature this can be extremely difficult to find out.

1.4.6   Litigation

Another aspect is litigation: a CSP may be forced to hand over data stored in the cloud, as illustrated by the US vs. Weaver case [50], where Microsoft was requested via a trial subpoena rather than a warrant to provide emails handled by their Hotmail service. A government only needs to show the requested material is relevant to the case for a subpoena, whereas for a warrant, probable cause must be demonstrated. In order to avoid a similar situation occurring with non-governmental entities, subscribers to cloud services could include contractual provisions in the service agreement that govern the CSP's response to any subpoena requests from such entities.

1.4.7 Legal Uncertainty

Legal frameworks have been instrumental and key to the protection of users' personal and sensitive information. As considered briefly in Sect. 1.3.1, in Europe, there is national legislation based upon an EU Directive; in the USA, there is a patchwork of legislation according to sector, information and/or geographical area; and in many other countries worldwide, analogous frameworks apply. The fundamental concepts of such frameworks are in the main technology neutral, and their validity would still apply to cloud computing. Nevertheless, such frameworks—along with the associated tools, advice and national legislation—need to be constantly updated and adjusted with current and future technologies in mind. There is currently a dialogue between organizations, regulators and stakeholders to ensure that the regulatory framework does adapt to new frameworks and business models without eroding consumers' trust in the systems that are deployed. In particular, the dynamically changing nature of cloud computing, potentially combined with cross-jurisdictional interactions, introduces legal aspects that need to be carefully considered when processing data.

There are existing legal constraints on the treatment of users' private data by cloud computing providers. Privacy laws vary according to jurisdiction, but EU countries generally only allow PII to be processed if the data subject is aware of the processing and its purpose, and place special restrictions on the processing of sensitive data (e.g. health or financial data), the explicit consent of the data owner being part of a sufficient justification for such processing [51]. They generally adhere to the concept of *data minimization*, that is, they require that personally identifiable information is not collected or processed unless that information is necessary to meet the stated purposes. In Europe, data subjects can refuse to allow their personally identifiable data to be used for marketing purposes [17]. Moreover, there may be requirements on the security and geographical location of the machines on which personally identifiable data is stored [51]. European law limiting cross-border data transfers also might prohibit the use of cloud computing services to process this data if data would be stored in countries with weak privacy protection laws, and notification may be required [52].

Since cloud technology has moved ahead of the law, there is much legal uncertainty about privacy rights in the cloud and it is hard to predict what will happen when existing laws are applied in cloud environments.

Areas of uncertainty still under current discussion include that the procedure of anonymizing or encrypting personal data may be regarded as regulated 'processing', requiring consent, and it is not clear whether that processing for the purpose of enhancing users' privacy is exempt from privacy protection requirements. Specifically, it can be unclear in practice whether or not data that will be processed is personal data or not, hence whether or not there are legal responsibilities associated with its processing. Anonymization and pseudonymization processes, such as key-coding/obfuscation; fragmenting; deleting 'identifying information' such as names, IP addresses, etc.; encryption), may in some circumstances result in personal data but in others not result in personal data under the current definition, and indeed it may not be obvious whether or not the anonymized/pseudonymized data is personal data or not. It follows that it may not be clear, for example, whether or not certain data can be sent outside the EU, or other actions can be performed that are restricted by EU [53].

In general, the legal situation is subject to change: legislation has not yet been updated to address the challenges above, and courts have not yet ruled many cases specifically related to cloud computing.

1.4.8 Privacy Conclusions

In summary, we are seeing the biggest change in privacy since the 1980s and there is uncertainty in all regions. Cloud (and its inherent pressure towards globalization) is helping strain traditional frameworks for privacy. Policymakers are pushing for major change—fast-tracking concepts of fairness, placing more emphasis upon accountability (see Sect. 1.7) and driving increased protection. This includes the draft US Privacy Bill of Rights and the EU data protection framework currently under consideration [21, 22].

Cloud computing offers significant challenges for organizations that need to meet various global privacy regulations, including the complexity of existing global legislation necessitating legal advice. Cloud faces the same privacy issues as other service delivery models, but it can also magnify existing issues, especially transborder data flow restrictions, liability and the difficulty in knowing the geographic location of processing and which specific servers or storage devices will be used. In addition, care must be taken to delete data and virtual storage devices, especially with regard to device reuse; this is considered further in the following section and is both a privacy and a security issue. More broadly, security is an aspect of privacy that is considered further in the next section—hence, many of the issues raised in that section, including the difficulties in enforcing data protection within cloud ecosystems, may be seen to also be privacy issues.

1.5 Security Issues for Cloud Computing

As we shall discuss further in Sect. 1.6.2, security often tops the list of cloud user concerns. Cloud computing presents different risks to organizations than traditional IT solutions. There are a number of security issues for cloud computing, some of which are new, some of which are exacerbated by cloud models and others that are the same as in traditional service provision models. The security risks depend greatly upon the cloud service and deployment model. For example, private clouds can to a certain extent guarantee security levels, but the economic costs associated with this approach are relatively high.

At the network, host and application levels, security challenges associated with cloud computing are generally exacerbated by cloud computing but not specifically caused by it. The main issues relate to defining which parties are responsible for which aspects of security. This division of responsibility is hampered by the fact that cloud APIs are not yet standardized. Customer data security raises a number of concerns, including the risk of loss, unauthorized collection and usage and generally the CSP not adequately protecting data.

There are a number of different ways of categorizing security risks; moreover, these fit into a broader model of cloud-related risks. For example, according to the Cloud Security Alliance [4], the top threats to cloud computing are abuse and nefarious use of cloud computing, insecure interfaces and APIs, malicious insiders, shared technology issues, data loss or leakage, account or service hijacking and unknown risk profile. They were unable to reach a consensus on ranking the degree of severity of these risks.

Abuse and nefarious use could cover a wide variety of threats, largely considered within Sect. 1.5.2 below (unwanted access), but could also include the type of threats considered in Sect. 1.4.3 above (unauthorized secondary usage) or abuse of cloud resources – for example, trying to use as much resource as possible (which could be quite high with a cloud model) without paying or in order to limit access for others. Insecure cloud interfaces and cloud APIs are considered within Sect. 1.5.5 below. Shared technology issues are considered within Sect. 1.5.4 (inadequate data deletion) and Sect. 1.5.7 (isolation failure). Malicious insiders could be considered with respect to a number of scenarios, but especially those considered in Sect. 1.5.2. Some aspects of data exposure have been covered in the previous section (covering privacy issues); others are considered in Sect. 1.5.6 (backup issues) and Sect. 1.5.2 (unwanted access). In this section, we also consider the relative lack of interoperability, assurance, transparency and monitoring in the cloud. In addition we consider how a gap in security can arise in cloud environments. For further details about cloud security issues, see, for example, [54–56].

1.5.1 Gap in Security

In general, security controls for the cloud are the same as those used in other IT environments. But as the customer cedes control to the cloud provider, there is a related risk that the CSP will not adequately address the security that they should be handling, or even that SLAs do not include any provision of the necessary security services.

This risk is dependent upon the service model used. The lower down the stack the cloud provider, the more security the consumer is responsible for: thus, the consumer of IaaS needs to build in security as they are primarily responsible for it, whereas in SaaS environments, security controls and their scope (as well as privacy and compliance) are negotiated into the contracts for service. The customer may need to understand how the cloud provider handles issues such as patch management and configuration management as they upgrade to new tools and new operating systems, as well as the IT security hardware and software that the cloud provider is using and how the environment is being protected. In the case of IaaS and PaaS, cloud providers need to clarify the kind of IT security the customer is expected to put in place. With SaaS, the customer still needs to provide access security through its own systems, which could either be an identity management system or a local access control application.

Furthermore, it may be difficult to enforce protection throughout the cloud eco-system. As discussed in Sect. 1.3.2, the CSP needs to implement 'reasonable security' when handling personal information. Different companies may be involved in the cloud supply chain, and this can make it difficult to ensure that such security is provided all the way along the chain. At present, clients often only know the initial CSP, and the standard terms and conditions of cloud computing service providers do not include any clauses ensuring the level of security provided: they provide no guarantee as to the security of data and even deny liability for deletion, alteration or loss related to data that is stored. As current terms of service are very much set in favour of the CSP [49], if anything goes wrong, it is often the customer that will be made liable.

1.5.2 Unwanted Access

There needs to be an appropriate level of access control within the cloud environment to protect the security of resources. Cloud computing may actually increase the risk of access to confidential information.

First, this may be by foreign governments: there can be increased risks due to government surveillance over data stored in the cloud, as the data may be stored in countries where previously it was not. Governments in the countries where the data is processed or stored may even have legal rights to view the data under some circumstances [6, 57], and consumers may not be notified if this happens. One example of this is US Patriot Act, as previously mentioned, that is an important concern for many customers considering switching to CSP models.

Second, as with other computing models, there is an underlying risk of unauthorized access that may be exacerbated if entities are involved in the provider chain that have inadequate security mechanisms in place (e.g. if they have inadequate vetting of internal IT staff who have highly privileged access). The risk of data theft from machines in the cloud can be by rogue employees of CSPs, by data thieves breaking into service providers' machines or even by other customers of the same service if there is inadequate separation of different customers' data in a machine that they share in the cloud. Attackers may also break into the networks of the CSP, subcontractors or co-hosted customers. Attackers may also use de-anonymization techniques (see [58]). The damage that can be caused in these cases can be greater than non-cloud environments, due to the scale of operation and the presence of certain roles in cloud architectures with potentially extensive access including CSP system administrators and managed security service providers.

In general, cloud storage can be more at risk from malicious behaviour than processing in the cloud because data may remain in the cloud for long periods of time and so the exposure time is much greater. On the other hand, there is more potential for usage of encryption in cloud storage [56].

1.5.3 Vendor Lock-In

Cloud computing, as of today, lacks interoperability standards. Competing architectural standards are being developed, including Open Virtualization Format [59], Open Cloud Computing Interface [60], Data Liberation Front [61], SNIA Cloud Data Management Interface (CDMI) [62] and SAML [63] with big cloud vendors pushing their own mutually incompatible *de facto* standards. Limitations include differences between common hypervisors, gaps in standard APIs for management functions, lack of commonly agreed data formats and issues with machine-to-machine interoperability of web services. The lack of standards makes it difficult to establish security frameworks for heterogeneous environments and forces people for the moment to rely on common security best practice. As there is no standardized communication between and within cloud providers and no standardized data export format, it is difficult to migrate from one cloud provider to another or bring back data and process it in-house.

1.5.4 Inadequate Data Deletion

Another major issue for cloud is to ensure that the customer has control over the lifecycle of their data, and in particular deletion, in the sense of how to be sure that data that should be deleted really are deleted and are not recoverable by a CSP. There are currently no ways to prove this as it relies on trust, and the problem is exacerbated in cloud because there can be many copies of the data (potentially held by different entities and some of which may not be available) or because it might not be possible to destroy a disk since it is storing other customers' data.

The risks of data exposure vary according to the service model. Using IaaS or PaaS, one or more VMs are created in order for a program to be run within those—when the task is finished, the VMs and the temporary disk space are released. In fact, IaaS providers can provide storage and VM services which are complementary but allow for persistency of data between usage of multiple VMs. An allocated VM could be started to carry out a task and stopped once the task is completed; this is logically separate from managing the lifecycle of a VM (as the VM can be deleted when the data are no longer needed). Using a SaaS approach, on the other hand, the customer is one of the users of a multi-tenant application developed by the cloud service provider, and the customers' data is stored in the cloud, to be accessible the next time the customer logs in. The data would only be deleted at the end of the lifecycle of the data, if the customer wishes to change service provider, etc. There is a correspondingly higher risk to the customer if hardware resources are reused than if dedicated hardware is used.

1.5.5   Compromise of the Management Interface

In public cloud service provision, the management interfaces are available via the Internet. This poses an increased risk compared to traditional hosting providers because remote access and web browser vulnerabilities can be introduced and in addition access can be given via these interfaces to larger sets of resources. This increased risk is present even if access is controlled by a password.

1.5.6   Backup Vulnerabilities

Cloud service providers make multiple copies of data and place them in different locations to provide a high level of reliability and performance. This serves as a form of backup, although it can lead to additional liabilities and threats from attackers. There is still the potential for the data to be lost, particularly with Storage as a Service. A popular solution is a type of hybrid storage cloud, where an appliance is placed at the customer's site and backup data is stored there with a replicated copy sent to a cloud storage service provider. Indeed, one of the top threats identified by CSA [4] is 'data loss or leakage', where records may be deleted or altered without a backup of the original content. A record might be unlinked from a larger context, making it unrecoverable; data could be stored on unreliable media, and if there is a key management failure, then data could be effectively destroyed. There have already been cases where backup was provided as an optional extra for a storage service, and a failure in that service resulted in the complete loss of the data of users that had not paid that premium. However, in general, cloud services can be more resilient than traditional services.

1.5.7   Isolation Failure

Multi-tenancy raises a security concern that one consumer may influence the operations or access data of other tenants running on the same cloud [64]. Multi-tenancy is an architectural feature whereby a single instance of software runs on a SaaS vendor's servers, serving multiple client organizations. The software is designed to virtually partition its data and configuration so that each client organization works with a customized virtual application instance. In such a SaaS model, the customers are users of multi-tenant applications developed by CSPs, it is likely that personal data and even financial data are stored by CSP in the cloud, and it is the responsibility of the CSP to secure the data. There is a risk that the mechanisms that separate storage, memory or routing between different tenants might fail, and hence, for example, other tenants could access sensitive information.

Some providers use job scheduling and resources management [65], but most cloud providers use virtualization to maximize hardware utilization. Virtual machines (VMs) are sandboxed environments and therefore completely isolated from each other. This assumption makes it safe for users to share the same hardware. However, this security can sometime break down, allowing attackers to escape the boundaries of this sandboxed environment and have full access to the host [66]. The use of virtualization can introduce new security vulnerabilities, such as cross-VM side-channel attacks, where the attacker breaches the isolation between VMs allowing extraction of data via information leakage due to the sharing of physical resources [67]; virtual network attacks; inadequate data deletion before memory is assigned to a different customer (cf. Sect. 1.5.4) or 'escape' to the hypervisor, where an attacker uses a guest virtual machine to attack vulnerabilities in the hypervisor software [68].

1.5.8 Missing Assurance and Transparency

One approach to privacy and security is to leave protection to the service provider. We have discussed above in Sect. 1.5.1 how expectations in this regard typically vary according to the service model. The cloud customer can in many case transfer risk to the cloud provider (e.g. via SLAs). However, not all risks can be transferred, and ultimately the cloud customer may be legally accountable (e.g. in its role as the data controller). Moreover, the consequences of failure may include reputational damage, legal liability or even business failure, and this is unlikely to be fully compensated for.

So, cloud customers need to obtain assurance from cloud service providers that their data will be protected properly. They may also require that they are notified about security and privacy incidents. Some cloud providers provide information about their data-handling practices, security mechanisms and offer related assurance, for example, SAS-70 type II certification. This type of approach is taken for accounting data, in any case. ENISA has developed a Cloud Computing Information Assurance Framework [69] for this purpose.

However, in some cases, it can be difficult to take this approach, particularly in cases of multiple transfers of data, for reasons considered in the previous section. Other drawbacks include that standard SaaS business models involve repurposing of customer data and furthermore that cloud computing terms of service typically offer no compensation if the customer's data is stolen or misused.

Various security policy and risk assessment frameworks exist, including good practice guides from UK CESG [70]; NIST 800 series [71]; ISO 27001 [72] and

27002 [73] Information Security Management; ISO 31000 Risk Management [74]; and CSA's [54], ENISA's [7] and Shared Assessments' analysis [75] of risks involved in migration to cloud environments. However, in general, current risk assessment methods have not been designed for use in a cloud computing setting. Liability assignment is also particularly difficult in an international context. Furthermore, it is very difficult and resource-demanding to detect and then prove that electronic data has been compromised and to identify the perpetrator. What is reported to the police is just a small percentage of all violations detected [76].

In current certification schemes, certificates are awarded to traditional, monolithic software systems and become invalid when a system is used in an open, dynamic environment, as in the mash-ups of different services deployed in the cloud. However, CSA's Trusted Cloud Initiative [77] is working towards certification of 'trusted clouds'.

Lack of technology support arises because current multijurisdictional regulatory frameworks are extremely complex and teams with strong interdisciplinary skills are needed to address these problems, which are rarely formed. UK ICO has published Privacy Impact Guidelines [78] and a business case for investing in proactive privacy protection, but the certification of properties such as privacy has had only a limited take up to date.

Cloud-based storage of data that requires privacy assurance (such as personal data) is almost always deployed in private clouds. Heterogeneous cloud infrastructures make it difficult to have effective controls to check privacy compliance (often offered as an optional extra) in an automated way, and the end user has no means to verify that his/her privacy requirements are being fulfilled. Effective and profitable utilization of cloud services relies on data transfer and storage across services and different cloud infrastructures (which may have different jurisdictional restrictions).

Furthermore, end-user agreements are stated in natural languages, making it hard for computer programs to assess whether application providers respect data usage agreements. Existing technologies filter information in different ways, including privacy-enhanced access control [79], data loss prevention techniques [80], redaction [81], various privacy-enhancing technologies [82] and database proxies like Informatica's dynamic data masking tool [83]. W3C has produced a number of standards, including P3P [84] (which is now discontinued although the concepts have subsequently been built on [85]) and tracking standards [86]. Existing auditing frameworks manually verify the adequacy of the data-handling controls used [87–89]. These procedures are extremely costly.

Automated assurance is necessary to quickly evaluate the evidence that obligations with respect to personal data handling and business compliance requirements are being carried out (for instance, the collection of events showing who created a piece of data, who modified it and how and so on). Governance, risk management and compliance (GRC) frameworks (e.g. RSA eGRC [90]) are a common means of automating compliance in enterprises but do not provide much breadth or strong co-design of technical and legal mechanisms, and although they can target specific regulations, they rarely deal with concepts like privacy and transparency, with the notable exception of recent work within CSA [91].

An open problem is how to find a balance between data provenance and related privacy or other regulatory constraints in the cloud, where physical perimeters are not clearly delimited. The lack of tools to support data localization and transfer across services and cloud infrastructures creates barriers to cross-border considerations and different jurisdictional restrictions [43]. Incompatibilities between jurisdictions affect privacy assurance, and even within the EU, regulatory requirements are defined at a national level and can differ.

1.5.9   Inadequate Monitoring, Compliance and Audit

There are a number of issues related to maintaining and proving compliance when using cloud computing. If a cloud customer migrates to the cloud, their previous investment in security certification may be put at risk if the CSP cannot provide evidence of their compliance with the relevant requirements and does not enable the cloud customer to audit its processing of the customer's data. Furthermore, it may be difficult to evaluate how cloud computing affects compliance with internal security policies. Certain kinds of compliance (such as PCI DSS) may actually not be achievable within a public cloud infrastructure. The cloud customer may want to monitor that SLAs have been met, but the infrastructure may be very complex and not suited either for provision of the appropriate information or for analysis at the right level.

CSPs need to implement internal compliance monitoring controls, in addition to an external audit process. It may even be that a 'right to audit' clause is included in cloud contracts to allow customers to audit the cloud provider, particularly when the customer has regulatory compliance responsibilities. The cloud computing environment presents new challenges from an audit and compliance perspective, but existing solutions for outsourcing and audit can be leveraged. Transactions involving data that resides in the cloud need to be properly made and recorded, in order to ensure integrity of data, and the data owner needs to be able to trust the environment such that no untraceable action has taken place. However, provision of a full audit trail within the cloud, particularly in public cloud models, is still an unsolved issue. In addition, transactional data is a by-product with unclear ownership, and it can be hard to anticipate which data to protect, as even innocuous-seeming data can turn out to be commercially sensitive [45]. Methods for monitoring the cloud's performance are currently being explored by the CloudAudit working group [91].

Nor are there efficient mechanisms for gathering convincing evidence from verified log data in distributed multi-tenancy environments, even if cloud providers would be willing to provide this. Although there are several existing log approaches, they do not fit cloud computing very well [92]. For example, the EGEE LB log solution [93] in grid computing is mostly used for debugging purposes only. Chukwa [94] is a large-scale log collection and analysis framework built on top of the Hadoop and MapReduce framework; it requires the ownership of all the machines that have data to be logged, which is not realistic in a multi-provider cloud environment.

Security Information and Event Management (SIEM or SIM/SEM) solutions [95], including, for example, RSA enVision [96] and HP ArcSight [97], provide a standardized approach to collect information and events, store and query and provide degrees of correlation, usually driven by rules. SIEM solutions do not cover business audit and strategic (security) risk assessment but instead provide inputs that need to be properly analysed and translated into a suitable format to be used by senior risk assessors and strategic policymakers. This is a painful and quite often manual process, prone to mistakes and errors. Risk assessment standards such as ISO 2700x [72, 73], NIST [98], etc., operate at a macro-level and usually do not fully leverage information coming from logging and auditing activities carried out by IT operations.

Similarly, there exist a number of frameworks for auditing a company's IT controls, most notably COSO [99] and COBIT [100]. Also, trust services [101] provide a set of principles enabling auditors and CPAs to assess the quality and usefulness of security controls implemented in an enterprise's infrastructure. With all of these, the gap between low-level monitoring and logging and high-level requirements is not efficiently bridged or well automated.

A few tools for monitoring cloud integrity exist, but in limited scope: Amazon CloudWatch [102] allows EC2 users to do real-time monitoring of their CPU utilization, data transfers and disk usage. Haeberlen has provided a primitive audit for cloud [103] and proposed an approach for accountable virtual machines [104]. HyTrust Appliance [105] is a hypervisor-consolidated log report and policy enforcement tool that logs from a system perspective. Chen and Wang of CSIRO have produced a prototype in which CSPs are made accountable for faulty services and a technique which allows identification of the cause of faults in binding web services and have presented this as 'accountability as a service' [106].

Further consideration of audit mechanisms for the cloud is given in Chap. 4.

1.5.10   Security Conclusions

There are a number of security issues for cloud, and these depend upon the service provision and deployment models. A number of open issues remain, including audit. Availability may be an issue for public clouds—the future speed and global availability of network access required to use them may prevent widespread adoption in the short to medium term.

Overall, security need not necessarily suffer in moving to the cloud model, because there is scope for security to be outsourced to experts in security and hence in many cases greater protection than previously can be obtained. The major issues are probably to do with selection of service providers with suitable controls in place and to do with privacy and are context-dependent.

1.6 Trust Issues for Cloud Computing

This section builds upon the analysis given in Sect. 1.3 to briefly consider the main trust issues for cloud computing. We consider the concerns of cloud customers, who may be either citizen end users, or else organizations using cloud (providing information to CSPs that may be personal information of their customers, business-confidential information, information about end users or employees, etc.). We also consider weak trust relationships within the cloud service provision ecosystem and the lack of consensus about the trust management approaches to be used for cloud.

1.6.1 Trust in the Cloud

In traditional security models, a security perimeter is set up to create a trust boundary within which there is self-control over computing resources and where sensitive information is stored and processed. For example, the corporate firewall often marks this boundary. The network provides transit to other trusted end hosts, which operate in a similar manner. This model held for the original Internet, but does not do so for public and hybrid cloud. The security perimeter becomes blurred in the sense that confidential information may be processed outside known trusted areas as these computing environments often have fuzzy boundaries as to where data is stored and/or processed. On the other hand, in order to obtain the service, consumers need to extend their trust to the cloud service provider, and so this can provide a point of friction, as considered further below.

In assessing cloud computing provision, mechanisms to provide dynamic technological-based trust need to be used in combination with social and technological mechanisms for providing persistent trust: if software processes provide information about the way in which information is stored, accessed and shared within a cloud, that information can only be trusted if entities that are trusted vouch for the method of providing the information and assessing the information. Depending upon the context, these entities could be consumer groups, auditors, security experts, regulators, companies with proven reputation, established CSPs, etc. Moreover, trust relationships can be very much at the centre of certain security and privacy solutions: for instance, in particular for key escrow and other forms of key distribution and secret sharing, audit, compliance checking and pseudonymization. There is also a strong link with policy development: if personal or business critical information is to be stored in the cloud, trust attains a new level of importance and CSPs need to embrace such an approach [107].

1.6.2 Lack of Consumer Trust

Of the European citizens surveyed in June 2011 about their attitudes on data protection [108], it was found that authorities and institutions—including the European Commission and the European Parliament (trusted by 55 % of people surveyed)—are trusted more than commercial companies. In fact, less than one-third trust phone companies, mobile phone companies and Internet service providers (32 %), and just over one-fifth trust Internet companies such as search engines, social networking sites and email services (22 %). Furthermore, 70 % of Europeans, according to this study, are concerned that their personal data held by companies may be used for a purpose other than that for which it was collected. In a recent Cloud Industry Forum survey, the results of 'how do you trust an online provider?' were reputation (29 %), recommendation from trusted party (27 %), trial experience (20 %), contractual (20 %) and others (4 %) [3].

Organizations handling personal information have a legal and moral obligation of ensuring privacy and thereby demonstrating the trustworthy nature of their service. Important questions to address include whether data is safe across all of the cloud, it is handled based upon users' expectations, data handling is compliant with laws and regulations, data is under control along its complete lifecycle, appropriate use and obligations are ensured along the processing chain and there are standards or general practices in place for operating in the cloud. There is a lack of confidence about cloud, and the answers to these questions at present, as seen from the results of a number of recent surveys considered below.

Business users recognize the cloud's advantages in speeding innovation, accelerating business processes and reducing time to revenue. Correspondingly, businesses are already moving to the cloud: an IDC study found that 70 % of businesses are considering or already using private clouds [109].

However, CIOs are more wary. A recent study by Forrester found that business is adopting cloud 2.5 times faster than IT operations [110]. Enterprise IT executives cite well-founded concerns about the challenges of maintaining security, service levels and governance seamlessly across the entire IT value chain [111]. They also want to be sure the decisions they make today about cloud technology suppliers do not prevent them from innovating in the future. Hence, a number of critical challenges need to be addressed in order to encourage cloud adoption in enterprises. These key barriers to cloud adoption include:

- 79 % were concerned about vendor lock-in [2].
- 75 % were worried about cloud performance and availability [2].
- 70 % of CIOs said cloud data security is a major concern [112].
- 63 % were concerned about integrating internal and external services [2].

Figure 1.2 shows the percentage of respondents ranking the top three barriers to moving to cloud computing, based on the McKinsey Global Survey results in October 2010 (where n is the total number of respondents), and how security was the top concern for IT executives. Similarly, security was rated the top challenge of

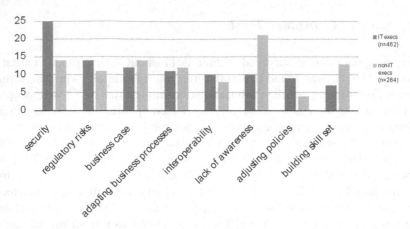

Fig. 1.2 Barriers to cloud technology

the cloud model in the IDC 2009 cloud user survey [2], and concerns about security also topped the list of primary barriers chosen as stopping UK businesses from making the transition to cloud computing, with lack of confidence coming second in a recent Cloud Industry Forum survey [3]. Similarly, in a recent 2010 survey by Fujitsu Research Institute [113] on potential cloud customers, it was found that 88 % of potential cloud consumers are worried about *who* has access to their data, and demanded more awareness of what goes on in the backend physical server. According to an interview study on the views of security and user experience experts on trust in cloud services [114], the most important factor affecting perceived trust in cloud services is brand, with security and privacy as the second most important aspect and transparency and reliability as the third most important aspect, with good auditing and agreement policies also being deemed important. Businesses are sceptical about the promises that many cloud vendors and suppliers are making: 62 % of respondents felt that when looking for a supplier, a code of practice would be important, while a further 28 % considered it essential in their selection process [3].

Since customers lack control of cloud resources, they are not in a good position to utilize technical mechanisms in order to protect their data against unauthorized access or secondary usage or other forms of misuse. Instead, they must rely on contracts or other trust mechanisms to try to encourage appropriate usage, in combination with mechanisms that provide compensation in the event of a breach, such as insurance, court action or penalties for breach of SLAs.

When it is not clear to individuals why their personal information is requested, or how and by whom it will be processed, this lack of control and lack of visibility of the provider supply chain will lead to suspicion and ultimately distrust [115]. There are also security-related concerns about whether data in the cloud will be adequately protected, as considered above. As a result, customers may hold back from using cloud services where personally identifiable information is involved, without an understanding of the obligations involved and the compliance risks faced, and assurance that potential suppliers will address such risks. This is particularly the case where sensitive information is involved, for example, financial and healthcare information.

1.6.3   Weak Trust Relationships

Trust relationships at any point in the cloud service delivery chain may be weak, but exist in order that a service can be provided quickly. Significant business risk may be introduced in a way that is not transparent when a cloud transaction is initiated, due to loss of control in passing sensitive data to other organizations and the global-ized nature of cloud infrastructure. Organizations that contract out key business processes may not even know that contractors are subcontracting, or even if they do, contract requirements regarding data protection measures may not be propagated down the contracting chain.

Trust along the chain from the customer to cloud providers at all levels may be non-transitive, and in particular the customer may not trust some of the subcontrac-tors (XaaS providers). Indeed, due to a lack of transparency, they may not even be aware of the identity of the cloud providers in this chain. In particular, 'on-demand' and 'pay-as-you-go' models may be based on weak trust relationships, involve third parties with lax data security practices, expose data widely and make deletion hard to verify. In order to provide extra capacity at short notice or in real time, new pro-viders could be added to the chain for which there is not sufficient chance to make adequate checks about their identity, practices, reputation and trustworthiness.

1.6.4   Lack of Consensus About Trust Management
Approaches to Be Used

There is a lack of consensus about what trust management approaches should be used for cloud environments. The inherent complexity of trust, the subjectivity of some factors and the difficulty of contextual representation makes trust measure-ment a major challenge. Artz and Gil [116] provide facets of trust that can be mea-sured for assessment purposes. Standardized trust models are needed for verification and assurance of accountability, but none of the large number of existing trust mod-els to date is adequate for the cloud environment [117]. There are many trust models which strive to accommodate some of the factors defined by Marsh [118] and others [119], and there are many trust assessment mechanisms which aim to measure them. These tend to be developed in isolation, and there has been little integration between hard and soft trust solutions. No suitable metrics exist for accountability, only a very high-level consideration to date [120]. Furthermore, there is no current consensus on the types of evidence required to verify the effectiveness of trust mechanisms [121]. Although the CloudTrust protocol [122] defines some categories, it has not covered others such as legal liability of the parties involved.

1.6.5 Trust Conclusions

Trust is widely perceived as a key concern, for end-user consumers, organizational customers and regulators. Lack of consumer trust is a key inhibitor to adoption of cloud services. People are suspicious about what happens to their data once it goes into the cloud. They are worried about who can access it and how it will be copied, shared and used, and they feel that they are losing control. Companies who change from carrying out their computing in-house to using the public cloud are not so much concerned any more about the health of servers, but instead the confidentiality and security of their data. Regulators fear that jurisdictional controls and compliance will weaken with cloud. All parties are concerned about potential access by certain foreign governments if sensitive data is moved to be stored within those countries.

Ultimately, usage of the cloud is a question of trade-offs between security, privacy, compliance, costs and benefits. Trust is key to adoption of SaaS, and transparency is an important mechanism. Furthermore, trust mechanisms need to be propagated right along the chain of service provision. We consider in the following section some solutions to these issues.

1.7 Approaches to Addressing Privacy, Security and Trust Issues

In this section, we present a brief overview of solutions and research in progress that aim to help address the concerns of privacy, security and trust in the cloud.

Overall, progress in this area demands that there should be consistent and co-ordinated development in three main dimensions:

- *Innovative regulatory frameworks*: such as accountability [123], which can facilitate both the operation of global business and provision of redress within cloud environments [124].
- *Responsible company governance*: whereby organizations act as a responsible steward of the data which is entrusted to them within the cloud, ensuring responsible behaviour via accountability mechanisms [125] and balancing innovation with individuals' expectations—Privacy by Design [126–128] being a way of achieving this.
- *Supporting technologies*: these include privacy-enhancing technologies [82, 129], security mechanisms [130], encryption [131], anonymization [132], etc.

By using a combination of these means, users and citizens can be provided with reassurance that their personal data will be protected, and cloud deployments can be made compliant with regulations, even within countries where such regulation is relatively strict.

We discuss in the rest of this book a number of mechanisms that illustrate promising approaches addressing the privacy, security and trust concerns considered above. Many of these mechanisms bridge the dimensions described above, or provide the basis for services that can be offered to organizations in order to enhance privacy and security. In particular, Chap. 2 bridges all three areas by considering law enforcement, Chap. 3 discusses how technical means can support regulatory compliance, and Chap. 4 shows how technology can help with corporate governance and provision of assurance. Chaps. 5 and 6 discuss technical mechanisms for enhancing security in the cloud, based upon trusted technologies. Chapters 7 and 8 consider the mitigation of information-security risks within an enterprise, based upon technical and procedural means.

1.8 Conclusions

In this chapter, we have assessed some of the key privacy and security issues involved in moving to cloud scenarios and set out the basis of some approaches that address the situation. Many of these themes are developed and explored in the subsequent chapters of this book.

Cloud models of service provision and the closely related capacity for big data processing and extended data mining allow new innovative approaches based upon increased value of personal information. At the same time, this increased business use of personal information can be very contentious, and so mechanisms need to be provided so that individuals can retain control over it. In particular, more information is known, recorded and accessible, making it difficult for people not to be judged on the basis of past actions. Profiling of individuals by business is becoming much more extensive and powerful, and governments, too, are connecting information about citizens, and their ability for much stronger surveillance is steadily increasing, making 'Big Brother'-type scenarios more possible over time.

Current cloud services pose an inherent challenge to data privacy because they typically result in data being present in unencrypted form on a machine owned and operated by a different organization from the data owner. There are threats of unauthorized uses of the data by service providers and of theft of data from machines in the cloud. Fears of leakage of sensitive data [4] or loss of privacy are a significant barrier to the adoption of cloud services [5, 51]. These fears may be justified. For instance, in 2007, criminals targeted the prominent CSP Salesforce.com and succeeded in stealing customer emails and addresses using a phishing attack [44]. Moreover, there are laws placing geographical and other restrictions on the processing by third parties of personal and sensitive information. These laws place limits on the use of cloud services as currently designed.

The large pools of resources made available through cloud computing are not necessarily located in the same country nor even on the same continent. Furthermore, the dynamic expansion or shrinkage of a cloud makes it difficult to keep track of what resources are used and in which country. This makes compliance with regulations related to data handling difficult to fulfil. Auditing is also a challenging task due to the volatility of the resources used.

The advantages of cloud computing—its ability to scale rapidly (through subcontractors), store data remotely (in unknown places) and share services in a dynamic environment—can become disadvantages in maintaining a level of assurance sufficient to sustain confidence in potential customers. These new features raise issues and concerns that need to be fully understood and addressed. Some of these issues will be shared with other paradigms, such as service-oriented architectures (SOA), grid, web-based services or outsourcing, but often, they are exacerbated by cloud. Privacy and security solutions need to address a combination of issues, and this may require new and even unique mechanisms rather than just a combination of known techniques for addressing selected aspects. The speed and flexibility of adjustment to vendor offerings, which benefits business and motivates cloud computing uptake, brings a higher risk to data privacy and security. This is a key user concern, particularly for financial and health data, and the associated lack of trust can be a key business inhibitor for cloud computing in domains where confidential or sensitive information is involved.

Responsible management of personal data is a central part of creating the trust to underpin adoption of cloud-based services and thereby to encourage customers to use cloud-based services. Privacy protection builds trust between service providers and users: accountability and privacy by design provide mechanisms to achieve the desired end effects and create this trust. This management can span a number of layers: policy, process, legal and technological. It is universally accepted as best practice that such mechanisms should be built in as early as possible into a system's lifecycle. Indeed, conforming to legal privacy requirements and meeting client privacy and security expectations with regard to personal information require corporations to demonstrate a context-appropriate level of control over such data at all stages of its processing, from collection to destruction.

In this chapter, we have stressed the importance of context to privacy and security requirements. As a result, solutions often need to be tailored to a specific context. In general, customers considering cloud services should consider their organization's operational, security, privacy and compliance requirements to see what approach would best suit them. Technology may help this decision-making process.

In summary, cloud providers need to safeguard the privacy and security of personal and confidential data that they hold on behalf of organizations and users. In particular, it is essential for the adoption of public cloud systems that consumers and citizens are reassured that privacy and security is not compromised. It will be necessary to address the problems of privacy and security raised in this chapter in order to provide and support trustworthy and innovative cloud computing services that are useful for a range of different situations.

Acknowledgements The influence and input contributing to development of the ideas in this chapter of various colleagues is gratefully acknowledged, notably Daniel Pradelles.

References

1. Mell, P., Grance, T.: A NIST definition of cloud computing. National Institute of Standards and Technology. NIST SP 800–145. http://www.nist.gov/itl/cloud/upload/cloud-def-v15.pdf (2009)
2. IDC: Enterprise Panel, Sept. http://www.slideshare.net/JorFigOr/cloud-computing-2010-an-idc-update (2009)
3. Cloud Industry Forum: Transition to the Cloud: The case for a code of practice. CIF Report. http://www.cloudindustryforum.org/downloads/transition-to-the-cloud.pdf (2011)
4. Cloud Security Alliance: Top Threats to Cloud Computing. v1.0, Mar (2010)
5. Horrigan, J.B.: Use of cloud computing applications and services. Pew Internet & American Life project memo, Sept (2008)
6. Uniting and Strengthening America by Providing Appropriate Tools Required to Intercept and Obstruct Terrorism Act (USA PATRIOT ACT) Title V, s 505 (2001)
7. Catteddu, D., Hogben, G. (eds.): Cloud computing: Benefits, risks and recommendations for information security. ENISA Report, Nov. http://www.enisa.europa.eu/activities/risk-management/files/deliverables/cloud-computing-risk-assessment/ (2009)
8. Marchini, R.: Cloud Computing: A Practical Introduction to the Legal Issues. BSI, London (2010)
9. McKinley, P.K., Samimi, F.A., Shapiro, J.K., Chiping, T.: Service clouds: a distributed infrastructure for constructing autonomic communication services. In: Dependable, Autonomic and Secure Computing, IEEE, 12–14 Dec 2011, Sydney, Australia, 341–348 (2006)
10. Warren, S., Brandeis, L.: The right to privacy. Harv. Law Rev. **4**, 193 (1890)
11. Westin, A.: Privacy and Freedom. Atheneum, New York (1967)
12. American Institute of Certified Public Accountants (AICPA) and CICA: Generally accepted privacy principles. Aug. http://www.aicpa.org/interestareas/informationtechnology/resources/privacy/generallyacceptedprivacyprinciples/downloadabledocuments/gapp_prac_%200909.pdf (2009)
13. Solove, D.J.: A taxonomy of privacy. Univ. Pennsylvania Law Rev. **154**(3), 477, Jan. http://papers.ssrn.com/sol3/papers.cfm?abstract_id=667622 (2006)
14. Nissenbaum, H.: Privacy as contextual integrity. Washington Law Rev. **79**, 101–139 (2004)
15. Nissenbaum, H.: Privacy in Context: Technology, Policy and the Integrity of Social Life. Stanford University Press, Stanford (2009)
16. Swire, P.P., Bermann, S.: Information Privacy: Official Reference for the Certified Information Privacy Professional, CIPP. International Association of Privacy Professionals, York (2007)
17. European Commission: Directive 95/46/EC of the European Parliament and of the Council of 24 October 1995 on the protection of individuals with regard to the processing of personal data and on the free movement of such data. http://ec.europa.eu/justice/policies/privacy/docs/95-46-ce/dir1995-46_part1_en.pdf (1995)
18. Privacy Protection Study Commission: Personal privacy in Information society, United States Privacy Protection Study Commission fair information practices. http://epic.org/privacy/ppsc1977report/ (1977)
19. Organization for Economic Co-operation and Development (OECD): Guidelines for the protection of personal data and transborder data flows. http://www.oecd.org/document/18/0,3746,en_2649_34223_1815186_1_1_1_1,00.html (1980)
20. Safe Harbor website: http://export.gov/safeharbor/ (2012)
21. The White House: Consumer data privacy in a networked world: a framework for protecting privacy and promoting innovation in the global digital economy, Feb. http://www.whitehouse.gov/sites/default/files/privacy-final.pdf (2012)
22. European Commission: Proposal for a Directive of the European Parliament and of the Council on the protection of individuals with regard to the processing of personal data by competent

authorities for the purposes of prevention, investigation, detection or prosecution of criminal offences or the execution of criminal penalties, and the free movement of such data, Jan. http://ec.europa.eu/justice/data-protection/document/review2012/com_2012_10_en.pdf (2012)

23. ISO: 27001: Information Security Management – Specification with Guidance for Use. ISO, London (2005)
24. Rousseau, D., Sitkin, S., Burt, R., Camerer, C.: Not so different after all: a cross-discipline view of trust. Acad. Manage. Rev. **23**(3), 393–404 (1998)
25. Baier, A.: Trust and antitrust. Ethics **96**(2), 231–260 (1986)
26. Gambetta, D.: Can we trust trust? In: Gambetta, D. (ed.) Trust: Making and Breaking Cooperative Relations. Basil Blackwell, New York (1988)
27. Nooteboom, B.: Social capital, institutions and trust. Rev. Soc. Econ. **65**(1), 29–53 (2007)
28. Sitkin, S., Roth, N.: Explaining the limited effectiveness of legalistic 'remedies' for trust/distrust. Org. Sci. **4**, 367–392 (1993)
29. Wang, Y., Lin, K.-J.: Reputation-oriented trustworthy computing in e-commerce environments. Internet Comput. IEEE **12**(4), 55–59 (2008)
30. Singh, S., Morley, C.: Young Australians' privacy, security and trust in internet banking. In: Proceedings of the 21st Annual Conference of the Australian Computer-Human Interaction Special interest Group: Design: Open 24/7 (2009)
31. Osterwalder, D.: Trust through evaluation and certification. Soc. Sci. Comput. Rev. **19**(1), 32–46 (2001)
32. Best, S.J., Kreuger, B.S., Ladewig, J.: The effect of risk perceptions on online political participatory decisions. J. Inform. Technol. Polit. **4**, 5–17 (2005)
33. Chang, E., Dillon, T., Calder, D.: Human system interaction with confident computing: the megatrend. In: Proceedings of the Conference on Human System Interactions, Krakow, Poland (2008)
34. Jaeger, P.T., Fleischmann, K.R.: Public libraries, values, trust, and e-government. Inf. Technol. Libr. **26**(4), 35–43 (2007)
35. Nissenbaum, H.: Can trust be secured online? A theoretical perspective. Etica e Politica, 2 (1999)
36. Giff, S.: The influence of metaphor, smart cards and interface dialogue on trust in e-commerce. M.Sc. project, University College, London (2000)
37. Nielsen, J.: Trust or bust: communicating trustworthiness in web design. Jacob Nielsen's Alertbox. http://www.useit.com/alertbox/990307.html (1999)
38. Huynh, T.: A personalized framework for trust assessment. ACM Symp. Appl. Comput. **2**, 1302–1307 (2008)
39. Leiven, R.: Attack resistant trust metrics. Ph.D. thesis, University of California, Berkeley (2003)
40. Ziegler, C.N., Lausen, G.: Spreading activation models for trust propagation. In: EEE 2004, IEEE, Taipei (2004)
41. Kosko, B.: Fuzzy cognitive maps. Int. J. Man-Mach. Stud. **24**, 65–75 (1986)
42. Pearson, S., Casassa Mont, M., Crane, S.: Persistent and dynamic trust: analysis and the related impact of trusted platforms. In: Herrmann, P., Issarny, V., Shiu, S. (eds.) Trust Management, Proc. iTrust 2005, LNCS 3477, pp. 355–363. Springer-Verlag, Berlin/Heidelberg/Paris (2005)
43. Gellman, R.: Privacy in the clouds: risks to privacy and confidentiality from cloud computing. World Privacy Forum. http://www.worldprivacyforum.org/pdf/WPF_Cloud_Privacy_Report.pdf (2009)
44. Greenberg, A.: Cloud computing's stormy Side. Forbes Magazine, 19 Feb (2008)
45. Fratto, M.: Internet evolution. The Big Report, Cloud Control. http://www.internetevolution.com/document.asp?doc_id=170782 (2009)
46. Hall, J.A., Liedtka, S.L.: The Sarbanes-Oxley Act: implications for large-scale IT outsourcing. Commun. ACM **50**(3), 95–100 (2007)
47. Reidenberg, J.: Technology and internet jurisdiction. Univ. Pennsylvania Law Rev.1, SSRN eLibrary (2005)
48. Kohl, U.: Jurisdiction and the Internet. Cambridge University Press, Cambridge (2007)
49. Mowbray, M.: The fog over the Grimpen Mire: cloud computing and the law. Script-ed J. Law, Technol. Soc. **6**(1), 132–143 (Apr 2009)

50. Goldberg, N.M., Wildon-Byrne, M.: Securing communications on the cloud. Bloomberg Law Rep.—Technol. Law. 1(10). http://www.infolawgroup.com/uploads/file/Goldberg%20Article. pdf (2009)
51. Salmon, J.: Clouded in uncertainty—the legal pitfalls of cloud computing. Computing Magazine, 24 Sept. http://www.computing.co.uk/computing/features/2226701/clouded-uncertainty-4229153 (2008)
52. Crompton, M.:, Cowper, C., Jefferis, C.: The Australian Dodo Case: an insight for data protection regulation. World Data Protection Report. 9(1), BNA (2009)
53. Hon, K.: Personal data in the UK, anonymisation and encryption. Queen Mary University of London, 9 June. http://www.cloudlegal.ccls.qmul.ac.uk/Research/49700.html (2011)
54. Cloud Security Alliance: Security guidance for critical areas of focus in cloud computing. v2.1, English language version, Dec. http://cloudsecurityalliance.org/guidance/csaguide.v2.1.pdf (2009)
55. Mather, T., Kumaraswamy, S., Latif, S.: Cloud Security and Privacy. O'Reilly, Sebastopol, CA (2009)
56. Vaquero, L., Rodero-Merino, L., Morán, D.: Locking the sky: a survey on IaaS cloud security. Computing 91, 93–118 (2011)
57. Regulation of Investigatory Powers Act: Part II, s 28, UK (2000)
58. Narayanan, A., Shmatikov, V.: Robust deanonymization of large sparse datasets. IEEE Symp. Sec. Privacy (S&P) 111–125 (2008). doi:10.1109/SP.2008.33
59. VMWare: Virtual appliances. http://www.vmware.com/appliances/getting-started/learn/ovf. html (2012)
60. Open Cloud Computing Interface (OCCI): http://occi-wg.org/ (2012)
61. Google: Data liberation front. http://www.dataliberation.org/ (2012)
62. SNIA: Cloud data management interface. http://www.snia.org/cdmi (2012)
63. OASIS. Security Assertion Markup Language (SAML). http://www.oasis-open.org/ standards#samlv2.0 (2005)
64. Wei, J., Zhang, X., Ammons, G., Bala, V., Ning, P.: Managing security of virtual machine images in a cloud environment. In: Proceedings of the CCSW '09. ACM, New York, pp. 91–96 (2009)
65. Google App Engine: http://code.google.com/appengine
66. Kortchinsky, K.: CLOUDBURST: A VMWare Guest to Host Escape Story. BlackHat, Las Vegas (2009)
67. Ristenpart, T., Tromer, E., Shacham, H., Savage, S.: Hey, you, get off of my cloud: exploring information leakage in third-party compute clouds. In: Proceedings of CCS'09, ACM, Chicago, Nov (2009)
68. IBM: X-force® 2010 mid-year trend and risk report. Aug. ftp://public.dhe.ibm.com/common/ ssi/ecm/en/wgl03003usen/WGL03003USEN.PDF (2010)
69. ENISA: Cloud computing information assurance framework. In: Catteddu, D., Hogben, G. (eds.), Nov. http://www.enisa.europa.eu/act/rm/files/deliverables/cloud-computing-information-assurance-framework (2009)
70. UK Cabinet Office and CESG: HMG information assurance maturity model and assessment framework. www.cesg.gov.uk/publications/Documents/iamm-assessment-framework.pdf (2010)
71. Jansen, W., Grance, T.: Guidelines on security and privacy in public cloud computing. NIST Special Publication 800–144, Dec (2011)
72. International Organisation for Standardisation (ISO): ISO/IEC 27001:2005 Information technology—security techniques—information security management systems—requirements. http://www.iso.org/iso/catalogue_detail?csnumber=42103 (2005)
73. ISO: ISO/IEC 27002:2005 Information technology—Security techniques—Code of practice for information security management. http://www.iso.org/iso/catalogue_detail?csnumber=50297 (2005)
74. ISO: ISO 31000:2009 Risk management—Principles and guidelines. http://www.iso.org/iso/ catalogue_detail?csnumber=43170 (2009)
75. Shared Assessments: Evaluating cloud risk for the enterprise. The Santa Fe Group, Oct. http:// www.sharedassessments.org/media/pdf-EnterpriseCloud-SA.pdf (2010)
76. Hagen, J.M., Sivertsen, T.K., Rong, C.: Protection against unauthorized access and computer crime in Norwegian enterprises. J. Comput. Secur. 16(3), 341–366 (2008)

77. CSA: Trusted cloud initiative. http://www.cloudsecurityalliance.org/trustedcloud.html (2012)
78. Information Commissioner's Office (ICO): Privacy impact assessment handbook. Version 2, June. http://www.ico.gov.uk/for_organisations/data_protection/topic_guides/privacy_impact_assessment.aspx (2009)
79. Ardagna, C.A., et al.: Exploiting cryptography for privacy-enhanced access control. J. Comput. Soc. **18**(1), 123–160 (2010) (IOS Press)
80. Data Loss Prevention: http://datalossprevention.com/ (2012)
81. Bier, E., et al.: The rules of redaction: identify, protect, review (and repeat). Secur. Privacy, IEEE **7**(6), 46–53 (2009)
82. Information Commissioner's Office UK ICO: Data protection guidance note: Privacy enhancing technologies: http://www.ico.gov.uk/upload/documents/library/data_protection/detailed_specialist_guides/privacy_enhancing_technologies_v2.pdf (2007)
83. Informatica: Dynamic data masking. http://www.informatica.com/au/products_services/data_masking/Pages/index.aspx (2012)
84. Cranor, L.: Web Privacy with P3P. O'Reilly and Associates, Sebastopol, CA (2002)
85. EnCoRe: Ensuring Consent and Revocation project: http://www.encore-project.info (2012)
86. Cachin, C., Schunter, M.: A cloud you can trust. Dec. http://spectrum.ieee.org/computing/networks/a-cloud-you-can-trust/4 (2011)
87. SAS 70: http://sas70.com/
88. SysTrust and WebTrust: http://www.webtrust.org/
89. RSA Archer: eGRC. http://www.emc.com/security/rsa-archer.htm (2012)
90. CSA: GRC stack. http://www.cloudsecurityalliance.org/grcstack.html (2012)
91. CSA: CloudAudit. http://cloudaudit.org/CloudAudit/Home.html (2012)
92. Takabi, H., Joshi, J.B.D., Ahn, G.: Security and privacy challenges in cloud computing environments. Secur. Privacy, IEEE **8**(6), 24–31 (2010)
93. EGEE project: Logging and Bookkeeping (LB) service. http://egee.cesnet.cz/en/JRA1/LB/ (2012)
94. Chuckwa: http://incubator.apache.org/chukwa/ (2012)
95. Nicolett, M., Kavanagh, K.M.: Critical capabilities for security information and event management technology, Gartner Report (2011)
96. RSA: EnVision platform. http://www.rsa.com/experience/envision/3n1/ (2012)
97. HP: ArcSight. http://www.arcsight.com/ (2012)
98. Stoneburner, G., Goguen, A., Feringa, A.: Risk management guide for information technology systems: recommendations of the National Institute of Standards and Technology. Special publication 800–30, July (2002)
99. Committee of Sponsoring Organisations of the Treadway Commission (COSO): http://www.coso.org (2012)
100. ISACA: http://www.isaca.org (2012)
101. American Institute of CPAs (AICPA): http://www.aicpa.org/INTERESTAREAS/INFORMATIONTECHNOLOGY/RESOURCES/TRUSTSERVICES/Pages/default.aspx (2012)
102. Amazon: CloudWatch. http://aws.amazon.com/cloudwatch/ (2012)
103. Haeberlen, A.: A case for the accountable cloud. ACM SIGOPS OS Rev. **44**(2), 52–57 (2010)
104. Haeberlen, A., et al.: Accountable virtual machines. In: Proceedings of the OSDI'10, USENIX, Vancouver, Canada (2010)
105. HyTrust: http://www.hytrust.com/product/overview/ (2012)
106. Chen, S., Wang, C.: Accountability as a service for the cloud: from concept to implementation with BPEL. In: Proceedings of the 6th IEEE World Congress on Services, IEEE, pp. 91–98 (2010)
107. Jaeger, P., Lin, J., Grimes, J.: Cloud computing and information policy: computing in a policy cloud? J. Inf. Technol. Polit. **5**, 269–283 (2008)
108. European Commission: Attitudes on data protection and electronic identity in the European Union. June. http://ec.europa.eu/public_opinion/archives/ebs/ebs_359_en.pdf (2011)

109. IDC: Cloud computing attitudes, Survey, Doc.#223077 (2010)
110. Forrester Research, Inc.: Ignoring cloud risks: a growing gap between I&O and the business. Mar (2011)
111. Forrester Research, Inc.: You're not ready for internal cloud. July (2010)
112. Goldman Sachs: Equity Research, Jan (2011)
113. Fujitsu Research Institute: Personal data in the cloud: a global survey of consumer attitudes. http://www.fujitsu.com/downloads/SOL/fai/reports/fujitsu_personaldata-in-the-cloud.pdf (2010)
114. Uusitalo, I., Karppinen, K., Arto, J., Savola, R.: Trust and cloud services – an interview study. In: Proceedings of the CloudCom 2010, IEEE, Indianapolis (2010)
115. Lacohé, H., Crane, S., Phippen, A.: Trustguide Final Report, October. DTI Sciencewise Programme. www.trustguide.org (2006)
116. Artz, D., Gil, Y.: A survey of trust in computer science and the semantic web. Web Semant. Sci. Serv. Agents World Wide Web 5, 58–71 (2007)
117. Li, W., Ping, L.: Trust model to enhance security and interoperability of cloud environment. In: Cloud Computing. Lecture Notes in Computer Science, vol. 5931, pp. 69–79. Springer, Berlin (2009)
118. Marsh, S.: Formalising trust as a computational concept. Doctoral dissertation, University of Stirling (1994)
119. Banerjee, S., Mattmann, C., Medvidovic, N., Golubchik, L.: Leveraging architectural models to inject trust into software systems. In: Proceedings of SESS '05, pp. 1–7. ACM, New York (2005)
120. The Centre for Information Policy Leadership (CIPP): Demonstrating and measuring accountability: a discussion document. Accountability Phase II—The Paris Project. http://www.huntonfiles.com/files/webupload/CIPL_Accountability_Phase_II_Paris_Project.PDF (2010)
121. Shin, D., Ahn, G.-J.: Role-based privilege and trust management. Comput. Syst. Sci. Eng. J. 20(6), 401–410 (2005)
122. CSA: Cloud trust protocol https://cloudsecurityalliance.org/research/ctp/ (2012).
123. Weitzner, D.J., Abelson, H., Berners-Lee, T., Feigenbaum, J., Hendler, J., Sussman, G.J.: Information accountability. Commun. ACM 51(6), 87 June (2008)
124. Pearson, S., Charlesworth, A.: Accountability as a way forward for privacy protection in the cloud. In: Jaatun, M.G., Zhao, G., Rong, C. (eds.) Proceedings of the 1st International Conference on Cloud Computing (CloudCom 2009), Beijing, Dec. LNCS, vol. 5931, pp. 131–144. Springer, Berlin (2009)
125. Pearson, S., et al.: Scalable, accountable privacy management for large organizations. In: INSPEC 2009, IEEE, Sept, pp. 168–175 (2009)
126. Information Commissioners Office: Privacy by design. Report. www.ico.gov.uk (2008)
127. Cavoukian, A., Taylor, S., Abrams, M.: Privacy by design: essential for organizational accountability and strong business practices. Identity Inf. Soc. 3(2), 405–413. http://www.springerlink.com/content/96852p1667mwl665/ (2010)
128. Cavoukian, A.: Privacy by design: origins, meaning, and prospects for assuring privacy and trust in the information era. In: Yee, G. (ed.) Privacy Protection Measures and Technologies in Business Organizations: Aspects and Standards, pp. 170–208. IGI Global, Hershey (2012)
129. Camenisch, J., Fischer-Hübner, S., Rannenberg, K. (eds.): Privacy and Identity Management for Life. Springer, Heidelberg (2011)
130. Kamara, S., Lauter, K.: Cryptographic cloud storage. In: Financial Cloud and Data Security. LNCS, vol. 6054, pp. 136–149. Springer, Berlin (2010). doi:10.1007/978–3–642–14992–4_13
131. Gentry, C.: Fully homomorphic encryption using ideal lattices. In: 41st ACM Symposium on Theory of Computing (STOC), pp. 169–178. ACM, New York (2009)
132. Spiekermann, S., Cranor, L.F.: Engineering privacy. IEEE Trans. Software Eng. 35(1), 67–82, Jan/Feb (2009)

Recommended Reading

Camenisch, J., Fischer-Hubner, S., Rannenberg, K. (eds.): Privacy and Identity Management for Life. Springer, Berlin (2011)

Catteddu, D., Hogben, G. (eds.): Cloud computing: benefits, risks and recommendations for information security. ENISA Report. http://www.enisa.europa.eu/act/rm/files/deliverables/cloud-computing-risk-assessment (2009)

Cavoukian, A., Taylor, S., Abrams, M.: Privacy by design: essential for organizational accountability and strong business practices. Identity Inf. Soc. 3(2), 405–413. http://www.springerlink.com/content/96852p1667mwl665/ (2010)

Cloud Security Alliance (CSA): Security Guidance for Critical Areas of Focus in Cloud Computing. v2.1, English language version, Dec. http://cloudsecurityalliance.org/guidance/csaguide. v2.1.pdf (2009)

Cofta, P.: The trustworthy and trusted web. Foundations Trends Web Sci. 2(4), 243–381 (2011)

Craig, T., Ludloff, M.E.: Privacy and Big Data. O'Reilly, Sebastopol, CA (2011)

Gellman, R.: Privacy in the clouds: risks to privacy and confidentiality from cloud computing. World Privacy Forum. www.worldprivacyforum.org/pdf/WPF_Cloud_Privacy_Report.pdf (2009)

Information Commissioners Office: Privacy by design. Report, Nov. www.ico.gov.uk (2008)

Mather, T., Kumaraswamy, S., Latif, S.: Cloud Security and Privacy. O'Reilly, Sebastopol, CA (2009)

Pearson, S.: Toward accountability in the cloud. IEEE Internet Comput., IEEE Comput. Soc. 15(4), 64–69, July/Aug (2011)

Pearson, S., Casassa Mont, M.: Sticky policies: an approach for privacy management across multiple parties. IEEE Comput. 44(9), 60–68, Sept (2011)

Schwartz, P.M.: Data Protection Law and the Ethical Use of Analytics, CIPL. http://www.huntonfiles.com/files/webupload/CIPL_Ethical_Undperinnings_of_Analytics_Paper.pdf (2010)

Solove, D.J.: Nothing to Hide: The False Tradeoff between Privacy and Security. Yale University Press, New Haven (2011)

The Royal Academy of Engineering: Dilemmas of Privacy and Surveillance: Challenges of Technological Change. Mar. www.raeng.org.uk/policy/reports/default.htm (2007)

Yee, G. (ed.): Privacy Protection Measures and Technologies in Business Organizations: Aspects and Standards. IGI Global, Hershey (2012)

Part II
Law Enforcement and Audits

Chapter 2
Accessing Data in the Cloud: The Long Arm of the Law Enforcement Agent

Ian Walden

Abstract When placing data in the cloud, users inevitably have concerns about unauthorised access to such data, exposing commercial secrets and breaching individual privacy. While such threats are primarily directed towards organised crime, access by law enforcement agencies in the course of an investigation has itself become a heightened privacy and security concern, particularly in relation to US authorities in a market where US-based cloud providers dominate. From a law enforcement perspective, the cloud represents the latest manifestation of a transnational environment within which they have to operate, presenting a multitude of conflicting laws. This chapter examines how rules, at a European and international level, attempt to balance the needs of law enforcement with the needs of users and providers of cloud services.

Keywords Cloud computing • Confidentiality • Conflict of laws • Contract • Crime • Criminal law • Cybercrime • Data disclosure • Data privacy • Data protection • Data retention • EU • European Union • Evidence • Forensics • Interception • Internet • Jurisdiction • Law enforcement • Law enforcement agencies • Legal issues • Privacy • Security • Surveillance • Telecommunications

2.1 Introduction

As cloud services become a mainstream ICT solution for business, consumers and governments, so the security and privacy issues will assume increasing significance. To the extent that cloud services are used for criminal activities or targeted by

This chapter was written under the auspices of the Queen Mary, University of London Cloud legal Project: http://www.cloudlegal.ccls.qmul.ac.uk/index.html

I. Walden (✉)
Centre for Commercial Law Studies, Queen Mary, University of London, London, UK
e-mail: i.n.walden@qmul.ac.uk

S. Pearson and G. Yee (eds.), *Privacy and Security for Cloud Computing*,
Computer Communications and Networks, DOI 10.1007/978-1-4471-4189-1_2,
© Springer-Verlag London 2013

organised crime, then public law enforcement agencies (LEAs) will want and need to obtain access to data held in cloud services for forensic purposes during the course of an investigation. Such forensic data may be held on systems controlled by a suspect, a victim or an innocent third party (collectively referred to as 'cloud users'), often located in foreign jurisdictions or where the location is unknown. The potential for law enforcement access can, however, generate its own commercial security and privacy concerns for cloud users. The launch of Microsoft Office 365 in June 2011, for example, was accompanied by expressions of concern that Microsoft would not guarantee that data of European customers could not be accessed by agencies acting under US jurisdiction [17]. Similar such concerns were behind the Dutch government appearing to suggest that US-based suppliers of cloud services may be 'excluded' from supplying public authorities handling government or citizen data due to the risk of access by US authorities [18]. In addition, some European providers have even tried to make a virtue out of their 'non-US' status, calling for certification schemes that would indicate where data is protected from such access.[1]

This chapter examines the legal framework governing law enforcement access to data in a cloud environment, giving particular attention to European Union and international law, specifically the Council of Europe Cybercrime Convention,[2] governing the obtaining of data for investigative and prosecutorial purposes. Consideration is given to how such rules interact and potentially conflict with other laws, particularly data protection and evidential rules. It is suggested that current fears voiced about US-based cloud providers are more a consequence of their current dominance in the global cloud market,[3] while concerns about the potential reach of US law enforcement agents, particularly under the 'Patriot Act',[4] reflect widespread ignorance about powers already available to LEAs in many, if not most, leading jurisdictions. A greater source of concern lies in the differential privacy regimes between Europe and the USA and a particular lack of clarity in the field of criminal law.

The exercise of LEA powers raises a number of jurisdictional questions that are examined in this chapter. First is the question of territorial reach: When does the exercising of LEA powers in the cloud reach their territorial limit, thereby becoming potentially unlawful in the domestic jurisdiction of the LEA, as well as in the foreign territory in which they were exercised? Second, what obligations does a service provider have to assist an LEA in the course of an investigation, from delivering up data in response to a request to the retention of data and the implementation of an intercept capability? Third, how may LEA powers differ between obtaining data which is 'at rest' within a cloud service, as opposed to data 'in transmission' to, from or within the cloud service?[5] Finally, where data is obtained *ultra vires* (i.e. beyond the power of the LEA) in breach of legal rules, what impact may that have on its evidential value?

Each of these issues presents a boundary issue for LEAs, service providers and cloud users and a boundary between lawful and unlawful behaviours or regulated and unregulated activities. Such boundaries are by no means unique to cloud-based activities, but are brought into sharper focus by the anticipated shift to cloud computing by users, whether as individuals or businesses. Clarifying how and when those boundaries apply and what mechanisms and procedures have been adopted, or are proposed, to address the needs of LEAs in a cloud environment are examined in this chapter. First, however, we need to consider some of the forensic challenges for law enforcement in a cloud computing environment.

2.2   Forensic Challenges in the Cloud

Cloud users depend on various 'service providers' for their use of the cloud, of which three broad categories are distinguished for our purposes:

- A cloud service provider, who has a direct contractual relationship with the subscriber to the service, whether offering a SaaS, PaaS, IaaS or other variant [4]
- A cloud infrastructure provider, who provides the cloud service provider with some form of infrastructure,[6] such as server farms and processing capacity, including persistent storage
- A communication service provider, who provides the transmission service enabling the cloud user to communicate with the cloud service provider

Both cloud users and service providers may become the focus of attention in an LEA investigation, through the utilisation of either covert investigative techniques, such as surveillance or interception, or the exercise of coercive powers, such as production or search and seizure orders, to directly obtain the forensic material. The layered nature of cloud computing services means that an LEA request could be served against a cloud infrastructure provider, such as Amazon Web Services, without either the cloud service provider, such as Dropbox, or the cloud user being aware that such a request has been made in respect of data entrusted by the user with his service provider.

Obtaining computer-derived evidence, whether 'at rest' or 'in transmission', raises formidable forensic challenges, which have been examined elsewhere [1, 2]. While methods of forensic analysis and the tools are fairly well established, some specific forensic challenges of cloud computing can be seen in four key areas:

- *Multiplicity* – Data held by the service provider is likely to be replicated within the cloud for reasons of performance, availability, backup and redundancy. These multiple copies are likely to be stored across different 'virtual' and physical machines, sometimes in different jurisdictions. As such, when responding to an LEA request, a cloud service provider may have the capability of choosing to retrieve the data from multiple locations.
- *Distributed storage* – Techniques widely used in cloud computing, such as 'sharding' or 'partitioning', mean that the data will likely be stored as fragments across a range of machines, logically linked and reassembled on demand, rather than as a single contiguous data set.
- *Protected data* – The cloud user may submit data in a protected form, i.e. using cryptographic techniques, which render the data opaque to the cloud service provider [7]. As such, when requesting data disclosure by a service provider, an

LEA may not be able to obtain intelligible material. In addition, the various service providers may apply their own cryptographic mechanisms to the submitted data, during transit and storage, which will need to be removed for LEA access.

- *Identity* – With a stand-alone PC, it can be difficult to establish an adequate forensic link between the relevant evidential data, the virtual identity of the user and a real-world person. These identity problems are more complex in a cloud environment, where there is a need to establish a link between the data held in the cloud; the user device from which data was created, submitted to or accessed from; the cloud service[7] and an individual user.

For the first three, the generic concern is one of access, locating the relevant data and reassembling or converting it into intelligible form. A fundamental principle of digital forensics is that data obtained for law enforcement purposes should not be altered through the process of obtaining, especially the metadata relating to the evidential content.[8] While client-side analysis will continue to offer valuable forensic material, remote data retrieval will likely become the norm in a cloud environment, which increases the likelihood that data changes will occur, especially where access is obtained through cloud APIs[9] and architectures that are unknown to the investigators. As such, the competence of investigators to testify about the authenticity of the process of obtaining, especially data changes attributable to their actions, may be compromised.

A shift to remote data retrieval will increase LEA reliance on cooperation from cloud service providers. Otherwise, access to the material could be obtained through a user's access device, whether a suspect or not, under coercion, voluntarily or surreptitiously. In both scenarios, however, the location of the data at the moment it is retrieved for the purpose of investigation may be unknown and unknowable, in terms of the actual machines upon which the data is stored, and therefore the territory or territories in which it can be said to reside. It may be forensically possible for the cloud service or cloud infrastructure provider to identify precisely the machines on which the data resides at the time of a request, although more likely *ex post* than prior to the data being retrieved. As a consequence, consideration needs to be given to the impact that the inability to establish location, referred to as the 'loss of location',[10] has on the exercise of law enforcement powers and the evidential value of cloud-derived material. Alternatively, where data fragments are located in different jurisdictions, it would be possible to resolve a single location prior to disclosure to the LEA, i.e. when and where the data is reassembled, which could be used as a proxy for determining the legality or enforceability of a request.

Remote data retrieval also differs in nature from the seizure of a suspect's device for forensic analysis. While the latter involves the taking of property, in the former, a copy is generally obtained of the relevant data, which raises questions about the appropriate legal characterisation of the copied data. Whether such a breach of confidentiality constitutes an interference with a person's 'possessions', engaging article 1 of Protocol 1 of the European Convention on Human Rights (ECHR), or his privacy, under article 8 of the Convention, may be uncertain.[11] The Cybercrime Convention refers both to the seizure and copying of data, although it does not make clear whether the distinction has legal consequence.[12] However, an earlier Council of Europe Recommendation suggested a principle of equality, whereby data that is functionally equivalent to a traditional document should be treated as the same for the purposes of procedural law governing search and seizure.[13]

2.3   Exercising LEA Powers

The Council of Europe Convention on Cybercrime (2001) is the leading public international law instrument harmonising substantive and procedural criminal law, with some 47 signatures, including non-European states such as the United States.[14] Key objectives of the Convention are to enable the investigation and prosecution of cybercrime within the domestic jurisdiction, as well as facilitate international cooperation against transborder cybercrimes under Chapter III of the Convention. As such, the Convention's provisions represent agreement amongst the signatories about the appropriate exercise of law enforcement powers in cyberspace, including a cloud environment.

It is expressly recognised in the Convention, at article 15, that the exercise of LEA powers inevitably interferes in the rights and freedoms of individuals, especially the right to privacy (art. 8), and therefore, any such measures must meet the criteria laid down in the ECHR: 'in accordance with the law', to meet a 'legitimate interest' and only to the extent that such interference is necessary and proportionate. For the purposes of this chapter, we are primarily concerned with the first of these, the legality of the exercise of LEA powers.

In general, the powers exercised by LEAs are expressly conferred by statute and may either be exercised in the course of carrying out duties conferred upon the LEA or require further and specific authorisation, granted by judicial, executive or administrative entities.[15] Further authorisation is usually relevant to the exercise of covert or coercive powers, which is the primary concern of this chapter. A failure to obtain appropriate authorisation would generally render the LEA conduct unlawful, unless express immunity is granted (e.g. RIPA, s. 80 'General saving for lawful conduct'). While a law enforcement officer may engage in conduct as any normal person without such conduct constituting an 'exercise of power' *per se*, certain conduct may be considered unlawful on the basis that the person, as a public official, is an agent of the state.[16]

Where an LEA exercises conferred powers, the legislation granting such powers is usually expressly stated to be, or presumed to be, limited to the territorial jurisdiction of the domestic state.[17] As such, an LEA would be acting unlawfully if it exercised powers outside the jurisdiction, although a domestic exercise of powers may have an extraterritorial effect. Conversely, any domestic protections controlling such exercise of LEA powers would also be generally limited to acts carried out within the domestic jurisdiction,[18] although whether such protections are available to 'any person' within the jurisdiction or only nationals may vary.[19]

When considering the legality of the 'exercise' of an LEA power, a further distinction should be made between the obtaining of the authorisation and the conduct carried out in furtherance of that authorisation. In respect of the former, legality issues may arise if an LEA engages in conduct without obtaining the required authorisation, or the authorisation process is procedurally flawed. In respect of the latter, a validly granted authorisation may be served on an entity to which it is not applicable or on an entity residing outside the jurisdiction. While the authorisation process itself may be 'in accordance with the law', the act of serving it may render it unlawful or, at least, unenforceable.

The powers referred to in the Convention can be broadly divided into measures exercised against cloud users and those against service providers. The requirement to enable the 'expedited preservation of stored computer data' (art. 16), while potentially applicable to any persons, is most likely to be used against an innocent third party, such as a cloud service provider, rather than a suspect. The preservation and disclosure of 'traffic data' is again primarily directed at service providers. 'Traffic data' is defined in the following terms:

> any computer data relating to a communication by means of a computer system, generated by a computer system that formed a part in the chain of communication, indicating the communication's origin, destination, route, time, date, size, duration, or type of underlying service. (art. 1(d))

This would include forensic material held by all three types of service provider outlined above and, indeed, the provision expressly recognises that 'one or more service providers' may have been involved in the transmission of the communication (art. 17(1)(b)). The Convention's data preservation obligations are potentially applicable across all types of cloud service provider, in contrast to the imposition of wholesale data retention obligations under EU law, applicable only to communication service providers. The contrast may be less stark, however, depending on how widely the latter category is defined (discussed further below) and how the preservation regime operates. In the USA, for example, the authorities can issue 90-day blanket data preservation orders against all three types of cloud service providers, which are renewable for an additional 90-day period (18 U.S.C. § 2703(f)).

The expedited preservation of forensic material is the first stage of an investigation, LEA access to such data will often comprise a separate procedure, subject to different authorisation procedures. The Convention distinguishes two forms of production order, one being issued against a person who is in 'possession or control' of computer data, while the other is for a service provider to disclose 'subscriber information' (art. 18). The former requires the person to be located 'in its territory', although the data may be held elsewhere, while a request for subscriber information can extend to any service provider 'offering its services in the territory', which could obviously mean that an order may be served where both entity and data resides in a foreign jurisdiction.

'Possession and control' reflects the terminology commonly found in the national law of signatories to the Convention.[20] 'Possession' would seem a narrower concept than 'control', even though it may extend beyond physical possession to constructive possession under certain legal systems.[21] The concept of having 'control' over data could be viewed from a managerial perspective, an ability to determine the purpose and means of processing,[22] from a technical perspective, whether the person is capable of remotely accessing the data, for example, under 'follow the sun' support services, or from legal perspective, as having legal rights in respect of the data, 'whether legislative, executive, administrative, judicial, contractual or consensual',[23] which reflects the Convention's approach with respect to the substantive offences. A court is likely to give consideration to the nature of the relationship between a parent company and its subsidiary,[24] which would appear to offer cloud providers the possibility of designing their corporate governance structure in a manner that could ensure that an EU-based subsidiary of a US cloud provider is legally immune from a production order issued under US law against that subsidiary. This is the converse of the current situation in Europe, where local subsidiaries of US service providers often decline to respond to domestic LEA requests on the grounds that they do not have rights of access to data held by their US parent.[25] Such Balkanisation of the cloud will be unappealing for cloud providers in terms of the efficacy of the technological infrastructure, but may be a necessary response to security and privacy concerns.

In providing for a second category of production order in relation to 'subscriber information' held by a service provider, the Convention suggests the need for a distinct regime governing access to such data. 'Subscriber information' relates to information held by a service provider 'relating to subscribers of *its* services' (art. 18(3)), which would exclude a cloud infrastructure provider from receiving data requests about users of a service supplied by a separate cloud provider over its infrastructure, as well as possibly resulting in approaches to a multitude of providers before locating the relevant one. In the UK, for example, the procedure for LEA access to 'subscriber data' arises through administrative self-authorisation, rather than requiring judicial sanction, which would be the norm when the same request is made to a cloud user.[26] Such differential treatment, while clearly advantageous to LEAs, raises concerns about the quality of oversight given to disclosures by service providers. In the USA, similar disclosure obligations in respect of subscriber and customer data made against providers of 'electronic communication services' and 'remote computing services' would be judicially authorised (18 U.S.C. § 2703(c)), while requests for financial records may be made under an administrative subpoena (31 U.S.C. § 5318(k)(3)).

Although many LEA powers can be viewed as coercive in the sense that they require a person to act in a certain manner, search and seizure powers represent one of the most intrusive forms of exercise of power provided for in the Convention (art. 19). As a consequence, such powers are generally subject to judicial authorisation and are only utilised against a suspect in an investigation, for example, a cloud user, rather than an innocent third party who is simply in possession of relevant forensic material, for example, a cloud service provider. The latter will generally receive a production order, as described above. However, to the extent that a search and seizure order is executed against a cloud user, then it will obviously likely impact on the cloud service provider.

In terms of cloud-located data, the Convention provides that an initial search may be extended to other computer systems connected to the user's system, for example, a cloud service provider, where that other system is within the territory and such remote data access is lawful or accessible from the user's system (art. 19(2)).[27] While accessibility is straightforward, determining legality may require that an LEA be able to determine the location of the systems being utilised by a 'domestic' cloud service provider for the storage of the cloud user's data. This is likely to be extremely difficult, particularly in a timely fashion demanded by the investigators, unless the service provider has structured its service on a jurisdictional basis.[28] To address this problem, the Convention provides for Member States to enable LEAs direct access to data stored in foreign territories.

Article 32 provides that a domestic LEA may access data in another territory without authorisation of the foreign state or the need to comply with mutual legal assistance procedures in one of two circumstances: where the data is 'publicly available (open source) stored computer data' or where the domestic LEA 'obtains the lawful and voluntary consent of the person who has a lawful authority to disclose the data...'. The former relates to the condition of the data itself, while the latter is concerned with the persons who have authority over the data.

These two circumstances do not preclude other conduct being authorised under national law, rather it represents a position acceptable to all parties to the Convention.[29] For 'publicly available' data, the implication is that it can be accessed without further authorisation, although such data may obviously be subject to other rules controlling further use of any information obtained, such as copyright and data protection law. Where implied authorisation cannot be assumed, i.e. where the data is placed behind some form of access control mechanism, then 'lawful and voluntary consent' is required to prevent law enforcement personnel from the investigating state committing offences under computer integrity laws of the jurisdiction in which the cloud resource resides. Who is capable of granting such consent?

The wording of the provision does not use the 'possession or control' criterion used in respect of the production orders, focusing instead on the person 'who has the lawful authority to disclose the data', although the nature of the distinction being implied between the two phrases is unclear. In a cloud environment, the cloud user will clearly have such authority. The cloud service provider is also likely to have such authority, generally obtained through the contractual arrangement entered into with the user. In a recent survey of cloud standard terms of business, virtually all cloud service providers reserve the right to disclose customer data, both stored by customers and generated by their use of the service, in certain specified circumstances. Such circumstances range from a high threshold, such as the receipt of a valid court order, to a low threshold based on the service provider's discretion or perception of its best interests.[30] In the former situation, serving a domestic court order on a foreign cloud service provider may render the order unenforceable [11]; therefore, many providers state a lower threshold, accepting requests from recognised LEAs or in circumstances where there is a clear and immediate need to disclose in the public interest, such as a danger to life. Cloud providers may also accept an obligation to notify a user on receipt of an LEA request, to the extent compatible by law, which would empower the customer to consider legal avenues to protect the data from disclosure.[31] Lack of provider clarity and customer awareness about such contractual reservations is one reason for the recent expressions of concern about LEA access in a cloud environment. In April 2011, for example, Dropbox was forced to change the wording used in a 'help' article to reflect an amendment made to its terms of service. It had stated that 'Dropbox employees aren't able to access user files', part of the security assurances made to its customers relating to its use of encryption. However, its terms incorporate a provision enabling it to hand over user data in compliance with a valid court order, which required it to clarify that its employees are 'prohibited' from accessing user files, rather than being unable to access them.[32]

'Lawful' is deployed twice in article 32(b), first in respect of authority of the person to disclose the data and then with regard to the consent granted by the person. In respect of the former, although a cloud provider is likely to have contractually reserved authority to disclose data, as noted above, that does not preclude the need to assess other legal rules that might prohibit any such disclosure. Such laws may be designed to protect national interest or rights-based concerns. The UK's Protection of Trading Interests Act 1980, for example, was specifically passed to restrain the extraterritorial reach of US regulatory agencies [8]. Under the Act, the government retains the power to prohibit compliance with a requirement to produce to a foreign 'court, tribunal or authority' any commercial document or information 'which is not within the territorial jurisdiction' of the foreign country (s. 2). Data protection laws, examined further below, also impose a layer of legal constraints over the processing of personal data, which can supersede any contractual authority the cloud provider may have obtained from the cloud user. From the requesting state's perspective, the impact that such conflicts of law may have on the 'lawful' nature of the request itself may vary between jurisdictions. In the USA, for example, the leading case of *United States v. Bank of Nova Scotia* 691 F.2d 1384 (11th Cir. 1982) held that a breach of law in the foreign state did not invalidate the enforceability of a domestic LEA request.

Although controversial, article 32 is not the only example of international agreement enabling domestic LEAs to carry out an investigation in a foreign territory without the need to follow interstate mutual legal assistance procedures. Under Title III of the EU 'Convention on Mutual Assistance in Criminal Matters' (2000),[33] the issue of transborder interception is addressed. At the time of drafting, two technical scenarios were of concern, satellite and mobile communication systems. With the former, the footprint of a satellite system extends over multiple jurisdictions, but the available point of interception may be a so-called 'gateway' located in a single jurisdiction.[34] Thus, a lawful intercept of a person located in territory A may require technical assistance from territory B. This may be termed the 'remote assist scenario', which could equally be applicable to a cloud-based Communications as a Service (CaaS). In the second scenario, mobile network coverage in border areas may enable an interception authorised in territory A of persons located in territory B with no requirement for technical assistance from territory B. This may be termed the 'spillover scenario'.

The Convention details two different procedures by which extraterritorial intercepts may be carried out in the 'remote assist' scenario. First, the intercepting state can issue a request to the state where the intercept capability is located, based on traditional MLA procedures. Alternatively, however, the service provider in territory A may carry out the interception by 'remote control'[35] in territory B in accordance with article 19, which does not require notification to an authority in territory B. The wording used seems to conceive of 'control' in a purely technical sense, although clearly such control may be organisational, when dealing with a single entity with multiple sites, or contractual, where the intercept is carried out by another service provider. A third procedure, under article 20, is applicable to the 'spillover scenario', which requires an authority in territory A to notify the relevant authority in territory B, who may permit or refuse the extraterritorial interception.

The 'article 19' procedure represents a surrender of territorial control over interception for the state where the 'gateway' is located, while extending the jurisdictional reach of criminal procedure for the requesting state, so it may only prove an acceptable solution within the context of the European Union, with its broader political and legal remit to establish an 'area of freedom, security and justice' (Treaty on European Union, art. 3(2)). In addition, the loss and the gains are unlikely to be shared equally between Member States, since the location of 'gateways' is likely to be driven by business imperatives, such as favourable tax regimes or low-cost infrastructure, which is likely to result in a clustering of 'gateways' in certain states.

Articles 20 and 21 of the Cybercrime Convention permit the real-time collection or recording of traffic data and the interception of communication content. Two scenarios are envisaged, the first involving conduct carried out solely by the 'competent authorities', i.e. the LEA, and the second being where a service provider is required and compelled to engage in the conduct. As discussed further below, the concept of a service provider is broadly defined and would seem to encompass all three types of service provider we have highlighted.

The Convention attempts to distinguish between LEA access to 'stored computer data', i.e. data 'at rest', and data obtained 'real time', i.e. 'in transmission', whether traffic data or content. The implication being, as with 'subscriber information', that separate procedures are likely to exist authorising LEAs to gather such data. While differential treatment may be justifiable in public policy terms, including on privacy grounds, the problem for LEAs and service providers is whether a distinction between data at rest and data in transmission is technically meaningful and an appropriate boundary in a cloud environment. For example, when a user posts a message on a SaaS application for subsequent retrieval, is the message in the course of transmission until it has been 'read' or stored [10]? Alternatively, should LEA access to automated intra-cloud transmissions of data occurring in accordance with load balancing algorithms be treated as an act of interception or a request for stored data?

The potential consequences of a blurred boundary between data at rest and in transmission in a cloud environment can be significant. An individual's rights in the content of their communications may be significantly eroded. Cloud service providers will face legal, procedural and operational uncertainties with regard to their obligations to obtain and deliver up data that has been requested by an investigator. Finally, LEAs will be faced with legal uncertainties about the appropriate procedures to be complied with when carrying out an investigation or risk obtained data being excluded evidentially.

2.4 International Cooperation

As noted already, the challenge for LEAs in a cloud environment is that there is a high likelihood that the evidence being sought is outside the territorial jurisdiction of the LEA and the suspect being investigated. Where evidence is located outside the domestic jurisdiction with a foreign cloud provider not subject to domestic jurisdiction, an investigative LEA is generally faced with four possible courses of action:

- Initiate formal mutual legal assistance (MLA) arrangements to obtain assistance from a foreign LEA.
- Engage in informal cooperation with the foreign LEA.
- Liaise directly with the foreign service provider requesting voluntary assistance.
- Engage directly with the material being sought.

Chapter III of the Council of Europe Cybercrime Convention is designed to facilitate the first and second of these through improved international cooperation. Broadly speaking, two forms of cooperation are addressed, the provision or exchange of information, which may be directly or indirectly evidential, and the delivery-up of the suspect, the notion of extradition.

The provision of information under formal MLA procedures has historically been notoriously complex, slow and bureaucratic, which is particularly unsuitable for cloud-based investigations. In 2004, for example, a US-based hosting and cloud company, Rackspace, received a subpoena, pursuant to a MLA Treaty, requesting delivery-up of certain log file information pertaining to a media organisation, Indymedia.[36] The originating request came from a public prosecutor in Italy. To comply with the request for the information, Rackspace chose to shut down the identified host server, which was in London not the USA, and deliver up drives to the FBI, on the grounds that they were unable to locate the requested files within the mandated delivery timescales. The case raises a number of issues of interest. First, execution of a legitimate bilateral MLA request required implementation in a third country, the UK, but with no involvement from domestic law enforcement or apparent consideration of the legality of such action under English law.[37] Second, the nature of the timescales involved in complying with the order meant that Rackspace felt the need to exceed the terms of the request, an inevitable tension between the need for speed, being facilitated by Convention initiatives to reduce procedural lag, and the ability of a requested party to respond in a lawfully compliant manner. The example also illustrates that even a lawfully obtained and served order can still result in potential unlawfully obtained material.

While data preservation is a relatively straightforward process, accessing the requested data may be considerably more problematic. The Convention attempts to address this legacy through a number of mechanisms that, in part, effectively blur the line between the provision of formal and informal assistance. While such blurring can improve the efficiency of international cooperation, it also raises questions about the legality of such cooperation and the impact that it may have on the rights of those under investigation and those who experience collateral interference.

The first tool for improving international cooperation lies in the reforms made to substantive criminal law. The harmonisation of offences and their extended jurisdictional reach means that cloud-based criminal conduct is more likely to result in an offence being committed simultaneously in multiple jurisdictions. Under traditional MLA procedures, a domestic LEA would have to evidence that the conduct being investigated constituted, theoretically, an offence of minimum seriousness in both the requesting and requested jurisdiction, the so-called 'double criminality' principle. However, in a cloud-based environment, there is a greater likelihood that a perpetrator may be held to have engaged in the types of criminal conduct addressed in the Convention in both the state in which he is located as well as the state in which the data is located, for example, criminal content such as child sexual abuse images (art. 9) or the storage of devices designed for criminal conduct against the confidentiality, integrity and availability of computer systems (art. 6). In such a situation, the foreign LEA can choose to investigate the alleged conduct without a formal request having been received, on the basis that the investigated conduct also constitutes an offence in their territory.

A second mechanism for improving informal cooperation is through encouraging national LEAs to spontaneously (i.e. proactively) disclose information to foreign LEAs where it appears relevant to conduct seemingly connected to the foreign territory, rather than waiting for the foreign LEA to commence an investigation and initiate a formal MLA request (art. 26). Such exchanges of information are obviously largely dependent on how good relations are between the various countries involved, as well as the attitudes and opinions of the people on the ground within the LEAs. The Convention also tries to encourage such good relations through requiring each party to establish a designated point of contact, available 24/7, with the appropriate technical and legal expertise and ability to facilitate communications and expedite requests for assistance (art. 35).

The final course of action noted above, i.e. direct engagement, does not require cooperation between LEAs and was partly addressed in the previous section in respect of legitimising certain extraterritorial conduct by LEAs under article 32 of the Convention. However, another mode of investigation that has been raised in a cyber context is the possibility of an LEA actively interfering with an online resource associated with a suspect, such as cloud service, in order to obtain evidence. Such interference could clearly constitute the commission of a criminal offence by the LEA, in the domestic and, or, foreign jurisdiction, such as an illegal access under the Convention (art. 2). A statutory defence or immunity from prosecution would therefore be required for such conduct, as well as an authorisation and supervision regime. Such LEA conduct, especially in a multi-jurisdiction context, is fraught with difficulties, on grounds of principle, legality and practicality, and is not therefore considered further in this chapter.

2.5   European Criminal Procedure

As with other areas of criminal procedure, different rules and procedures exist, or are being established, for the movement of evidence between EU Member States compared with the procedures governing the movement of such evidence with non-EU states. At the moment, MLA between Member States is governed by the Council of Europe's 'European Convention on Mutual Assistance in Criminal Matters' (1959),[38] which has been amended on a couple of occasions,[39] as well as supplementary EU measures, specifically the 'Schengen Convention'[40] and the 'Convention on Mutual Assistance in Criminal Matters' (2000), discussed above.

The 1959 and 2000 Conventions, based on mutual legal assistance, are progressively being supplanted by other European measures designed to facilitate the handling of evidence between Member States, based on the principle of mutual recognition, as specified in the Treaty on the Functioning of the European Union, art. 82(1). In 2003, a Decision on the execution 'of orders freezing property and evidence' was adopted by the Council.[41] This enables an LEA in one Member State to request the securing of potential evidence in another Member State against potential destruction, transfer or disposal, through an expedited procedure. The measure builds on article 16 of the Convention, which calls for the expedited preservation of stored computer data, by providing a cross-border mechanism. However, the mechanism does not provide for the data to be transferred to the requesting state, which is subject to a separate procedure.

In 2008, the European Evidence Warrant (EEW)[42] was adopted, which Member States should have transposed into national law by 19 January 2011 (art. 23(1)). Under the EEW measure, a request for evidence issued by an 'issuing authority', which may be a judge, an investigating magistrate or public prosecutor (art. 2(c)), in one Member State would be recognised and directly enforced by the 'executing authority' in the recipient Member State. However, due to the political sensitivities involved in establishing such procedures, the EEW is being established in two stages. This current instrument only covers 'evidence which exists and is readily available',[43] while evidence that requires further investigative activities to be carried out in the executing state, such as real-time interception and covert surveillance, as well as access to data retained by a communications service provider under the Data Retention Directive,[44] cannot be obtained under the current EEW (art. 4(2)).

An EEW request takes the form of a standard document, translated by the issuing authority into the official language of the executing authority, which can be treated by the executing authority in the same manner as a domestic request, with the requested information being obtained in a manner considered most appropriate by the executing authority, but 'without delay and…no later than 60 days after receipt of the EEW' (art. 15(3)). Verification of 'double criminality' is not required for the recognition or execution of an EEW, unless it involves the use of search and seizure powers (art. 14(1)). In the latter circumstance, verification is also not required for certain designated offences where they are punishable in the issuing state by a custodial sentence of at least 3 years (art. 14(2)). The list of offences includes child pornography, fraud, computer-related crime, racism and xenophobia and counterfeiting and piracy of products, as well as infringements of intellectual property rights and sabotage. Member States have also retained the right, in exceptional cases, to refuse to execute an EEW where the offence has been committed wholly or partly in the executing state (art. 13(f)(1)), based on the territoriality principle, which may result in multi-state jurisdictional negotiations taking place at an evidential stage, rather than when deciding where to prosecute. This can be criticised for creating new obstacles to the transfer of evidence that are not present under traditional MLA procedures.

In April 2010, a second measure of mutual recognition was proposed by certain Member State governments, 'regarding the European Investigation Order in criminal matters' ('EIO').[45] The proposal forms part of the 'Stockholm Programme',[46] adopted by the European Council in December 2009, and is designed to replace the current fragmentary regime with a 'comprehensive system for obtaining evidence in cases with a cross-border dimension'.[47] It would apply to almost all investigative measures, including those requiring the ongoing gathering of evidence, such as real-time surveillance, although it is proposed that certain forms of conduct would remain outside the regime, including the interception of satellite transmission that would remain subject to the 2000 Convention, as outlined above. Once the evidence has been obtained, it would be transferred 'without undue delay' to the issuing state.[48]

The EIO proposal has generated much controversy and dispute concerning both the appropriateness of its legal basis as well as the scope and implications of its provisions [14]. However, were it to be adopted, it would facilitate LEA access to cloud-derived data held within the European Union, if that can be determined!

2.6   LEA/Service Provider Relations

Where evidence is located outside the territory, another course of action available to an LEA is to liaise directly with the service provider. The success of liaising with a foreign service provider will obviously depend on a range of factors, including the provision made in the contractual terms with the customer for the disclosure of data, as discussed above. Where the foreign service provider has a domestic presence, even though distinct from the service relevant to the investigation, is also likely to impact on relations. Facebook, for example, may store evidential material on servers in the USA relating to its cloud services, but its presence in the UK means that there is a domestic route through which LEA requests can be channelled to the foreign entity.[49] The manner in which such a request is treated by the recipient foreign entity will obviously vary according to internal corporate policy, but any multinational corporation is likely to be mindful of any impact that any adverse decision may have on the position of its domestic entity. In September 2010, Google launched its 'transparency report' to publicise the numbers of domestic and foreign LEA requests it receives for user information, as well as the extent to which such requests were fully or partially complied with.[50] The stated aim is to contribute to 'discussions about the appropriate scope and authority of government requests'.

In 2008, a conference organised by the Council of Europe adopted a set of 'Guidelines for the cooperation between law enforcement and internet service providers against cybercrime'.[51] In similar fashion to the international cooperation measures detailed in the Convention, the Guidelines are designed to structure the interactions that take place 'in an efficient manner with due consideration to their respective roles, the cost of such cooperation and the rights of citizens' (para. 7). Similar to relations between states, effective cooperation will often depend on building a 'culture of cooperation' between service providers and LEAs (para. 11), although detailed in written procedures[52] and achieved through appropriately trained and resourced points of contact. However, whether one views the existence of such a culture in simply positive terms or as a potential cause for concern, in terms of facilitating non-legal disclosures of data, will depend on your perspective and trust in the participating entities. The decision by Amazon to terminate the provision of hosting services to WikiLeaks, purportedly under pressure from the US administration, is an example of such concerns.[53]

The Guidelines specifically refer to requests made to foreign service providers, stating that LEAs 'should be encouraged not to direct requests directly to non-domestic Internet service providers', but should make use of interstate procedures contained in international cooperation treaties.[54] This wording is obviously an implicit recognition that direct liaison with foreign service providers does take place, even if the recommendation is against such practices. In addition, indirect requests made through the domestic branch of the foreign service provider would not be covered by this recommendation. It is also interesting to note that the Guidelines do not have a complementary recommendation for service providers, encouraging them not to disclose in response to a request from a foreign LEA!

From the perspective of service providers, the Guidelines recommend that they be encouraged to cooperate with LEAs, including through reporting incidents of criminality which come to their attention.[55] Similar to the provisions under the Convention encouraging spontaneous information disclosure by foreign LEAs, compliance with this recommendation would effectively circumvent the need to comply with MLA procedures. Service providers are also recommended to establish 'criminal compliance programmes', which would detail their internal procedures, including 'the extent that a service provider operates in multiple countries'.[56] From a cloud perspective, mapping a service provider's footprint of operations and data centres would be of particular value to LEAs in terms of facilitating the serving of data requests, but not necessarily identify the jurisdiction in which the data resides at the time of the request.

Another critical factor in the relationship between LEAs and service providers is how the 'service' is characterised in law. Under the Convention, measures may be taken against a 'service provider' defined in the broadest possible terms, encompassing all three cloud-related service providers outlined at the start of the chapter:

i. any public or private entity that provides to users of its service the ability to communicate by means of a computer system, and
ii. any other entity that processes or stores computer data on behalf of such communication service or users of such service. (art. 1(c))

Unfortunately, however, this terminology does not map neatly onto EU regulatory concepts. Under EU law, a distinction is made between the provision of 'electronic communication services' ('ECS') and 'information society services' ('ISS'):

> 'electronic communications service' means a service normally provided for remuneration which consists wholly or mainly in the conveyance of signals on electronic communications networks, including telecommunications services and transmission services in networks used for broadcasting, but exclude services providing, or exercising editorial control over, content transmitted using electronic communications networks and services; it does not include information society services, as defined in Article 1 of Directive 98/34/EC, which do not consist wholly or mainly in the conveyance of signals on electronic communications networks.[57]

The latter ISS are primarily regulated under the 'Electronic Commerce' Directive.[58] Taking our three types of service provider, the first two are widely seen as an ISS, while the provider of the communication service would be an ECS, although it would depend on the nature of the service being supplied in the particular circumstances. So, for example, the emergence of Communications as a Service ('CaaS') as a variety of cloud offering providing enterprises with the functionality of an in-house communications system,[59] could be seen as an ECS or, alternatively, as an 'associated facility' or 'associated service',[60] which also form part of the EU communication regime distinct from the provision of ISS. The boundary is particularly blurred given the potential variety of approaches that could be adopted for interpreting the phrase 'mainly in the conveyance of signals', from quantitative to qualitative measures, including the imputed intention of suppliers or the perception of consumers. As such, this creates legal and regulatory uncertainty for service providers, as well as LEAs.

Two key EU measures where this uncertainty becomes manifest are the Communications Privacy Directive (02/58/EC) and the Data Retention Directive (06/24/EC). Both contain provisions obliging Member States to adopt measures relevant to LEA access to data processed by service providers.

Under article 5(1) of the Communications Privacy Directive, Member States are required to prohibit the 'listening, tapping, storage or other kinds of interception or surveillance of communications and the related traffic data by persons other than users', except as authorised under article 15(1), which includes 'the prevention, investigation, detection and prosecution of criminal offences'. The prohibition is applicable against all persons, including the service provider and LEAs, but is only applicable to communications being transmitted by means of 'a public communications network and publicly available electronic communication services'. Communications carried over non-public networks and services would not therefore be subject to the EU regime, although they are covered by the analogous Convention provisions (art. 21) and national legislation may extend the scope of any such prohibition.[61] As such, for intra- or inter-cloud communications, uncertainty exists as to whether such communications are subject to the additional protections granted under the Directive.

While article 15(1) permits Member States to authorise interception or surveillance by LEAs, it does not further specify the conditions under which such authorisation may take place. By contrast, the Convention states that competent LEAs should be empowered to either carry out acts of interception or to compel a service provider 'within its existing capability' to carry out the interception or assist LEAs (art. 21(1)). In many states, however, the procedural regime goes beyond the Convention provision by requiring that certain entities specifically implement a lawful intercept capability to enable LEAs to carry out or compel the interception of communication content.[62] Such build obligations are generally only imposed upon providers of communication networks or services,[63] as a regulated activity, which returns us to the boundary issue of whether a cloud provider can be characterised as an ECS or ISS.

Similarly, under the Data Retention Directive, the obligations to retain data are placed upon 'providers of publicly available electronic communication services'. The regulatory boundary issue has been examined in detail by the Data Retention Experts Group,[64] in relation to webmail and web-based messaging, which is an example of a cloud-based SaaS, whether provided to corporate or consumers. The Position Paper considers various operational scenarios, such as a person leaving a message on a website for another user, and concludes that the majority constitute an ISS, rather than an ECS, and therefore fall outside the scope of the Data Retention Directive.[65]

That this characterisation issue is a real problem can be seen in an important case recently examined in Belgium involving Yahoo! Inc. In this case, a public prosecutor requested the disclosure of certain data from Yahoo! regarding certain fraudulent conduct carried out using Yahoo! webmail accounts, under article 46*bis* of the Belgium Criminal Procedure Code. Yahoo! refused to disclose on two grounds: (a) Yahoo! Inc., being based in the USA, was not subject to Belgian jurisdiction, and therefore, the request should have been made through MLA procedures, and (b) the service was not an 'electronic communication service' and therefore not subject to the relevant order [6]. The lower court held that Yahoo! had unlawfully refused to disclose and imposed a €55 k fine, with an additional €10 k for every day they continue to refuse to comply.[66] On appeal, the court held that Yahoo! was not a 'provider of an electronic communication service' and could not therefore be required to cooperate.[67] The Supreme Court, however, held that the Court of Appeal had been wrong to exempt Yahoo! from the application of the criminal procedure provisions on the basis that the service was not an 'electronic communication service' under the Belgian Electronic Communications Act 2005, as the scope of the concept under criminal law was broader than that under regulatory law.[68] The decision was referred back to the Court of Appeal for reconsideration, which subsequently decided that Yahoo! Inc. was not subject to Belgian jurisdiction,[69] although this is also to be appealed.

A similar regulated boundary issue exists under US federal criminal law in respect of access to stored 'communications and transactional records', with a distinction made between providers of 'electronic communication services' and 'remote computing services',[70] which has procedural implications.[71] While the latter, defined as 'the provision to the public of computer storage and or processing services by means of an electronic communication system', would seem to most closely match that of a cloud service provider, the US courts have struggled with the issue of characterisation in a similar manner to the Belgian courts [5, 12]. In *Crispin v. Christian Audigier Inc*. 717 F.Supp.2d 965, (C.D.Cal.2010), the court held that Facebook and MySpace could be either an ECS or a RCS, in respect of wall postings and comments. Elsewhere, however, US law has circumvented such problems through the adoption of expansive catch-all definitions. Under the Foreign Intelligence Surveillance Act, for example, authorisation can be given to specifically target the surveillance of persons 'outside the United States', with the assistance of an 'electronic communication service provider' defined in terms that encompasses all possible types of cloud and communications provider.[72]

The characterisation of cloud services from a regulatory perspective has important governance implications which go beyond the scope of this chapter. In the context of law enforcement requests for assistance, however, regulatory characterisation can impact directly on the legality of a law enforcement request and the obligation of the service provider to comply, potentially resulting in disputes between them.

2.7   Law Enforcement and Data Protection

Cloud user concerns about the long-arm reach of US law enforcement lie as much in the perceived threat to personal privacy as that of commercial secrecy.[73] To address such concerns, the EU harmonising procedural measures discussed previously are complemented by a measure to protect personal data.[74] The measure was necessary because such matters fall outside the scope of the general data protection regime, i.e. Directive 95/46/EC.[75] This is an area where the Commission has proposed reform following the abolition of the pillars by the Lisbon Treaty.[76]

The 2008 Decision is primarily directed to the exchange of personal data between law enforcement bodies, 'competent authorities', within the EU Member States. However, it also details those conditions under which it would be permissible for a competent authority to transfer such data onwards to a 'third State or international bodies', which include the need for 'consent' from the authority where the data originated and that the receiving entity 'ensures an adequate level of protection'.[77] As such, personal data obtained from an EU-based cloud user or service provider may be transferred by an EU domestic authority to a US LEA under mutual legal assistance procedures in a manner designed to safeguard the rights of data subjects. An MLA agreement between the USA and the EU was signed in 2003, with provisions on the use of personal data, including detailing the range of purposes for which the data may be used.[78] Other than purpose limitation, however, no 'generic restrictions with respect to the legal standards of the requesting state' may be imposed, although additional conditions can be specified in 'a particular case'.[79]

The more concerning scenario for EU cloud users, raised at the start of this chapter, is where a US LEA directly addresses a request to a cloud service provider that it produces personal data stored by cloud users in facilities located within the EU. As already noted, such a request is likely to be a lawful exercise of powers, provided the recipient provider has reserved its rights to disclose under its terms of business. European data protection law, however, adds an additional compliance layer that could result in a breach of the law of the state in which the recipient provider, as data controller, is established or has 'equipment' on which the cloud user data resides, the 'requested provider's state' (art. 4)[13].

As noted above, the general data protection regime does not encompass 'activities of the State in areas of criminal law'. This is clearly not applicable to the scenario outlined in the previous paragraph because the requested provider's state is not involved in the making or serving of the request. The EU regime both permits processing activities when carried out for law enforcement purposes (art. 7(e)), as well as exempting certain processing activities from some obligations where the processing is necessary for reasons which include the 'prevention, investigation, detection and prosecution of criminal offences' (art. 13). What the regime does not disapply, however, are the provisions governing the transfer of personal data outside of the EEA, articles 25 and 26. As such, for a cloud provider to respond to a request for personal data from a US LEA, the provider must be able to legitimise such transfer under the existing rules.

Article 25 provides that transfers to a third country may take place where there is 'an adequate level of protection', such adequacy being determined in 'the light of all the circumstances surrounding a data transfer', including sectoral laws, professional rules and security measures.[80] US federal law enforcement bodies, for example, are subject to the Privacy Act 1974, which broadly reflects the provisions of the EU regime, although it is only applicable to 'individuals', defined as 'a citizen of the United States or an alien lawfully admitted for permanent residence' (5 USC § 552a(a)(2)). The process by which a determination of 'adequacy' is made can vary, from the default position being that of the data controller in the first instance[81] to reliance on a Commission finding of 'adequacy'.[82] In terms of the former, therefore, a cloud provider could decide that a transfer is adequate on the basis of specific representations made by the requesting authority, such as domestic judicial over-sight of the subpoena under which the data is requested. It would also seem arguable that the existence of the EU-US MLA agreement could be viewed as providing an assurance of 'adequacy' in respect of disclosures to US LEAs, which could be relied upon by cloud providers, even though the data protection provisions detailed in it fail, on the face of it, to meet the minimum criteria laid down by the Article 29 Working Party: content principles and procedural/enforcement mechanisms.[83] In respect of a Commission decision facilitating disclosures, a precedent exists in the EU agreement on 'adequacy' entered into with the USA concerning the 'safe harbour privacy principles'[84] and the disclosure of passenger name records to the US Department of Homeland Security.[85]

Where the cloud provider determines that 'adequacy' is not present, then an exemption will need to be relied upon under article 26. The most relevant exemption for this discussion is where the transfer is 'necessary or legally required on important public interest grounds'.[86] The scope of the 'public interest' exemption has been considered by the Article 29 Working Party in two situations concerning disclosures for law enforcement purposes: the operation of the whistle-blowing schemes under the US Sarbanes-Oxley Act and the disclosure of financial data by SWIFT.[87] In these opinions, the Working Party held that the important public interests had to be related to an EU Member State to avoid circumvention of the regime, thereby preventing reliance on US public interest claims. What the opinions fail to address, however, is the process by which a public interest claim advanced by a requesting LEA can be held to concurrently engage a public interest of the recipient EU state. As noted earlier, the transnational nature of many serious crimes, such as terrorist acts, coupled with harmonisation of substantive criminal law principles, increasingly means that criminal conduct involves the commission of offences in multiple jurisdictions. Where a requesting LEA claims a 'dual' public interest,[88] would a cloud provider be expected, or indeed be able, to look behind such a claim? Would it, for example, be expected to seek confirmation from a domestic LEA?

While the European data protection regime contains provisions that try to balance the potentially conflicting interests of privacy and law enforcement, such provisions are strictly limited to jurisdictions held to have 'adequate' protections in place. As such, despite the extended jurisdictional reach granted LEAs under the Cybercrime Convention, current data protection rules may render such disclosure by a cloud provider unlawful. Uncertainty over the treatment of personal data processed in a criminal context, however, represents an obstacle to cloud computing, which needs to be addressed as part of the current reform process.

2.8   Using Cloud-Derived Evidence

It is beyond the scope of this chapter to examine different national rules governing the admissibility of cloud-derived evidence in criminal proceedings, although the applicable rules will generally vary depending on how the cloud-derived evidence is characterised from an evidential perspective. Stricter controls are generally placed over the use of testimonial and hearsay evidence, compared with real evidence generated by machines.[89] Most cloud-derived evidence is likely to fall into the latter category.

It is important to recognise that data obtained from a cloud-based service may be excluded from use in court proceedings on a number of grounds. Statutory rules may exclude certain types of evidence. In the UK, for example, evidence obtained through interception is generally inadmissible, which may impact on the recording of a suspect's communication with his cloud service. In addition, a court generally has jurisdiction[90] to exclude evidence in certain circumstances if that evidence is considered to undermine or cause real prejudice to the defendant's right to a fair trial, as enshrined in article 6 of the ECHR. Article 6 does not, however, contain rules on the admissibility of evidence; therefore, the European Court of Human Rights cannot exclude evidence simply on the basis that such evidence was obtained unlawfully.[91]

Evidence gathered by an LEA may be excluded, either as a matter of law or at the discretion of the court, if the evidence was obtained in breach of law. Such a breach may result from the conduct of an LEA investigator exceeding the jurisdiction granted to the LEA, or the conduct itself being illegal under the substantive criminal code.

In terms of the former, considerations of exclusion will often depend on whether the conduct was an intentional flaunting of the applicable rules or simply a mistake made in good faith.[92] The legality of conduct may obviously differ between the foreign jurisdiction, where the evidence was obtained, and the domestic jurisdiction, where the evidence is being adduced, which may impact on the domestic court's treatment of such evidence. In the UK, for example, a breach of foreign legal procedures would only lead to the exclusion of real evidence if the nature of the breach was considered to amount to an act of bad faith on behalf of the domestic LEA [9]. On the other hand, in the United States, a request for evidence obtained from a foreign computer system to be suppressed on the grounds that it breached constitutional protections was denied by the court on the grounds that the protection was not applicable to property outside the United States.[93] As a consequence, for example, a breach of data protection rules in the course of obtaining evidence may not constitute a bar to the admissibility of cloud-derived evidence, all other things being equal.

Evidence gathered in another state may also face admissibility challenges, where the rules governing the collection of evidence may differ from the state in which the evidence is subsequently used, especially those governing the use of testimonial and hearsay evidence. As a general rule, however, evidence gathered under formal MLA procedures, through a 'letter rogatory' or 'commission rogatoire', will be admissible as evidence in the requesting state. Although such procedures are available to both the prosecution and defence, mechanisms designed to streamline the efficiency of these procedures are generally put in place to assist the prosecution,[94] potentially undermining the 'equality of arms' required under the right of fair trial.[95]

The EIO proposal, outlined above, provides that an issuing state may request that its 'authorities' be able to assist the authorities of the executing state in the execution of the EIO.[96] This is not intended to constitute a grant to the LEAs of the issuing state of any extraterritorial powers in the territory of the executing state; rather it is intended to forestall admissibility challenges to the evidence when relied upon in future proceedings in the issuing state, through the direct involvement of the domestic authorities in the evidence gathering process.

Even if admissible in court, whether cloud-derived evidence is given evidential weight will often depend on the ability of the party adducing the evidence to show that the material is authentic and has integrity and an appropriate account can be rendered of how the material was handled from the moment it was obtained until its presentation in court. All computer-derived evidence is vulnerable to alteration and, in a cloud environment, the service providers may be required to verify the provenance of data purportedly obtained from their service.

2.9 Conclusion

In this chapter, a number of legal issues facing LEA investigators when gathering forensic data from a cloud environment have been examined. First, when exercising investigative powers granted to them by the state, particularly where they are covert or involve coercion, LEAs must be concerned that such powers are not exceeded, either in terms of application or territorially. As we have seen, *issues of application* may arise due to uncertainty as to the characterisation of the evidence being 'at rest' or 'in transmission', or the entities against which such powers may be exercised, while *issues of territoriality* arise from the multi-jurisdictional nature of cloud computing. By exceeding such powers, the LEAs may be acting illegally, which is a concern in its own right, exposing LEAs to liability and potentially infringing the rights of others, as well as impacting on the evidential use or value of the material gathered in the course of the investigation.

Within Europe, there is a need to address the uncertainty over the regulatory boundary between the provision of communication services and cloud-based services, as the characterisation of a service has important implications in terms of the regulatory obligations of the service provider and their relationship with LEAs. Although rules in the Member States governing the investigative process, for example, policing operational matters, are not substantially harmonised at an EU level, there is evidence of an overlap between EU regulatory concepts and national rules, which contributes to the uncertain legal position. A second area of uncertainty is found in the application of current data protection rules to the transfer of personal data outside Europe for the purposes of a criminal investigation. The piecemeal approach that has resulted from the restricted competence of the community in the area of criminal law has placed cloud users and providers in an uncertain legal position, which can deter the take up of such services.

International rules governing the transborder gathering of evidence, 'mutual legal assistance', are unsuited to cloud-based processing activities, as with other forms of computer and networking environments. Reforms have taken place over the past 10 years to try and improve the situation, especially through resort to more informal interstate mechanisms, based on harmonised legal systems as well as building trusted networks of LEA experts. The primary concern with greater reliance upon informal procedures is that of accountability, ensuring that LEAs do not exceed their powers and inappropriately interfere with individual rights. As Boister warns, 'law enforcement effectiveness tends to predominate over values like international legality, at the expense of legitimacy' [3].

Part of the response has also resulted in sovereignty concessions being made in limited circumstances in order to legalise certain extraterritorial conduct by LEAs. While such initiatives can be viewed as eroding traditional sovereign rights, they can also represent an extraterritorial extension of criminal procedure jurisdiction that may actually strengthen sovereignty in a transnational cloud environment.

Another component of this shift to informality is greater cooperation between LEAs and service providers. For transborder investigations, this cooperation takes the form of domestic LEAs directly or indirectly (i.e. through a domestic entity) contacting foreign service providers with requests for data. Such requests shift the concern over legality from the requesting LEA to the responding service provider. However, our research indicates that cloud service providers generally provide for the possibility of law enforcement disclosures of customer data in their standard terms of business, thereby facilitating informal cooperation with LEAs, while mitigating the legal risks.

The legality of gathering evidence in a cloud environment is obviously only part of the challenge facing LEAs in an investigation. Considerable technical forensic issues will confront LEAs. Where cloud-derived material is obtained, its admissibility as evidence and evidential weight may be challenged not only on the basis of the conduct of the LEA in the course of gathering such material but also the quality of the forensic process itself, which will depend in large part on the systems and conduct of cloud service providers.

Endnotes

1. See 'Deutsche Telekom wants 'German Cloud' to shield data from US', *Business Week*, 14 September 2011.
2. CETS No. 185, entered in force 1 July 2004 ('the Convention').
3. For example, CRN's 'Cloud 100: The Top 100 Cloud Computing Vendors Of 2011', available at http://www.crn.com/news/cloud/index/100-cloud-computing-vendors.htm
4. The full title is: 'Uniting and Strengthening America by Providing Appropriate Tools Required to Intercept and Obstruct Terrorism Act of 2001', *Pub. Law*. 107–156.
5. The distinction between data 'at rest' and 'in transmission' does not denote the technical state of the data since data held by a cloud service provider, i.e. 'at rest' may be regularly 'in transmission' between internal resources of the service provider, for example, using load balancing. Rather the phrases are used to indicate a legal distinction between LEA powers of access to data.
6. For the purpose of this article, 'infrastructure' refers to any component of the cloud service, not an IaaS.
7. Particularly as user applications may be configured not to record such interactions, for example, Microsoft Internet Explorer's 'InPrivate' browsing setting [15].
8. For example, ACPO, *Good Practice Guide for Computer based Electronic Evidence*, 4th ed., October 2008.
9. Application programming interfaces specify the manner in which software programs communicate with each other.
10. See Spoenle, J.: 'Cloud Computing and cybercrime investigations: Territoriality vs. the power of disposal', Council of Europe Discussion paper, 31 August 2010 (2010).
11. See, for example, *Veolia ES Nottinghamshire Limited v. Nottingham County Council & ors* [2010] EWCA Civ 1214, at paras 117–122.
12. The Explanatory Report purposely leaves flexibility to States, see paras. 137 and 187.
13. Council of Europe Recommendation No R(95)13, 'concerning problems of procedural law connected with information technology', at Principle 4.
14. Number of signatories is correct as of 14 November 2011. The United States ratified the Convention in January 2007 and the United Kingdom in May 2011.
15. For example, in the UK, for example, access to stored data generally occurs under a judicial warrant (e.g. Police and Criminal Evidence Act 1984, s. 9); the interception of data in transmission requires an executive warrant (Regulation of Investigatory Powers Act 2000 ('RIPA'), s. 5), while access to communications data occurs under an administrative authorisation (Ibid., s. 22).
16. For example, the incitement of crime through the actions of 'agent provocateurs' may breach an individual's right to a fair trial, under art.6 of the ECHR. See *Teixeira de Castro v. Portugal* (1998) 28 EHRR 101.
17. For example, for an express limitation, see the Police Act 1996, s. 30(1), while the presumption was recently restated in *R (Al-Skeini) v. Secretary of State for Defence* [2008] 1 AC 153, 45.
18. For example, *Zheng v. Yahoo! Inc.*, 2009 WL 4430297 at *4, No. C-08–1068 MMC (Dec. 2, 2009), where representatives of the China Democracy Party tried unsuccessfully to bring an action for violation of the ECPA.

19. For example, *Suzlon Energy Ltd v. Microsoft Corp.*, (2011), US Court of Appeals for the 9th Circuit, unreported, where the court held that the ECPA protected the domestic communications of any person not just US citizens.

20. Under UK law, the terminology is 'possession, custody or power' (e.g. Terrorism Act 2000, Sch. 5, para. 5), while US law refers to 'possession, custody or control' (e.g. Federal Rules of Civil Procedure, at Rules 26 and 34; Federal Rules of Criminal Procedure, Rule 16).

21. Convention Explanatory Report, at para. 173.

22. Similar to the EU data protection law, i.e. Directive 95/46/EC, art. 2(d).

23. Convention Explanatory Report, at para. 38.

24. For example, *United States v. Vetco, Inc.*, 691 F.2d 1281 (9th Cir. 1981), where the court required the US entity to produce data held by a subsidiary outside of the US.

25. For example, the Yahoo! Belgium case discussed below.

26. Regulation of Investigatory Powers Act 2000, Part I, Chapter II. It should be noted, however, that the Protection of Freedoms Bill 2011, cl. 37, will amend this to require judicial authorisation in respect of requests made by 'local authorities'.

27. In the UK, the Police and Criminal Evidence Act 1984, s. 20, contains a similar provision.

28. For example, Amazon offers its customers 'regional zones', i.e. a US or European cloud. See further [4], at p. 28.

29. However, the provision does not represent consensus among Council of Europe member states. In particular, Russia does not accept art. 32(b) and wants it either amended or a supplementary agreement between the parties as to its meaning, prior to becoming party to the Convention.

30. [4] at 4.9. For Apple's recently launched iCloud service, the privacy policy states that it will disclose personal information if necessary 'by law, legal process, litigation, and/or requests from public and governmental authorities within or outside your country of residence', as well as where Apple 'determine that for purposes of national security, law enforcement, or other issues of public importance, disclosure is necessary or appropriate' (www.apple.com/privacy).

31. For example, Microsoft Online Services, Trust Center, 'Data Use Limits' states that, in the first instance, Microsoft will redirect an LEA to the customer, while if required to respond to the LEA request, it will 'use commercially reasonable efforts to notify the enterprise customer in advance of any production unless legally prohibited' (available at www.microsoft.com/online/legal/v2/?docid=23, as of 4 November 2011).

32. Sherman, M.: At Dropbox, even we can't see your dat- er, nevermind (19 April 2011), available at http://www.bnet.com/blog/technology-business/-8220at-dropbox-even-wc-cant-see-your-dat-8211-er-nevermind-8221-update/10077 (2011).

33. The Convention on Mutual Assistance in Criminal Matters between the Member States of the European Union established by Council Act of 29 May 2000 (OJ C 197, 12.7.2000). An Explanatory Report has been published at OJ C 379, 29.12.2000, p. 7.

34. The 'gateway' may be the earth station controlling the telemetry, tracking and operation of the satellite.

35. Explanatory Report at para. 20.

36. See generally www.eff.org/Censorship/Indymedia/

37. In response to Parliamentary questions from MPs, Richard Allan and Jeremy Corbyn (20.10.04, Col. 725 W), John McDonnell MP (27.10.04, Col. 1278 W) and Lynne Jones (11.11.04, Col. 895 W), to Home Office minister Caroline Flint, who replied: 'I can confirm that no UK law enforcement agencies were involved in the matter'.

38. CETS No. 30, entered into force 12 June 1962. The Council of Europe includes non-EU member states.

39. An additional Protocol was adopted in 1978 (CETS No. 99) and a Second Additional Protocol in 2001 (CETS No. 182).

40. Convention implementing the Schengen Agreement (OJ L 239/19, 22.09.2000), at arts. 48–53.

41. Council Framework Decision 2003/577/JHA of 22 July 2003 on the execution in the European Union of orders freezing property or evidence; OJ L 196/45, 2.8.2002.

42. Council Framework Decision 2008/978/JHA of 18 December 2008 on the European evidence warrant for the purpose of obtaining objects, documents and data for use in proceedings in criminal matters; OJ L 350/72, 30.12.2008.
43. See Press Release from the Justice and Home Affairs Council Meeting, 9409/06 (Presse 144), 1–2 June 2006.
44. Directive 2006/24/EC on the retention of data generated or processed in connection with the provision of publicly available electronic communications services or of public communications networks and amending Directive 2002/58/EC, OJ L 105/54, 13.4.2006.
45. Council of the European Union, 2010/0817 (COD), 29 April 2010 ('EIO Proposal').
46. 'The Stockholm Programme – An open and secure Europe serving and protecting citizens' (OJ C 115/1), 4.5.2010.
47. Ibid., at 3.1.1., para. 4.
48. EIO Proposal, at art. 12(1).
49. In May 2011, Twitter announced it was opening a London office at a time when it was accused of facilitating breaches of a privacy injunction against the footballer Ryan Giggs and subject to a court order requiring it to deliver up details concerning its users.
50. Available at http://www.google.com/transparencyreport/
51. Available at http://www.coe.int/t/dghl/cooperation/economiccrime/cybercrime/documents/lea_isp/default_EN.asp
52. For example, mandatory sign-off by in-house counsel.
53. For example, The Guardian, 'WikiLeaks website pulled by Amazon after US political pressure', 2 December 2010.
54. Guidelines, at para. 36.
55. Ibid., at para. 42. Service providers are not, however, expected to 'actively search for facts or circumstances indicating illegal activities'.
56. Ibid., at para. 50.
57. Directive 2002/21/EC on a common regulatory framework for electronic communications networks and services (OJ L 108/33, 24.4.2002), at art. 2(c).
58. Directive 2000/31/EC on certain legal aspects of information society services, in particular electronic commerce, in the Internal Market (OJ L 178/1, 17.7.2000).
59. See, for example, http://www.caas.com/Pages/default.aspx
60. Framework Directive, at art. 2(e) and (ea), respectively.
61. For example, under the UK Regulation of Investigatory Powers Act 2000, s. 2, it is an offence to intercept a transmission carried by means of a private telecommunication system.
62. For example, Belgium, Germany, Netherlands, Italy, Mexico, Russia, Spain, Switzerland and the UK.
63. Note, however, the ongoing dispute between RIM, the manufacturer of the Blackberry device and law enforcement agencies in Saudi Arabia and India: for example, http://www.arabian-business.com/blackberry-s-response-rim-statement-in-full-339572.html
64. Commission Decision 2008/324/EC setting up the 'Platform on Electronic Data Retention for the Investigation, Detection and Prosecution of Serious Crime' group of experts; OJ L 111/11, 23.4.2008.
65. DATRET/EXPGRP (2009) 2 Final – 03 12 2009.
66. Court of Dendermonde, Not. nr. DE 20.95.16/08/26, 2 March 2009.
67. Court of Appeal of Ghent of 30 June 2010.
68. Supreme Court, Nr. P.10.1347.N, 18 January 2011.
69. 12 October 2011.
70. 18 U.S.C. § 2510(15) and § 2711(2), respectively.
71. 18 U.S.C. § 2703(a) and (b), respectively.
72. 50 USC § 1881(a)(4). These provisions were inserted in by the FISA Amendments Act of 2008, s. 701(b)(4).
73. For example, European Parliament resolution 'on the interception of bank transfer data from the SWIFT system by the US secret services' (P6_TA-PROV(2006)0317), which raises concerns about privacy as well as 'large-scale forms of economic and industrial espionage'.

74. Council Framework Decision 2008/977/JHA on the protection of personal data processed in the framework of police and judicial co-operation in criminal matters (OJ L 350/60, 30.12.2008) ('2008 Decision').
75. OJ L 281/31, 23.11.1995, at art. 3(2).
76. See Commission Communication, 'A comprehensive approach on personal data protection in the European Union', COM (2010) 609 final, 4.11.2010, at 2.3. See also Commission proposed Directive of the European Parliament and Council 'on the protection of individuals with regard to the processing of personal data by competent authorities for the purposes of prevention, investigation, detection or prosecution of criminal offences or the execution of criminal penalties, and the free movement of such data' COM(2012) 10 final, 25.1.2012.
77. 2008 Decision at art. 13.
78. OJ L 181/34, 19.7.2003, at art. 9. The Agreement entered into force on 1 February 2010, after all Member States had aligned their bilateral MLAs with the US.
79. Ibid., art. 9(2).
80. Ibid., at 25(1) and (2), respectively.
81. For example, UK, Data Protection Act 1998, Sch. I, Pt. I, para. 8; Germany, Federal Data Protection Act, s. 4(b)(5).
82. Supra n. 106, at art. 25(6).
83. WP12 'Transfers of personal data to third countries: Applying Articles 25 and 26 of the EU Data Protection Directive', July 1998.
84. Council Decision 2000/520/EC, L 215/7, 25.8.2000, which expressly permit derogation 'to the extent necessary to meet....law enforcement requirements'.
85. Council Decision 2006/729/CFSP/JHA (OJ L 298/27, 27.10.2006), extended by Council Decision 2007/551/CFSP/JHA.
86. Supra n. 106, art. 26(1)(d).
87. Opinion 1/2006 'on the application of EU data protection rules to internal whistle-blowing schemes in the fields of accounting, internal accounting controls, auditing matters, fight against bribery, banking and financial crime', WP 117, 1.2.2006; Opinion 10/2006, 'on the processing of personal data by the Society for Worldwide Interbank Financial Telecommunication (SWIFT)', WP 128, 22.11.2006.
88. Analogous to the 'double criminality' requirement in international criminal law.
89. For example, even hearsay evidence recorded and stored by a cloud service provider is real evidence of the fact the recording was made.
90. Such jurisdiction may arise under statute (e.g. criminal procedure code) or be inherent to the court (e.g. abuse of process). See, for example, the US exclusionary doctrine based on the 'fruit of the poisonous tree' metaphor.
91. *Schenk v. Switzerland* (1991) 13 E.H.R.R. 242.
92. For example, *Herring v. United States* 555 US (2009).
93. *United States v. Gorshkov*, 2001 WL 1024026 (W.D. Wash. 2001), at *3.
94. Ibid., at p. 46.
95. See *Jespers v. Belgium* (1981) 27 DR 61 and *X v. FRG* (1984) 8 E.H.R.R. 225.
96. EIO Proposal at art. 8(3).

References

Book

1. Casey, E.: Handbook of Digital Forensics and Investigations. Academic, London (2009)
2. Walden, I.: Computer Crimes and Digital Investigations. OUP, Oxford (2007)

Journal Article

3. Boister, N.: Transnational criminal law? Eur. J. Int. Law. **14**, 953, 960 (2003)
4. Bradshaw, S., Millard, C., Walden, I.: Contracts for clouds: a comparative analysis of terms and conditions for cloud computing services. Int. J. Law Inf. Technol. **19**(3), 187–223 (2011)
5. Couillard, D.A.: Defogging the cloud: applying fourth amendment principles to evolving expectations in cloud computing. Minn. Law Rev. **93**, 2205 (June 2009)
6. de Hert, P., Kopcheva, M.: International mutual legal assistance in criminal law made redundant: a comment on the Belgian Yahoo! case. Comput. Law Secur. Rev. **27**, 291–297 (2011)
7. Hon, K., Millard, C., Walden, I.: The problem of 'personal data' in cloud computing – what information is regulated? Int. Data Privacy Law **1**(4), 211–228 (2011)
8. Kapranos Huntley, A.: The Protection of Trading Interests Act 1980: some jurisdictional aspects of enforcement of antitrust laws. Int. Comp. Law Quart. **30**, 213–216 (1981)
9. Loof, R.: Obtaining, adducing and contesting evidence from abroad: a defence perspective on cross-border evidence. Crim. Law Rev. **1**, 40–57 (2011)
10. O'Floinn, M., Ormerod, D.: Social networking sites, RIPA and criminal investigations. Crim. Law Rev. **10**, 766–789 (2011)
11. Reidenberg, J.: Technology and internet jurisdiction. Univ. Pa. Law Rev. **153**, 1951 (2005)
12. Robinson, W.J.: Free at what cost?: cloud computing privacy under the stored communication act. Georgetown Law J. **98**, 1195 (April 2010)

Online Article (No DOI Available)

13. Hon, W.K., Hörnle, J., Millard, C.: Data protection jurisdiction and cloud computing – when are cloud users and providers subject to EU data protection law? The Cloud of Unknowing, Part 3 (September 7, 2011). Available at SSRN: http://ssrn.com/abstract=1924240 (2011)
14. Peers, S.: The proposed European investigation order: assault on human rights and national sovereignty. Statewatch Analysis, May 2010. Available at http://www.statewatch.org/analyses/no-96-european-investigation-order.pdf and http://www.statewatch.org/analyses/no-112-eu-eio-update.pdf (2010)
15. Schwerha IV, J.J.: Law enforcement challenges in transborder acquisition of electronic evidence from 'cloud computing providers' (January 15, 2010). Available at http://www.coe.int/t/dghl/cooperation/economiccrime/cybercrime/Documents/Reports-Presentations/2079_reps_IF10_reps_joeschwerha1a.pdf (2010)
16. Spoenle, J.: Cloud computing and cybercrime investigations: territoriality vs. the power of disposal (August 31, 2010). Available at http://www.coe.int/t/dghl/cooperation/economic-crime/cybercrime/Documents/Internationalcooperation/2079_Cloud_Computing_power_disposal_31Aug10a.pdf (2010)
17. Whittaker, Z.: EU demands answers over Microsoft's Patriot Act Admission (September 19, 2011). http://www.zdnet.com/blog/igeneration/eu-demands-answers-over-microsofts-patriot-act-admission/11290 (2011, September 19)
18 Whittaker, Z.: Dutch government to ban U.S. providers over Patriot Act concerns. ZdNet, 19 Sept 2011. http://www.zdnet.com/blog/btl/dutch-government-to-ban-us-providers-over-patriot-act-concerns/58342?tag=search-results-rivers;item3 (2011)

Chapter 3
A Privacy Impact Assessment Tool
for Cloud Computing

David Tancock, Siani Pearson, and Andrew Charlesworth

Abstract In this chapter, we consider requirements for Privacy Impact Assessments
(PIAs) carried out within a cloud computing environment and explain how a PIA support
tool may be constructed. Privacy is an important consideration in cloud computing, as
actual or perceived privacy weaknesses will impact legal compliance, data security, and
user trust. A PIA is a systematic process for evaluating the possible future effects that a
particular activity or proposal may have on an individual's privacy. It focuses on understanding the system, initiative, or scheme; identifying and mitigating adverse privacy
impacts; and informing decision-makers who must decide whether the project should
proceed and in what form (Stewart B, Privacy impact assessments. PLPR 3(7):61–64,
1996. http://www.austrii.edu/au/journals/PLPR.html. Accessed 30 October 2011).

Keywords Cloud • Privacy • Privacy Impact Assessment • Regulation

3.1 Introduction

A Privacy Impact Assessment (PIA) [1] is a systematic process for identifying and
addressing privacy issues in an information system that considers the future consequences for privacy of a proposed action [2]. It is thus, in part, a predictive exercise

S. Pearson
Cloud and Security Lab, HP Labs, Long Down Avenue, Bristol BS34 8QZ, UK
e-mail: Siani.Pearson@hp.com

A. Charlesworth
Centre for IT and Law, University of Bristol, Queens Road, Bristol BS8 1RJ, UK
e-mail: csdjt@bristol.ac.uk; a.j.charlesworth@bris.ac.uk

D. Tancock (✉)
Department of Computer Science, University of Bristol,
Merchant Venturers Building, Woodland Road, Clifton, Bristol BS8 1UB, UK
e-mail: csdjt@bristol.ac.uk

S. Pearson and G. Yee (eds.), *Privacy and Security for Cloud Computing*,
Computer Communications and Networks, DOI 10.1007/978-1-4471-4189-1_3,
© Springer-Verlag London 2013

designed to prevent or minimise adverse privacy outcomes. Typically, PIAs usually take the form of a series of steps, posing and answering questions and considering options, although they can also be more holistic in nature. In some jurisdictions, an expected deliverable of the PIA process is a document, such as a PIA report [3]. PIAs are primarily a proactive process, whereas other related business processes such as privacy issue analysis, privacy audits, or privacy law compliance checking can be proactive and reactive. For example, a privacy audit can be done in a proactive manner as part of an organisation's attempt to protect private data without it being required by an outside agency or it can be done in a reactive manner by scrutinising existing projects to ensure their continuing conformity with internal rules and external requirements [4]. A PIA permits organisations to design privacy into new systems during the design and development stages, reducing the risk that costly retrofitting of privacy safeguards will be required after implementation.

While a PIA may be perceived primarily as a management tool (i.e. as a threat/ risk assessment process), it can be used as a tool for enhancing individual privacy. By surfacing privacy issues at an early stage, and providing system designers with relevant knowledge, as well as the impetus to tackle those issues at the architectural level, PIAs can facilitate the raising of a system's privacy baseline without undue impact on its functionality [5].

Privacy rights are protected and advanced by convincing agencies and businesses to carry out a PIA for the following reasons: to demonstrate legal compliance, to allow organisations to develop better policies, to save money, to develop a culture of privacy protection, to prevent adverse publicity, and to mitigate risks in advance of resource allocation. In the case of cloud computing, the goal of enhancing end user trust by decreasing the risk of exposure of end user's information is particularly important because there is a perceived lack of consumer trust with respect to cloud scenarios specifically where sensitive information is involved.

This chapter considers the possibility of developing a PIA decision support tool for a cloud environment. The structure of this chapter is organised as follows. In Sect. 3.2, we provide some background information on PIAs within major jurisdictions. Section 3.3 considers the problems and issues of privacy and security in the cloud and discusses the challenges of deploying a PIA tool for this environment, which provides the motivation for our approach. In Sect. 3.4, we present details of a PIA tool for cloud environments, outlining what the tool does, how the tool works, and its architecture. In Sect. 3.5, we discuss and present details of the methodology used for our PIA tool including the software development methodology, data collection, analysis, results, and modelling. In Sect. 3.6, we cover related work previously carried out within the context of privacy and security in cloud computing and evaluate whether elements of these approaches are suitable for the proposed tool. Section 3.7 considers the planned next steps for the proposed tool. In Sect. 3.8, we briefly provide conclusions.

3.2 Background

In this section, we discuss PIA processes in different jurisdictions and provide examples of PIAs that have been recently undertaken by government agencies and private organisations.

Our analysis of the various guidance materials indicates that PIAs vary across jurisdictions – sometimes substantially – and that there are many interrelated dimensions. The following subsections describe five major dimensions that we have identified.

3.2.1   The Level of Prescription

The first dimension that affects the type of PIA relates to levels of prescription within different jurisdictions. The requirements for conducting PIAs within different jurisdictions are by "legislation" (e.g. required by law), prescribed by binding "policy" or "recommended" by those with no legal authority (e.g. privacy commissioners), and the landscape can be very complex.

For example, in the Canadian province of Ontario, all three levels of prescription exist for PIAs [6]. Section 6 of the Regulation to the "Personal Health Information Protection Act" (PHIPA) mandates PIAs for Health Information Network Providers (HINP), when two or more Heath Information Custodians (HIC) use electronic means to disclose Personal Health Information (PHI) to one another [7]. In this respect, the legislative and policy drivers for this come from the government. Furthermore, PIAs are required by policy at the detailed design phase or when requesting funding approval for product acquisition or system development work, where those projects involve changes in the management of personal information held by government programmes or otherwise affect client privacy.

The Ontario PIA process is very much seen as part of, or complimentary to, the mandated threat risk assessment process and is designed primarily to aid management decision-making processes. Moreover, it is the responsibility of the information and privacy commissioner to ensure that government and health-care practitioners and organisations abide by the FIPPA and MFIPPA Acts [8]. The commissioner also provides policy advice and training in the areas of freedom of information (FOI) and privacy including PIAs.

In addition, since the "Data Handling Procedures in Government" report published in June 2008 [9], PIAs in the United Kingdom (UK) are mandatory from all government departments that introduce new policy or processes that involve the use of personal data. Thus, all UK government departments will introduce PIAs to ensure that privacy issues are factored into plans from the start and check that they have been carried out as an integral part of the risk management assessment process.

Our analysis also identifies that organisations can conduct PIAs in the absence of any level of prescription (i.e. required by law, prescribed by binding policy, or recommended by those with no legal authority) and instead are based upon self-regulation. The motivations for conducting self-regulation PIAs are based upon the perception of the benefits. For example, private sector organisations typically conduct self-regulated PIAs when they are concerned about reputation.

The next section considers the application of PIAs in private and public sectors, which again affects the type of PIA used.

Table 3.1 Statistical report of Canada's PIAs and PPIAs

Privacy Impact Assessments	Amount
Number of PIAs initiated	172
Number of PIAs completed	89
Number of PIAs forwarded to the Office of the Privacy Commissioner of Canada	78
Preliminary Privacy Impact Assessments	**Amount**
Number of PPIAs initiated	104
Number of PPIAs completed	99

3.2.2 Application of PIAs in Private and Public Sectors

In this section, we discuss the application of PIAs in private and public sectors. In jurisdictions in which PIAs are being currently applied, there is a longer history of regulation within organisations in the public sector than in the private sector. For example, in Canada, New Zealand (NZ), Australia, and the United States (US), public sector privacy legislation has generally predated that for the private sector. Therefore, most PIA requirements apply to public sector organisations such as government ministries or departments and types of public bodies or agencies. However, it is increasingly difficult to determine the limits of the public sector PIAs under current conditions. This is because many public agencies that are outside government ministries now have extensive experience with PIAs. This includes organisations in the health sector, higher education, and statistical agencies. Although there is evidence that PIAs are conducted within the private sector (e.g. self-regulation), we do not know the extent of this in the absence of a mandate. However, private sector organisations have been mentioned by oversight bodies (e.g. privacy commissioners) and central agencies (e.g. Treasury Board of Canada) in relation to conducting PIAs in high-risk situations or initiatives [4]. For example, the Treasury Board Secretariat (TBS) of Canada states in a report of 2010 that 276 PIAs and a short form of PIA called Preliminary Privacy Impact Assessments (PPIAs) were initiated, of which 188 were completed, as illustrated in Table 3.1 [10].

The UK Information Commissioner's Office (ICO) also states in its "Annual Review" of 2010 that "over 300 PIAs have been started across central government and their agencies" [11].

As discussed in Sect. 3.2.4, the PIAs involved in this process include both full-scale PIAs (i.e. those that conduct a more in-depth internal assessment of privacy risks and liabilities) and small-scale PIAs (i.e. those that are less formalised and require less exhaustive information gathering and analysis) [4]. Thus, some examples of PIAs that have been conducted in the UK are outlined in Table 3.2.

However, as illustrated in Table 3.3, some organisations in the UK employ external consultants to carry out a PIA either because they do not possess the necessary skills in-house or because they wish the PIA to be perceived as being as independent as possible from potential influences within the organisation.

Table 3.2 Examples of PIAs conducted in the UK

Organisation	Year of publication	Project/procedure assessed	Type of PIA
Individual electoral registration	2011	Introduction of new policy to help rebuild public confidence in the security of electoral registration	Full scale
UK Anti-Doping	2010	The disclosure of personal data to UK Anti-Doping by the Serious Organised Crime Agency	Small scale
Northern Ireland Statistics and Research Agency (NISRA)	2010	2011 census for Northern Ireland	Full scale
Office for National Statistics (ONS)	2009	2011 census for England and Wales	Full scale
UK Border Agency	2009	Exchange of fingerprint information with immigration authorities in Australia, Canada, United States, and New Zealand	Small scale
National Policing Improvement Agency	2009	Electronic exchange of police intelligence across England and Wales via the Police National database	Full scale

Table 3.3 Examples of PIAs outsourced in the UK

Organisation	Type of privacy impact accessed	Consultancy employed
Aegate (Pharmaceutical authentication services)	Use of RFID technologies to authenticate prescription pharmaceuticals at point of sale	Enterprise Privacy Group
Department for Transport	National time-distance-place road pricing policy. This charges vehicles based on when, where, and how much they drive	Enterprise Privacy Group
Phorm Inc	Behavioural targeted advertising	80/20 Thinking Ltd

Analysis of the outsourced PIAs suggests that in traditional approaches such as an internal distributed network, external consultants (e.g. independent experts, regulators, civil society groups, professional bodies and charities) often bring considerable experience to the PIA process, lending impartially to the process. However, the experiences found in the UK concerning difficulties in organisations conducting PIAs seem to be replicated in most of the jurisdictions studied. These include internal stakeholder resistance such as project managers who often perceived PIAs to be a burden and public relations managers who were wary of engagement with external stakeholders.

In addition, security officers sometimes considered PIAs to be a threat to their expertise, and consequently, employees in that position in the organisation or acting as external stakeholders may often be reluctant to engage with an organisation conducting a PIA. This is through either lack of interest, lack of trust, or lack of resources [2].

Moreover, an exercise such as that conducted by 80/20 Thinking Ltd cannot be accurately described as a PIA, given that the technology and its applications were already fully developed and in use in business operations at the time of the PIA exercise. These exercises might be more accurately characterised as a privacy audit or compliance check [12].

In the next section, we consider the conditions and circumstances for conducting PIAs in the jurisdictions.

3.2.3 Initial Screening

There is variance in the mechanisms for determining the conditions and circumstances for conducting PIAs. Some jurisdictions have developed screening tools to help organisations to determine whether or not to conduct a PIA for any given initiative or to identify privacy issues that may require further analysis.

Commonly, an initial screening exercise is conducted to determine if a PIA should be completed according to the rules or recommendations in the jurisdiction. This can be as simple as determining whether personal information is involved or take the form of a structured instrument that poses a series of questions, as in NZ [13] and the UK [14].

The US screening process is a form called a Privacy Threshold Analysis [15]. Those completing the form provide a variety of information about the system, answering specific questions tailored to their operational context, and the Privacy Office makes an assessment that determines whether or not a PIA is required.

In contrast, within Canada, a Preliminary PIA (PPIA) is similar to a screening tool [8].

In the next section, we discuss the scale of the PIA processes that are conducted in all jurisdictions, as this can vary considerably.

3.2.4 The Scale of the PIA Process

Generally, there are two different types of PIAs conducted in all jurisdictions although the names and the processes vary. For example, names attributed to a short form of PIA are "small-scale" (e.g. UK), "PPIA" (e.g. Canada), and "Privacy Scan" or "Privacy Impact Statement" in other jurisdictions. The short form of PIA is similar to a full-scale PIA but is less formalised and requires less exhaustive information gathering and analysis, usually focusing on specific aspects of a project [4]. A full-scale PIA conducts a more in-depth internal assessment of privacy risks and liabilities. It analyses privacy risks, consults widely with stakeholders on privacy concerns, and brings forward solutions to accept, mitigate, or avoid such concerns. The process guidelines for a full-scale PIA tend to be more comprehensive and suggest the various stages of the process. For example in Australia, the process for conducting a PIA consists of five stages [16]: project description, mapping the information flow, privacy impact analysis, privacy management, and recommendations.

In contrast, the Ontario PIA process consists of three main stages: conceptual analysis, data flow analysis, and follow-up analysis. However, the Ontario PIA process ensures client privacy is considered throughout the business redesign or project development cycle, particularly at the conceptual stage, the final design approval and funding stage, the implementation and communications stage, and at the post-implementation audit or review stage [8].

In the UK, the processes involved in conducting a PIA are again similar to PIAs conducted in other jurisdictions and consist of the following [14]:

- *Initial assessment*: Examines the project at an early stage, identifies stakeholders, assesses privacy risks, and decides whether a PIA is necessary or not and if so, what level of PIA is required.
- *Small-scale PIA*: This is less formalised and requires less exhaustive information gathering and analysis and usually focuses on specific aspects of a project.
- *Full-scale PIA*: This consists of five phases that are usually conducted in sequence and include the following [14]:

  o *Preliminary*: Establishes and ensures a firm basis for the PIA, so that it can be conducted effectively and efficiently
  o *Preparation*: Makes the arrangements needed to enable the following phase (i.e. consultation and analysis) to run smoothly
  o *Consultation and analysis*: Identifies problems early on, discovers effective solutions, and ensures that the design is adapted to include those solutions
  o *Documentation*: Documents the PIA process and the outcomes and delivers a PIA report
  o *Review and audit*: Ensures that the undertakings arising from the consultation and analysis phase are actually within the running system or implemented project

- *Privacy law compliance check*: Examines compliance with statutory powers, duties, and prohibitions in relation to the use and disclosure of personal information.
- *Data protection compliance check*: Examines compliance with the Data Protection Act of 1998. An organisation usually conducts this check when the project is more fully formed.

In the next section, we consider the people involved in conducting PIAs in all jurisdictions.

3.2.5 Who Conducts PIAs

PIAs are usually completed by a senior analyst or a manager with ongoing programme administration responsibilities. The various guidance material suggests a team or committee approach and stipulates what types of expertise should be drawn in to the PIA. This can include, with varying degrees of participation, the following personnel [2]: programme and project managers, privacy policy makers, legal advisors, records management staff, information technology or data security experts, communications staff, and other functional specialists.

3.2.6 Current PIA Tools

As considered above in Sect. 3.2, the processes involved in conducting PIAs across jurisdictions sometimes vary substantially. One important difference is in the PIA tools that each jurisdiction uses. For example, in Canada, the TBS provides an e-learning tool for government employees interested in learning more about privacy and PIAs and how to complete them. The e-learning tool consists of two courses (e.g. Overview and Manage/Monitor) and a PIA assistant to help users complete PPIAs and full PIAs [17].

In contrast, the US Department of Homeland Security (DHS) employs a PIA tool called the Privacy Threshold Analysis that helps users determine whether a PIA is required under the E-Government Act of 2002 and the Homeland Security Act 2002 [18]. In the UK, the PIA Guidelines provide a number of screening questions to help users decide whether a full-scale PIA or a small-scale PIA is warranted. The Guidelines also include a number of questions for a privacy law compliance check and a Data Protection Act (1998) compliance check. Templates are also included within the Guidelines for Data Protection compliance and the Privacy and Electronic Communications Regulations (PECR) [14].

The evaluation processes involved in these PIA tools consist of simple questionnaires, whereby most of the questions require a "yes" or "no" response. Analysis of the PIA tools suggests that they are mainly based upon a simple "decision-tree" approach. This approach is commonly used for simple reasoning, as it is both a knowledge representation scheme and a method of reasoning about that knowledge. In addition, the PIA tools produced by the different jurisdictions are mainly procedure-based (e.g. whereby a number of specified steps are used to reach the desired outcomes), and their granularity is coarse-grained (e.g. consist of fewer larger components). Finally, the PIA tools are Web applications where both data and the applications are at the server-side; therefore, they do not take into account the cloud or any of its characteristics (e.g. on-demand self-service, ubiquitous network access, location-independent resource planning, rapid elasticity, and pay for use).

Furthermore, we contend that deploying a PIA tool (i.e. a tool that is based upon questionnaires in which answers provided by the user addresses the complexity of privacy compliance requirements by highlighting privacy risks and compliance issues) can lead to negative perceptions by organisations and end users including [19]:

- Some organisations find it very difficult to relinquish control or trust third parties to manage their applications and data.

- Some organisations are worried about security and weak data protection in cloud applications.
- Some markets require industry-specific business applications (e.g. military systems) for which solutions such as the software as a service (SaaS) solution are not available.
- Organisations without clear objectives and defined business processes are sometimes no better off with a cloud solution than with an on-premise solution.

3.2.7   Future PIAs

We have seen above that a number of PIAs have been carried out in various jurisdictions and that pressure is mounting from regulators for this approach to be used more widely.

Privacy rights can be protected and advanced by convincing agencies and businesses to carry out a PIA for the following reasons: to demonstrate legal compliance, to allow organisations to develop better policy, to save money, to develop a culture of privacy protection, to prevent adverse publicity, and to mitigate risks in advance or resource allocation.

However, as business becomes more global and moves to the cloud, it will become increasingly difficult to carry out the analysis needed and so more help will be required from a technical standpoint.

Moving PIAs onto the cloud and potentially across and between legal jurisdictions, including processes that are outsourced and data that crosses organisational boundaries, increases risk factors and legal complexity. Therefore, in the next section, we discuss the problems and issues of privacy and security in the cloud and explain further the challenges of deploying a PIA tool for this environment, before considering solutions later in this chapter.

3.3   Issues for Privacy, Security, and PIAs in the Cloud

In this section, we consider the problems and issues of privacy and security in the cloud and discuss the challenges of deploying a PIA tool in this environment, which provides the motivation for our approach.

As discussed in Chap. 1, there are a number of privacy, security, and trust issues associated with the cloud including [20] lack of user control, potential unauthorised secondary usage, data proliferation, transborder data flow and dynamic provisioning, access, availability, backup, multi-tendency, and lack of standardisation. Of these issues, data proliferation, transborder data flow, dynamic provisioning, and virtualisation are very important to PIAs in the cloud. For example, data proliferation is a feature of cloud and this happens in a way that may involve the PIA tool being accessed by multiple customers from different organisations that reside in different jurisdictions, whereby data is not controlled by the data owners. However, Cloud

Service Providers (CSP) ensure availability by replicating data in multiple data centres; therefore, it is difficult to guarantee that a copy of the PIA tool and its data or its backups are not stored or processed in a certain jurisdiction or that all these copies of the PIA tool and its data are deleted if such a request is made. This is because customers of the PIA tool cannot be sure that the PIA tool and its data is in one jurisdiction or that copies that are deleted are really deleted and are not recoverable by a CSP, as currently there are no ways to prove this as it relies on trust.

Furthermore, the movement of data, governance, and accountability of the PIA tool becomes more complex when it moves onto the cloud and potentially across and between legal jurisdictions. This is because processes may be outsourced and knowing the jurisdictions involved can be quite difficult. Moreover, transferring data stored in the cloud to other jurisdictions may violate local laws, because of the difficulty of asserting which specific server or storage device is used, due to the dynamic nature of the cloud [20].

Virtualisation introduces similar concerns due to the separation of the logical entities being assessed from the underlying physical resources. Thus, virtual machines (VMs) are environments that are completely isolated from each other. Although virtualisation makes it safe for users to share the same hardware, the underlying physical resources are the responsibility of the CSP. However, these environments can sometime break down, allowing attackers to escape the boundaries of this environment and have full access to the host. Therefore, organisations should maintain their security based on sound security practices including keeping software up to date with security patches, using secure configuration baselines, and using host-based firewalls, antivirus software, or other appropriate mechanisms to detect and stop attacks.

However, we believe that a cloud-based PIA tool is a novel approach. This is because at the time of writing (e.g. February 2012), no such tool exists. Thus, the PIA tool can provide significant value in increasing trust as a commercial service, in spite of the number of challenges it faces in deployment. This is because we contend that the PIA tool can be accessed in the same way the cloud is delivered: "as a service". Indeed, the same five characteristics of the cloud (i.e. on-demand self-service, ubiquitous network access, location-independent resource pooling, rapid elasticity, and pay per use) that are used to deploy and access existing applications and tools may be used to deploy and access the PIA tool especially the metering that is already built in for billing and service-level assurance.

In the next section, we discuss our approach for a cloud-based PIA tool.

3.4   Development of a PIA Tool for Cloud Computing

In this section, we present details of a PIA tool for cloud environments, outlining what the tool does, how the tool works, and its architecture.

The PIA tool addresses the complexity of privacy compliance requirements for organisations (both public and private sector), by highlighting privacy risks and compliance issues for individuals within the organisation who are not experts in privacy and security, so they can identify solutions in a given situation. This will allow organisations to identify potential issues at an early stage and hence avoid costs associated with pursuing development paths that are unlawful or pose a higher risk than an organisation can accept or insure against. Where PIAs are mandatory for public sector organisations, the tool can provide evidence that due process has been followed for the purpose of reporting and audit. More specifically, it can help decision-makers within organisations to decide whether a new project (in a broad sense, encompassing scheme, notion or product, etc.) that they wish to develop should go ahead, and if so in what form (i.e. what restrictions there are, what additional checks should be made, etc.). The tool could be run at several stages during the lifetime of a project development process, each time producing different output and advice appropriate to that stage.

The PIA tool also addresses privacy and security risks in the cloud that may be raised, as part of its analysis about the project. This analysis includes those aspects mentioned in the previous section, in relation to the particular context involved: who the cloud service provider is, what their trust rating is, what security and privacy mechanisms they use, as well as other factors that are not specifically cloud-related, for example, to what extent the current project involves sensitive information and for what purposes personal data will be used.

User input for the PIA tool contains project information, such as project name, organisation name, region, brief project description, project lead, and contact details. This is followed by a descriptive analysis of the project such as outlining project documents, identifying stakeholders, and identifying early privacy risks in order to determine if a PIA is required. For example, the user may wish to describe how the organisation collects or obtains personal information or explain if personal information will be transferred outside their jurisdiction including details of the receiving countries. Output for the PIA tool is a report displaying information in several sections: introduction, project and contact details, the summary of findings (which indicates if the PIA tool has found the project to be either compliant or not), risk summary (which indicates the levels of risk associated with each privacy domain), and details of other compliance/non-compliance issues, such as security, transparency, and transborder data flows. Furthermore, the PIA tool provides detailed information about policies in relation to which the project is not compliant or is only partially compliant. In these situations, the tool provides detailed reasons for the partial or non-compliance by highlighting the specific legislation concerned, risks, standards, policies, etc. Finally, recommendations are displayed indicating what the user (organisation) must do to resolve these issues. Throughout the report, clear visual indicators are displayed; these indicate the issues that appear to be compliant with the requirements (i.e. legislation), require further attention, or have failed.

Although our focus for the tool is on privacy and data protection, this approach is also applicable in a broader sense as it can apply to other compliance areas, such as data retention, security, and export regulation.

The following section provides more details of how the tool works.

3.4.1   Architecture and Knowledge Representation

In this section, we discuss the architecture and knowledge representation of the PIA tool. There are a number of traditional programming approaches (e.g. Java, Python, C#, and other object-oriented languages), available for developing a Web-based PIA tool that can address the generic requirements for a PIA system including the collection of data such as project and contact information, the processing of data, and the display of data (e.g. report). Our approach for the PIA tool is a decision support system (DSS) based on a type of expert system [21]. A number of different approaches are available for developing a rule-based system (e.g. expert system) that stores and manipulates knowledge and interprets information in a useful way including Drools [22] and VisiRule [23].

The architecture of the PIA tool that we are currently developing and prototyping is illustrated in Fig. 3.1. This represents one approach (i.e. client-server) of a Web-based PIA tool that can address privacy and cloud environments that is based upon our choice of using the Corvid Runtime environment for a single organisation [24].

The PIA tool has a knowledge base (KB) that is created and updated by privacy experts on an ongoing basis. The experts can be within the organisation (i.e. in-house) or can be outsourced externally (i.e. external consultants). Thus, generic rules for privacy and data protection legislation from a number of jurisdictions (e.g. the UK Data Protection Act 1998, the US Privacy Act 1974) are created and entered into the KB by the experts using a specific user interface (UI). This is important as the tool is to be deployed within a cloud environment, whereby organisations from different jurisdictions may ask to use the application. Initially, the tool will cover jurisdictions that currently conduct PIAs including the UK, the USA, Australia, NZ, and Canada.

There are two types of users: end users (who fill in a questionnaire from which a PIA report is generated) and domain experts (who create and maintain the KB). Typically, users interact with the PIA tool via the Corvid Java runtime that can be Web based (e.g. delivered either as an applet or servlet) or fielded as a standalone Java application [24].

The architecture uses the Corvid servlet runtime [24] that delivers Hyper-Text Markup Language (HTML) pages that contain session-specific data and variables that are sent to the user's browser. Therefore, all processing is done on the server with only HTML pages sent to the client's machine, and it can handle multiple users when questions or results are displayed. Since the servlet engine is already running, starting a new session is very quick as the user does not have to wait for an applet and KB to download. In addition, the full power of HTML and any extensions supported by the browser such as Extensible Markup Language (XML), JavaScript, or Java Server Pages (JSP) can be used to design the user interface screens. This allows for far more complex and sophisticated interfaces to be built than can be done using the Corvid applet approach.

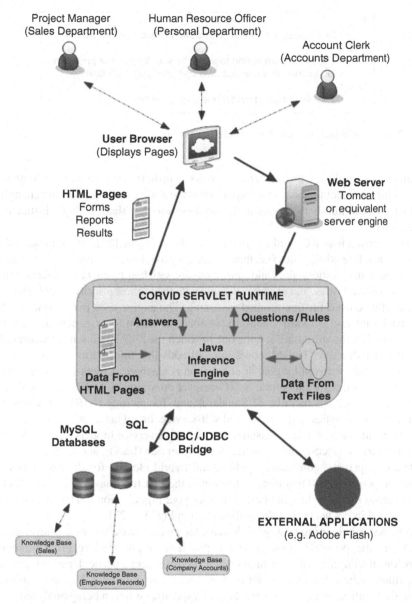

Fig. 3.1 PIA tool architecture for single organisation

The PIA tool may also use multi-tenancy, whereby a single instance of the PIA application may run on a server, serving multiple clients (i.e. tenants) within the organisation. Therefore, it is possible with this architecture to have different KBs for different departments within the organisation that have different privacy and

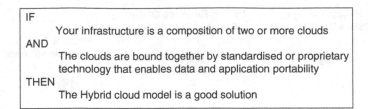

IF
    Your infrastructure is a composition of two or more clouds
AND
    The clouds are bound together by standardised or proprietary
    technology that enables data and application portability
THEN
    The Hybrid cloud model is a good solution

Fig. 3.2 Heuristic representation of cloud infrastructure question

organisational policies and acceptable risks. Furthermore, we believe that this architecture is scalable because the system has the ability to accommodate changing load such as the number of users in the organisation that share a single instance of the PIA tool.

Our approach uses a Corvid Exsys rules (i.e. Java) engine [25], which makes inferences by deciding which rules (i.e. those created by the domain expert that are directly associated with questionnaires and questions) are satisfied by facts or objects, prioritises the satisfied rules, and executes the rule with the highest priority. Ontologies can additionally be used for fine-grained reasoning. The engine uses two distinct modes (e.g. backward and forward chaining). In forward chaining (e.g. data-driven), the engine searches the rules until it finds one in which the "IF" condition is known to be true. It concludes the "THEN" condition and adds this information to its data and continues in this way until a goal or conclusion is reached. A meta-level description of the privacy rules for this phase is "IF <trigger conditions> THEN <action>". For example, the National Institute of Standards and Technology (NIST) provides five essential characteristics (e.g. on-demand self-service, broad network access, resource pooling, rapid elasticity, and measured service), three service models (e.g. SaaS, platform as a service (PaaS), and infrastructure as a service (IaaS)), and four deployment models (e.g. private, community, public, and hybrid clouds) for their definition of cloud computing [26]. Therefore, a question in the PIA tool may ask the user "Is the Hybrid cloud infrastructure the best option for your organisation?" This question can be converted into a heuristic rule, as illustrated in Fig. 3.2 [27].

In backward chaining (e.g. goal driven), the engine searches for top-level goals, which are the possible answers to the problem or potential recommendations. Therefore, the engine can determine what it needs to meet a particular goal including determining when that goal is met or that a goal cannot be met. However, to meet this determination, the tool requires data on a specific situation being analysed. This data can come from other rules, external sources such as databases and spreadsheets, or asking the user additional questions. For example, an organisation might like to use a cloud provider that uses Representational State Transfer (REST) Web resources and supports multiple accounts with different key management techniques for each customer. The engine checks the rules to find one that would be relevant to making this decision, as illustrated in Fig. 3.3 [27]:

Although in this case the engine has found a potentially useful rule, without more data, it cannot determine if this rule should be used. This is because the engine does not know how many multiple accounts are allowed for each customer by Windows

---

IF

    Representational State Transfer (REST) Web resources are used
by the organisation

AND

    Multiple user accounts for each customer are required

THEN

    Windows Azure AppFabric Access Control Service
is a good choice

Fig. 3.3   Heuristic representation of REST/multiple accounts question

---

IF

    Multiple accounts for each customer is greater than 6

THEN

    Windows Azure is not a good choice

Fig. 3.4   Heuristic representation of new goal

Azure [28]. Therefore, the engine searches for a rule that can tell it something about the maximum number of multiple accounts, as illustrated in Fig. 3.4 [27]:

Although the original rule (i.e. goal) is not forgotten, it is temporarily superseded by the new rule (i.e. new goal). However, to use this rule, the engine needs to know the maximum number of multiple accounts per customer the organisation requires. Thus, this answer may come from a database, a different program, other rules, or by asking the user directly, as the engine determines where and how to get the needed data. This process of having one goal requiring data leading to another goal from the highest level to the lowest level is how the engine in the PIA tool uses backward chaining [27]. In addition, as data becomes available, lower level goals are met and are dropped off the chain and continue until the engine is able to determine which of the conditions for the initial top-level goals are true. Similarly, this approach is used to reason about transborder data flow and other data protection requirements.

Although we use this particular inference engine to run rules, the approach is not reliant on any particular inference engine or specific format beyond the processing of "IF/THEN" rules, and so a variety of mechanisms could be used from production rules systems to "Clips" or "Prolog".

In Sect. 3.5, we provide further details of our approach for our PIA tool including the software development methodology, data collection, analysis, results, and modelling.

The following section will provide more details of our specialised tool, including how it may be used in a cloud environment.

3.4.2   Cloud Deployment of PIA Tool

This section considers the deployment of our PIA tool in a cloud environment and its architecture. The possible deployment of our PIA tool is based upon the advantages and disadvantages between the cloud service models and the major cloud deployment models [26]. As previously discussed in Sect. 3.4.1, there are three cloud service models to consider including:

- *IaaS*: physical hardware such as servers, disks, and networks are abstracted into virtual servers and virtual storage
- *PaaS*: this provides a platform built upon the abstracted hardware that can be used by developers to create cloud applications such as the PIA tool
- *SaaS*: this provides our PIA tool as a service that enables customers to use the cloud without complexities of hardware, the Operating System (OS), or even the PIA tool's installation

For our PIA tool, the SaaS service model appears to be appropriate, whereby the end users (i.e. customers) of the tool do not actually have to own the platforms. However, when deploying our PIA tool as a SaaS service, as with all of the other cloud service models, there is a common set of technological challenges including [29]:

- *User interface flexibility*: UIs must be easy for the end users to use and meet the needs of the customer.
- *Productivity*: The solution for our PIA tool must provide a highly productive environment that focuses on industry best practices.
- *Operational excellence*: Our PIA tool must be always available and scale to the maximum size required.
- *Security and compliance*: The solution for our PIA tool must ensure that the data and application are accessed only by those who are registered to use it.
- *Multi-tenancy*: The solution for our PIA tool must be able to support from one user to many.
- *Integration*: The solution must be able to have the ability to easily integrate with other applications by supporting all relevant standards.
- *Personalisation*: This ensures that our PIA tool must look and work as the tenant and end users want it to. However, each tenant may want different UIs and questions for their particular organisational needs.
- *Costs*: As discussed in this section, initial costs of the deployment of our PIA tool depend upon the adopted solution. However, tenant and end user costs are on a pay-per-use basis.

One of the key elements discussed in the list above is multi-tenancy. In deploying our PIA tool as a SaaS service, multi-tenancy provides several options including [29]:

- *Isolated tenancy*: Whereby our PIA tool, databases, and infrastructure are isolated and are hosted per tenant as separate instances
- *Infrastructure tenancy*: Whereby our PIA tool and databases are isolated, although the infrastructure is shared and hosted in a virtual environment
- *Application tenancy*: Whereby our PIA tool and the infrastructure are shared by all tenants, although the databases are isolated
- *Shared tenancy*: Whereby our PIA tool, database, and infrastructure are all shared by the tenants

Table 3.4 Comparison of multi-tenancy models

Tenancy models

	Isolated	Infrastructure	Application	Shared
Time to market	Short	Short	Long	Longest
Infrastructure costs	High	High	Low	Low
Economies of scale	Very poor	Poor	High	Highest
Scalability	Poor	Poor	High	Highest
Provisioning	Difficult	Difficult	Easy	Easy
Admin/mgmt costs	Very high	High	Low	Low
Target tenants	Dissimilar	Dissimilar	Similar	Similar
Allows for application changes	No	No	Yes (except DBs)	Yes
Coding difficultly	Easier	Easy	Less difficult	Difficult
Implementation of service-level agreements (SLAs)	Easier	Easy	Less difficult	Difficult
Containment	Easier	Easy	Less difficult	Difficult

In considering which option to choose for our PIA tool as a SaaS service that involves multi-tenancy, a comparison is made of the different models as illustrated in Table 3.4.

The application multi-tenancy model is more suited to our PIA tool because of several reasons including the initial costs are reasonably low, the scalability is high, and the target tenants for our PIA tool are similar in nature (i.e. they will be using our application to check if their projects require PIAs). Therefore, the deployment of our PIA tool as a SaaS application is illustrated in Fig. 3.5.

There are various different options for how this might be provided within a cloud environment. For example, one option may be to deploy our PIA tool in a private cloud infrastructure, whereby the tool is provided as a service for a single organisation. Private clouds rely on virtualisation (e.g. storage and server) and treat hardware as a pool of resources that can be allocated to various functions. Thus, our PIA tool may be managed by the organisation or a third party (e.g. cloud provider) and may exist on premise or off premise [30]. The advantages of using this option relate to control, governance, security, availability, and speed of access. In contrast, the disadvantages of using this option for our PIA tool are minimal elasticity, costs, and scalability since the organisation is responsible for setting up, maintaining, and growing the infrastructure as necessary [31, 32].

Another option is to deploy our PIA tool as a SaaS application in a community cloud. In this cloud, the infrastructure may be shared by multiple organisations and supports a specific community that has shared concerns (e.g. mission, security requirements, policy, jurisdiction, and compliance considerations). Again, this cloud may be managed by the organisation or a third party and may exist (e.g. hosted) on premise or off premise [30]. Some advantages of using this option for our PIA tool are elasticity and a pay-for-use on-demand service. However, because community clouds target a specific industry or concern, some disadvantages for the

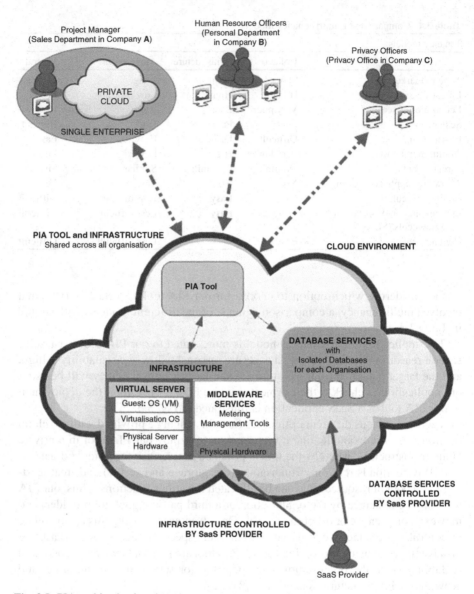

Fig. 3.5 PIA tool in cloud environment

infrastructure exist including low visibility, control, trust, and higher costs due to specialisation in support of specific customer requirements [31, 32].

A possible benefit to PIAs in the community cloud involves the use of a communal KB that may have several PIA questionnaires that represent the needs of the multiple organisations. Thus, the KB can be shared, updated, and maintained by all organisations in the community, and knowledge (such as answers and PIA decisions) is therefore shared between all organisations.

Table 3.5 Advantages/disadvantages of hybrid cloud

Hybrid cloud	
Advantages	Disadvantages
Maximum flexibility	Most of the disadvantages for both private and public clouds (for their respective components)
Dedicated resources on-site (via private cloud)	Additional layer of software is needed to provide governance and brokerage between the cloud services
Pay-per-use resources off-site (via public or community cloud)	Policy must be defined indicating which services and datasets are allowed in which part of the cloud
Off-site resources are pay for what is used. Turn the service off when done	The broker/governance component is an additional software component requiring additional IT skills to operate and manage
Elasticity when needed	
Immediate self-service	

A third option for our PIA tool is deploying it as a SaaS application in a public cloud. This infrastructure is made available to the general public or a large industry group and is owned by an organisation or cloud provider that sells cloud services [30]. Again, in a public cloud, there is no purchase of physical infrastructure, and the organisation (i.e. client) can use the services on a pay-for-use basis (e.g. on-demand self-service) with maximum elasticity. However, using this option for our PIA tool in the public cloud can lead to several disadvantages and issues for the organisation including low visibility, control, and trust. For example, our PIA tool collects information (i.e. contact information such as name, e-mail, and telephone numbers) and produces results and reports that organisations may regard as sensitive data or may regard their exposure as a high risk to the organisation.

This is because the cloud provider takes responsibility for the software and services. Furthermore, governance and policy enforcement is still emerging in public clouds, and from a security perspective, multi-tenancy provides added complexity [31, 32].

A fourth option is to deploy our PIA tool in a hybrid cloud. A hybrid cloud is the composition of two or more clouds (e.g. private, community, or public) that remain unique entities but are bound together by standardised or proprietary technology that enables data and application portability such as the use of cloud bursting for load balancing between the clouds [29]. In this scenario, the sensitive data collected by our PIA tool is stored on its own private servers in a private cloud behind a firewall away from the Internet. Therefore, published PIA results and reports that are then ported to the public cloud for customers would not contain sensitive information. Thus, our PIA tool would use public clouds for less sensitive tasks such as the PIA questionnaires but use a private cloud for vital processing tasks. However, like all cloud deployment models, the hybrid cloud has advantages and disadvantages, as illustrated in Table 3.5 [31, 32].

A public cloud deployment introduces a third party that may lead to several disadvantages and issues including low visibility, control, security, privacy, and trust, as discussed in Chap. 1.

Another consideration is the network bandwidth constraints and cost. For example, if a decision is made to move some of our PIA tool's infrastructure to a public cloud, disruption in the network connectivity between our tool's clients and the cloud service may affect the availability of our cloud hosted PIA tool. Moreover, on a low bandwidth network, there is a possibility that the interaction between our PIA tool and its customers (i.e. users) may also be affected.

There are additional factors to consider before selecting the use between private, community, and public clouds for our PIA tool. One important factor is the amount of storage and time our PIA tool is to be deployed. For example, 10 terabytes (TB) of storage supplied by a cloud provider for 5 years may involve a high pricing structure for our PIA tool in order to recover costs. On the other hand, if our PIA tool uses a temporary storage plan for 1 year, it may be cost-effective to use this private cloud. However, if the plan is to use a community cloud, the costs would be shared between all participating organisations. Thus, it can be seen that one of the factors dictating the use between private, public, or community clouds is the size of storage and how long the storage for our PIA tool is intended to be used.

Of course, cost may not be the only consideration in evaluating which type of deployment cloud model is best for our PIA tool, as some application services such as Salesforce.com (i.e. a popular customer relationship management (CRM) cloud service) offers unique features such as specialised management tools [30]. In addition, other public cloud providers offer services such as capacity planning, procurement, and the management of data centres.

Also there is the context in which our PIA will be deployed. For example, is our tool intended for the UK-based customers only (i.e. those who operate solely in the UK) or for UK customers who operate globally? This difference is critical because sensitive information can mean one thing in the UK under the Data Protection Act 1998, but sensitive information can mean completely something else especially in other countries such as those outside the European Union (EU).

In general, since the deployment models (i.e. private, public, and community) have different characteristics and even different business drivers such as cost, the best solution for our PIA tool may be a hybrid solution that involves all three models.

In the next section, we provide some examples of user interfaces (UIs) that are part of the PIA tool.

3.4.3 Examples of PIA Tool UIs

This section considers the functionality and appearance of some of the PIA tool UIs. However, the examples shown are not the final production UIs, rather those designed as of the time of writing (March 2012).

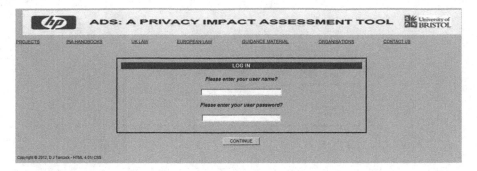

Fig. 3.6 Log-in page

Our PIA tool uses Java servlets that display HTML templates to end users via standard browsers. Typically, the call to start our PIA tool is done with a Uniform Resource Locator (URL) [27]: http://www.myServer.com/CORVID/corvidsr? KBNAME=../../MyApps/MySystem.cvr

The initial screen of our PIA tool consists of a log-in screen that prevents unauthorised users entering our application, as illustrated in Fig. 3.6.

The log-in system asks for specific user names and passwords that allow different user access modes for the tool (i.e. administrator, customer and stakeholder). In a further instantiation, the tool would be integrated with a dedicated authentication mechanism that allow role-based access.

Upon completion of a successful log-in by users, our PIA tool automatically loads a file that contains project contextual information including: contact details, project details, previous PIAs and similar project information, and stakeholder details. This information is the result of previous usage of the tool by those users, although some information may be derived automatically via the login process e.g. via an enterprise directory system.

In the next section, we describe the functionality and appearance of our PIA tool if the end user selects the administrator mode.

3.4.3.1   Administrator Mode

This section discusses the functionality and appearance of our PIA tool when authorization to the administrator mode is successful. The administration main page provides the user with options, as illustrated in Fig. 3.7 . For example, the administrator can view projects, customers and stakeholders in a particular project, or use specific utilities that help maintain our PIA tool. For this particular implementation, restrictions are placed on the layout of some screens by the underlying application used, but future plans include creation of more flexible interfaces for such screens, e.g. via a taskbar.

Projects are listed in a table that displays information including: the overal status of the project, the project name, organisation name, contact name, the date the proj-

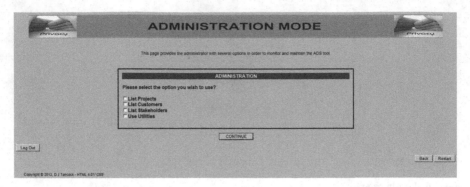

Fig. 3.7 Administration mode

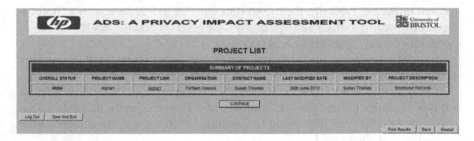

Fig. 3.8 Project list

ect was completed or last modified, the person who completed or modified the project and the project description, as illustrated in Fig. 3.8. However, due to the limitations of the servers taht the tool is currently using (i.e. Corvid and Tomcat 7) the returned data is text. It is anticipated that for businesses that use their own servers for the tool the overall status field in the display would include an image that represents the privacy risk.

To access the project the user clicks the project link. A detailsed HTML page is returned that displays the project information, as illustrated in Fig. 3.9. Contact information and stakeholder details can be accessed, in a sanitised form if appropriate for the viewer.

Utilities currently under development such as the web browser, mail log analyser, firewall analyser and multi-router analyser that help the administrator to maintain the tool are accessed via the 'Utilities' checkbox.

3.4.3.2 Stakeholder Mode

This section describes the functionality and appearance of the stakeholder mode. This mode allows stakeholders to view completed reports for particular projects and allows stakeholders to provide feedback without going through the main questionnaires.

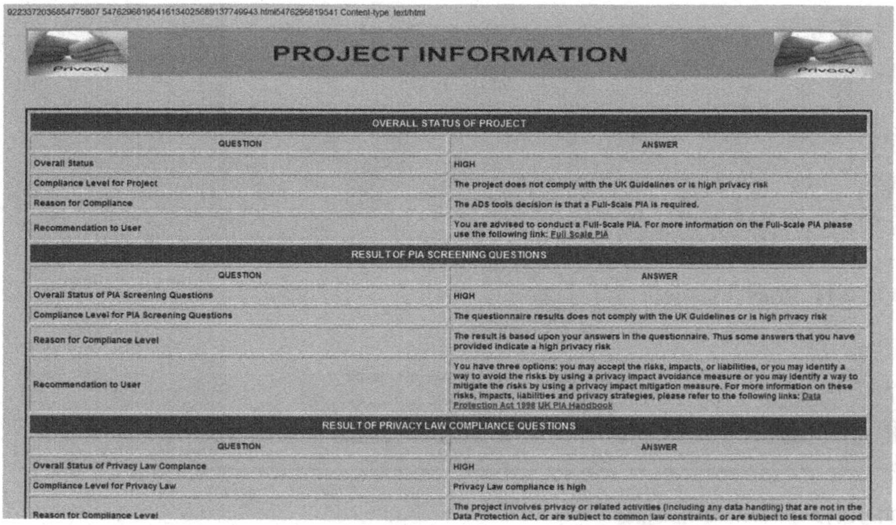

Fig. 3.9 Project information

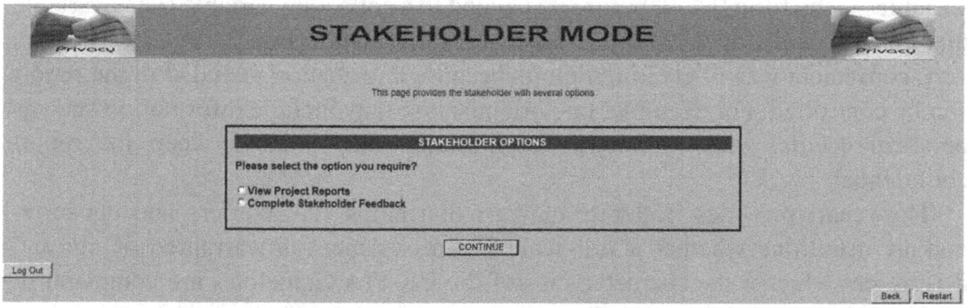

Fig. 3.10 Stakeholder options

Access and permissions to particular projects that stakeholders are involved with is provided by our tool in several ways. First, a log-in screen is used, whereby users must provide a user name and password that authorised access to a project. Second, permissions are set in the database via the "GRANT" option to restrict stakeholders to particular database tables where the project name equals the stakeholder ID. In addition, organisations can control permissions and access to reports by setting the Internet Protocol (IP) address to individual or group computers because it is often desirable to share a report among others or to have the PIA tool dynamically build a Web page that can be widely accessed. Once authorised, the stakeholder is forwarded to the options page, as illustrated in Fig. 3.10.

One option for a stakeholder is to view the reports for the project. Thus upon clicking "View Project Reports" they are forwarded to the view reports page, as illustrated in Fig. 3.11. Report creation involves the use of a separate HTML template that formats the contents and appearance of the report by using embedded

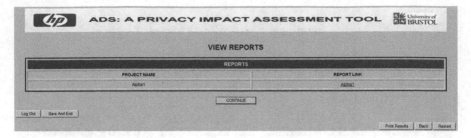

Fig. 3.11 Report list screen

Fig. 3.12 Embedded variables

variables in the form [[...]], before it is added to a collection variable (i.e. a variable that contains a list of strings) and saved, as illustrated in Fig. 3.12 [27]. This is a very convenient way of creating reports because information included in the report can be controlled. For example, one organisation may include information such as personal details, whereas another organisation may want to keep the report confidential.

The report provides in-depth analysis that helps stakeholders and decision-makers determine whether a full-scale PIA assessment is warranted or not and determines whether the characteristics of the UK PIA Guidelines are complaint or non-compliant with the criteria. In addition, the report provides specific reasons for the compliance status and gives advice to the user. The recommendation also includes embedded HTML links to specific information that helps the user understand the advice given by the tool. However, due to the limitations of the servers that the PIA tool currently uses the report displayed is mainly text, as illustrated in Fig. 3.13. However, a display such as a histogram may be developed that indicates the levels of risk associated with each key characteristic.

In addition, the stakeholders can complete a questionnaire about any report that they have read. The questionnaire consists of several questions that encourage communication between the stakeholders involved in the project and the project team, as illustrated in Fig. 3.14, and that allow free text input and ideally attachment of ancillary relevant information. Upon completion of the questionnaire the PIA tool automatically creates a report. Thus interaction between the project team and the stakeholder completed questionnaire is achieved and archived within the customer mode.

In the next section, we consider the customer mode that allows end users to conduct or modify a full-scale PIA initial assessment.

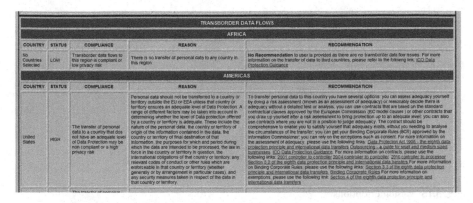

Fig. 3.13 Sample of completed report

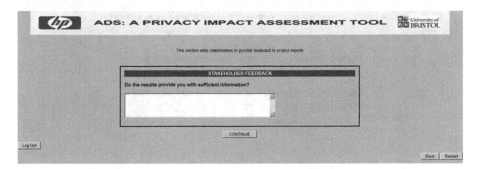

Fig. 3.14 Sample of stakeholder form

3.4.3.3   Customer Mode

This section describes the functionality and appearance of our PIA tool in the customer mode. The initial customer screen provides several options for users including: the ability to view stakeholder feedback, to conduct a new PIA assessment, the ability to view reports, and the ability to edit an existing PIA assessment, as illustrated in Fig. 3.15.

In both options "conduct a new PIA assessment" and "edit an existing PIA assessment", a specific "user ID" is used to build a unique identifier for saved data for that particular customer, as illustrated in Fig. 3.16. However, in a production version of our PIA tool, there would be a combination of user ID and password to assure that each user's data is protected.

This functionality allows customers to answer some questions and quit mid-session during the PIA assessment, with the ability to return to the same session later as this can be very useful for situations including [28]:

• When there are many questions in the questionnaires that takes the user a long time to answer them.

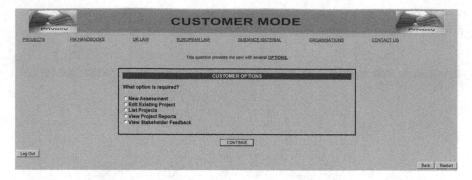

Fig. 3.15 Customer options

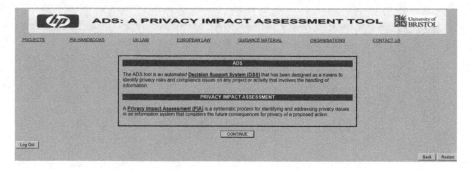

Fig. 3.16 Welcome page

- When there are questions that the end user may not be able to immediately answer.
- When there arc questions that require input from several different users, each providing different answers to some questions.

A new assessment typically begins with a welcome page that briefly describes the objective of the tool and gives a brief explanation of what a PIA is. For example, the objective of the tool describes it as being designed as a means to identify privacy risks and compliance issues on any project or activity that involves the handling of information, as illustrated in Fig. 3.17. The main functionality of the page consists of a navigation bar and a submit button (i.e. Continue or OK) that forwards the user to the next page. The navigation bar contains buttons which provide a number of activities and information for the user including:

- *Projects*: Navigates to a different HTML template that lists all previous PIAs and similar projects conducted either by the organisation or by the individual
- *PIA handbooks*: A drop down menu that contains hyperlinks to different PIA handbooks that have been published by major jurisdictions

Fig. 3.17 Current risk level

Fig. 3.18 Current progress

- *UK legal topics*: A drop down menu that contains hyperlinks to different UK legal documents including current legislation, regulations, and codes of practice
- *European law*: A drop down menu that contains hyperlinks to different European Directives involving privacy
- *Legal organisations*: A drop down menu that contains hyperlinks to different legal organisations including privacy commissioners websites, privacy advocates, groups, and organisations
- *Contact us*: Navigates to a different HTML template in which the user can e-mail comments and suggestions about the tool or PIAs

The PIA tool can collect a variety of information from databases, files, or by manual user input. For example, contact project, stakeholder, previous PIAs and similar project information, as illustrated in Fig. 3.18. Thus, information is collected via a series of questions that contain free text boxes for user input. HTML hyperlinks are also used in the templates to provide links to instructional help, descriptions, and other websites. Although this information is in the internal results that our PIA tool produces, as previously discussed in Sect. 3.4.3.2, currently in the implementation provided the external reports may not contain this information.

Our tool also provides users with several help pages during a PIA assessment run. For example, at certain stages of the assessment, current risk status and progress HTML pages appear to the users that indicate the risk associated with the

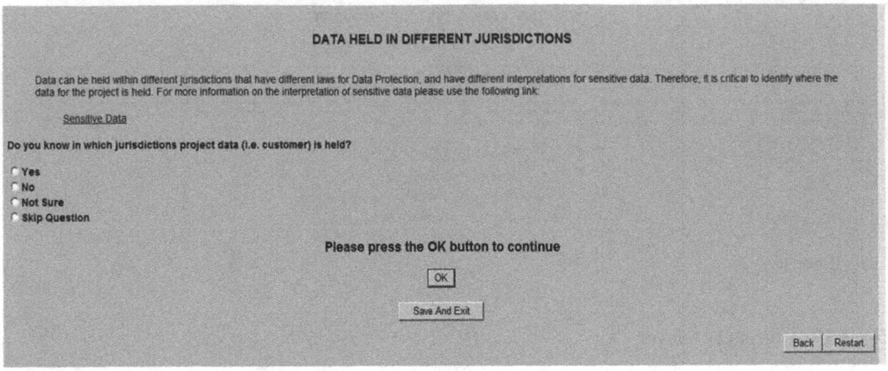

Fig. 3.19 Question on customer data held in jurisdictions

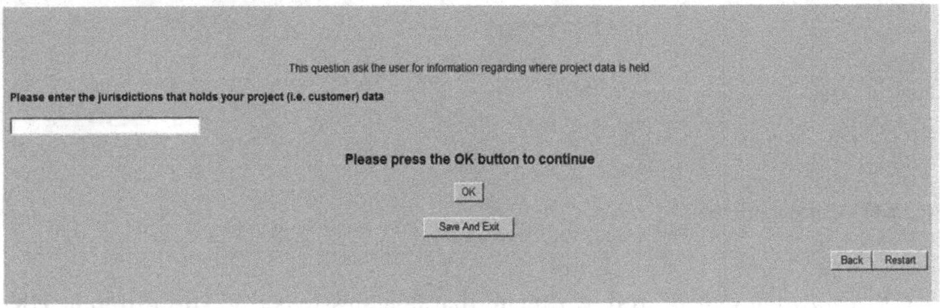

Fig. 3.20 Question for manual user input

project at that particular stage and how much of the questionnaire has been completed, as illustrated in Fig. 3.19 and Fig. 3.18.

Typically, the evaluation of questions contained in our tool depends upon the user selecting a single answer from a number of radio buttons. For example, a cloud-related question about customer data held in data centres within different jurisdictions is illustrated in Fig. 3.20 [33]. Therefore, if the user selects any of the possible options, they are given a number of following questions to extract further information. For example, if the user selects "yes" a further question is asked that records the values entered by the user via a free text box (e.g. names of jurisdictions that holds the customer data), as illustrated in Fig. 3.21. These values are then saved in the database in order to produce the results and following report.

However, if the user answers "No" to the question (i.e. Fig. 3.20), a further question asks the user for further information, as illustrated in Fig. 3.22. The possible answers to this follow-up question are "yes" or "no", whereby "yes" triggers a new question that is similar to Fig. 3.20, whereby the user manually enters the values for the jurisdictions supplied by the cloud provider. On the other hand, if the user selects "no", our PIA tool records this answer and provides a recommendation in the results to the user to contact their cloud provider as soon as possible.

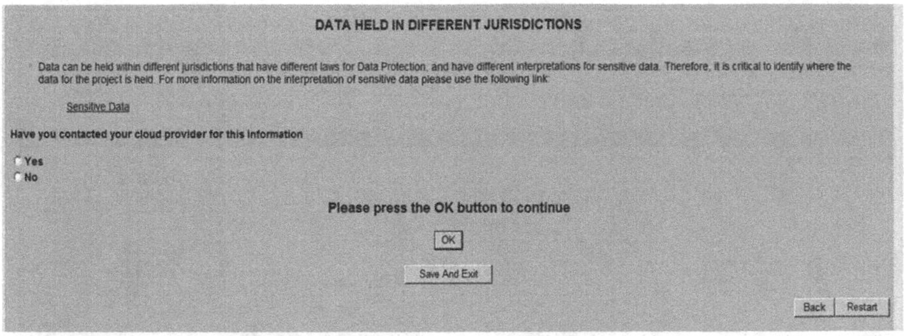

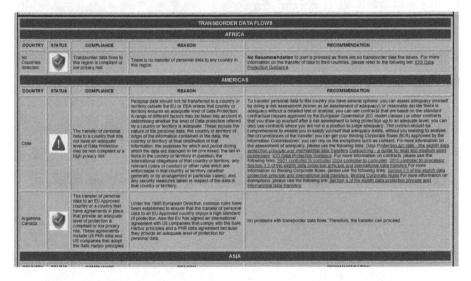

Fig. 3.21 Question on contacting cloud provider

Fig. 3.22 Question for different jurisdictions

Finally, if the user answers "not sure", a further question is then provided by our PIA tool in the form of a list, as illustrated in Fig. 3.23. In this list, the user can select multiple answers to the question including:

• The selection of multiple answers that are provided in the list including the "other" option, whereby the user can manually enter a value
• The selection of "None" that clears the list and records a value of "no counties have been entered by the user for this particular session" in the database

In addition, the list may be modified to allow the user to select a "not sure" option. In this case, the question is drilled down further to include simple separate questions about cloud providers that provide "yes/no" answers.

Basically, the tool uses rules to generate an output results page and also an audit trail. The output results page provided by our PIA tool is ultimately based on the answers provided by end users, as illustrated in Fig. 3.24.

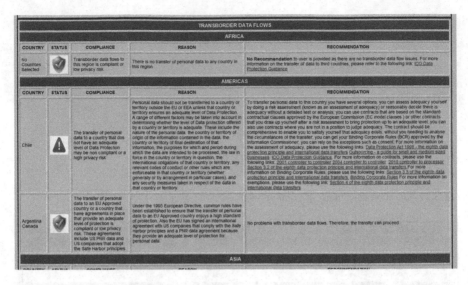

Fig. 3.23 Sample of results page

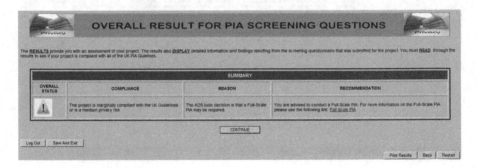

Fig. 3.24 Overall results page

The output of the questionnaire (being the answers provided by the user) is matched against the "THEN" condition of the business rules: the corresponding action within the rules contains code that assesses associated risk and groups output into characteristics and categories (transborder data flows, compliance with legislation, jurisdictions, etc.).

The results page provides an in-depth analysis that helps decision-makers determine whether the category is complaint or non-compliant with the UK PIA Guidelines. Although, our tool may use any criteria such as legislation or PIA Guidelines from another particular jurisdiction. In addition, the results provide specific reasons for the compliance status and gives advice to the user. However, at the time of writing (March 2012), the results displayed by the tool are mainly text with a few images. Therefore, in the next iteration of the PIA tool, a display such as

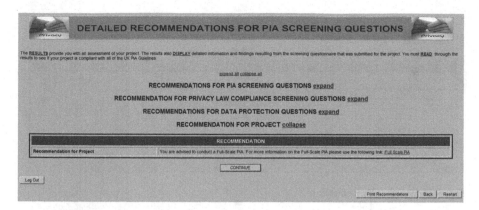

Fig. 3.25 Detailed recommendations page

a histogram may be developed that indicates the levels of risk associated with each key characteristic.

Part of the analysis carried out by the tool is to consider legal aspects, such as the UK-US safe harbour process for US companies to comply with the European Directive 95/46/EC on the protection of personal data [34]. The tool has to take into account the rules associated with transborder data flows and cross-border PIAs [35, 36]; moreover, the tool has to consider global organisations and their binding corporate rules. To achieve this, the tool will have a representation of policies related to different legal jurisdictions and will take these policies into account as they apply to a given context.

After the results page, a decision is made by our PIA tool regarding whether the initial full-scale PIA assessment should continue to the privacy law and data protection compliance checks or whether an initial small-scale PIA assessment should be conducted by the organisation, as illustrated in Fig. 3.25. Thus, if our tool recommends that the compliance checks are required, the user is forwarded to the compliance checks upon clicking the "OK" button. However, if the recommendation is that an initial small-scale PIA assessment should be conducted, our tool automatically creates a report.

The privacy law and data protection compliance checks follow the same formats previously described in this section. Thus, three questions are initially asked for the privacy law compliance checks, and a results page is then produced by our PIA tool, which is based upon the users' answers. In addition, the data protection compliance check consists of one question and a displayed results page. Finally, a results page is produced and displayed by our PIA tool that includes the results from the compliance checks and a report is created.

In summary, our PIA tool helps organisations to ensure privacy concerns are met and supports enterprise accountability, supplying employees with sufficient information and guidance to ensure that they design and conduct their projects in compliance with privacy requirements, such as those outlined in the UK PIA Guidelines of 2009 [14]. In addition, our PIA tool identifies what the user (organisation) must do to resolve these issues.

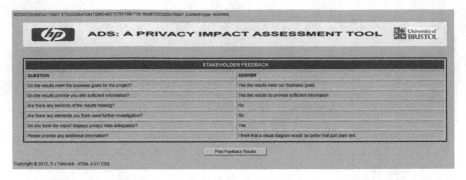

Fig. 3.26 Stakeholder feedback

In the next section, we consider the development suite for our PIA tool, whereby experts can edit and modify questions and rules.

3.4.3.4   Expert Mode and Development Suite

This section discusses the development suite that allows experts to edit and modify questions and rules. The development suite for our PIA tool has been modified into an external file (i.e. a cvd file) that can reside outside the infrastructure on the experts' computer. However, the cvd file must have a link to the cvr file, as illustrated in Fig. 3.26.

However, the cvd file is updated only when the system is saved, whereas the cvr file on the server is updated whenever the system is run by the browser.

The development suite incorporates easy access to our PIA tools internal processes that allow the expert to edit and modify existing questions, rules, and risk levels or create new features without using the application. This is achieved by the expert accessing internal "blocks" including:

- *Logic blocks*: These blocks are made up of rules that can be defined by tree diagrams or stated as individual rules, whereby each block may contain many rules or only a single one. Thus, logic blocks are treated in our PIA tool as objects and are a convenient way to use a group of related rules.
- *Action blocks*: These blocks use a spreadsheet style approach to describe the logic of our PIA tool processes. Thus, action blocks use a procedural approach to solve problems by asking a series of questions.
- *Command blocks*: These blocks control how our PIA tool operates such as what actions to take and what order to perform actions. Fundamentally, these blocks control what variables our PIA tool will try to derive values for and what logic blocks will be used to perform that function. Also, command blocks control the procedural flow of our PIA tool including how the system chains, what blocks to execute, and what results to display.

In the next section, we discuss the confidence variable that is used in our PIA tool to reach a "best fit" for several decisions and conclusions our tool makes.

3.4.3.5   Confidence Variable

This section describes the confidence variable that is used in our PIA tool. A confidence variable is intended to calculate an overall confidence value for the variable. Usually, this is the confidence or likelihood that the result is an appropriate recommendation or solution to the problem that our PIA tool solves. Confidence variables can also be used in other ways, but in all cases, the variable will be given one or more numeric values which will be combined via a formula to produce the overall confidence value.

In our PIA tool, the confidence variable is called "risk level" and is used to measure the probability that the answers in the questionnaire will be selected by the user. The calculation of our confidence variable "risk level" is done by using the sum method, whereby the single value for each question is added together; thus, positive values increase the confidence and negative values decrease the confidence. However, there are other ways of calculation such as average, independent, dependent, multiplication, and the mycin method [27].

Therefore, from and including the technology question in the initial full-scale PIA assessment questionnaire, each possible answer is assigned a value that reflects its confidence. For example, in Table 3.6, risk level values have been assigned to both the technology and identifiers questions.

The use of this feature enables our PIA tool to make multiple simultaneously possible recommendations with differing degrees of confidence to reach a "best fit" for several decisions and conclusions that are then presented to the user. For example, a current status page that may have three possibilities (i.e. the risk level to the project is high, medium, or low) is displayed several times during the assessment run to help the user objectively view the status of the project after a particular set of questions, as illustrated in Fig. 3.27.

Another stage where our PIA tool makes use of the confidence variable "risk level" is in the project summary that is displayed in the results page. Again, this uses a mathematical formula to reach the "best fit" for the project status from three possibilities (i.e. project status is high, low, or medium), as illustrated in Fig. 3.28.

Finally, the confidence variable "risk level" is used in the tool's full-scale PIA decision. Again, this is a mathematical formula that is similar to Fig. 3.28, whereby different recommendations are displayed to the user, as previously described in Sect. 3.4.3.3.

This feature is used to calculate the answers provided by the user in the questionnaire with the result of the confidence variable "risk level" being an appropriate solution (i.e. displays an compliance indicator and advice to the user for the project status) Thus, in our PIA tool, if the confidence variable "risk level" assigned to each question were modified to meet the needs of an organisation who interprets each question differently, the PIA results and the following report will reflect the change.

This provides an effective solution, whereby KBs can be created that have different values for each question that produce different results and reports. For example, an organisation may have several versions of the KB for different departments.

Table 3.6 Risk levels assigned to questions

Risk levels assigned to questions

Question	Possible answer	Risk level
Technology	Yes	20
	No	−10
	Not sure	0
	Skip question	10
Technology list	Smart cards	12
	Biometrics	15
	Mobile phone location systems	8
	Global positioning systems	7
	Intelligent transport systems	7
	Visual surveillance	14
	Digital image and video recording	16
	Profiling techniques	10
	Data mining techniques	11
	Logging of electronic traffic	8
	Other	9
	None	−10
Identifiers	Yes	10
	No	−10
	Not sure	0
	Skip question	6
Identifiers list	Digital signature initiative	9
	Multipurpose identifier	7
	Document with identifiable information	10
	Regulation schemes	7
	Biometric identifiers	11
	Other	8
	None	−10

Fig. 3.27 Link from cvd file to cvr file

```
[RiskLevel]>70
  → [StatusIndicator.ADD]  <IMG SRC="redwarning.jpg">
  → [StatusCompliance.ADD]  The project does not comply with the requirements or is high privacy risk
  → [StatusReason.ADD]  Based upon the users answers to the screening process questionnaire the privacy risk level is high
  → [StatusRecommendation.ADD]  You have 3 options: you may accept the risks, impacts, or liabilities; or you may identify a way to avoid the risks by using a privacy impact avoidance measure; or you may identify a way to mitigate the risks by using a privacy imp
[RiskLevel]<45
  → [StatusIndicator.ADD]  <IMG SRC="greenshield.jpg">
  → [StatusCompliance.ADD]  The project does comply with the requirements or is low privacy risk
  → [StatusReason.ADD]  Based upon the users answers to the screening process questionnaire the privacy risk level is low
  → [StatusRecommendation.ADD]  You may have 3 options: you may accept the risks, impacts, or liabilities; or you may identify a way to avoid the risks by using a privacy impact avoidance measure; or you may identify a way to mitigate the risks by using a privacy
[RiskLevel]>46&[RiskLevel]<=70)
  → [StatusIndicator.ADD]  <IMG SRC="yellow.jpg">
  → [StatusReason.ADD]  The project is marginally compliant with the UK PIA Guidelines or is medium privacy risk.
  → [StatusReason.ADD]  Based upon the users answers to the screening process questionnaire the privacy risk level is medium
  → [StatusRecommendation.ADD]  You may have 3 options: you may accept the risks, impacts, or liabilities; or you may identify a way to avoid the risks by using a privacy impact avoidance measure; or you may identify a way to mitigate the risks by using a privacy
```

Fig. 3.28 Command block showing formulas to display project status

In addition, a global organisation may have different KBs that reflect the PIA Guidelines of several jurisdictions.

In the next section, we discuss the decision-making process of our PIA tool.

3.4.3.6   Decision Making in Our PIA Tool

This section describes the reasoning and decision making of our PIA tool. It appears that simple decision trees that automate business rules are functionally limited by two main factors: the rules are typically black and white with no leeway for special cases and the complexity of logic that can be represented is quite limited such as "yes/no" answers based upon simple logic.

Our PIA tool is different in that it is able to handle very complex problem-solving tasks, involving probabilistic reasoning folding together many factors in reaching a conclusion and recommendation. For example, a typical business rule for stakeholders involved in projects may be "No reports after 10 days", whereby the rule engine would implement this as a simple rule "If days since report created > 10 then refuse access", but what would happen if one of the stakeholders wanted to access the report on day 11? Our PIA tool can be designed to access the stakeholders' history, consider factors that may have delayed the stakeholder in accessing the report, and advise the project manager to make an exception or contact the stakeholder directly, rather than an absolute "NO".

This type of reasoning and decision making in our tool is achieved by the inference engine (IE), allowing complex probabilistic backward chaining (discussed later in this section) logic to be used to solve complex problems in a manner comparable to a human expert. The IE in our tool is used to analyse and combine the individual rules to solve the larger problem and determines [27]:

- What possible answers there are to the problem
- What data is needed to determine if a particular answer is appropriate
- If there is a way to derive or calculate the needed data from other rules
- When enough data is available to eliminate a possible answer, and stop asking unnecessary questions related to it
- How to differentiate between remaining answers
- Which answer is most likely based upon the rules

Backward chaining in our PIA tool is "goal driven", whereby the top-level goals are the possible answers to the problem or potential recommendations. The IE can determine what it needs to meet a particular goal including determining when that goal is met or that a goal cannot be met. Thus, the IE analyses what data is needed to determine if the first possible goal is appropriate for the user. To make this determination, our PIA tool requires data on the specific situation being analysed.

This data can come from other rules, external sources such as databases and spreadsheets, or by asking the user additional questions. Therefore, the IE checks the rules to find one that would be relevant to making this decision. For example, if the HTML report template discussed in Sect. 3.4.3.2 had an embedded variable such as [[ContactAddress]] that did not have a specific rule associated to it. The IE in our tool will ask the user for this value before creating the report because this becomes the new goal of our tool, whereby it supersedes the original goal "create Report". This process of having one goal requiring data, which leads to another goal, can be repeated many times in our tool. Thus, as data becomes available, lower levels goals are met and are dropped off the chain until the IE is able to determine which of the conditions for the initial top-level goal are met, and the recommendation is then presented to the user.

Our PIA tools IE also uses the forward chaining "data-driven" method, whereby the data is already available in the logic of the rules. In this case, the rules are tested sequentially to see what conclusions result. Moreover, in our PIA tool, backward and forward chaining methods are combined, whereby forward chaining is used to run top-level rules and backward chaining is used to derive needed values from other rule modules such as the confidence variable "risk level".

In the next section, we consider the aspects of storing sensitive data in a shared cloud environment and how our PIA tool may minimise the risk.

3.4.4 The PIA Tool and Sensitive Data in the Cloud

This section discusses the storage of sensitive data in the cloud and how our PIA tool may minimise the risk.

Sensitive data encompasses a wide range of information including ethnic or racial origin, political opinion, religious beliefs, memberships, physical or mental health details, criminal or civil offences, as well as PII that relates to customer and contact details [34]. However, as discussed briefly in Sect. 3.4.2, the definition of sensitive data may vary across jurisdictions.

Our PIA tool can record information including contact name, telephone number, project lead name, and stakeholder details. However, answers in the initial full-scale PIA questionnaire may be interpreted by organisations as confidential data, although in some cases organisations may be willing to accept the risk. In addition, the KB itself could be classed as confidential by organisations if the KB was customised to suit their particular needs. For example, if the data gathered and also the customised KB is combined with company policies. To minimise risks, encryption of personal data is feasible, and strongly advisable, if using simple storage. Thus, the PIA tool can make use of a network appliance (or server), called a cloud storage gateway [37].

A cloud storage gateway can provide encryption, authentication, and authorisation, but it is a server that resides at the customer premises and exposes cloud storage services as if they were local storage devices [37]. The gateway is typically packaged as a virtual machine (VM) and translates cloud storage Application Programming Interfaces (APIs), including Representational State Transfer (REST) or Simple Object Access Protocol (SOAP), to block-based storage protocols such as Internet Small Computer System Interface (iSCSI) or Fibre Channel. Additionally, the cloud storage gateway uses local caching to alleviate latency issues and can translate file-based interfaces such as the Network File System (NFS) or Common Internet File System (CIFS) with seamless integration. This is largely due to the fact that cloud storage gateways use standard network protocols and can translate traditional file-based protocols to cached object-oriented storage. An advantage of using this approach is that the administrator (i.e. expert) can modify or update the rules and templates of the PIA tool very easily and quickly without corrupting the application files that are copied by the cloud provider.

Another advantage of using a cloud storage gateway for our PIA tool is the ability to update, at regular intervals, the main files of our PIA tool (i.e. cvr file which is the java runtime servlet file and HTML files that can be accessed in a browser) that are stored in the cloud. For example, Nasuni [37] terms this a "synchronous snapshot". Thus, after the initial push (where all files are copied to the public cloud and moved into the cache), the snapshot checks each file chunk for changes within the file tree. It then tags new files and altered, corrupted, old, chunks of data as dirty. New files are chunked, and all of the dirty data is then compressed and encrypted. The snapshot then sends each encrypted chunk to the specified cloud and receives the associated keys that allow it to retrieve files in the event of a restore or a cache miss. Once both files and directories have been pushed to the cloud, the snapshot generates a new root directory and tears down the snapshot, ready to start all over again. Therefore, the snapshot uses a number of protection techniques including the duplication, compression, and encryption of each file, before sending them to the cloud. However, the snapshot only forwards changes between the original files and the most recent version and pushes out only what is necessary, thus reducing potential storage costs. Moreover, many cloud storage gateways facilitate the use of encryption techniques and frameworks (e.g. RSA, OpenPGP), whereby the gateway has no access to customer data, as all encryption and decryption happens at the user site.

Also, data at rest which may be used by the PIA tool is generally not encrypted because the problem is that encryption limits data use. In particular, searching and indexing the data becomes problematic. For example, if data is stored in clear text, one can efficiently search for a document by specifying a keyword. This is impossible to do with traditional, randomised encryption schemes. However, there are solutions to this problem including predicate and homomorphic encryption, and private information retrieval (PIR) [38].

Moreover, the data held by the tool cannot be encrypted if processed in the cloud, as it is not yet possible to process encrypted data in an efficient way. Note that techniques for doing this in a non-efficient way are possible including Yao's protocol for secure two-party computation [39], Gentry's fully homomorphic encryption scheme [40], and obfuscation (discussed further in Sect. 3.6).

An important factor is that our tool collects information in the form of project and contact details (i.e. names, telephone numbers, and e-mail addresses) that may be considered by organisations and jurisdictional law (i.e. UK Data Protection Act 1998 and EU Directive (95/46/EC)) as sensitive data. Thus, an issue arises when our PIA tool is deployed as a SaaS using an UK cloud provider and accessed by customers that are outside the UK and EU (i.e. transborder data flow restrictions).

In jurisdictions such as the USA, a solution is provided by a framework called "safe harbour". The framework bridges the differences between the US approach on privacy protection with that taken by the EU Directive. Thus, the US organisations who self-certify to the US-EU safe harbour framework ensures the UK cloud provider that they provide adequate privacy protection, as defined by the EU Directive [41].

However, for jurisdictions that do not have any frameworks or agreements with the EU, a possible solution may be the use of redaction software to obscure or remove sensitive information such as names, telephone numbers, and e-mail addresses from our tools results prior to display. For example, RapidRedact [42] is a tool that can be used with our PIA tool to remove the sensitive information and keep it private and confidential. The solution for sensitive data that may be in reports is discussed in Sect. 3.4.3.2 (i.e. Fig. 3.12), whereby manual HTML templates are created using embedded variables. Thus, if an organisation wishes to leave out project, contact, and stakeholder information, all they have to do is omit the variables (i.e. ProjectName, ContactName, etc.).

In the next section, we outline the development methodology adopted for our PIA tool.

3.5   Development Methodology for a PIA Tool in Cloud Computing

In this section, we present details of the methodology used for our PIA tool including the software development methodology, data collection, analysis, results, and modelling.

Stakeholders (i.e. approximately 25) who were generally interested in a PIA tool of some description were initially contacted via e-mail and telephone. These consisted of several backgrounds including software development, security, privacy, records management, networking, and PIAs. Out of the 25, 11 stakeholders were chosen to participate in gathering requirements and providing feedback for our PIA tool and were chosen because of their working experience with PIAs, records management, security, and privacy in organisations in the UK. Typically, feedback from initial conversations and e-mails from the 11 participating stakeholders were mixed but were very encouraging in that several ideas were put forward including the use of open-ended questions for gathering our tools requirements, the use of semi-structured interviews, and the use of MoSCoW rules (discussed in Sect. 3.5.1). The use of MoSCoW rules in gathering requirements for our PIA tool was important, as it helped dictate the style of the interview questionnaire. In addition, after several conversations and e-mails, arrangements were made with the participating stakeholders to hold interviews at their organisations.

The software methodology chosen for the development of the PIA tool is the Dynamic Systems Development Method (DSDM) framework [43]. This is because the framework provides a flexible yet controlled process that can be used to deliver solutions in tight project timescales (i.e. 3–6 months). Furthermore, a fundamental assumption of the framework is that nothing is built perfectly first time but that as a rule of thumb 80 % of the solution can be produced in 20 % of the time that it would take to provide the total solution. This is in contrast to the classical, sequential "waterfall" approach, whereby the next step cannot be started until the current step is completed that results in projects being delivered late, usually over budget, or fail to meet business needs since time is not spent reworking the requirements. Moreover, the DSDM framework incorporates several important techniques that benefit the development of the PIA tool including [43]:

- *Timeboxing*: This is a planning technique that divides the development into time periods (i.e. usually 4–6 weeks long with each part having its own set deadline and a set of deliverables).
- *MoSCoW prioritisation*: This technique reaches a common understanding with stakeholders on the importance they place on the delivery of each requirement of the PIA tool. Thus, *M* equates to "must" have, *S* equates to "should" have, *C* equates to "could" have, and *W* equates to "won't" have.

In the next section, we discuss data collection, data analysis, and present a summary of findings for our PIA tool.

3.5.1   Data Collection, Analysis, and Findings

In this section, we consider data collection, data analysis, and present a summary of findings of the requirements for our PIA tool.

Prior to any data collection, it was agreed with participating stakeholders that the MoSCoW rules were set at the values:

- *Must have* => 4 points
- *Should have* =< 3 points
- *Could have* => 2 points
- *Won't have* => 1 point

These values were set because there was no indication of how many stakeholders would answer questions about the requirements for a PIA tool. Furthermore, an agreement was reached that the development would initially try to deliver all the *M*, *S*, and *C* requirements, but the *S* and *C* requirements will be the first to go if the delivery timescale looks threatened. Moreover, agreements were made that the value of "very high" corresponded to the MoSCoW rule of "must" have, and the values of "low, very low" corresponded to the rule of "won't" have.

The collection of data consists of a questionnaire (e.g. formulated to include both close-ended and open-ended questions) that is used to elicit from target stakeholders their emotional opinions about privacy, PIAs, and the requirements for our PIA tool [44]. To satisfy the research objectives, the study's methodology employed a series of ten semi-structured interviews with a mixture of private and public sector stakeholders in four geographical locations in the UK: the county borough of

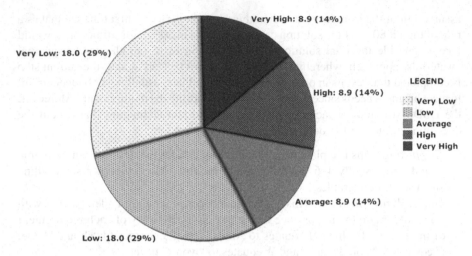

Fig. 3.29 Findings for separate stakeholder analysis page

Torfaen, the metropolitan area of Bristol, the home counties including London, and Essex. Interviews, each lasting approximately 45 min–1 h were conducted between July and September 2011. They were segregated into privacy/security officers, record officers, and information officers to enhance the opportunity for different discussions, opinions, and perspectives.

Analysis of the raw data indicates that opinions and perspectives of the topics discussed differed significantly between the interested parties. For example, regarding the issue of whether privacy was an important factor within their organisation, privacy officers naturally "valued highly" this factor. However, records and information officers suggested that privacy was "not important" or a major concern. Moreover, most stakeholders interviewed (e.g. 80 %) agreed that PIAs are necessary and that they should be adopted for their organisation and that PIAs must start at the "beginning of development". In addition, one of the most notable findings to emerge from the study is that 70 % of the stakeholders interviewed desire an automated PIA tool to help them in this process.

To convert the raw data into requirements (i.e. functional and non-functional), each stakeholder's answer relating to the functionality of the PIA tool is given a value based upon the agreed MoSCoW rules. For example, one question in the questionnaire is about whether the PIA tool should incorporate a stakeholder analysis screen, whereby the findings of this particular question are illustrated in Fig. 3.29.

Each value (e.g. very high, low) is then given a number of points such as high = 4 points. These are then multiplied with the percentage of stakeholders answering that particular value for the question. For example, 14 % of stakeholders answered this question very high, which equates to $14 \times 5 = 70$. This formula is then applied to all

Table 3.7 MoSCoW rules applied to UI questions

Prioritised list of user interfaces for PIA tool	
Name of user interface	MoSCoW rule
Security log-in	Could have
Welcome	Should have
Project information	Must have
Contact information	Must have
Stakeholder analysis	Could have
Communication strategy	Won't have
Environmental scan	Could have
Questionnaire	Must have
Display of results	Must have
Report	Must have

values of the question to give the total number of points for the question (e.g. 255 points). To convert this number into the agreed MoSCoW rule, the total number of points for the question is then divided by 100 (the total percentage) to compute the average value. For example, using this formula, the average value of the question is 255/100 = 2.55, which equates to the MoSCoW rule of "could" have for the question. This method is the applied to all of the other questions about the functionality of the PIA tool, as illustrated in Table 3.7.

Furthermore, correlation techniques such as pattern matching are applied to the raw data to reveal common stakeholder phrases and words such as "I must have that", "I don't like that" or "that is good", and it appears that these phrases and words can be directly interpreted into MoSCoW rules to give the requirements for our PIA tool [44]. For example, a number of functional and non-functional requirements for the project information UI are illustrated in Table 3.8.

In the next section, we discuss modelling the user requirements for our PIA tool.

3.5.2 Modelling of User Requirements for Our PIA Tool

In this section, we discuss modelling the user requirements for our PIA tool. In DSDM, the term modelling refers to Unified Modelling Language (UML) diagrams [43]. To illustrate modelling the user requirements for our PIA tool, we use the project information requirements discussed in the previous section. For example, Table 3.9 describes the use case requirements in detail.

The use case description in Table 3.9 is then converted into a use case diagram. For example, the third iteration for the functionality of the project information screen is illustrated in Fig. 3.30, and the activity diagram for the project name is illustrated in Fig. 3.31.

In the next section, we consider validation of our PIA tool.

Table 3.8 Requirements for project information UI

Requirements for project information

Functional requirements

Name	Label	Requirement
Interface	Project name	String data entry only
	Project title	String data entry only
	Project description	String data entry only
	Project lead	String data entry only
	Telephone no.	Numeric data entry only
Business		Data entered by user is stored in database
		Clicking the Back button moves the user request to the Welcome screen
		Clicking the Restart button moves the user request to the Start screen
		Clicking the OK button moves the user request to the next question
Regulatory/ compliance		The database will have a functional audit trial
Security		Administrators can edit and delete project information

Non-functional requirements

Name	Label	Requirement
User		User must be able to access the project information 23 h a day, 7 days a week
		User is not allowed to delete project information
System		System must be unavailable between midnight and 1.00 am for backups

Table 3.9 Use case requirements for project information UI

Use case requirements of project information

Use case	Description
View project information	User views the project information screen
Enter project name	User enters a string that represents the project name
Enter project title	User enters a string that represents the project title
Enter project lead	User enters a string that represents the name of the project leader
Enter telephone no.	User enters a numeric value that represents the telephone number of the project leader
Enter project description	User enters a string that represents the description of the project
Restart button	If user clicks this button, the system re-starts the process
Back button	If user clicks this button, the system moves back to the last screen or question viewed
OK button	If user clicks this button, the system moves forward to the next screen or question

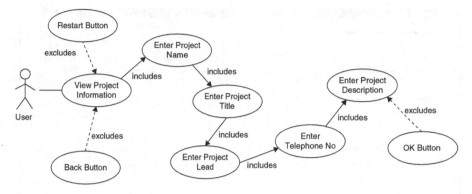

Fig. 3.30 Use case diagram for project information UI

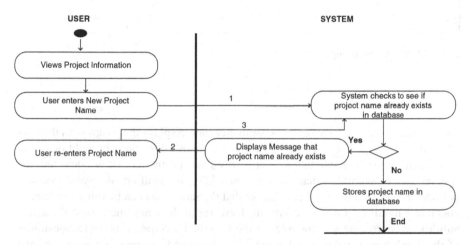

Fig. 3.31 Activity diagram for project name use case

3.5.3 Validation of Our PIA Tool

This section discusses validation of our PIA tool. Testing our PIA tool is important as it helps to provide quality assurance, verification and validation, and reliability estimation. Corvid provides a validation function, as illustrated in Fig. 3.32 [27].

This function enables automating very large numbers of tests, along with setting various warning tests to check for specific types of issues in the system.

Validation testing in Corvid allows for a specific logic block or subset of a system (e.g. single or multiple variables) to be tested, allowing thorough testing of even large systems. Once the parameters for the validation test are set, the tests run automatically without additional user input. Thus, Corvid displays the number of tests that will

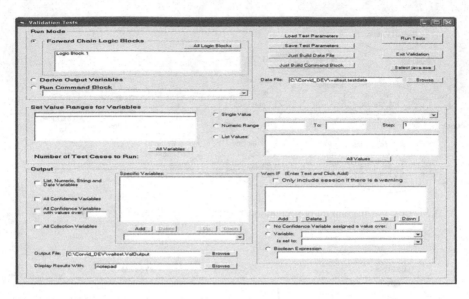

Fig. 3.32 Validation testing in Corvid

have to be run based on the selected parameters and displays the progress as the tests are being executed. For larger tests, they can be allowed to run over night or longer as needed. A file is generated with any errors and problems that are detected and special system warnings that are generated [27]. In addition, the validation test parameters can also be saved to a file, so that the same tests can be run again later to check any modifications to the system. However, it does not understand the actual validity and correctness of the rules in the system. Therefore, it is the responsibility of the developer to make sure that the actual logic and advice given is correct, and only the author and domain expert can assure that a system is giving the correct answers and advice. For example, a specific logic block may be used to set the value for a variable that is based upon user input. Thus, it may be easier to test this block separately from the rest of the system to analyse whether it is setting the correct values. This allows the developer to focus on this detail without the influence of the rest of the system and once that part is validated the logic block can be used in a more extensive test. Moreover, the process of user validation (e.g. tests carried out by the users on the functionality of the PIA tool) has not started, so there is currently no feedback from users on the tool. It is hoped that this process will be completed in the near future.

In the next section, we consider related work in the areas of privacy and security in cloud computing to evaluate whether these approaches are suitable to aid enhancement of our PIA tool.

3.6   Related Work

In this section, we consider related work in the areas of privacy and security in cloud computing to evaluate whether these approaches are suitable to aid enhancement of our PIA tool.

Accountability as a way forward for privacy protection in the cloud is considered by Pearson and Charlesworth [45]. They propose the incorporation of complementary regulatory, procedural, and technical provisions that demonstrate accountability into a flexible operational framework to address privacy issues within a cloud computing scenario. They believe that accountability is a useful basis for enhancing privacy in many cloud computing scenarios, as corporate management can quickly comprehend its links with the recognised concept of, and mechanisms for achieving, corporate responsibility. Accountability in this context is corporate data governance (i.e. the management of the availability, usability, integrity, and security of the data used, stored, or processed within an organisation), and it refers to the process by which a particular goal – the prevention of disproportionate (in the circumstances) harm to the subjects of PII – can be obtained via a combination of public law (legislation, regulation), private law (contract), self-regulation, and the use of privacy technologies (system architectures, access controls, machine readable policies). The approach taken requires a combination of procedural and technical measures to be used and co-designed. In essence, this would use measures to link organisational obligations to machine readable policies and mechanisms to ensure that these policies are adhered to by the parties that use, store, or share that data, irrespective of the jurisdiction in which the information is processed. Companies providing cloud computing services would give a suitable level of contractual assurances, to the organisation that wishes to be accountable, that they can meet the policies (i.e. obligations) that it has set, particularly PII protection requirements. Furthermore, technology can provide a stronger level of evidence of compliance and audit capabilities. However, while the approach appears to be a practical way forward, it has limitations. For example, while contracts provide a solution for an initial service provider to enforce its policies along the chain, risks that cannot be addressed contractually will remain, as data has to be unencrypted at the point of processing, creating a security risk and vulnerability due to the cloud's attractiveness to cybercriminals. Moreover, only large corporate users are likely to have the legal resources to replace generic SLAs with customised contracts.

Obfuscation, as a first line of defence is described by Pearson et al. [46]. This chapter describes a tool called "privacy manager", which they believe reduces the risk to the cloud computing user of their private data being stolen or misused and also assists the cloud computing provider to conform to privacy law. The idea is that instead of being present unencrypted in the cloud, the user's private data is sent to the cloud in an encrypted form, and the processing is done on the encrypted data. The output of the processing is de-obfuscated by the privacy manager to reveal the correct result. The obfuscation method uses a key which is chosen by the user and known by the privacy manager but is not communicated to the service provider. Thus, the service provider is not able to de-obfuscate the user's data, and the un-obfuscated data is never present on the service provider's machines.

Although some obfuscation methods are highly susceptible to known plaintext attacks [46], this does at least protect the data from opportunistic data thieves with access to cloud databases because it ensures that the data is never present in the database in the clear.

Use of DSSs for cloud computing and PIAs is a very new field and there are few systems available. Those that are available for cloud computing are found in the areas of clinical decision applications [47] and life science enterprise solutions [48]. However, very recently, there has been a step change in DSS for PIAs (such as privacy expert systems). Typically, a DSS has a KB that needs to be created and updated periodically by experts on an ongoing basis and a mechanism (e.g. a rules engine, decision tree, or dedicated queries to databases) by which output can be generated, based upon user input via questionnaires. Within this context, we will discuss briefly two DSSs that are at the cutting edge of research.

PRAIS [49] is a research project that has developed a prototype DSS tool for context-sensitive privacy-aware information sharing in children's social care. The DSS is based on the architecture developed for the Identity Governance Framework (IGF) [50], where information sharing is based on a pull model. This means that the recipients are alerted that information is being made available to them, after which it is retrieved from the source. PRAIS uses the IGF architecture as its design choice because it allows the owner of the information to retain liability for the data and to audit each use by using the pull model. Therefore, PRAIS is a DSS tool that enables personnel working with personal information to assess the privacy implications of information sharing actions dynamically and to share information with confidence, whether verbally or electronically. This has been achieved by accommodating the daily routines of social care staff from the outset, whereby it manages users consent and the needs and requests of information from the participants.

However, analysis suggests that the scope of PRAIS is very narrow as it is not intended that the DSS will ever make decisions on behalf of properly trained personnel but instead will assist social care practitioners in making privacy-aware decisions where required. Therefore, it appears that the DSS is designed to assist in the professional's decision-making process and not to replace it. Moreover, one of the main findings is that although PRAIS can be used for sharing information electronically, this may not necessarily be its primary purpose. This is because in social care, information is often shared in multi-agency meetings or over the telephone. Thus, the system can be used by practitioners on an ad hoc basis to explore privacy implications where information may be shared verbally. In summary, PRAIS in its current format is not applicable for the UK PIA tool although some approaches such as the use of an expert system may be considered.

Hewlett Packard's Privacy Advisor (HPPA) is an expert system that captures data about business processes to determine their privacy compliance [51, 52]. The tool helps organisations to ensure privacy concerns are met and supports enterprise accountability, supplying employees with sufficient information and guidance to ensure that they design and conduct their projects in compliance with organisational privacy policies. HPPA uses a rules engine for which rules are defined that are used both to generate questions that are customised to the employee's specific situation and to codify HP's privacy rulebook and other information sources. Based on the employee's response to these questions, it automatically generates an output report that includes analysis of possible privacy risks and a checklist of actions that the employee should take in order to mitigate these risks. This tool has been rolled out to employees within HP.

Analysis of this tool indicates that the methods and techniques used in HPPA are well suited for the UK PIA tool, such as the use of its knowledge representation and inference methods (i.e. rules, dynamic questionnaires, and report generation), and knowledge management (i.e. user modes, interfaces, and its reasoning about global requirements and regulations). However, it will be necessary to modify HPPAs methods and techniques to fit the UK PIA tool because HPPA is based on a customised set of organisational policies, which would need to be different for other organisations; therefore, it is not generic.

A new self-assessment tool, aimed at private sector organisations, particularly small- and medium-sized businesses, was recently launched in Canada (e.g. May 2011). The tool developed jointly by the federal, Alberta and British Columbia privacy commissioners' offices is called "Securing Personal Information: A Self-Assessment Tool for Organizations", where it is hoped that the tool may help businesses better safeguard the personal information of customers and employees and may help prevent breaches of PII [53].

The tool is a detailed online questionnaire that helps organisations gauge how well they are protecting personal information and meeting compliance standards under Canada's private sector privacy law on both federal and provincial levels. The questionnaire is complex and not easy to navigate, as it involves dozens of "yes" or "no" questions divided up into 17 different categories including network security, access control, incident management, and database security. However, it offers some flexibility by allowing users to focus on areas most relevant to their own enterprise. The goal of the tool is for organisations to be able to answer "yes" to each question, and at the end of the process, results for the minimum and higher levels of security are tabulated separately.

The main disadvantage of the tool is that its usage is voluntary, and hence, a comprehensive evaluation of an organisation's internal policies may not be easy to complete. This can also be the case because users who are not experts may have difficulty in understanding the questions. For example, the questions under the assessment "risk management" section indicate that an IT expert is required to provide answers.

Similar tools exist and are freely available from vendors such as Microsoft [54]. For example, the Microsoft "Security Assessment Tool" is also designed to help find weaknesses in an IT security environment and offers a download that takes a snap shot of an organisations current security state. However, the new tool from Canada's privacy commissioners focuses on privacy and protecting personal information rather than the more common security paradigm of protecting intellectual property.

Analysis of these tools indicates that they are composed of simple decision trees that follow a straightforward approach that provides advice based on users answers. For example, the user starts at the first question, and whether they answer "yes" or "no", they are forwarded to the next question, until they reach the end of the questionnaire when a report is produced based upon their answers. As discussed in Sect. 3.4.3.6, these simple decision trees do not allow for complex reasoning as the rules are typically black and white with no leeway for special cases such as global regulations and transborder data flows, and the complexity of logic that can be represented is quite limited such as "yes/no" answers that is based upon simple logic.

Sander and Pearson [55] outline a DSS for cloud computing that aids selection of appropriate cloud service providers (CSPs). Their approach is a semi-automated DSS tool that gathers context relating to CSPs and inputs to a rule-based system to trigger decisions about whether or not to use that CSP and/or to determine additional stipulations that would need to be made. The tool helps to determine appropriate actions that should be allowed and assesses risk before personal information is passed on through the cloud. For each customer enterprise, an administrator will set up the original questionnaire according to the policies that the customer (i.e. the enterprise) wishes to check or use the default setting offered by the assessment service. When a customer wishes to assess different CSPs offering a service, providers will use the tool via a Web interface in order to provide answers to the questionnaire, and the results will be sent back to the enterprise that wishes to choose between the service providers. These results include reports and automatically generated ratings, which will allow the administrator to distinguish between them. This tool is similar to the HPPA tool, in that it is a form of expert system using a set of intermediate variables (IMs) to encode meaningful information and to drive the questionnaire generation.

Although there are some similarities between this tool, HPPA and our PIA tool, there are significant differences in architecture and deployment, the underlying mechanism for the knowledge representation and for generating questionnaires, and the rules, report structure, and output.

The next section will discuss next steps associated with the development of our PIA tool.

3.7 Next Steps

As the prototype for the tool is only at the first iterative stage, our next planned steps include the following:

1. Conducting another round of stakeholder meetings that includes a presentation of the working tool. This is for validation purposes and to elicit further user requirements.
2. Developing the tool further to include all necessary, and some preferable, requirements.
3. Considering a cloud storage gateway provider for provision of infrastructure that protects the PIA tool's customer data in the cloud.

3.8 Conclusions

We are currently developing a PIA tool that can be used in a cloud environment to identify potential privacy risks and compliance issues. The tool addresses the inherent complexity and helps both expert and non-expert end users with identifying and addressing privacy requirements for a given context. As part of this approach, we provide mechanisms for privacy experts and other authorised non-technical personnel to modify the KB in our tool in an intuitive way.

If our PIA tool is used as a SaaS application itself, regulatory issues such as transborder data flow can be involved because personal information may need to be accessed from and transferred to different jurisdictions.

References

1. Stewart, B.: Privacy impact assessments. PLPR **3**(7), 61–64 (1996). http://www.austrii.edu/au/journals/PLPR.html. Accessed 30 Oct 2011
2. Warren, A., Bayley, R., Bennett, C., Charlesworth, A., Clarke, R., Oppenheim, C.: Privacy impact assessments: international experience as a basis for UK guidance. Comput. Law Secur. Rep. **24**(3), 233–242 (2008). doi:10.1016/j.clsr.2008.03.003
3. Tancock, D., Pearson, S., Charlesworth, A.: Analysis of privacy impact assessments within major jurisdictions. In: Privacy Security and Trust (PST), 2010 Eighth Annual International Conference, Ottawa, Ontario, Canada, 17–19 Aug 2010, pp. 118–125 (2010). doi: 10.1109/PST.2010.5593260
4. Tancock, D., Pearson, S., Charlesworth, A.: The emergence of privacy impact assessments. http://www.hpl.hp.com/techreports/2010/HPL-2010-63.pdf (2010). Accessed 30 Oct 2011
5. Cavoukian, A.: Privacy by design: the 7 foundational principles. http://www.ipc.on.ca/images/Resources/7foundationalprinciples.pdf (2009). Accessed 30 Oct 2011
6. Charlesworth, A.: Jurisdictional report for Canada: privacy impact assessments. International Study of Their Application and Effects (Appendix C). http://www.ico.gov.uk/upload/documents/library/corporate/research_and_reports/lbrouni_piastudy_appc_can_2910071.pdf (2007). Accessed 26 Oct 2011
7. eHealth Ontario: Privacy impact assessment policy version 2. http://www.ehealthontario.on.ca/pdfs/Privacy/PrivacyImpactAssessmentPolicy.pdf (2008). Accessed 27 Oct 2011
8. Cavoukian, A.: Privacy impact assessment guidelines for the Ontario Personal Health Information Protection Act. http://www.ipc.on.ca/images/Resources/up-phipa_pia_e.pdf (2005). Accessed 23 Oct 2011
9. UK Cabinet Office: Data Handling Procedures in Government: Final Report. http://www.cabinetoffice.gov.uk/sites/default/files/resources/final-report.pdf (2008). Accessed 21 Nov 2011
10. Treasury Board Secretariat Canada: Info source bulletin number 33B: statistical reporting. http://www.infosource.gc.ca/bulletin/2010/b/bulletin33b/bulletin33b03-eng.asp (2010). Accessed 15 Nov 2011
11. Information Commissioners Office: Information Commissioners annual report 2009/10. http://www.ico.gov.uk/upload/documents/library/corporate/detailed_specialist_guides/annual_report_2010.pdf (2010). Accessed 14 Nov 2011
12. 80/20 Thinking Ltd: Privacy impact assessments for Phorm Inc. http://www.8020thinking.com/news/9.html?task=view (2008). Accessed 26 Oct 2011
13. The Office of the Privacy Commissioner of New Zealand: Privacy impact assessment handbook. http://privacy.org.nz/assets/Files/Brochures-and-pamphlets-and-pubs/48638065.pdf (2009). Accessed 27 Oct 2011

14. Information Commissioners Office: Privacy impact assessment handbook. http://www.ico.gov.uk/handbook/June.2009 (2009). Accessed 30 Oct 2011
15. Department of Homeland Security: Privacy Threshold Analysis (PTA). http://www.dhs.gov/xlibrary/assets/privacy/DHS_PTA_Template.pdf (2007). Accessed 30 Oct 2011
16. Australian Government: Office of the Privacy Commissioner: Privacy Impact Assessment Guide. http://www.privacy.gov.au/index.php?option=com_icedoc&view=types&element=guidelines&fullsummary=6590&Itemid=1021 (2010). Accessed 29 Oct 2011
17. Treasury Board Secretariat Canada: Welcome to the PIA e-learning tool. http://www.tbs-sct.gc.ca/pgol-pged/piatp-pfefvp/index-c-eng.asp (2003). Accessed 13 Nov 2011
18. United States Department of Homeland Security: Privacy threshold analysis (PTA). http://www.dhs.gov/xlibrary/assets/privacy/DHS_PTA_Template.pdf (2007). Accessed 15 Nov 2011
19. Vallini, M.: Software as a Service (SaaS) Ethical Issues. http://www.marcovallini.com/documentazione/saas_ethical_issues.pdf (2009). Accessed 24 Oct 2011
20. Pearson, S., Benameur, A.: Privacy, security and trust issues arising from cloud computing. In: Cloud Computing Technology and Science (CloudCom), 2010 Second Annual International Conference, 30 Nov –3 Dec, pp. 693–702 (2010). doi: 10.1109/CloudCom.2010.66
21. Giarratano, J.: Expert Systems: Principles and Programming. Thomson Learning, Boston, Massachusetts, Canada (2005)
22. J Boss Community: Drools: Business logic integration/platform. http://www.jboss.org/drools (2011). Accessed 22 Nov 2011
23. Logic Programming Associates Ltd: LPA VisiRule 1.5. http://www.lpa.co.uk/vsr.htm (2011). Accessed 20 Nov 2011
24. Corvid ExSys: Overview of Corvid Knowledge Automation Expert System Software. http://www.exsys.com/pdf/AboutCORVID.pdf (2008). Accessed 18 Oct 2011
25. Corvid ExSys: Java-based Expert System Knowledge Automation Development and Deployment Technologies White-Paper. http://www.exsys.com/pdf/ExsysCORVIDWhitePaper.pdf (2009). Accessed 20 Oct 2011
26. Mell, P., Grance, T.: The National Institute of Standards and Technology (NIST) Definition of Cloud Computing Version 15. http://www.nist.gov/itl/cloud/upload/cloud-def-v15.pdf (2009). Accessed 19 Nov 2011
27. Corvid ExSys: ExSys Corvid Manual Version 5.2.1. http://www.exsys.com/PDF/CorvidManual.pdf (2009). Accessed 16 Oct 2011
28. Microsoft: What is the Windows Azure Platform? http://www.microsoft.com/windowsazure/ (2011). Accessed 21 Nov 2011.
29. Sitaram, D., Manjunath, G.: Moving to the Cloud. Elsevier, Waltham (2012)
30. Sosinsky, B.: Cloud Computing Bible. Wiley, Indianapolis (2011)
31. Rhoton, J.: Cloud Computing Explained, 2nd edn. Recursive Press, London (2010)
32. Trusted Computing Group: TCG Architecture Overview Version 1.4. http://www.trustedcomputinggroup.org/resources/tcg_architecture_overview_version_14   (2010). Accessed 12 Nov 2011
33. European Network and Information Security Agency: Cloud Computing: Benefits, Risks and Recommendations for Information Security. http://www.enisa.europa.cu/act/rm/files/deliverables/cloud-computing-risk-assessment/at_download/fullReport.pdf (2009). Accessed 17 Nov 2011
34. Solove, D.J.: Understanding Privacy. Harvard University Press, Cambridge (2008)
35. Organization for Economic Co-operation and Development (OECD): Guidelines Governing the Protection of Privacy and Transborder Flow of Personal Data. OECD, Geneva (1980)
36. Karol, T.: A guide to cross-border privacy impact assessments. http://www.isaca.org/Knowledge-Center/Research/ResearchDeliverables/Pages/A-Guide-To-Cross-Border-Privacy-Impact-Assessments.aspx (2009). Accessed 30 Oct 2011
37. Nasuni: http://www.nasuni.com/ (2011). Accessed 30 Oct 2011
38. Bethencourt, S., Chan, J., Song, D., Perrig, A.: Multi-dimensional range query over encrypted data. In: IEEE Symposium on Security and Privacy. [City Not Specified] http://www.cs.berkeley.edu/~bethenco/oakland07rangequery.pdf (2007). Accessed 19 Feb 2012
39. Yao, A.C.: How to generate and exchange secrets. In: 27th Symposium on Foundation of Computer Science (FoCS), 27–29 Oct 1986, pp. 162–167 (1986). doi: 10.1109/SFCS.1986.25

40. Gentry, C.: Fully homomorphic encryption using ideal lattices. In: 41st ACM Symposium on Theory of Computing (STOC), [Date not specified] June 2009, pp. 169–178 (2009). doi: 10.1145/1536414.1536440
41. Export.gov: Welcome to the U.S.-E.U. & U.S.-Swiss Safe Harbor Frameworks. 26 October 2011. http://export.gov/safeharbor/ (2011)
42. RapidRedact: Welcome to Redacta. 21 Feb 2012. http://www.redacta.co.uk/ (2012)
43. DSDM Consortium: Handbook Version 2.1. http://www.dsdm.org/atern-handbook/flash. html#/1/ (2011). Accessed 30 Oct 2011
44. Shull, F., Singer, J., Sjoberg, D.: Guide to Advanced Empirical Software Engineering. Springer, London (2010)
45. Pearson, S., Charlesworth, A.: Accountability as a way forward for privacy protection in the cloud. In: Jaatun, M., Zhao, G., Rong, C. (eds.) Cloud Computing, vol. 5931, pp. 131–144. LNCS. Springer, Berlin/Heidelberg (2009). doi:10.1007/978–3–642–10665–1_12
46. Pearson, S., Shen, Y., Mowbray, M.: A privacy manager for cloud computing. In: Jaatun, M., Zhao, G., Rong, C. (eds.) Cloud Computing, vol. 5931, pp. 90–106. LNCS. Springer, Berlin/ Heidelberg (2009). doi: 10.1007/978–3–642
47. Preimesberger, C.: IBM, Aetna Join for New Cloud-Based Health Care Support System. http:// www.eweek.com/c/a/Health-Care-IT/IBM-Aetna-Join-for-New-CloudBased-Health-Care-Support-System-667092/ (2010). Accessed 30 Oct 2011
48. CambridgeSoft: ChemBioOffice Cloud – An Integrated Decision Support System for CHDI. http://chembionews.cambridgesoft.com/WhitePapers/Default.aspx?whitePaperID=43 (2010). Accessed 30 Oct 2011
49. Harbird, R., Ahmed, M., Finkelstein, A., McKinney, E., Burroughs, A.: Privacy Impact Assessment with PRAIS. http://www.cs.ucl.ac.uk/staff/A.Finkelstein/papers/hotpets.pdf (2007). Accessed 30 Oct 2011
50. Liberty Alliance Project: ID governance – identify privacy and access policy, marketing requirements document. http://www.projectliberty.org/ (2007). Accessed 30 Oct 2011
51. Pearson, S., Sander, T., Sharma, R.: Privacy management for global organizations. In: Garcia-Alfaro, J., Navarro-Arribas, G., Cuppens-Boulahia, N., Roudier, Y. (eds.) Data Privacy Management and Autonomous Spontaneous Security, vol. 5939, pp. 9–17. LNCS. Springer, Berlin/Heidelberg. doi:10.1007/978–3–642–11207–2_2
52. Pearson, S., Rao, P., Sander, T., Parry, A., Paull, A., Patruni, S., Dandamudi-Ratnakar, V., Sharma, P.: Scalable, accountable privacy management for large organizations. INSPEC 2009: 2nd International Workshop on Security and Privacy Distributed Computing, Enterprise Distributed Object Conference Workshops (EDOCW 2009), IEEE, Auckland, New Zealand, 1–4 Sept 2009, pp. 168–175
53. Office of the Privacy Commissioner of Canada: Securing Personal Information: A self Assessment Tool for Organisations. http://www.priv.gc.ca/resource/tool-outil/security-securite/english/AssessRisks.asp?x=1 (2011). Accessed 26 Oct 2011
54. Microsoft: Microsoft Security Assessment Tool Version 4.0. http://www.microsoft.com/download/en/details.aspx?displaylang=en&id=12273 (2009). Accessed 27 Oct 2011
55. Sander, T., Pearson, S.: Decision support for selection of cloud service providers. Int. J. Comput. GTSF. 1(1) (2010)

Chapter 4
Understanding Cloud Audits

**Frank Doelitzscher, Christoph Reich, Martin Knahl,
and Nathan Clarke**

Abstract Audits of IT infrastructures can mitigate security problems and establish
trust in a provider's infrastructure and processes. Cloud environments especially lack
trust due to non-transparent architectures and missing security and privacy measures
taken by a provider. But traditional audits do not cover cloud computing-specific
security. To provide a secure and trustable cloud environment, audit tasks need to
have knowledge about their environment and cloud-specific characteristics.
Furthermore, they need to be automated whenever possible to be able to run on
a regular basis and immediately if a certain infrastructure event takes place, like
deployment of a new cloud instance. In this chapter, research about cloud-specific
security problems and cloud audits gets presented. An analysis about how traditional
audits need to change to address cloud-specific attributes is given. Additionally, the
agent-based "Security Audit as a Service" architecture gets presented as a solution
to the identified problems.

Keywords Audit • Cloud • Security • Security Audit as a Service • Trust

4.1 Introduction

This section introduces the topic of cloud computing and audits and covers different cloud environment types. It also discusses why security audits of clouds are
necessary.

F. Doelitzscher (✉) • C. Reich • M. Knahl
Cloud Research Lab, Furtwangen University, Furtwangen im Schwarzwald, Germany
e-mail: Frank.Doelitzscher@hs-furtwangen.de

N. Clarke
Centre for Security, Communications and Network Research, University of Plymouth,
Plymouth, UK

School of Computing and Security, Edith Cowan University, Perth, WA, Australia

S. Pearson and G. Yee (eds.), *Privacy and Security for Cloud Computing*,
Computer Communications and Networks, DOI 10.1007/978-1-4471-4189-1_4,
© Springer-Verlag London 2013

Table 4.1 What the cloud provider controls [2]

Layer	Software as a Service	Platform as a Service	Infrastructure as a Service
Facility	√	√	√
Network	√	√	√
Hardware	√	√	√
Operating system	√	√	?
Middleware	√	?	–
Application	√	–	–
User	–	–	–

Cloud computing is not a new technology; in fact, it combines known and established technologies, such as virtualization and infrastructure management to provide IT services as an on-demand model. It mainly provides three service delivery models: Infrastructure as a Service (IaaS), Platform as a Service (PaaS) and Software as a Service (SaaS). The US National Institute of Standards and Technology identifies in its definition [1] on cloud computing the following main cloud characteristics:

- *On-demand self-service*: Cloud customer can provision and manage computing power and network storage without any human interaction with a service provider.
- *Broad network access*: Cloud resources are accessed via the network (mostly the Internet) using standardized Internet protocols.
- *Resource pooling*: A provider's computing and storage resources are shared between multiple customers as a multi-tenant model. A customer has no control or knowledge over the exact physical location where their data is stored or where their rented resources are executed.
- *Rapid elasticity*: Resources can be deployed elastically and scaled rapidly to fulfil the current demand by scaling up and down automatically. Cloud customers pay only for actually used resources and services.

NIST's definition has evolved into a *de facto* standard for cloud computing. But one major characteristic that comes with cloud computing is that parts of an IT infrastructure's trust boundary are moving to a third-party provider. An implication is a certain loss of hardware governance for the cloud user. Table 4.1 shows which cloud service model, either the cloud provider or the cloud customer, is in control of a certain layer [2]. Maintaining consistent security across boundaries is complex and challenging for information security professionals [3]. The Cloud Security Alliance defined a cloud model consisting of seven layers: facility, network, hardware, operating system, middleware technology, application and user.

Since security is still a considerable challenge for classic IT environments, it is even more for cloud environments due to its characteristics, such as seamless scalability, shared resources, multi-tenancy, access from everywhere, on-demand availability and third-party hosting. Although existing recommendations (ITIL), standards (ISO 27001:2005) and laws (e.g. Germany's Federal Data Protection Act) provide well-established security and privacy rule sets for data centre providers, research has shown that additional regulations have to be defined for cloud environments [4, 5]. In classic IT infrastructures, security audits and penetration tests are used to document a data centre's compliance to security best practices or laws. The major shortcoming of a traditional security audit is that it only provides a snapshot of an environment's security state at the time of the audit. This is adequate since classic IT infrastructures do not change that frequently. However, because of the mentioned cloud characteristics above, it is not sufficient for auditing a cloud environment. A cloud audit needs to consider the point of time when the infrastructure changes and the ability to decide if this change gives rise to a security gap or an infrastructure misuse. Knowledge of the underlying business processes is needed, for example, to decide if an up-scaled cloud service is caused by a higher demand of business requests or by hacker misuse.

The following examples assist in illustrating the need for cloud audits [6]:

- Hackers stole credentials of Salesforce.com's customers via phishing attacks (2007).
- T-Mobile customers lost data due to the "Sidekick disaster" of Microsoft cloud (2009).
- Botnet incident at Amazon EC2 infected customer's computers and compromised their privacy (2009).
- Hotmail accounts were hacked due to technical flaws in Microsoft software (2010).
- Amazon customer services were unavailable for multiple days, and data was lost due to a logical flaw in the cloud storage design (2011).

This book chapter is structured as follows: Sect. 4.2, "The role of auditing in addressing cloud specific security issues", first identifies the most important security issues to be considered when moving a service to a cloud. A comparison between traditional IT outsourcing and cloud computing is provided. For each identified security issue, a classification of the affected core principles of information security is given. Then the question of how audit approaches can mitigate the identified security issues gets discussed. Other related research work in corresponding areas is introduced.

Section 4.3, "Cloud audits", defines different IT security audit types and discusses how classic audits need to change to consider the special characteristics of cloud computing environments and their security. Important challenges for cloud audits are discussed, and the main questions are presented which a cloud audit needs to answer. Existing IT security audit industry standards for traditional data centres are analysed and supplemented by the new emerging standards for cloud environments.

Section 4.4, "Use cases for cloud audits", introduces possible use cases for cloud audits as (a) audit of a non-Cloud IT, (b) audit of Cloud IT from the cloud customer point of view and (c) audit of Cloud IT from the cloud provider point of view.

Section 4.5, "Security audit as a service," then presents a cloud incident detection architecture as a possible enabler to perform cloud audits while respecting cloud-specific characteristics and challenges. The Security Audit as a Service (SAaaS) architecture uses the concept of utilizing autonomous agents for monitoring a cloud infrastructure. The advantage of using audits gets discussed, followed by the introduction of the concept of security service-level agreements (SSLA). The SAaaS architecture is presented, and an early SAaaS agent prototype is shown.

Section 4.6, "Evaluation", discusses how the presented SAaaS architecture helps to mitigate challenges for auditing cloud infrastructures. It provides early experiences in building audit agents for a private cloud environment.

Finally, Sect. 4.7, "Conclusions and future work", concludes this chapter and shows future work.

Suggestions for further reading are given in "Recommended reading".

4.2 The Role of Auditing in Addressing Cloud-Specific Security Issues

This section will identify the most important security issues that should be considered when moving a service to a cloud. First, a comparison between traditional IT housing, IT outsourcing and cloud computing is given. Afterwards, two types of cloud security issues get identified, and the most critical security issues of each type are presented. For each security issue, a classification of affected core principles of information security is done. Then a discussion follows how an audit approach can mitigate the identified cloud-specific security problems.

4.2.1 Cloud Security Issues

Security issues are the most cited reason in current literature, economic studies and the press that hinder enterprises to adopt cloud computing intensively. A detailed analysis of the actual security impact is not easy to find because very often security problems are declared as cloud security problems, although they already exist in traditional IT-outsourcing scenarios and are merely exacerbated in cloud environments. This section will list cloud security problems and compare them to similar problems already known from traditional IT outsourcing. In addition, often basic, well-established security terms, as *risk*, *threat* or *vulnerability*, get mixed without regard to their respective definitions. However, for a well-defined risk analysis of building or moving a service to a cloud computing environment, this is important. Therefore, all cloud security issues presented in this section will be classified into its respective nature. Furthermore, affected core principles of information security, such as availability, confidentiality, integrity, etc., are listed for each security problem.

4.2.2 Cloud Computing vs. Classic IT Outsourcing

In our definition of traditional "IT outsourcing", we combine the two most common models existing on the market: "IT housing" and "outsourcing". In IT housing, a customer provides its own hardware, for example, server, and just runs them in a data centre of a service provider. He is only providing the necessary infrastructure components, like network components, cooling or power. Administration of the hardware stays with the customer. In outsourcing, a customer rents the complete infrastructure from a service provider, including any hardware and software. Administration is done by the service provider.

In traditional IT outsourcing, working or business processes get partly or fully externalized to a third-party service provider. A customer is renting a certain infrastructure and using it exclusively, which is called "single-tenant model". An extension of infrastructure or service requires a prior communication with the service provider. Long contract durations are characteristic for traditional IT outsourcing. In cloud computing, a customer is also renting a certain infrastructure but shares them most of the time with other customers. This is identified as the "multi-tenant model". Scalability of the rented service is simple, automatable and adaptable without prior interaction of the cloud provider. Cloud computing contracts are flexible in duration and can vary from just a couple of minutes to years. A number of research papers (e.g. [7–9]) have identified cloud security and privacy problems. They all have in common the following differentiation of identified cloud-specific security problems:

• Amplified cloud security problems (amplified CSP): problems already known from traditional, distributed IT environments but amplified through cloud computing attributes
• Specific cloud security problems (specific CSP): security problems which arise due to cloud computing's special characteristics

Sometimes, security issues which are frequently found in state-of-the-art cloud offerings are also defined as a separate class [10], but in our opinion, they also correlate to either one of the aforementioned defined classes.

4.2.3 Amplified Cloud Security Problems

Amplified cloud security problems (amplified CSP) mainly originated from underlying technologies upon which cloud computing is substantially built, such as virtualization technology, Web applications and multi-tenant software architectures. Furthermore, we include to amplified CSP problems originating in well-known and commonly established security best practices which are difficult or impossible to implement in a cloud computing environment. The following amplified CSP have been identified:

A1. Misuse of Administrator Rights/Malicious Insiders

Misuse of administrator rights is a severe problem already known in traditional IT. In a recent survey [11], among 300 IT professionals, 26% admitted that at least one staff member has abused a privileged login to access information. In cloud computing, this threat is amplified. Virtual machines (VMs) are mostly provided as managed root servers. The cloud provider is responsible for the underlying host system and has always access to the VMs running on the host through the hypervisor. A misuse through malicious insiders is possible and hard to detect due to a general lack of transparency into provider process and procedure. This affects the following core principles of information security: confidentiality, authenticity, authorization, integrity, data protection, accountability and non-repudiation.

A2. Missing Transparency of Applied Security Measures

In traditional IT outsourcing, this risk is mitigated by a well-defined regulation: The customer (IT housing) or the provider (IT outsourcing) is responsible for the application of security measures. They must be communicated to the customer. Providers can prove their compliance to baseline security measures with ISO 27001 or PCI DSS certificates. In cloud computing, there is a lack in transparency regarding applied provider security measures and processes. The underlying hardware infrastructure gets masqueraded to protect it from attacks. Cloud customers currently need to trust the provider that they are compliant to current security standards. Amazon Web Services announced in December 2010 that the AWS data centre, infrastructure and services are compliant to ISO 27001 and PCI DSS Level 1 [12]. However, to date, no agreed standard criteria for running a secure cloud infrastructure exist. This affects the following core principles of information security: integrity, availability and data protection.

A3. Missing Transparency with Security Incidents

Since computing systems are completely owned by the customer in IT housing, they are responsible for securing all evidence in case of a security incident. In IT outsourcing, this responsibility is transferred to the service provider which employs skilled personnel, for example, an own Computer Emergency Response Team (CERT). In cloud computing, customer and provider need to work together to collect all information of a security incident. Problems with hardware must be mapped to the different customer cloud resources to react to incidents and initiate correct problem management. But a standardized procedure is currently missing. Current cloud offers available in the market do not offer a transparent process for its customers on how security incidences are detected, which efforts are taken by the provider to mitigate it and how the provider supports its customer during the investigation phase. This is an increased risk in cloud computing. This affects the following core principles of information security: data protection, integrity, availability and non-repudiation.

A4. Shared Technology Issues

This threat includes the problem of sharing physical resources with multiple customers as well as the problem of misconfigured VMs that endangers other resources. In IT housing, this threat only applies for misconfiguration of security parameters and is limited to one corresponding customer. In IT outsourcing, the provider is fully responsible to configure running services securely. In cloud computing, this is caused by the use of virtualization and their lack of isolation. It can be categorized into:

- VM isolation: If one customer runs an improperly configured VM in the cloud, this also endangers other VMs running on this specific host. An attacker could use a VM as an entry point to get access to the host machine through a hypervisor flaw to gain inappropriate levels of control or influence on the underlying platform. Exploits seem rare but have already been demonstrated by Kortchorski [13] and Rutkowska [14]. Although few successful attacks are published so far, increasing code complexity in hypervisor software amplifies this threat.
- Memory/cache isolation: Often, the underlying components that make up this infrastructure, for example, GPUs or CPU caches, were not designed to offer strong isolation properties for a multi-tenant architecture [15]. These resources need to be quickly allocated and deallocated to fulfil a current demand. Well-established measures for secure data wiping might not be applicable. So far, no cloud provider discloses information on how shared resources get securely wiped before being reassigned to a different customer. Furthermore, by getting a default root access to a VM in current IaaS offering enlarges the attack vector of breaking through the isolation of shared resources. Certified Common Criteria compliant hypervisor software (minimum EAL 4) could mitigate this threat [16].
- I/O isolation: If there are problems with the virtual network (bridge software), traffic sniffing can be undertaken by an attacker.

This affects the following core principles of information security: integrity, availability, data protection, confidentiality, authentication and non-repudiation.

A5. Data Life Cycle in Case of Provider Switch or Termination

This threat does not exist in IT housing since data and computing resources remain the property of the customer if he changes the housing provider. In IT outsourcing, service-level agreements control how data is transferred to a customer or how storage devices need to be securely wiped or disposed of. In cloud computing, this threat is increased due to shared usage of resources. Customers need to define special rules for end of contract scenarios regulating how data gets exported from the cloud and how a provider has to securely erase customer's data [15]. This affects the following core principles of information security: data protection and confidentiality.

A6. Monitoring of Service-level agreements

IT housing and IT outsourcing can easily log events per user. In a cloud, several multi-tenant applications running in a virtualized environment need special tools to monitor service-level agreements. New tools for hypervisor, virtualized networking, monitoring, etc., must be available. This affects the following core principles of information security: availability and integrity.

4.2.4 Specific Cloud Security Problems

Due to our prior definition, we are speaking of specific cloud security problems (specific CSP) when they originate or affect at least one of NIST's cloud characteristics.

B1. Unclear Data Location

In traditional IT outsourcing, a customer always knows where and from whom its data gets stored and processed. Mostly, customers can physically visit a data centre to inform themselves personally about the security measurements a provider has taken for data protection. Germany's Data Protection Act §11 (1) states that where other bodies are commissioned to collect, process or use personal data, the responsibility for compliance within the provisions of this Act and with other data protection provisions shall rest with the principal [17]. From the interpretation of this Act, users must know the exact location of their data and their cloud providers' court of jurisdiction. An export or movement of data is not possible without prior notification of the customer. In current cloud computing offerings, customers do not have the possibility of knowing where the data gets stored or processed. Only a very rough decision about a cloud data centre's continental location can be made, for example, AWS data centre in Northern Ireland. Nevertheless, currently, there is no way to prove if data is not outsourced by a cloud provider. A current court decision about legitimate access of US governmental agencies to data of US-originated firms even of data centres located outside of US area of jurisdiction [18] strongly amplifies this risk. This affects the following core principles of information security: data protection, confidentiality and availability.

B2. Abuse and Nefarious Use of Cloud Resources

Characteristic for cloud computing is fast access to numerous virtual machines within a very short time frame. This attracts not only legally acting enterprises or organizations but also individuals and organizations with more malicious intent. It has never been easier for an attacker to get legal access to a high-performance computing environment. Amazon's cloud was already used to host malware (e.g. Trojans).

Also, the Zeus botnet (a phishing Trojan that steals banking information) was known to be hosted on virtual machines within the Amazon cloud. Another possibility would be to aggregate many VMs and use them to DDoS a single target and thereby prevent others to use its services. While this threat mainly addresses the cloud provider, the cloud customer can also be affected. As a result of the Zeus botnet, big parts of Amazon's IP address range was blacklisted on spam lists causing e-mails from "good" customers, running their mail server on Amazon, being rejected as well. This issue affects the following core principles of information security: availability.

B3. Missing Monitoring

A security incident within a cloud environment should get detected and eliminated by the cloud provider. If customer data is in danger, this should be communicated. To our best knowledge, no cloud provider so far runs an information policy system that will inform the customer automatically. But especially in cases of personal data processing, for example, credit card information, it could be important for a cloud customer to know if a security problem exists so he can stop the service to guarantee data protection and integrity and minimize risk for its own systems. For a sustainable risk analysis of running a service in a cloud, it is important to know:

- Which data protection measures exist to secure the cloud environment (antivirus protection, intrusion detection systems (IDS), measures for denial of service (DoS) detection and prevention, patch and change management)
- History of service breakdowns
- Measurements taken for availability, backup, reliability and data recovery
- Installed software versions at cloud host systems
- Tracking of administrative access of cloud provider service personnel
- What information and support are available during a service breakdown or a security incident

For monitoring security of large IT infrastructures, a best practice approach is to run intrusion detection systems (IDS) with distributed sensors as input feeds. But this approach breaks down for cloud infrastructures, mainly because of the complexity and frequently changing environment driven by the users. Traditional IDS setups are built around a single monolithic entity, which is not adaptive enough to do data collection and processing in an efficient and meaningful way [19]. This affects the following core principles of information security: non-repudiation, availability, data protection and confidentiality.

B4. Insecure APIs

Cloud resources are mostly deployed, controlled, orchestrated and managed through specific cloud application programming interfaces (APIs) offered by the provider. The security and availability of general cloud services are dependent upon the security of these basic APIs. From authentication and access control to encryption and activity monitoring, these interfaces must be designed to protect against both accidental and malicious attempts to circumvent policy [15]. Since third-party providers essentially build their services upon these APIs, for example, a load balancer service, a complex architectural layer gets inserted which needs to be subject to careful investigation. Standardized protocols and measurements for secure software development (Microsoft Secure Development Lifecycle (SDL) or Software Assurance Maturity Model (SAMM) of the Open Web Application Security Projects (OWASP)) address this threat. This affects the following core principles of information security: confidentiality, integrity, availability, non-repudiation, data protection and accountability.

B5. Missing Monitoring of Cloud Scalability

One reason of using a cloud infrastructure is to benefit from its scalability attributes. In this context, it is most often used to deal with usage peeks, for example, if a new version of software gets released and huge download requests are expected. Characteristic to peeks is that they are mostly foreseeable and limited to a certain time frame. Therefore, cloud users design their cloud application to start new instances if a certain threshold is reached to provide service availability. This introduces two new challenges for cloud security:

B5.1 IaaS upscaling – business driven: Since a user's infrastructure can change rapidly (grow, shrink) in case of a peek scenario, a monitoring system needs to be aware of the peek situation and the defined scalability thresholds.

B5.2 IaaS upscaling – attack driven: Most of the time, scalability thresholds, like "maximum number of new VMs to be created", get defined once, mostly during the design phase for the first peek event. If the peek was managed well by the thresholds, they stay, defined, although they might be not needed anymore (e.g. until the next major version release). This enables a new cloud-specific attack: financial damage due to nefarious abuse of cloud resources. An attacker can cause the creation of new cloud instances up to the scalability threshold by creating a huge number of allowed requests, which do not result in any successful business case but could be caused by, for example, distribution of malicious software. This affects the following core principles of information security: availability and accountability.

B6. Missing Interoperability of Cloud Provider

To minimize the potential damage of a provider downtime or in case of a provider change, interoperability between different cloud providers is very important. Current cloud offerings are not compatible with each other due to the usage of customized VM formats or proprietary APIs. A migration of cloud resources from one provider to another is not possible. This increases the risk of vendor and data lock-in.

For example, a customer of a Microsoft Azure database service cannot use it with a service developed and running on the Cloud App Engine [16]. Standards are necessary to mitigate this risk. First developments are started with the following projects:

- Open Cloud Computing Interface
- Open Virtualization Format (OVF)
- OpenStack Cloud Software – Rackspace Hosting, NASA

Furthermore, a detailed strategy needs to be defined between provider and cus-tomer, which regulates data formats, perpetuation of logic relations and total costs in case of a provider change [16]. This affects the following core principles of infor-mation security: availability.

4.2.5 How Audit Approaches Can Help

After outlining the cloud-specific security issues, we now want to discuss how cloud audit approaches can address them. To support the argument, we present other related research work taking place in the area.

Due to the loss of hardware governance in cloud computing, customers need to trust the provider that data does only get stored on the providers' storage compliant to applying data protection laws. This can result in *unclear data location*. Ries et al. present in [20] a geolocation approach based on network coordinate systems and evaluate the accuracy of three prevalent systems. Furthermore, Massonet et al. discuss in [21] the problem for IT security audits if federated cloud infrastructures are spanned across different countries. They introduce an existing federated cloud monitoring infrastructure to monitor in which country data is actually saved without compromising cloud isolation. In the presented approach, collaboration is required between the cloud infrastructure provider, the user of the cloud and the service provider. The proposed architecture is validated by an e-Government case study with legal data location constraints. A cloud audit system needs to prove that data is only stored at the agreed storage location (e.g. cloud provider's data is stored in Germany) and not transferred to other locations. This could be achieved by analysing data access operations to show when and by which subject (process or person) data was accessed and may be transferred.

Detecting an *abuse and nefarious use of cloud resources* can be a challenging task. Just evaluating VM usage data, like CPU and memory usage, or the number of open network connections can result in a false-positive decision, especially since enterprises use cloud computing to satisfy demand peeks or use cloud for calculation of intense operations, for example, high-performance computing (HPC). To filter out nefarious use of a cloud infrastructure, an audit system has to combine usage and network data of the cloud-wide network. Due to the distributed nature of cloud computing, information about network flow has to be collected at many different physical locations. To get the whole picture, however, this data has to be analysed in the overall context. Therefore, this information then needs to be correlated with the time of occurrence and a snapshot of the current infrastructure status (e.g. running VMs, demand) to that specific time. In Sect. 4.5, a first draft of such an audit architecture gets presented where techniques of behaviour analysis and anomaly detection are used to distinguish between "normal" and nefarious use of cloud resources.

4.2.5.1 Missing Monitoring and Cloud Scalability

Jonathan Spring describes in [2] and [22] how monitoring of cloud infrastructures can be done. He utilized a seven-layered model of cloud infrastructures established by the Cloud Security Alliance and gives ideas about what can be monitored at each layer. Tancock introduces in [23] a privacy impact assessment decision support tool that can be integrated within a cloud computing environment. The authors show that privacy weaknesses impact legal compliance, data security and user trust in cloud environments. The presented system is a systematic process for evaluating the possible future effects that a particular activity or proposal may have on an individual's privacy. With the system, presented risk analysis of moving a service to a cloud environment can be enhanced. A distributed monitoring facility can deliver the input to detect multiple cloud-specific security issues. The proposed audit architecture in Sect. 4.5 especially is designed to detect attacks on the scalability features in a cloud infrastructure. Audit systems which can evaluate if an infrastructure change is caused by an attack or due to real demand can help reduce false positives. Cloud audits can be used to prove the compliance to data protection laws and contractual service-level agreements of the provider if monitoring information cannot be disclosed due to customer data protection regulations.

To address the problem of *insecure APIs*, a cloud audit system can be used to verify that a cloud provider uses strong authentication and access controls for accessing the cloud services through the provided APIs. Furthermore, an audit can evaluate if API calls are only accepted and processed over encrypted communication paths to provide connection security. Also, the *missing interoperability of cloud providers* can be mitigated by cloud-specific audit checks. A cloud audit system needs to prove that standardized formats, protocols and interfaces are used to transfer and process data in the cloud. Furthermore, the usage of standardized formats also provides cloud users with a clear exit strategy to prevent provider lock-in situations. Section 4.3.3 presents current standardization activities regarding cloud protocols and cloud audits.

4.2.5.2 Audit of Cloud Computing Infrastructures

Wang et al. present in [24] a system to audit the integrity and security of public data cloud storage. Their solution allows a third-party auditor (TPA) to be able to efficiently audit the cloud data storage without demanding a local copy of data and it introduces no additional on-line burden to the cloud user. Therefore, they combine a public key-based homomorphic authenticator with random masking to achieve a privacy-preserving public cloud data auditing system.

Zhu et al. also present in [25] a system for "dynamic audit services for outsourced storages in clouds". The system uses fragment structures, random sampling and index hash tables, supporting provable updates to outsourced data and timely anomaly detection.

Table 4.2 summarizes the presented cloud security problems (amplified CSP and specific CSP) and classifies them according to their origin (IT outsourcing, virtualization or cloud computing). If known, real-world examples of security incidents resulting from a discussed problem are listed, and a short overview of countermeasures is given.

This section introduced the main differences between traditional IT outsourcing and cloud computing. Amplified cloud security problems (amplified CSP) and specific cloud security problems (specific CSP) were presented, and a classification of affected core principles of information security was given for every identified problem. Further on, it was discussed how audit approaches can help mitigate the identified cloud-specific security problems. Selected related work for certain problems was introduced. More work can be found in the "Recommended reading" section.

4.3 Cloud Audits

This section defines different IT security audit types and discusses how classic audits need to change to consider the special characteristics of cloud computing environments and their security. Important challenges for cloud audits are presented, and the main questions are given which a cloud audit should answer. This section finishes with a discussion of IT security audit industry standards for traditional data centres as well as new standards for cloud environments.

4.3.1 IT Security Audit Types

An audit can be defined as:

> Formal inspection and verification to check whether a standard or set of guidelines is being followed, records are accurate, or efficiency and effectiveness targets are being met. [26]

The audit of IT environments focuses upon a particular technology area, for example, network infrastructure. Generally, IT audits can be characterized into four areas: general controls audits, application control audits, network/infrastructure audits and system development audits. The IT security audit focuses upon security issues of the whole IT infrastructure and can be defined as the process of IT risk analysis and vulnerability assessment. Typically, these audits are part of a quality

Table 4.2 Overview of cloud security problems

No.	Problem	Origin	Incident examples	Affected security principle	Countermeasures
A1	Misuse of administrator rights/malicious insiders	OC	Liebermann password survey 2011	Confidentiality, authenticity, authorization, integrity, data protection, accountability, non-repudiation	Monitoring and alerting Disclosure of data protection policies of cloud provider employees
A2	Missing transparency of applied security measures	OC, V	Heartland data breach, 2009	Integrity, availability, data protection	Disclosure of security measures, for example, patch management, log files
A3	Missing transparency with security incidents	OC	Amazon Service Health Board history, 04/2011	Data protection, integrity, availability, non-repudiation	Detailed service-level agreements which regulate measures taken in case of security incidents
A4	Shared technology issues	OC, V	Amazon: BitBucket; Red- and blue-pill exploits J. Rutkowska, 2008; Cloudburst Kortchinsky, 2009; UDP flood attack in 2009	Integrity, availability, data protection, confidentiality, authentication, non-repudiation	Monitoring and alerting SLAs for patch management and secure configuration Consideration of installation and configuration best practices
A5	Data life cycle in case of provider switch or termination	OC	–	Data protection, confidentiality	Detailed exit strategy Confirmation of secure erase of data
B1	Intransparent data location	C	–	Data protection, confidentiality, availability	–
B2	Abuse and nefarious use of cloud resources	C	Zeus botnet, Trojan and malicious office documents in Amazon EC2, 2010	Availability	Stronger authentication measures Stronger verification of cloud user
B3	Missing monitoring	C	–	Non-repudiation, availability, data protection, confidentiality	Monitoring and alerting

B4	Insecure APIs	C	Attack of Amazon SOAP API, Nils Gruschka, 2009	Confidentiality, integrity, availability, non-repudiation, data protection, accountability	Only over-encrypted communication paths Use of strong authentication and access controls
B5	Missing monitoring of cloud scalability	C	Miscalculated bill of costs in Amazon EC2, ToasterNET 2011	Availability, accountability	Monitoring component which is aware of business processes to evaluate cloud scalability events
B6	Missing interoperability of cloud provider	C	EMC storage cloud closes, 2010; Iron Mountain ends cloud storage service, 2010	Availability	Use of standardized formats, protocols and interfaces Detailed exit strategy

Fig. 4.1 Steps of an IT audit

management process to reduce the number of security holes. IT security audits can be categorized into the following types:

- *Vulnerability assessment*: Its task is to expose known security problems in all services of an IT infrastructure. Broad and automated vulnerability scans are used to assess the weaknesses of the IT. Experts manually verify detected vulnerabilities.
- *Vulnerability audit*: It is a risk-based approach where IT is seen from the perspective of an attacker. It simulates an attack from malicious outsiders (hackers) by performing a penetration test. It is an intensive technical security audit with a high percentage of manual testing and verification.
- *Application security audit*: It is an intensive security audit of an application and its associated components (e.g. Web application security scanner).
- *Vulnerability management*: It specifies an automated vulnerability audit, and characteristics include automated, regular vulnerability scans and documentation of detected vulnerabilities in chronological order over multiple scans.

Figure 4.1 shows the process of a security audit: typical phases are definition, analysis, reporting, organization and validation. It is good practice to use the results of the validation phase as additional input for a future audit.

4.3.2 Classic IT Audits vs. Cloud Audits

For classical IT audits, today's standard is the Statements on Standards for Attestation Engagements No. 16 (SSAE 16) [27] report. SSAE 16 is an AICPA auditing standard for reporting on controls at service organizations (including data centres) in the United States. It requires that the auditor obtains a written assertion from management regarding the design and operating effectiveness of the controls being reviewed. This should minimize the IT risks, which is also applicable for cloud infrastructures, of:

- Loss of business focus of the service.
- Solutions failing to meet business and/or user requirements. The service is not performing as expected.
- Contractual (stated in SLA) discrepancies between the service user and the service provider.

- Compromised security and confidentiality.
- Invalid or incorrect processed transactions.
- Pure software quality (high number of failures).

With the appearance of cloud infrastructures, cloud-specific risks regarding IT security audits have been discussed and addressed by many researchers [8, 28], companies [15] and institutions [4, 9]. Broadly, it can be summarized as:

- *Greater dependency on the provider*: Access to data or the control of resources in the cloud is still very much provider dependent. The cloud resource access interfaces are complex, and the extra control interfaces increase the vulnerability of cloud infrastructures. The risk of data lock-in is high, and because of the appearance of many new cloud providers, the risk of bankruptcy should not be neglected. There is a lack of standardized access interfaces to the cloud.
- *Increase complexity of compliance with laws and regulations:* Although a service is hosted at a cloud provider, the customer is still responsible for the data and service quality to the service users. Thus, the laws and regulations of a cloud provider country might be quite different than from the cloud customers'. The nature of cloud computing is to hide the location of the resources to the customer. The processing and data location can be anywhere, which might violate laws (e.g. European law of privacy forces the location in Europe for personal private data).
- *Reliance on the Internet*: The organization's data stored in the cloud is only accessible through the Internet, which raises further security issues like data integrity, privacy and all kinds of attacks from this public environment.
- *Dynamic nature of cloud computing:* Processing and data location can be changed at any time because of load-balancing reasons or infrastructure failure. This causes many monitoring and controlling problems, and therefore, arguably the level of security decreases. Since the provider can scale the customer's infrastructure automatically, the user must have control of this to limit the number of instances and control of the costs. Otherwise, a denial of service eats up all the revenue of the business service.

For cloud computing, an audit needs to clarify the following questions:

- *Privileged user access*: Remember the provider has root access to the infrastructure and therefore can read unencrypted data on the cloud storage. So the number of administrators with root access should be minimized.
- *Regulatory compliance*: Customers are responsible for the data, even if it is in an external data centre. It has to be ensured that the provider takes care of backup, has reasonable data recovery times and strong encryption algorithms are used, if data encryption is needed.
- *Data confidentiality, integrity, privacy, availability and segregation*: In a cloud, the environment is typically shared among the customers. It is important to verify if that is secure. If the VM of another company is compromised, would my company VM be affected? Do you want to share a resource with your competitor? For many applications, resource sharing is acceptable, but for enterprise critical applications, you might want resources exclusively. Can a provider offer this? Special interest

should be taken in understanding how the data is segregated and secured at the cloud provider. Is the data replicated over multiple sites? Are backup strategies logically consistent? Is the data really encrypted? Is the data access limited to the customer's application? Is it possible to limit the data location to predefined areas? The cloud provider should transparently inform about the key management, access control, data segmentation, used encryption algorithms utilized, etc., of the cloud infrastructure. Additionally, business continuity plans and disaster recovery plans have to be defined in cooperation with the provider.

- *Investigative support*: Suppose the customer's resources are compromised. The provider might have problems in undertaking forensic analysis, since the logging in cloud environments are not user partitioned.
- *Monitor and control of cloud services*: Do customers get commercial service-level agreements (SLAs), which can be adapted to the needs of the customers? Will the customers be able to monitor and manage them afterwards? Do the cloud interfaces offer sufficient and reliable information for the integration, control and monitoring tasks? How does data which is stored, transmitted and processed outside the company get audited? Is there access to accounting information?
- *Data retention*: For data stored in a cloud, questions need to be answered: How long can data be stored? How are data archived? How much is budgeted to retain data? [29] For retaining data from the cloud, it is important to clarify the following: How can data be retrieved? How is data integrity maintained during this process? How is data removed/securely wiped from the cloud storage systems?

Service-level agreements are most often used to clarify the majority of these questions. Nevertheless, SLAs are no support for a cloud customer without enforcement or traceability. It is important to provide a customer with the ability to check log data (physical, virtual and logical), event transport and storage services as well as event processing rules derived from SLAs. From the technical point of view, the following challenges need to be covered [30]:

- *Loss of 1:1 mapping*: Due to the technology shifts towards VMs, virtual landscaped, location transparency is not clear for the customer.
- *Static gets variable*: Dynamic changes of IPs, data centres and servers dependant on demand, time of day, etc.
- *Audit analysis*: *data storm problem:* How can data be retrieved, correlated and extracted meaningfully in a permanently changing infrastructure (VM start and stop)?
- *Audit as a service*: For customers, it might be important to audit their business processes across multiple cloud providers.

4.3.3   Towards a Cloud Audit

Multiple industry standards exist regarding compliance, regulation and best practices. Compliance to these standards enables companies to perform IT security audits which fit to their infrastructure. Since cloud infrastructures are definitely a special kind of IT infrastructure, cloud service providers (CSP) need to consider what IT services customers are allowed to run on their infrastructure and which industry standards apply to that business model. Table 4.3 shows available industry standards and their special focus [31].

Over the past 2 years, new IT security standards appeared which are specialized for cloud infrastructures:

- CloudAudit A6: Automated Audit, Assertion, Assessment and Assurance API [32]
- EuroCloud Star Audit [33]
- Cloud Controls Matrix by Cloud Security Alliance [34]

CloudAudit A6: Its goal is to provide a common interface and namespace that allow cloud computing providers to automate the Audit, Assertion, Assessment and Assurance (A6) of their cloud environments. The interoperability between different clouds to avoid resource lock-in is important. It should be ensured that virtual machines can be controlled and hosted at different cloud sides. Therefore, the cloud provider should offer standardized interfaces to make the cloud more transparent in a secure and reliable way. One initiative is the DiffCloud interface, a language-independent REST-API.

EuroCloud Star Audit: Audit is a certificate for a SaaS cloud provider. It is the first specific certification for the Software as a Service model by the German EuroCloud Deutschland_eco e.V. [33]. The audit aims to establish a high level of security and transparency for users and providers alike. The audit starts with the provider's general profile; carries on with contract and compliance including data privacy protection, general security, operation and infrastructure and operation processes and goes as far as application and implementation. The audit consists mainly of six steps:

1. *Questionnaire*: The SaaS provider fills out a questionnaire about company profile, contract clauses, compliance, security and safety, infrastructure, business processes and implementation.
2. *Evaluation of questionnaire*: Auditors evaluate the questionnaire.
3. *Auditor interview*: Auditors interview the SaaS provider about questionnaire details, validity of certifications and implementation of documentation processes.
4. *On-site verification*: Auditors verify in an on-site visit questionnaire details, validity of certifications and documentation processes. This includes a visit of the provider's data centre if applicable.
5. *Evaluation and star ranking*: Auditors evaluate results based on a point-based evaluation matrix to decide which SaaS stars can be assigned. Detailed information about the matrix can be found in EuroCloud quick reference [35].
6. *Assignment of certificate*: The provider gets 1–5 SaaS EuroCloud stars assigned, dependent on the results of the evaluation. The certificate is valid for 24 months.

Cloud Security Control Matrix: Published by the Cloud Security Alliance, the Cloud Security Control Matrix (CCM) is designed to provide fundamental security principles as guidance for cloud providers and to assist prospective cloud customers in assessing the overall security risk of a cloud provider. It provides an overview of audit attributes for a cloud infrastructure and classifies which cloud service models as well as cloud infrastructure components are affected by this attribute. It furthermore

Table 4.3 Industry standards for IT security

	Control environment/ company level controls	Information security	IT service delivery/ operations	Systems development	Financial reporting system	Specific technologies or incremental requirements
Best practices guidance	COBIT COSO	ISO 27002	ITIL ISO 20000-2	CMM/ISO 21827	ITGI-SOX	ISO var. ANSI var. NIST var.
Certification/audit criteria/ requirement		ISO 27001	ISO 20000-1			
Regulatory/industry requirements		FFIEC HIPAA HITRUST NIST PCI ISO2700X			SOX PCAOB	EV SSL
Audit framework	SAS 70 SysTrust WebTrust BITS FISAP	PCAOB	WebTrust CA WebTrust EV GAPP			

provides information about which specific section of available audit industry standards (as listed in Table 4.2) is addressing the respective issue.

This section introduced different IT security audit types. It discussed the main challenges for traditional IT security audits and which questions need to be answered with respect to cloud-specific attributes. An overview of applicable industry standards for IT security audits was given, and new emerging standards for cloud audits were discussed.

4.4 Use Cases for Cloud Audits – Use case (a)

While cloud environments cause new challenges to traditional IT security audits due to their characteristics, they also enable new business cases to perform security audits on a regular basis. This section discusses the following possible use cases for cloud audits: (a) audit of non-Cloud IT, (b) audit of Cloud IT from the cloud customer point of view and (c) audit of Cloud IT from the cloud provider point of view.

4.4.1 Audit of Non-Cloud IT

A typical enterprise is running at least the following basic IT infrastructure:

- File server to store documents
- Web server to host company's website
- Mail server to provide e-mail services
- ERP system for financial transaction and reporting
- Internet connection and basic network services

Installation and maintenance are undertaken either by an external provider who charges per hour or an internal system administrator. Since some of these components are exposed to the Internet due to their very nature, IT security audits should be performed to provide a descent level of protection of data and system availability. But especially small and medium enterprises (SMEs) face the following problems:

- Costs of an IT security audit performed by a third-party security provider are out of proportion to the company's revenue and available IT budget.
- Security is also undertaken by the company's administrator; however, frequently, IT security-specific knowledge is missing. Priority is more commonly attributed to system maintenance and security controls rather than training.

Due to the cloud computing's pay on-demand model, "audit from the cloud" can be offered as depicted in Fig. 4.2. A cloud customer can rent an "audit VM", which was compiled by a security provider, including typical vulnerability assessment software like fingerprinting tools, port scanner and vulnerability scanners, like

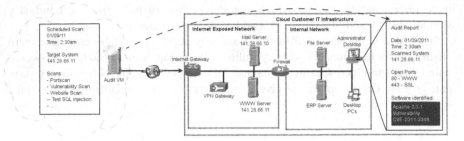

Fig. 4.2 Audit from the cloud

Nessus.[1] The tools are configured to start automatically in a logical order after the VM was booted, working through a list of target IP addresses of systems to be scanned. These will be the Internet-exposed systems of the customer. The results are conditioned in a standardized form to an audit report, which is sent to the customer's administrator. If security problems were identified (for example, an outdated version of Web server software), recommendations, (for instance, from the Common Vulnerability and Exposures (CVE)) database are given on how the problem can be fixed. A customer subscribed to this service schedules the scans to be performed either once or on a regular (for example, weekly) basis. Thus, common security problems like vulnerabilities due to outdated software, insecure configuration of services or compromised systems can be detected. So comprehensible documentation of a system's state gets created. After the scan is completed, the report gets mailed to the customer and the audit VM gets shut down. Customer benefits are:

- Pay on-demand model: Audit VM only costs during runtime.
- Security knowledge comes from an external provider who maintains the audit VM.
- Regular vulnerability assessment of Internet-exposed systems.
- Audit report in standardized format provided taking into account a system's security status over time.

It is imaginable that this service could be extended by scanning customer systems which are not directly exposed to the Internet. Therefore, an authorized SSH host key or VPN certificate of the audit VM could be imported to an internal customer gateway, allowing the audit VM to first establish a connection to a customer's data centre. Then internal systems can be included in the scan as well, as depicted in Fig. 4.2. There are already some companies on the market that offer a similar service to the described use case:

- Retina Cloud by eEye Digital Security [36]
- The Cloud Penetrator by SecPoint [37]
- Website security and antivirus scanner by Kyplex [38]

---

[1] Nessus: vulnerability scanner, http://www.tenable.com/products/nessus

4.4.2   Audit of Cloud IT from the Cloud Customer
Point of View – Use case (b)

In this use case, a cloud customer already uses a cloud offer and runs some instances (VMs) in a cloud. Due to the introduced cloud computing's characteristics and resulting problems, as already described in Sect. 4.2.2, "Cloud Computing vs. Classic IT Outsourcing", the customer faces the following problems:

* Missing monitoring of cloud instances
* Data security issues due to unknown data location and shared technology
* Missing auditability of the cloud provider due to missing transparency
* Loss of overview due to frequent infrastructure changes (VM start and stop)

In the traditional data centre scenario, the server landscape does not change often, and especially SME administrators know "their" systems by heart. In cloud computing, this can change due to the scalability of cloud resources. Dependent on the demand, the quantity of a customer's active cloud instances can increase and decrease quite frequently, for example, to fulfil a demand of service requests. Since cloud computing offers inexhaustible computing resources, users as well as administrators can pick up on this advantage quite fast. For example, getting an additional machine exclusively just to try out a new version of a certain piece of software was very unlikely in traditional IT environments; in cloud computing, this is only a couple of mouse clicks away at little cost.[2] Administrators like this because they can be satisfied quite quickly other running systems are not affected and there is no additional physical space needed. But this comfort can quickly lead to a loss of overview of the entire infrastructure, which is critical for securing it. Furthermore, in traditional data centres, security administrators harden systems and use a combination of firewall rules and intrusion detection system to secure it. But in the cloud, this is not applicable anymore due to the loss of control over hardware and shared technology issues.

To overcome these problems in this use case (b), each cloud instance and the corresponding cloud infrastructure, for example, virtual switches, VM hosts, router and switches, are monitorable. Therefore, an agent framework can be used, providing "audit agents" deployed at core components of a cloud infrastructure, as illustrated in Fig. 4.3. It shows the cloud reference architecture based on work from University of Los Angeles and IBM [39], which makes the most important security-relevant cloud environment components explicit [10]. By adding audit agents to every layer, transparency to the cloud infrastructure can be provided for the user. Each agent is producing events in case an ominous transaction was detected. The cloud customer will define security service-level agreements (SSLAs) regulating which components should be monitored and how, as well as alarm levels describing how the system automatically reacts in the event of a detected security incident.

---

[2] If a private cloud scenario is considered, costs come down to zero in currency terms, and just the available resources count.

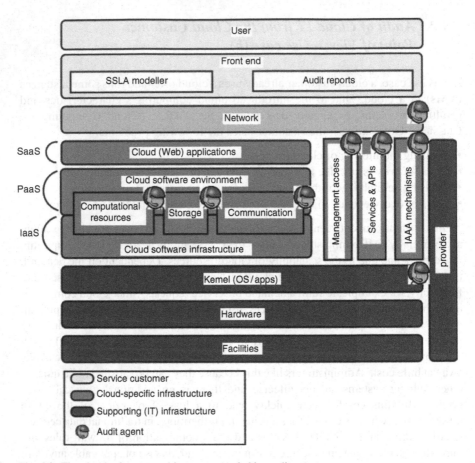

Fig. 4.3 The cloud reference architecture extended by audit agents

Additionally, the described audit system from use case (a) (described in 4.4.1) can be applied to internal cloud instances as well, extended by using the audit agent's events as additional input for the audit report.

The following advantages can be achieved for a cloud customer:

- Better overview of all customer-associated instances, possibly created from multiple accounts
- Transparency about cloud instances' security state
- Transparency about provider's administrative access (see Sect. 4.2.3 – A1)

The following open-source or research projects support this use case:

- CloudAudit A6 [32]
- Security Audit as a Service (SAaaS) [40]

4.4.3 Audit of Cloud IT from the Cloud Provider Point of View – Use case (c)

From the cloud provider's point of view, running and maintaining a cloud infrastructure are more challenging than a classic data centre. The reasons lie in cloud computing's characteristics, mainly its multi-tenant user model. To be successful, a cloud provider needs to prove the following:

- Compliance to laws, especially data protection laws
- Compliance to laws of all subtractors
- Isolation and adequate segregation of shared computing and storage resources
- Measurements taken for availability, service and data protection, for example, backups and comprehensive continuity-of-operations plan
- Measurements taken to secure the cloud network environment, for example, intrusion detection systems, firewalls and logging facilities
- Accordance of cloud infrastructure with audit requirements
- Logging of all administrative access to customer's cloud resources, for example, two-factor authentication for cloud administrators, codes of conduct and confidentiality agreements
- Customer-specific audit requirements

To fulfil this need, research [40] as well as governmental and industry security experts [16], for example, the German Federal Office for Information Security (BSI), recommends security audits and certificates as the preferred method of proof. Traditional IT security audits or penetration tests need to be adapted to a cloud's specific attributes, as described in the previous chapters. Principally, it is important to provide continuous monitoring of the cloud's security state over time. Due to the frequently changing infrastructure, the possibility that possible misusers of cloud resources are already within the cloud's network (currently most are authenticated by a credit card number) are facts that traditional intrusion detection systems cannot cope with. Therefore, a monitoring system built on audit agents as described in use case (b) can provide the following advantages for a cloud provider:

- Monitoring and detection of attacks against the cloud management system
- Monitoring of cloud usage behaviour to detect misuse of cloud resources (by legally registered cloud customer)
- Support of IT forensic investigations in case of successful attacks
- Displays security state of cloud infrastructure over time
- Proof of compliance to laws
- Possible interface to third-party security provider for an external audit

This section introduced three use cases of cloud audits. Use case (a) utilizes cloud resources to perform repeating vulnerability scans of a customer's IT infrastructure. Use case (b) describes the possibility of monitoring a customer's cloud instances overcoming the lack of traditional intrusion detection systems for cloud environments. Use case (c) discusses an audit from the view of cloud provider to run a secure cloud environment, detecting cloud-specific threats like misuse of cloud resources or attacks to the cloud management system.

4.5 Security Audit as a Service (SAaaS)

This section introduces the Security Audit as a Service (SAaaS) architecture as a possible cloud audit infrastructure. SAaaS uses the concept of utilizing autonomous agents for monitoring a cloud infrastructure to achieve the use cases presented in Sect. 4.4.

To address the lack of transparent monitoring of a cloud infrastructure, the Cloud Research Lab at Furtwangen University (HFU), Germany, is developing an incident detection system for cloud computing: "Security Audit as a Service (SAaaS)". Its development is funded by HFU and the Federal Ministry of Education and Research (BMBF), Germany. Two industry partners, a German cloud provider and a German IT security provider, are participating in the SAaaS project. It is built upon intelligent, autonomous agents collecting data directly at key points of a cloud infrastructure, analysing and aggregating information and distributing it with consideration to the underlying business processes. Therefore, a description format, the security service-level agreements (SSLA), will be developed which allows an organization to define monitoring events considering business process flows to decrease false-positive alarms. The usage of autonomous agents enables a behaviour anomaly detection of cloud components while maintaining the cloud-specific flexibility. SAaaS respects the following cloud-specific attributes:

- A high number and complexity of distributed systems
- An often-changing infrastructure (e.g. service scalability or user driven)
- An interpretation of the cloud activation in respect to business processes

First, the advantage of using agents to detect incidents will be discussed, followed by the introduction of security service-level agreements. Then the SAaaS architecture gets presented and an early SAaaS agent prototype is shown.

4.5.1 How Agents Can Improve Incident Detection

First, an agent can be defined as

> ...a software entity which functions continuously and autonomously in a particular environment ... able to carry out activities in a flexible and intelligent manner that is responsive to changes in the environment ... Ideally, an agent that functions continuously ... would be able to learn from its experience. In addition, we expect an agent that inhabits an environment with other agents and processes to be able to communicate and cooperate with them... [41]

Agents within the SAaaS architecture are running independently, not necessarily connected to a certain central instance; they are self-defending and self-acting. Therefore, we term them "autonomous". Agents can receive data from other instances, for example, a policy module, and distribute information to other instances, like other agents or an SAaaS event processing system. The "central" event processing system gets itself implemented as an agent, which can be scaled and distributed over multiple VMs.

Incident detection in cloud environments is a non-trivial task due to a cloud's characteristics. In particular, the frequently changing infrastructure poses a big challenge to the definition of "normal cloud usage behaviour". It is therefore important to have a high number of sensors capturing simple events. Simple events need to be preprocessed and abstracted to complex events, reducing the possibility "of event storms". Combined with knowledge about business process flows (see Sect. 4.5.2), it will be possible to detect security incidents in a frequently changing infrastructure while keeping the overall message count and therefore the resulting network load low. Furthermore, agents can also be added, removed or reconfigured during runtime, without altering other components. Thus, the amount of monitoring entities (e.g. network connections of a VM, running processes, storage access) of a cloud instance can be changed without restarting the incident detection system. Agents can also be updated to new versions (as long as their interface remains unchanged) without restarting the whole incident detection system or other already deployed SAaaS agents. By ordering agents in a hierarchical structure (multiple simple agents can exist on the same platform), preprocessing of simple events can reduce load on the cloud management network. Furthermore, this makes the system more scalable by reducing data sent to upper system layers. This procedure is introduced and used in [39].

Combining events from system agents (VM agent, host agent – see Fig. 4.4) and infrastructure monitoring agents (network agent, firewall agent), incident detection is not limited to either host- or network-based sensors which is especially important for the characteristics of cloud environments. Furthermore, using autonomous agents has advantages in case of a system failure. Agents can monitor the existence of co-located agents. If an agent stops for whatever reason, this does not stay undetected. Concepts of asymmetric cryptography or Trusted Platform Module (TPM) technology can be used to guarantee the integrity of a (re-)started agent. If an agent stops, damage is restricted to this single agent or a small subset of agents which are requiring information from this agent.

4.5.2 The Glue: Security Service-level agreements

Security service-level agreements (SSLAs) are service-level agreements with a strong emphasis on monitoring security service objectives. A customer's cloud instances always serve a certain business case. Therefore, security service-level agreements for business process flows are important. Consider the example depicted in Fig. 4.5: Given a typical

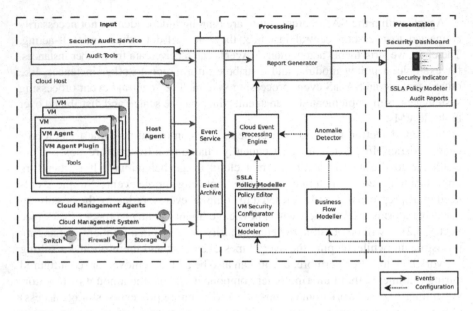

Fig. 4.4 Security Audit as a Service event processing sequence

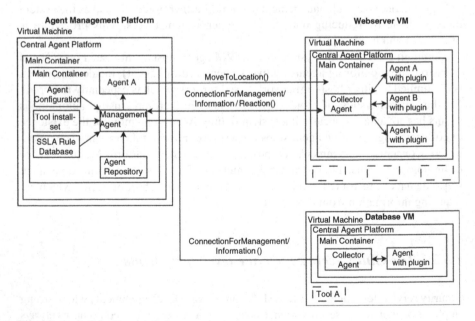

Fig. 4.5 Basic SAaaS agent design

Web application system consisting of a load balancer, a Web server and a database back end deployed exclusively at three VMs in a cloud. All VMs are equipped with SAaaS agents. The user's administrator installs each VM with its necessary software, for example, Apache Web server, Tomcat load balancer and MySQL database. After the functional configuration is finished, the monitoring configuration gets designed based upon security service-level agreements. These can be technical rules, like allowed user logins, allowed network protocols and connections between VMs or that the Web server configuration is finished and an alarm should be raised if changes to its config files are detected.

SSLA rules consider the system's business flow. For example, if a request (using the allowed protocols) to the load balancer or database VM without a preceding service request to the Web application is detected, this is rated as an abnormal behaviour which does not occur in a valid business process flow. Therefore, a monitoring event should be generated. SSLAs need to be modelled by the user, who is aware of its cloud instances and the underlying business process. Hence, a formal modelling description for cloud environments needs to be developed. A first high-level example of a modelled SSLA is shown in Listing 4.1.

Lines 4–19 describe possible technical rules, while lines 21–26 model a business flow rule. In this case, a request to the Web server is only valid if a preceding request was sent from the load balancer. Line 24 names the SAaaS agents, which need to be contacted to resolve this constraint. Line 31 defines which action to take in case of a detected monitoring event. This is a first example – the complete definition of the SSLA modelling language is future work. To reduce complexity, a graphical policy modeller needs to be developed. For typical cloud usage components, for example, a Web server, profiles will be prepared, which model necessary dependencies, like config directory, associated processes or used network protocols.

4.5.3 SAaaS Architecture

Figure 4.4 gives a high-level overview of the SAaaS architecture and how events are generated, preprocessed, combined and forwarded. It can be divided into three logical layers: input, processing and output.

Input Layer: The SAaaS architecture gets its monitoring information from distributed agents, which are positioned at key points of the cloud's infrastructure to detect abnormal activities in a cloud environment. Possible key points are running VMs of cloud users, the VM hosting systems, data storage, network transition points like virtual switches, hardware switches, firewalls and in particular the cloud management system. A VM agent integrates several monitoring and policy-enforcing tools. Therefore, it loads the necessary VM agent plug-ins to interact with standalone tools like the process monitor, an intrusion detection system or an antivirus. It gets installed on a VM as well as on a cloud host. A logging component records the chronological sequence of detected events building audit trails.

```
1 <system>
2 <id>webserver1</id>
3
4 <runningprocesses1>
5 <processname>/usr/sbin/apache</processname>
6 <allowedprotocol1>
7 <protname>tcp</protname>
8 <srcport>80</srcport>
9 <srcsystem>IPofloadbalancer</srcsystem>
10 ...
11 </allowedprotocol1>
12 ...
13 </runningprocesses1>
14
15 <freezedconfigdir1>
16 <path>/etc/apache2</path>
17 <allowedaccesstype>readonly</
allowedaccesstype>
18 <allowedaccesser>runningprocesses1</
allowedaccesser>
19 </freezedconfigdir1>
20
21 <request1>
22 <name>Webapplicationrequest</name>
23 <precedingconstraint>loadbalancersentrequest</
precedingconstraint>
24 <constraintvalidator>SAaaSloadbalanceragent<
constraintvalidator>
25 ...
26 </request1>
27
28 <incidentalarm1>
29 <name>Webserverconfigchanged<name>
30 <origin>freezedconfigdir1</origin>
31 <action>email1</action>
32 ...
33 </incidentalarm1>
34 ...
35 </system>
```

Listing 4.1 SSLA example

Processing Layer: Each SAaaS agent receives security policies from the SSLA policy modeller component. Through security policies, each agent gets a rule set (its intelligence) specifying actions in case of a specific occurrence (e.g. modification of a config file which is considered "final" as no modifications are applied during "normal" operations). Thus, every occurrence gets first preprocessed by an agent, which reduces communication between VM agents and the cloud management agent. Self-learning algorithms will be evaluated to improve an agent's intelligence. The security service-level agreements policy modeller consists of a policy editor, a

VM security configurator and a semantic correlation modeller to enable cloud user to design SSLA and security policies. An example for an SSLA rule could be: "In case of a successfully detected rootkit attack on a VM running on the same cloud as a user's VM, the user VM gets moved to a different host to minimize risk of further damage". Whereas a security policy could state: "In case a modification attempt of a file within/etc./php5/gets detected, deny it and send an email to the cloud administrator". Security policies get sent from the security audit service to the corresponding agents. Using the monitoring information of the distributed agents in combination with the SSLAs, a cloud behaviour model is built up for every cloud user. SSLAs are also used as input for the cloud management agent to detect user overlapping audit events. Forwarded higher-level events are processed by a complex event processing engine. It is also fed with the modelled business flows from the Business Flow Modeller to aggregate information and detect behaviour anomalies. Countermeasures can then be applied to detect early and prohibit security or privacy breaches. The Report Generator conditions events and corresponding security status as well as auditing report results in a human friendly presentation.

Presentation layer: As a single interaction point to cloud users, the security dashboard provides usage profiles, trends, anomalies and cloud instances' security status (e.g. patch level). Information is organized in different granular hierarchies depending on the information detail necessary. At the highest level, a simple three-colour indicator informs about a user's cloud services overall status. Communication between distributed agents and the security dashboard is handled by an event service. Events will use a standardized message format which is not yet defined. Our first prototype implements the Intrusion Detection Message Exchange Format (IDMEF). Events are also stored in an Event Archive.

4.5.4 SAaaS Agent Prototype

For the SAaaS architecture, we evaluated existing agent frameworks with the following requirements:

- Agents can be deployed, moved and updated during runtime.
- Agent performance.
- Open-source software platform.
- Documentation and community support.

As a result, we chose the Java Agent Development Platform (JADE), which enables the implementation of multi-agent systems and complies with FIPA1 specifications. Furthermore, it already provides a user interface, which alleviates agent creation, deployment and testing. Figure 4.5 illustrates a basic agent architecture we already assumed in the SAaaS use case discussed in Sect. 4.4. It shows three SAaaS VM agents. Agents live in an agent platform, which provides them with basic services such as message delivery. A platform is composed of one or more containers. Containers can be executed on different hosts thus achieving a distributed platform. Each container can contain zero or more agents [42]. To provide monitoring

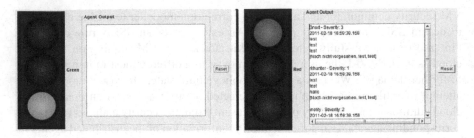

Fig. 4.6 Security dashboard prototype

functionality, a VM agent interacts through agent plug-in with stand-alone tools, like process monitor, intrusion detection system or antivirus scanner, as depicted in Fig. 4.5. To harness the potential of cloud computing, an agent can be deployed to a VM on demand according to the SSLA policies a user defines. Different agents based on modelled business processes are stored within an agent repository. To be able to move a JADE agent to a running cloud instance, the Inter-Platform Mobility Service (IPMS) by Cucurull et al. [43] was integrated. This supports the presented advantage of deploying agents on demand if a designed business process flow was started – although this implementation has been reserved for future work.

As a first prototype, a two-layered agent platform was developed, consisting of a VM agent running inside a VM and a cloud management agent running as a service at a dedicated VM feeding information to a security dashboard. The test bed is HFU's research cloud environment CloudIA [44], which is based on OpenNebula. Since all VMs in the test bed are Linux based, only open-source Linux tools were considered during the research. Two tool-agent notification mechanisms were implemented:

(a) The tool sends agent-compatible events directly to the agent plug-in.
(b) The tool writes events in a proprietary format into a log file, which gets parsed by an agent plug-in.

As for mechanism (a), the file system changes monitoring tool inotify was used, whereas for mechanism (b) fail2ban, an intrusion prevention framework was chosen. For demo purposes, a simple Web front end was written, which offers to launch several attack scenarios on a VM. Before/after tests were performed to validate that an attack was detected and (depending on the plug-in configuration) prohibited. A prototype version of the security dashboard, depicted in Fig. 4.6, informs about occurring events. Figure 4.6 [left side] shows the VM's state before an attack. After launching an attack, the security dashboard indicator light changes its colour as defined in a simple severity matrix and gives short information about the monitored event (Fig. 4.6 [right side]).

In this section, the Security Audit as a Service (SAaaS) architecture was presented as a possible architecture to mitigate cloud-specific security problems. It was shown how the usage of autonomous agents and security service-level agreements provide cloud user and cloud provider with a transparent monitoring and incident detection system, which considers cloud-specific attributes. An early prototype of a JADE cloud agent was shown.

4.6 Evaluation

This section will evaluate the presented SAaaS architecture against specific cloud security problems as described in Sect. 4.2.

In regard to the introduced cloud security problems, mainly "B3 Missing Monitoring", the following advantages can be achieved by the SAaaS architecture:

- Message reduction by business process awareness
- Cloud-wide incident detection
- Detection of cloud misusage and attacks against cloud scalability
- Better cloud monitoring and audit

We will now consider each of these in turn.

4.6.1 Message Reduction by Business Process Awareness

Traditional IDS would produce too many messages when monitoring a cloud environment due to a lack of flexibility regarding frequent infrastructure changes. With SAaaS, in case a monitoring event is produced, it first will be processed by the agent, which is initiating the event. Afterwards, this agent informs all other agents which are also involved in the current business case (agent group). This is important to reduce the overall messages sent to the cloud event processing system especially in large cloud computing environments. Imagine an expected high load on the load balancer can result in a high number of events produced by the load balancer's agent. Since the events are expected, they again result in a high load on the Web server and the database whose corresponding agents could produce again a high number of events. By informing the business flow participating agents (Web server agent, database agent) with an abstract message (e.g. 100 db access events expected), false-positive event messages will be prevented. For cloud audit, this can also be a possibility to prevent data storms by using special audit-aware agents.

4.6.2 Cloud-Wide Incident Detection

With the presented SAaaS, the security state of the entire cloud environment, especially the cloud management system, will be monitored. Of interest are customer data and data path, administrative actions concerning customer's instances (e.g. patch management), incident response time, backup restore time, etc. This way, cross-customer monitoring is used by the cloud provider as well as third parties, like a security service provider, to ensure the overall cloud security state. Standardized interfaces enable security audits of a cloud infrastructure, which can lead to a cloud security certification. This addresses cloud security problem B3, missing monitoring in cloud infrastructure, and helps bring assessable security features to cloud computing.

4.6.3   Detection of Cloud Misusage and Attacks Against Cloud Scalability

Several incidents of misused cloud resources were reported during the last few years, as described in Sect. 4.1. Mostly cloud instances of customers were infected and used in a botnet to send spam messages or distribute malicious code. Effective cloud monitoring needs to be aware of business processes to detect an event of possible misuse of cloud scalability. With the introduced SAaaS architecture, VM agents monitor cloud instances' behaviour. If an instance gets compromised to serve a hacker's needs, this leads to an abnormal behaviour, detected by the monitoring system. Furthermore, since SAaaS agents are business flow aware by the SSLA rules, attack-driven IaaS up- or downscaling can be detected and prevented. This addresses cloud security problems B2, abuse and nefarious use of cloud resource, and B5, missing monitoring of cloud scalability.

4.6.4   Better Cloud Monitoring and Audit

Cloud customers so far have just limited possibilities to monitor their cloud instances. This leads to a problem of lack of trust in cloud computing technology and provider. In a SAaaS-enabled cloud infrastructure, user VMs are equipped with agents. Users define security service-level agreements, describing which VM components are to be monitored, which behaviour of this VM is considered "normal" and how to alert in case of system security suspicion, for example, an open network connection without a preceding legitimate request. The status gets conditioned in a user-friendly format accessible easily through a Web portal – the SAaaS security dashboard. Continuous monitoring creates transparency about the security status of a user's cloud instances, hence increasing the user's trust into the cloud environment. Furthermore, with SAaaS agents monitoring at key points in the infrastructure of a cloud, customers can be warned if a security problem occurred in their cloud instances environment, for instance, in a VM which is running on the same cloud host. The user can model with the SSLAs in a fine-grained manner if they want to take a certain risk or if further actions are required to protect their instance. This could result, for example, in the migration of a VM to a different cloud host or a shutdown of the VM and the start of a twin VM at a different cloud data centre.

Administrative action done by a cloud provider's staff to cloud instance hosting systems or customer's cloud instances misusing their rights given by the hypervisors can also be detected by intelligent interconnection of different SAaaS agents. Fine-grained modelled SSLAs combined with SAaaS host agents could warn a user if a cloud provider neglects its duty of patch management to software running on cloud hosts, for example, hypervisor software. This addresses the cloud security problems A1, misuse of administrator rights; A2, missing transparency of applied security measure; and B1, intransparent data location. It can also mitigate problem A4, shared technology issues, and A5, data life cycle in case of provider switch or termination.

Continuous monitoring and the standardized reporting of the SAaaS agents described in the cloud audit use cases in Sects. 4.4.1 and 4.4.2 help customers to ensure the compliance of IT security best practices and help them to fulfil their responsibility to data protection laws. Continuous monitoring also helps cloud provider to prove compliance to IT security best practices and laws to customers and third-party IT security service providers. This is necessary for IT forensics if a security incident need to be tracked over time over multiple cloud instances or cloud hosts. This could lead to a possible "cloud security certification", which still needs to be defined by security experts, governments and industry. This addresses cloud security problem B3, missing monitoring in cloud infrastructure. It also mitigates problem A4, shared technologies issues.

This section showed how the presented SAaaS architecture helps to address the specific cloud security problems A1, misuse of administrator rights; A2, missing transparency of applied security measures; A4, shared technology issues; A5, data life cycle in case of provider switch or termination; B2, abuse and nefarious use of cloud resource; B3, missing monitoring in cloud infrastructure; and B5, missing monitoring of cloud scalability.

4.7 Conclusion and Future Work

Before concluding this chapter, a quick look into future work of cloud computing audits is given. The "Recommended reading" section lists more literature which discusses selected topics of this chapter in more detail.

4.7.1 Future Work in Cloud Audits

As for future work, more results from cloud computing security research needs to go into proposals for cloud-specific security standards. Germany's Federal Office for Information Security approaches this issue with their first guideline of security recommendations for cloud computing service providers [16]. But attacks to the cloud management system are not covered by this at all. As for the presented SAaaS architecture, we identified the following tasks: comprehensive research in anomaly detection algorithms, comprehensive research in complex event processing and the development of the SSLA policy modeller.

4.7.2 Conclusion

It has been shown that with cloud computing, there are amplified cloud security problems and specific cloud security problems which need to addressed, if an IT security audit of a cloud environment is used to prove compliance to IT security best practices and data protection laws. Different IT security audit types were presented, and it was discussed how classic audits need to change to consider the special characteristics of cloud computing environments. Important challenges for cloud audits and the main questions which a cloud audit needs to answer were presented. Existing IT security audit industry standards for traditional data centres were introduced and supplemented by the new emerging standards for cloud environments. After discussing possible use cases for audit from and for cloud environments, a first approach to mitigate the presented problems was given with the Security Audit as a Service (SAaaS) architecture. SAaaS tries to enable mutual trust and mutual auditability of cloud providers and cloud customers. An evaluation was given in which the introduced cloud specific security problems are addressed by the SAaaS architecture.

Acknowledgement This research is supported by the German Federal Ministry of Education and Research (BMBF) through the research grant number 01BY1116.

References

1. Mell, P., Grance, T.: Effectively and securely using the cloud computing paradigm. US National Institute of Standards and Technology, Tech. Rep., 2009. [Online]. Available: http://csrc.nist.gov/groups/SNS/cloud-computing
2. Spring, J.: Monitoring cloud computing by layer, Part 1. Secur. Privacy IEEE **9**(2), 66–68 (2011). March–April 2011
3. Mather, T., Kumaraswamy, S., Latif, S.: Cloud Security and Privacy: An Enterprise Perspective on Risks and Compliance. O'Reilly Media, Sebastopol, CA (2009)
4. Brunette, G., Mogull, R.: Security guidance for critical areas of focus in Cloud Computing V2. 1. CSA (Cloud Security Alliance), USA. Online: http://www.cloudsecurityalliance.org/guidance/csaguide.v2 (2009)
5. Dölitzscher, F., Reich, C., Sulistio, A.: Designing cloud services adhering to government privacy laws. In: Proceedings of 10th IEEE International Conference on Computer and Information Technology (CIT 2010), Bradford, West Yorkshire, UK, 29 June–1 July 2010, pp. 930–935 (2010)

6. Chung, M.: Audit in the cloud. http://www.slideshare.net/eburon/audit-in-the-cloud-kpmg. KPMG (2010)
7. Sotto, L.J., Treacy, B.C., McLellan, M.L.: Privacy and data security risks in cloud computing. Electron. Comm. Law Rep. Feb 2010 (2010)
8. Chen, Y., Paxson, V., Katz, R.H.: What's new about cloud computing security? EECS Department, University of California, Berkeley, Tech. Rep. UCB/EECS-2010-5, Jan 2010 (2010)
9. European Network and Information Security Agency: Cloud Computing Security Risk Assessment. Tech. Rep., Nov 2009 (2009)
10. Grobauer, B., Walloschek, T., Stocker, E.: Understanding cloud computing vulnerabilities. Secur. Privacy IEEE **9**(2), 50–57 (2011). March–April 2011
11. Liebermann Software: 2011 Survey of IT Professionals Password Practices and Outcomes. Tech. Rep., 2011 (2011)
12. Amazon Web Services: AWS achieves PCI DSS level 1 compliance and ISO 27001 certification. http://aws.amazon.com/de/about-aws/newsletters/2010/12/15/december-2010—pci-compliance-and-iso27001-certification//187-6806868-8856222 (2010, Dec) [Online]
13. Kortchinsky, K.: Cloudburst. Tech. Rep., June 2009. [Online]. Available: http://www.blackhat.com/presentations/bh-usa-09/KORTCHINSKY/BHUSA09-Kortchinsky-Cloudburst-PAPER.pdf (2009)
14. Rutkowska, J.: Xen owning trilogy: code, demos and q35 attack details. Sept 2008. [Online]. Available: http://theinvisiblethings.blogspot.com/2008/09/xen-0wning-trilogy-code-demos-and-q35.html (2008)
15. Cloud Security Alliance: Top Threats to Cloud Computing V1.0. [Online]. Available: https://cloudsecurityalliance.org/topthreats.html (2010)
16. Federal Office for Information Security: Security recommendations for cloud computing provider. Tech. Rep., 2011 (2011)
17. German Parliament: German Data Protection Act. Deutscher Taschenbuch Verlag, Munich (2010). ISBN: 3406561632
18. ComputerworldUK: Law Enforcement Agencies Access Rights to Your Cloud Data. http://blogs.computerworlduk.com/cloud-vision/2011/07/law-enforcement-agencies-access-rights-to-your-cloud-data/index.htm (2011, July)
19. Spafford, E.H., Zamboni, D.: Intrusion detection using autonomous agents. Comput. Netw. **34**(4), 547–570 (2000) (Recent Advances in Intrusion Detection Systems)
20. Ries, T., Fusenig, V., Vilbois, C., Engel, T.: Verification of data location in cloud networking, In: 2011 Fourth IEEE International Conference on Utility and Cloud Computing (UCC), Melbourne, Australia, Dec 2011. pp. 439–444
21. Massonet, P., Naqvi, S., Ponsard, C., Latanicki, J., Rochwerger, B., Villari, M.: A monitoring and audit logging architecture for data location compliance in federated cloud infrastructures. In: 2011 IEEE International Symposium on Parallel and Distributed Processing Workshops and PhD Forum (IPDPSW), Anchorage, Alaska, May 2011, pp. 1510–1517
22. Spring, J.: Monitoring cloud computing by layer, part 2. Secur. Privacy IEEE **9**(3), 52–55 (2011). May–June
23. Tancock, D., Pearson, S., Charlesworth, A.: A privacy impact assessment tool for cloud computing. In: 2010 IEEE Second International Conference on Cloud Computing Technology and Science (CloudCom), Indianapolis, IN, 30 Nov–3 Dec 2010, pp. 667–676
24. Wang, C., Wang, Q., Ren, K., Lou, W.: Privacy-preserving public auditing for data storage security in cloud computing. In: INFOCOM, 2010 Proceedings IEEE, San Diego, CA, March 2010, pp. 1–9
25. Zhu, Y., Ahn, G., Hu, H., Yau, S., An, H., Chen, S.: Dynamic audit services for outsourced storages in clouds. IEEE Trans. Serv. Comput. **99**, 1 (2011)
26. Office of Government Commerce: Service Operation Book (Itil). The Stationery Office, London (2007). No. 978-0113310463
27. American Institute of Certified Public Accountants: The SSAE16 Auditing Standard. http://www.ssae-16.com

28. Vaquero, L., Rodero-Merino, L., Morán, D.: Locking the sky: a survey on IAAS cloud security. Computing **91**, 93–118 (2011)
29. Sinclair, J.: Cloud Compliance Auditing – Closer 2011. SAP Research. http://www.slideshare. net/jonathansinclair86/closer-2011 (2011, May)
30. Sinclair, J.: Cloud Auditing. SAP Research. http://www.slideshare.net/jonathansinclair86/ cloud-auditing (2010, Oct)
31. Lundin, M.: Industry issues and standards – effectively addressing compliance requirements. *ISACA San Francisco Chapter, Consumer Information Protection Event* (2009, April)
32. A6: Cloudaudit. http://http://cloudaudit.org/ (2011)
33. EuroCloud Deutschland_eco e.V.: Eurocloud Star Audit SAAS Certificate. http://http://www. saas-audit.de (2011, Oct)
34. Cloud Security Alliance: Cloud Security Control Matrix: https://cloudsecurityalliance.org/ research/initiatives/cloud-controls-matrix/ (2011, Oct)
35. EuroCloud Deutschland_eco e.V.: Eurocloud Quick Reference. http://www.saas-audit. de/files/2011/04/110223-Quick_Reference_en.pdf (2011, Oct)
36. eEye: Retina Cloud. http://www.eeye.com/products/retina/cloud (2011)
37. Secpoint: Cloud Penetrator. http://www.secpoint.com/cloud-penetrator-web-vulnerability- scanner.html (2011)
38. Kyplex; Website Security and Anti Virus Scanner. http://www.securitywizardry.com/index. php/products/scanning-products/website-scanners/kyplex-website-antivirus.html (2011)
39. Youseff, L., Butrico, M., Da Silva, D.: Toward a unified ontology of cloud computing. In: Grid Computing Environments Workshop, 2008. GCE'08, Austin, TX, Nov 2008, pp. 1–10 (2008)
40. Doelitzscher, F., Reich, C., Knahl, M., Clarke, N.: An autonomous agent based incident detection system for cloud environments. In: Proceedings of 3rd IEEE International Conference on Cloud Computing Technology and Science (IEEE CloudCom 2011), Athens, Greece, 29 Nov–1 Dec (2011)
41. Bradshaw, J.M.: An Introduction to Software Agents. MIT Press, Cambridge, MA (1997)
42. Grimshaw, D.: JADE Administration Tutorial. http://jade.tilab.com/doc/tutorials/JADEAdmin. (2011, July)
43. Cucurull, J., Martí, R., Navarro-Arribas, G., Robles, S., Overeinder, B., Borrell, J.: Agent mobility architecture based on IEEE-FIPA standards. Comput. Commun. **32**(4), 712–729 (2009)
44. Sulistio, A., Reich, C., Dölitzscher, F.: Cloud infrastructure & applications – CloudIA. In: Proceedings of the 1st International Conference on Cloud Computing (CloudCom'09), Beijing, China, December (2009)
45. Halpert, B.: Auditing Cloud Computing: A Security and Privacy Guide. Wiley, Hoboken (2011). No. 978-0470874745

Recommended Reading

Security Issues of Cloud Computing

The most comprehensive survey about current literature addressing cloud security issues is given by Vaquero et al. in "Locking the sky" [28]. It categorizes the most widely accepted cloud security issues into three different domains of the Infrastructure as a Service (IaaS) model: machine virtualization, network virtualization and physical domain. It also proposes prevention frameworks on several architectural levels to address the identified issues.

Auditing Cloud Infrastructures

John Spring discusses in *Monitoring Cloud Computing by Layer, Part 1* [2] *and Part 2* [22] what a cloud monitoring system should cover to respect cloud-specific attributes.

Wang et al. present in their paper "Privacy-preserving public auditing for data storage security" [24] a system to audit integrity and security of public data cloud storage. Their solution allows a third-party auditor (TPA) to be able to efficiently audit the cloud data storage without demanding the local copy of data and introduce no additional on-line burden to the cloud user. Therefore, they combine the public key-based homomorphic authenticator with random masking to achieve a privacy-preserving public cloud data auditing system.

Auditing Cloud Computing: A Security and Privacy Guide [45] is a collection of papers which cover the topics of governance, audit, legal and service delivery of cloud infrastructures.

Part III
Security and Integrity

Chapter 5
Security Infrastructure for Dynamically Provisioned Cloud Infrastructure Services

Yuri Demchenko, Canh Ngo, Cees de Laat, Diego R. Lopez, Antonio Morales, and Joan A. García-Espín

Abstract This chapter discusses conceptual issues, basic requirements and practical suggestions for designing dynamically configured security infrastructure provisioned on demand as part of the cloud-based infrastructure. This chapter describes general use cases for provisioning cloud infrastructure services and the proposed architectural framework that provides a basis for defining the security infrastructure requirements. The proposed security services lifecycle management (SSLM) model addresses specific on-demand infrastructure service provisioning security problems that can be solved by introducing special security mechanisms to allow security services synchronisation and their binding to the virtualisation platforms' run-time environment. This chapter describes the proposed dynamically provisioned access control infrastructure (DACI) architecture and defines the necessary security mechanisms to ensure consistent security services operation in the provisioned virtual infrastructure. In particular, this chapter discusses the design and use of a security token service for federated access control and security context management in the generically multi-domain and multi-provider cloud environment.

Keywords Access control • Cloud infrastructure • DACI • IaaS • Security • Trusted computing

Y. Demchenko (✉) • C. Ngo • C. de Laat
University of Amsterdam, Amsterdam, The Netherlands
e-mail: mailto:y.demchenko@uva.nl

D.R. Lopez
Telefonica I+D, Madrid, Spain

A. Morales
RedIRIS, Madrid, Spain

J.A. García-Espín
I2CAT Foundation, Barcelona, Spain

S. Pearson and G. Yee (eds.), *Privacy and Security for Cloud Computing*, 167
Computer Communications and Networks, DOI 10.1007/978-1-4471-4189-1_5,
© Springer-Verlag London 2013

5.1 Introduction

Cloud technologies [1, 2] are emerging as a new way of provisioning virtualised computing and network infrastructure services on demand for collaborative projects and groups. Security in provisioning virtual infrastructure services should address two general aspects: supporting the secure operation of the provisioning infrastructure and provisioning a dynamic access control infrastructure as part of the provisioned on-demand virtual infrastructure.

The current cloud security model is based on the assumption that the user/customer should trust the cloud service provider (CSP). This is governed by the service level agreement (SLA) that in general defines mutual provider and user expectations and obligations. However, such an approach addresses only the first part of the problem and does not scale well with the potential need to combine cloud-based services from multiple providers when building complex infrastructures.

Cloud providers are investing significant efforts and costs into making their own infrastructures secure and achieving compliance with the existing industry security services management standards (e.g. Amazon Cloud recently achieved Payment Card Industry Data Security Standard (PCI DSS) compliance certification and Microsoft Azure Cloud claims compliance with ISO27001 security standards). However, overall security of cloud-based applications and services will depend on two other factors: security services implementation in user applications and binding between virtualised services and cloud virtualisation platforms. Advanced security services and fine-grained access control cannot be achieved without deeper integration with the cloud virtualisation platform and incumbent security services, which in its turn can be achieved with open and well-defined cloud IaaS platform architectures.

This chapter presents recent results of the ongoing research on developing architecture and framework for dynamically provisioned security services as part of the provisioned on-demand cloud-based infrastructure services. This chapter extends earlier published works by authors with the recent results and implementation experiences.

This chapter analyses the basic use cases and proposes an abstract model for on-demand infrastructure services provisioning. Section 5.3 provides a short description of the architectural framework for on-demand infrastructure services provisioning proposed in earlier authors' work [3, 4]. It is used as a basis to define the general security requirements to the security infrastructure. Section 5.4 discusses conceptual issues, basic requirements, proposed architectural solutions, supporting security mechanisms and practical suggestions for provisioning dynamically configured access control services as part of the provisioned on-demand cloud-based infrastructure services. This section summarises the earlier works by authors [5–7] and describes the proposed dynamically provisioned access control infrastructure (DACI). Section 5.5 describes the security token service that allows federated access control to distributed multi-domain cloud resources.

Consistent security services design, deployment and operation require continuous security context management during the whole security services lifecycle, which is aligned to the main provisioned services lifecycle. The proposed security services lifecycle management (SSLM) model addresses specific on-demand infrastructure service provisioning security problems that can be solved by introducing a special security mechanism to allow synchronisation of security services and their binding to virtualisation platform and run-time environment. This chapter discusses how these security mechanisms can be implemented by using Trusted Computing Group Architecture (TCG Architecture) and the functionality of the Trusted Platform Module (TPM) that is currently available in many computer platforms and supported by most VM management platforms. Section 5.4.5 describes the proposed security bootstrapping protocol that uses TPM functionality and can be integrated with DACI.

The practical implementation of DACI reveals a wide spectrum of problems related to distributed access control, policy and related security context management. This chapter discusses important security services and mechanisms that ensure consistency of the provisioned security infrastructure and its integration with user applications: authorisation tokens used for provisioning and authorisation session management and for security context exchange between infrastructure services and providers (Sect. 5.4.6) and the standard-based security token service as an important mechanism for inter-domain access control and identity management (Sect. 5.5).

5.2 Background

5.2.1 Cloud Computing as an Emerging Provisioning Model for Complex Infrastructure Services

Modern e-Science and high-technology industry require high-performance infrastructure to handle large volumes of data and support complex scientific applications and technological processes. Dynamicity of projects and collaborative group environment require that such infrastructure is provisioned on demand and capable of dynamic (re-)configuration. A large amount of currently available e-Science/research infrastructures is available on the grid, which in the case of Europe is coordinated by the European Grid Initiative (EGI) [8]. Future research infrastructures will inevitably evolve in the direction of using cloud resources and will combine both grid and cloud resources.

Currently large grid projects and cloud computing providers use their own dedicated network infrastructure that can handle the required data throughput but typically are over-provisioned. Their network infrastructure and security model are commonly based on the traditional VPN model that spreads worldwide, creates distributed environments for running their own geographically distributed services (like Google and Amazon) and provides localised access for users and local providers. Their service delivery business model and consequently security model are typically based and governed by a service level agreement (SLA) that in general defines mutual provider and user expectations and obligations.

Recently, cloud technologies [1, 2, 9] are emerging as infrastructure services for provisioning computing and storage resources and gradually evolving into general IT resources provisioning. Cloud computing can be considered as a natural evolution of grid computing technologies to more open infrastructure-based services. Cloud "elasticity", as recognised by researchers and technology practitioners, brings a positive paradigm shift in relation to the problem and the problem-solving infrastructure from sizing a problem to infrastructure to sizing infrastructure to the problem.

The current cloud services implement three basic service models: infrastructure as a service (IaaS), platform as a service (PaaS) and software as a service (SaaS). There are many examples of the latter two models, PaaS and SaaS, that are typically built using existing SOA (service-oriented architecture) [10] and Web Services or REST (representational state transfer) [11] technologies. However, the IaaS model, if intended to provision user or operator manageable infrastructure services, requires a new type of service delivery and operation framework that should also include security infrastructure integration with the user or enterprise legacy security infrastructure.

This chapter presents ongoing research aimed at developing an architectural framework that will address known problems in on-demand provisioning virtualised infrastructure services that may include both computing resources (computers and storage) and the transport network. The solutions for pooling, virtualising and provisioning computing resources are provided by current grid and cloud infrastructures. New solutions should allow the combination of IT and network resources, supporting abstraction, composition and delivery for individual collaborating user groups and applications.

5.2.2   General Use Case for Cloud-Based On-Demand Infrastructure Services Provisioning

One general use case for on-demand cloud-based infrastructure services provisioning can be considered: large project-oriented scientific infrastructure provisioning including dedicated transport network infrastructure. However, two different perspectives in developing infrastructure services can be considered – the users and application developers' perspective, on one side, and the providers' perspective, on the other side. Users are interested in uniform and simple access to resources and services that are exposed as cloud resources and can be easily integrated into the scientific or business workflow. Infrastructure providers are interested in infrastructure resource pooling and virtualisation to simplify their on-demand provisioning and extend their service offering and business model to virtual infrastructure provisioning.

Figure 5.1 illustrates the typical e-Science infrastructure that includes grid and cloud-based computing and storage resources, instruments, a control and monitoring

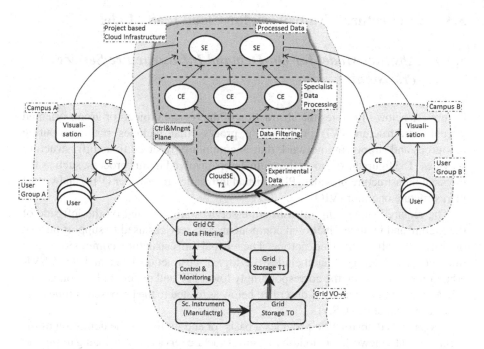

Fig. 5.1 Project-oriented collaborative infrastructure containing grid-based scientific instruments managed by grid VO-A, 2 campuses A and B, and cloud-based infrastructure provisioned on demand

system, a visualisation system and users represented by user clients. The diagram also reflects that there may be different types of connecting network links: high-speed and low-speed which both can be permanent for the project or provisioned on demand.

The figure also illustrates a typical use case when a high-performance infrastructure is used by two or more cooperative users/researcher groups in different locations. In order to fulfil their task (e.g. cooperative image processing and analysis), they require a number of resources and services to process raw data on distributed grid or cloud data centres, analyse intermediate data on specialist applications and finally deliver the result data to the users/scientists. This use case includes all basic components of the typical e-Science research process: data collection, initial data mining and filtering, analysis with special scientific applications and finally presentation and visualisation to the users.

With the growing complexity and dynamicity of collaborative projects and applications, they will require access to network control and management functions to optimise their performance and resources usage. Currently, the transport network, even if provided as a VPN, is set up statically or can only be reconfigured by a network engineer.

5.3   Architectural Framework for Cloud IaaS Model

5.3.1   Abstract Model for On-Demand Infrastructure Services Provisioning

Figure 5.2 below illustrates the abstraction of the typical project- or group-oriented virtual infrastructure (VI) provisioning process that includes both computing resources and supporting network that is commonly referred to as infrastructure services. The figure also shows the main actors involved in this process, such as the physical infrastructure provider (PIP), virtual infrastructure provider (VIP) and virtual infrastructure operator (VIO).

The required supporting infrastructure services are depicted on the left side of the picture and include functional components and services used to support normal operation of all mentioned actors. The virtual infrastructure composition and management (VICM) layer includes the logical abstraction layer and the VI/VR adaptation layer facing the correspondingly lower PIP and upper application layers. VICM-related functionality is described below as related to the proposed composable services architecture (CSA).

The proposed abstraction provides a basis for and motivates the definition of the architectural framework for cloud-based infrastructure services provisioning to support the main cloud IaaS features such as on-demand provisioning, elasticity, scalability, virtualisation, lifecycle management and combined compute and network resource

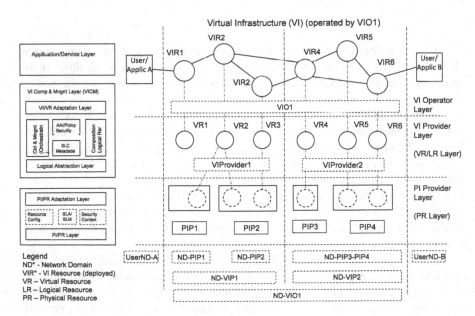

Fig. 5.2 Main actors, functional layers and processes in on-demand infrastructure services provisioning

provisioning. The proposed architectural framework comprises the following components discussed in this chapter:

- Infrastructure services modelling framework (ISMF)
- Composable services architecture (CSA)
- Service delivery framework (SDF)
- Dynamically provisioned security infrastructure that includes dynamically provisioned access control infrastructure (DACI) and related security services and mechanisms for inter-domain security context management

The proposed architecture is SOA (service-oriented architecture) [10] based upon and using the same basic operation principle as known and widely used SOA frameworks, which also provide a direct mapping to the possible VICM implementation platforms such as enterprise service bus (ESB) or the OSGi framework [12, 13].

The infrastructure provisioning process, also referred to as service delivery framework (SDF), is adopted from the TeleManagement Forum SDF [14, 15] with necessary extensions to allow dynamic services provisioning. It includes the following main stages: (1) an infrastructure creation request sent to VIO or VIP that may include both required resources and network infrastructure to support distributed target user groups and/or consuming applications, (2) infrastructure planning and advance reservation, (3) infrastructure deployment including services synchronisation and initiation, (4) an operation stage and (5) infrastructure decommissioning. The SDF combines in one provisioning workflow all processes that are run by different supporting systems and executed by different actors.

Physical resources (PR), including IT resources and network, are provided by physical infrastructure providers (PIP). In order to be included into VI composition and provisioning by the VIP, they need to be abstracted to logical resource (LR) that will undergo a number of abstract transformations possibly including interactive negotiation with the PIP. The composed VI needs to be deployed to the PIP which will create virtualised physical resources (VPR) that may be a part, a pool or a combination of the resources provided by PIP.

The deployment process includes distribution of common VI context, configuration of VPR at PIP, advance reservation and scheduling and virtualised infrastructure services synchronisation and initiation to make them available to application layer consumers.

The proposed abstract models allow outsourcing the provisioned VI operation to the VI operator (VIO) which is from the user/consumer point of view, providing valuable services of required resources consolidation – both IT and networks – and taking a burden of managing the provisioned services.

5.3.2 Dynamically Provisioned Cloud Security Infrastructure

The proposed architecture provides a basis and motivates development of the generalised framework for provisioning dynamic security infrastructure that includes

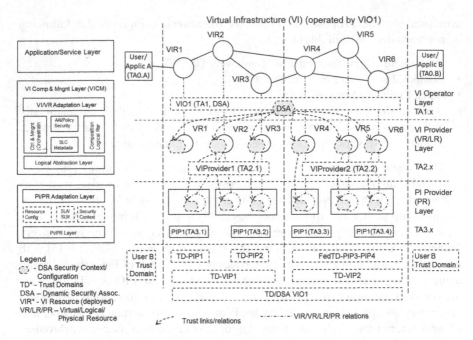

Fig. 5.3 Dynamic security association (*DSA*) to support security infrastructure provisioned on demand as a part of the overall infrastructure

the dynamically provisioned access control infrastructure (DACI), security services lifecycle management model (SSLM), common security services interface (CSSI) and related security services and mechanisms to ensure the consistency of the dynamically provisioned security services operation. The required security infrastructure should provide a common framework for operating security services at VIP and VIO layers and be integrated with the PIP and user legacy security services.

Figure 5.3 illustrates security and trust domain-related aspects in the infrastructure provisioning. It shows trust domains related to VIO, VIP and PIP that are defined by the corresponding trust anchors (TA) denoted as TA1, TA2 and TA3. The user (or requestor) trust domain is denoted as TA0 to indicate that the dynamically provisioned security infrastructure is bound to the requestor's security domain. The dynamic security association (DSA) is created as a part of the provisioning VI. It actually supports the VI security domain and is used to enable consistent operation of the VI security infrastructure.

5.3.3 Infrastructure Services Modelling Framework

The infrastructure services modelling framework (ISMF) provides a basis for virtualisation and management of infrastructure resources, including description, discovery, modelling, composition and monitoring. In this chapter, we mainly focus on the description of resources and the lifecycle of these resources. The described model in this section is being developed in the GEYSERS project [16].

5.3.3.1   Resource Modelling

The two main descriptive elements of the ISMF are the infrastructure topology and descriptions of resources in that topology. Besides these main ingredients, the ISMF also allows for describing QoS attributes of resources, energy-related attributes and attributes needed for access control.

The main requirement for the ISMF is that it should allow for describing physical resources (PR) as well as virtual resources (VR). Describing physical aspects of a resource means that a great level of detail in the description is required, while describing a virtual resource may require a more abstract view. Furthermore, the ISMF should allow for manipulation of resource descriptions such as partitioning and aggregation. Resources on which manipulation takes place and resources that are the outcome of manipulation are called logical resources (LR).

The ISMF is based on semantic Web technology. This means that the description format will be based on the Web Ontology Language (OWL) [17]. This approach ensures the ISMF is extensible and allows for easy abstraction of resources by adding or omitting resource description elements. Furthermore, this approach has enabled us to reuse the network description language [18] to describe infrastructure topologies.

5.3.3.2   Virtual Resource Lifecycle

Figure 5.4 illustrates relations between different resource presentations during the provisioning process stages that can also be defined as the virtual resource lifecycle.

The physical resource information is published by a PIP to the registry service serving VICM and VIP. This published information describes a PR. The published LR information presented in the commonly adopted form (using common data or semantic model) is then used by VICM/VIP composition service to create the requested infrastructure using a combination of (instantiated) virtual resources and interconnecting them with a network infrastructure. In its turn, the network can be composed of a few network segments run by different network providers.

It is important to mention that physical and virtual resources discussed here are in fact complex software-enabled systems with their own operating systems and security services. The VI provisioning process should support smooth integration into the common federated VI security infrastructure by allowing the definition of a common access control policy. Access decisions made at the VI level should be trusted and validated at the PIP level. This can be achieved by creating dynamic security associations during the provisioning process.

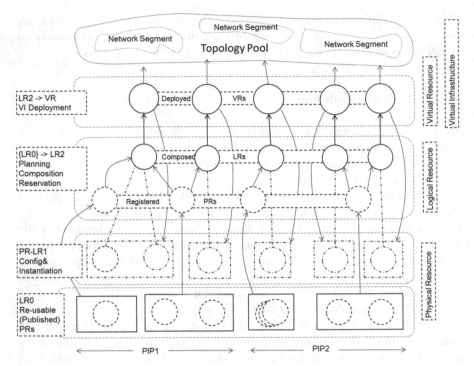

Fig. 5.4 Relation between different resource presentations in relation to different provisioning stages (Refer to Fig. 5.3 for the initial VI presentation)

5.3.4 Service Delivery Framework (SDF)

Service-oriented architecture (SOA) [10] allows for better integration between business process definition with higher abstraction description languages and dynamically composed services and provides a good basis for creating dynamically composable services that should also rely on the well-defined services lifecycle management (SLM) model. Most existing SLM frameworks and definitions are oriented on rather traditional human-driven services development and management. Dynamically provisioned and reconfigured services will require rethinking of existing models and proposing new security mechanisms at each stage of the typical provisioning process.

The service delivery framework (SDF) [14] proposed by the TeleManagement Forum (TMF) provides a common basis for defining software-enabled services [15] lifecycle management framework that includes both the service delivery stages and required supporting infrastructure services.

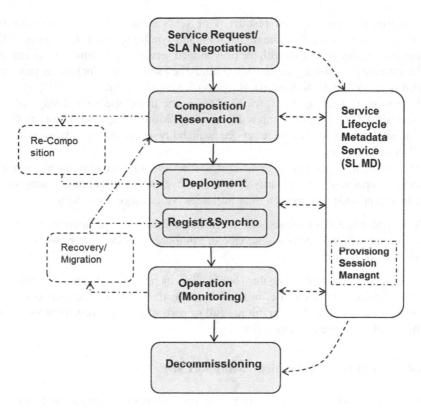

Fig. 5.5 On-demand composable services provisioning workflow

5.3.4.1 SDF Workflow

Figure 5.5 illustrates the main service provisioning or delivery stages:

Service request (including SLA negotiation). The SLA can describe QoS and security requirements of the negotiated infrastructure service along with information that facilitates authentication of service requests from users. This stage also includes generation of the global reservation ID (GRI) that will serve as a provisioning session identifier and will bind all other stages and related security context.

Composition/reservation, which also includes *reservation session binding* with GRI providing support for a complex reservation process in a potentially multi-domain multi-provider environment. This stage may require access control and SLA/policy enforcement.

Deployment, including services *registration and synchronisation*. The deployment stage begins after all component resources have been reserved and includes distribution of the common composed service context (including security context)

and binding the reserved resources or services to the GRI as a common provisioning session ID. The registration and synchronisation stage specifically targets possible scenarios with the provisioned services migration or re-planning. In a simple case, the registration stage binds the local resource or hosting platform run-time process ID to the GRI as a provisioning session ID.

*Operation (*including *monitoring).* This is the main operational stage of the provisioned on-demand composable services. Monitoring is an important functionality of this stage to ensure service availability and secure operation, including SLA enforcement.

Decommissioning. This stage ensures that all sessions are terminated, data are cleaned up and session security context is recycled. The decommissioning stage can also provide information to or initiate services usage accounting.

Two additional (sub-)stages can be initiated from the operation stage and/or based on the running composed service or component services state, such as their availability or failure:

Recomposition or replanning that should allow incremental infrastructure changes. *Recovery/migration* can be initiated by both the user and the provider. This process can use MD SLC to initiate full or partial resources re-synchronisation; it may also require recomposition.

5.3.4.2   Infrastructure Services to Support SDF

Implementation of the proposed SDF requires a number of special infrastructure support services (ISS) to support consistent (on-demand) provisioned services lifecycle management (similar to the above-mentioned TMF SDF) that can be implemented as a part of the CSA middleware.

The following services are essential to support consistent service lifecycle management:

- Service repository or service registry that supports services registration and discovery
- Service lifecycle metadata repository (MD SLC as shown in Fig. 5.3) that keeps the services metadata during the whole services lifecycle that include services properties, services configuration information and services state
- Service and resource monitor, an additional functionality that can be implemented as a part of the CSA middleware and that provides information about services and resources state and usage

5.3.5   The Composable Services Architecture

The infrastructure as a service provisioning involves dynamic creation of an infrastructure consisting of different types of resources together with necessary (infrastructure wide)

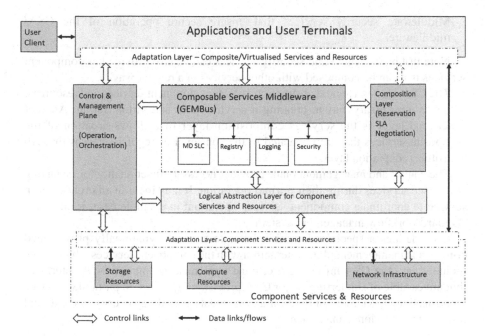

Fig. 5.6 Composable service architecture and main functional components

control and management planes, all provisioned on demand. The CSA proposed by authors [3] provides a framework for the design and operation of the composite/complex services provisioned on demand. It is based on component services virtualisation, which in turn is based on the logical abstraction of the (physical) component services and their dynamic composition. Composite services may also use the orchestration service provisioned as a CSA infrastructure service to operate composite service-specific workflow.

Figure 5.6 shows the major functional components of the proposed CSA and their interaction. The central part of the architecture is the CSA middleware that should ensure smooth service operation during all stages of the composable services lifecycle.

Composable services middleware (CSA-MW) provides a common interaction environment for both (physical) component services and complex/composite services, built of component services. Besides exchanging messages, CSA-MW also contains/provides a set of basic/general infrastructure services required to support reliable and secure (composite) services delivery and operation:

- Service lifecycle metadata service (MD SLC) that stores the services metadata, including the lifecycle stage, the service state and the provisioning session context.
- Registry service that contains information about all component services and dynamically created composite services. The registry should support automatic services registration.
- Logging service that can also be combined with the monitoring service.

- Middleware security services that ensure secure operation of the CSA/ middleware.

Note that both logging and security services can be also provided as component services that can be composed with other services in a regular way.

The CSA defines a logical abstraction layer for component services and resources, which is a necessary part in creating a services pool and virtualisation. Another functional layer is the services composition layer that allows creation of the composite services that are presented to the consumer as regular services through the (other) adaptation layer.

The control and management plane provides necessary functionality for managing composed services during their normal operation. It may include an orchestration service to coordinate component services operation; in a simple case, it may be a standard workflow management system.

CSA defines a special adaptation layer to support dynamically provisioned control and management plane interaction with the component services which, to be included into the CSA infrastructure, must implement adaptation layer interfaces that are capable of supporting major CSA provisioning stages, in particular, service identification, services configuration and metadata including security context, and provisioning session management.

5.3.6 GEMBus as a CSA Middleware Platform

The GÉANT Multi-domain service bus (GEMBus) is being developed as a middleware for composable services in the framework of the GÉANT3 project [19, 20]. GEMBus incorporates the SOA services management paradigm in on-demand service provisioning. GEMBus is built upon the industry accepted enterprise service bus (ESB) [12] and will extend it with the necessary functional components and design patterns to support multi-domain services and applications.

The goal of GEMBus is to establish seamless access to the network infrastructure and the services deployed upon it, using direct collaboration between network and applications, and therefore providing more complex community-oriented services through their composition.

Figure 5.7 illustrates the suggested GEMBus architecture. GEMBus infrastructure includes three main groups of functionalities:

- GEMBus messaging infrastructure (GMI) that includes, first of all, messaging backbone and other message handling supporting services such as message routing, configuration services, secure messaging and event handler/interceptors. The GMI is built on and extends the generic ESB functionality to support dynamically configured multi-domain services as defined by GEMBus.
- GEMBus infrastructure services that support reliable and secure composable services operation and the whole services provisioning process. These include such services as composition; orchestration; security, in particular, security token service; and also the important lifecycle metadata service, which is provided by the GEMBus environment/framework itself.

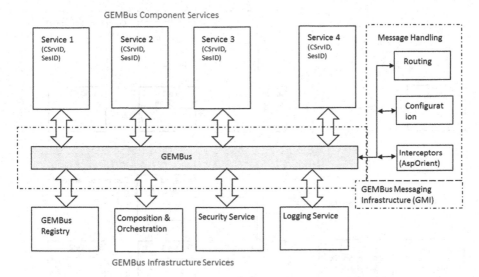

Fig. 5.7 GEMBus infrastructure, including component services, service template, infrastructure services and core message-processing services

- Component services, although typically provided by independent parties, need to implement special GEMBus adaptors or use special "plug-in sockets" that allow their integration into the GEMBus/CSA infrastructure.

The following issues have been identified to enable GEMBus operation in the multi-domain heterogeneous service provisioning environment:

- Service registries supporting service registration and discovery. Registries are considered as an important component to allow cross-domain heterogeneous service integration and metadata management during the whole services lifecycle.
- Security, access control and logging should provide consistent services and security context management during the whole provisioned services lifecycle.
- Service composition and orchestration models and mechanisms should allow integration with higher-level scientific or business workflows.
- Messaging infrastructure should support both SOAP-based and RESTful (conforming to a representational state transfer (REST) architecture) services [11].

The GEMBus and GMI, in particular, are built on top of the standard Apache/Fuse messaging infrastructure that includes the following components [21, 22]:

- Fuse Message Broker (Apache ActiveMQ) messaging processor
- Fuse Mediation Router (Apache Camel) normalised message router

The GEMBus services and applications can be deployed on standard Fuse or Apache ESB servers as component services that can be integrated with the standard OSGi [13] and Spring [23] compliant service development frameworks and platforms such as Fuse Services Framework/Apache CXF and Fuse ESB/Apache ServiceMix.

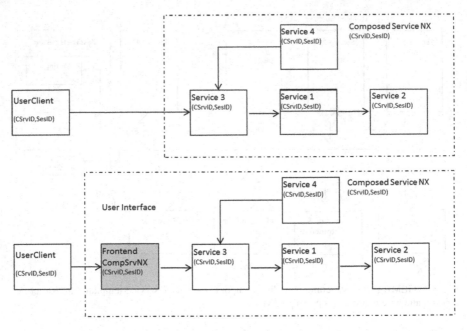

Fig. 5.8 Example of a composite service composed of services: service 1, service 2, service 3 and service 4

Figure 5.8 illustrates two examples of composite services that are composed of four component services. In the second case, the composite service contains a special front-end service that is created from the corresponding service template that should be available for specific kinds of applications. Examples of such service templates can be a user terminal (or rich user client) or a visualisation service. Requiring the GEMBus framework or toolkit to provide a number of typical service templates will provide more flexibility in delivery/provisioning composite services.

5.4 Cloud IaaS Security Infrastructure

5.4.1 General Requirements to Dynamically Provisioned Security Services

On-demand provisioning of cloud infrastructure services drives a paradigm change in security design and operation. Considering the evolutional relationship between grids and clouds, it is interesting to compare their security models. This is also important from the point of view that future e-Science infrastructures will integrate both grid-based core e-Science infrastructures and cloud-based infrastructures provisioned on demand. Grid security architecture is primarily based on the virtual organisations (VO) that are created by the cooperating organisations that share resources (which however remain in their ownership) based on mutual agreement between VO members and common VO security policy. In grids, VO actually acts as a federation of users and resources that enable federated access control based on the federated trust and security model [24, 25]. In general, the VO-based environment is considered as trusted.

In the clouds, data are sent to and processed in the environment that is not under the user or data owner control and potentially can be compromised either by cloud insiders or by other users sharing the same resource. Data/information must be secured during all processing stages – upload, process, store and stream/visualise. Policies and security requirements must be bound to the data, and there should be corresponding security mechanisms in place to enforce these policies.

The following problems/challenges arise from the cloud IaaS environment analysis for security services/infrastructure design:

- Data protection both stored and "on-wire" that includes, besides the traditional confidentiality, integrity and access control services, also data lifecycle management and synchronisation
- Access control infrastructure virtualisation and dynamic provisioning, including dynamic/automated policy composition or generation
- Security services lifecycle management, in particular, service-related metadata and properties, and their binding to the main services
- Security sessions and related security context management during the whole security services lifecycle, including binding security context to the provisioning session and virtualisation platform
- Trust and key management in provisioned on-demand security infrastructure and support for the dynamic security associations (DSA) that should provide fully verifiable chains of trust from the user client/platform to the virtual resource and the virtualisation platform
- SLA management, including initial SLA negotiation and further SLA enforcement at the planning and operation stages

The security solutions and supporting infrastructure to support the data integrity and data processing security should provide the following functionalities:

- Secure data transfer that possibly should be enforced with the data activation mechanism
- Protection of data stored on the cloud platform
- Restoration from the process failure that entails problems related to secure job/application session and data restoration

The security solutions and supporting infrastructure should support consistent security session management:

- A special session for data transfer that should also support data partitioning and run-time activation and synchronisation

Security Service Lifecycle

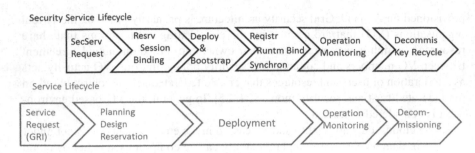

Fig. 5.9 The proposed security services lifecycle management model

- Session synchronisation mechanisms that should protect the integrity of the remote run-time environment
- Secure session failover that should rely on the session synchronisation mechanism when restoring the session

Wider cloud adoption by industry and integration with advanced infrastructure services will require implementing manageable security services and mechanisms for remote control of the cloud operational environment integrity by users.

5.4.2   Security Services Lifecycle Management Model (SSLM)

Most of the existing security lifecycle management frameworks, such as defined in the NIST Special Publication 800-14 "Generally Accepted Principles and Practices in Systems Security" [26], provide a good basis for security services development and management, but they still reflect the traditional approach to services and systems design driven by engineers. The defined security services lifecycle includes the following typical phases: initiation, development/acquisition, implementation, operation/maintenance and disposal.

Figure 5.9 illustrates the proposed security services lifecycle management (SSLM) model [5] that reflects security services operation in generically distributed multi-domain environments and their binding to the provisioned services and/or infrastructure. The SSLM includes the following stages:

- Service *request* and generation of the GRI that will serve as a provisioning session identifier (SessionID) and will bind all other stages and related security context [6, 7]. The request stage may also include SLA negotiation which will become a part of the binding agreement to start on-demand service provisioning.
- *Reservation* stage and *reservation session binding* with GRI (also a part of the general SDF/SLM) that provides support for a complex reservation process including required access control and policy enforcement.
- *Deployment* stage (including *Bootstrapping*) begins after all component resources have been reserved and includes distribution of the security context and binding

Table 5.1 Relation between SSLM/SLM stages and supporting general and security mechanisms

SLM/SDF stages	Request	Planning Reservation	Deployment	Operation	Decommissioning
SSLM Process/ Activity	SLA Negotiation	Serv/Rsr Compose Reserve	Configure Bootstrap Synchron	Orchestration / Session Management	Logoff Accounting
Supporting Mechanisms (M– mandatory, O- optional)					
SLA	M				O
Workflow		O		M	
Metadata	M	M	M	M	
Dynamic Security Association		O	M	M	
AuthZ SecCtx Management		M	M	M	
Logging		O	O	M	M

the provisioned virtualised resources and hosting platform to the GRI as a provisioning session ID.

- *Registration and synchronisation* stage (including *run-time binding*) that allows the whole virtual infrastructure to start synchronously and specifically targets possible scenarios with the provisioned services migration or failover. In a simple case, the registration stage binds the local resource or hosting platform run-time process ID to the GRI as a provisioning session ID.
- During the *operation* stage, the security services provide access control to the provisioned services and maintain the service access or usage session.
- *Decommissioning* stage ensures that all sessions are terminated, data are cleaned up and session security context is recycled.

The proposed SSLM model is compatible with the above-described SDF and extends the existing SLM frameworks with the additional stages "registration and synchronisation" that specifically target such security issues as the provisioned services/ resources restoration (in the framework of the active provisioning session) and provide a mechanism for remote data protection by binding them to the session context.

Table 5.1 explains what main processes/actions take place during the different SLM/SSLM stages and what general and security mechanisms are used:

- SLA – used at the stage of the service request placing and can also include the SLA negotiation process.
- Workflow is typically used at the operation stage as a service orchestration mechanism and can be originated from the design/reservation stage.
- Metadata are created and used during the whole service lifecycle and, together with security services, actually ensure the integrity of the SLM/SSLM.
- Dynamic security associations support the integrity of the provisioned resources and are bound to the security sessions.

- Authorisation session context supports integrity of the authorisation sessions during the reservation, deployment and operation stages.
- Logging can be actually used at each stage and is essentially important during the last 2 stages – operation and decommissioning.

The proposed SSLM model extends the existing SLM frameworks with the additional stages of "reservation session binding" and "registration and synchronisation" which especially target such scenarios as the provisioned services/resources restoration, re-planning or migration (in the framework of the active provisioning session) and provide a mechanism for remote data protection by binding them to the session context. An important role in these processes belongs to the consistent security context management and dynamic security associations that should be supported by the dynamic trust anchors binding and special bootstrapping procedure or protocol. However, it is perceived that implementing such functionality will require the service hosting platform that supports a Trusted Computing Group Architecture (TCG Architecture) [27, 28].

5.4.3 Dynamically Provisioned Access Control Infrastructure (DACI)

Developing a consistent framework for dynamically provisioned security services requires deep analysis of all underlying processes and interactions. Many processes typically used in traditional security services need to be abstracted, decomposed and formalised. First of all, it is related to security services setup, configuration and security context management that in many present solutions/frameworks is provided manually, during the service installation or configured out-of-band.

The general security framework for on-demand provisioned infrastructure services should address two general aspects: (1) supporting secure operation of the provisioning infrastructure which is typically provided by the providers' authentication and authorisation infrastructure (AAI) supported also by federated identity management services (FIdM) and (2) provisioning a dynamic access control infrastructure as part of the provisioned on-demand virtual infrastructure. The first task is primarily focused on the security context exchanged between involved services, resources and access control services. The virtualised DACI must be bootstrapped to the provisioned on-demand VI and VIP/VIO trust domains as entities participating in the handling initial request for VI and legally and securely bound to the VI users. Such security bootstrapping can be done at the deployment stage.

Virtual access control infrastructure setup and operation is based on the above-mentioned DSA that will link the VI dynamic trust anchor(s) with the main actors and/or entities participating in the VI provisioning – VIP and the requestor or target user organisation (if they are different). As discussed above, the creation of such a DSA for the given VI can be done during the reservation and deployment stage. The reservation stage will allow the distribution of the initial provisioning session

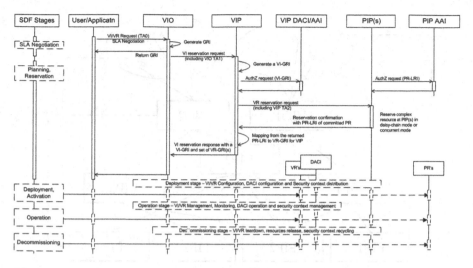

Fig. 5.10 Security context management during VI provisioning and operation

context and collection of the security context (e.g. public key certificates) from all participating infrastructure components. The deployment stage can securely distribute either shared cryptographic keys or another type of security credential that will allow validation of information exchange and application of access control to VI users, actors and services.

Figure 5.10 illustrates in detail the interaction between main actors and access control services during the reservation stage and includes also other stages of provisioned infrastructure lifecycle. The request to create VI (RequestVI) initiates a request to VIP that will be evaluated by VIP-AAI against access control polices, which will next be followed by a VIP request to PIP for required or selected physical resources PRs, which in turn will be evaluated by PIP-AAI. It is an SDF and SSLM requirement that starting from the initial RequestVI, all communication and access control evaluations should be bound to the provisioning session identifier GRI. The chain of requests from the user to VIO, VIP and PIP can also carry corresponding trust anchors TA0…TA2, for example, in a form of public key certificate (PKC) [29] or WS-Trust security tokens [30].

DACI is created at the deployment stage and controls access to and use of the VI resources; it uses dynamically created security association of the users and resources. The DACI bootstrapping can be done either by fully preconfiguring trust relations between the VIP-AAI and DACI or by using special bootstrapping registration procedure similar to those used in the TCG Architecture [22]. To ensure unambiguous session context and the identification of all involved entities and resources, the following types of identifiers are used committed PR@PIP or created VR@VIP resources:

- Global reservation ID (GRI) – generated at the beginning of the VI provisioning, stored at VIO and returned to the user as identification of the provisioning session and the provisioned VI

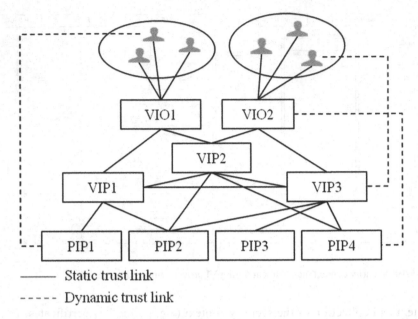

Fig. 5.11 Trust relationships in a multi-provider cloud environment

- VI-GRI – generated by VIP as an internal reservation session ID, which can be also refolded GRI, depending on the VIP provisioning model
- Local reservation ID (LRI) that can be generated by PIP or VIP to provide identification PR-LRI and VR-LRI of the committed or created PR@PIP and VR@VIP resources

5.4.4   Dynamic Security Associations Management

5.4.4.1   Trust Relations

Figure 5.11 describes relations between entities in the cloud infrastructure services provisioned on demand. PIPs own virtualised physical devices to offer virtual resources (VRs). VIPs are intermediate providers to compose and aggregate VRs from multiple PIPs into the virtual infrastructures (VIs), which are subscribed by VIOs. The end-users then may consume VRs in the VI associated with the VIOs' identifier. The involved actors form the cloud supply-chain service model from low-level providers (PIPs) to intermediate providers (VIPs), subscribers (VIOs) and end-users.

Providing trust between parties is basic for security services. This model has two types of trust relationship. The first one is static or direct trust between two direct parties based on SLA agreements. The second one is dynamic trust, the trust relation established during provisioning stages between indirect parties (i.e. VIO and PIPs, VI-end-users and VIPs). These relationships are dynamic because they are established and released during the VI provisioning phases.

According to various models in distributed systems including public key cryptography models (e.g. PKI or PGP) and recommendation-based models, trust relationships are assumed not to be transitive [31]. For example, if A trusts B and B trusts C, it cannot be concluded that A trusts C. In some specific conditions, the trust could be transitive [30] and A could trust C. In our approach, we select the transitive trust between parties as specified in [30] with a set of conditions, for example, with VI-end-users, VIO and VIP, VIO trusts VIP and recommends the trust to VI-end-users. VI-end-users then trust VIO as the recommender for trust relationships and could judge VIO's recommendations. With the above cloud supply-chain service model, recommendation paths or trust paths are formed from PIP to VIP, VIO and VI-end-users. This dynamic trust model can follow one of the following categories. The first one is an evidence-based model where entities establish a trust relationship based on evidence, such as cryptographic keys. The other one is a recommendation-based model [32]. For clouds, we propose to use the evidence-based model because direct/static trust relations are enforced by a SLA along with specific cryptographic parameters that can be provided as a provisioning session security context. Dynamic trust relations are established based on direct trust relations and other assumptions as specified above to satisfy conditional transitive trust.

5.4.4.2 Establishing Dynamic Trust Relationships

A trust relationship between two entities is described by a security association (SA). It contains agreed security attributes between parties. The SA may include cryptographic parameters (certificates, keys, algorithms, etc.) to help one endpoint assure another about its trustworthiness.

The direct/static trust relations described in the previous section are known as the static security association (SSA), while the dynamic trust relations can be defined as the dynamic security association (DSA). In the reference model, SSAs include SSA (VI-user, VIO), SSA (VIO, VIP) and SSA (VIP, PIP). The set of DSAs include DSA (VI-end-user, VIP), DSA (VI-end-user, PIP) and DSA (VIO, PIP).

Generic steps to establish dynamic trust relationship are as follows:

Conditions: SSA (A, B), SSA (B, C)
Goal: Establish the DSA (A, C)
Procedures:

1. A asks B to establish trust with C.
2. B retrieves its SA list to find SSA (B, A) and SSA (B, C). It then generates a new SA. This SA is sent back to A and C by protecting with SSA (B, A) and SSA (B, C), respectively.
3. A receives the generated SA. By verifying the SSA (B, A) protector, it adds the new generated SA to its SA list as the DSA (A, C).

4. C receives the generated SA and verifies it with SSA (C, B). Since it is valid, C adds the new SA, known as DSA (C, A), to its SA list.

For specific mechanisms such as PKI, PGP or SAML [33], the procedure needs to be modified to generate SA dynamically and sent to both indirect parties A and C. Further development of these mechanisms will require additional research.

5.4.5   Security Infrastructure Bootstrapping Protocol

This section describes the proposed security bootstrapping protocol that was proposed in the authors' papers [25] and [7] and is currently being implemented in the framework of the GEYSERS project [16].

The DACI trust model relies on a number of trust anchors residing at PIP, VIP and VIO and rooted in the VI provisioning request or SLA between user/customer and VI/cloud provider (in our model, VIP or VIO). However, to protect it from compromise (e.g. by cloning) and make it integrity protected, it needs to be bootstrapped to the virtualisation platform run-time environment. The proposed bootstrapping protocol uses a Trusted Computing Platform Architecture (TCG Architecture) and Trusted Platform Module (TPM) which can provide a trustworthy platform from which secure systems may be built. They can provide a static root of trust to allow booting a system to a known and trusted state by taking measurements and verifying each piece of software before it is executed [34].

In order to create a trusted computing environment, it is necessary to build an unbroken chain of trust from the most fundamental hardware (such as the BIOS and firmware) through to the operating system and virtualisation platform that hosts virtualised services and the DACI itself. The TPM can be configured to take measurements of each software component before it is executed. Only if the signature is valid will the system proceed. Software needs to be specifically designed to take advantage of these capabilities; as an example, such solutions and firmware are provided by Intel [35] and VMware [36].

The initial TPM-based platform initiation uses a special method for remote TPM attestation called direct anonymous attestation (DAA) [37] that actually requires a third-party role (the issuer) [26] that can be a part of cloud provider security infrastructure.

In order to authenticate the TPM-enabled system, the service provider would provide a signed package that contains relevant TPM public keys, system keys and valid trusted states for those machines. Next, a special Vanguard application is sent to a remote machine via the SCP protocol as an initial stage in the required service deployment. It determines the safety of the remote machine before more sensitive information or software is transferred to it. As part of the bootstrapping process a Vanguard application verifies the identity and state of the remote machine based on the fingerprint provided in the security package.

After verification, a trusted platform session token can be generated based on GRI or LRI that is then sealed by the TPM. It is included as a part of the general VI or DACI security context and can only be decrypted by the same TPM and only when in the same state [38]. This prevents the session from being decrypted on another machine and in effect binds the session to the machine in a trusted state. In order to defeat a cloning attack, an encryption key or other metadata can also be sealed to a TPM. When used to encrypt disk images, this prevents the images from being decrypted on another untrusted machine.

5.4.6 Security Context Management in DACI

Although DACI operates at the operation stage of the SSLM/SLM, its security context is bound to the overall provisioning process starting from the initial stage of the service request and SLA negotiation that will provide a trust anchor TA0 to the user/application security domain with which the DACI will interact during the operation stage. The RequestVI initiates the provisioning session inside which we can also distinguish two other types of sessions: reservation session and access session, which however can use that same access control policy and security context management model and consequently can use the same format and type of the session credentials. In the discussed DACI, we use the authorisation token (AuthzToken) mechanism initially proposed in the GAAA-NRP framework and used for authorisation session context management in multi-domain network resource provisioning [39, 40]. Tokens as session credentials are abstract constructs that refer to the related session context stored in the provisioned resources or services. The token should carry a session identifier, in our case GRI or VI-GRI.

When requesting VI services or resources at the operation stage, the requestor needs to include the reservation session credentials together with the requested resource or service description which in its own turn should include or be bound to the provisioned VI identifier in a form of GRI or VI-GRI. The DACI context handling service should provide resolution and mapping between the provided identifiers and those maintained by the VIP and PIP, in our case VR-LRI or PR-LRI. If session credentials are not sufficient, for example, in case delegation or conditional policy decision is required, all session context information must be extracted from AuthzToken and the normalised policy decision request will be sent to the DACI policy decision point (PDP) which will evaluate the request against the applied access control policy.

In the discussed DACI architecture, the tokens are used both for access control and signalling at different SSLM/SDF stages as a flexible mechanism for communicating and signalling security context between administrative and security domains (that may represent PIP or individual physical resources). Inherited from GAAA-NRP, the DACI uses two types of tokens:

- Access tokens that are used as AuthZ/access session credentials and refer to the stored reservation context.
- Pilot tokens that provide flexible functionality for managing the AuthZ session during the reservation stage and the whole provisioning process. A few types of the pilot token are defined that can communicate different domain-related context information during the services or resources reservation stage.

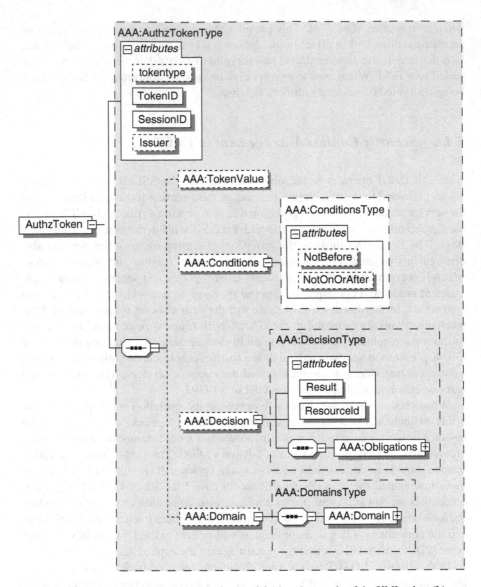

Fig. 5.12 Common access and pilot token data model (**a**) and example of the XML token (**b**)

Figure 5.12 illustrates the common data model of both access token and pilot token. Although the tokens share a common data model, they are different in the operational model and in the way they are generated and processed. When processed by the AuthZ service components, they can be distinguished by the token type attribute which is optional for access token and mandatory for pilot token.

(a) High-level access and pilot token data model

```
<AAA:AuthzToken
xmlns:AAA="http://www.aaauthreach.org/ns/AAA"
```

```
         Issuer="http://testbed.ist-
phosphorus.eu/phosphorus/aaa/TVS/token-pilot"
         SessionId="0912182e7f9c7d156028e77e3d6b460de8e4
937c"
     TokenId="a99b91e70307bdd329c9a0aec18bb4a3"
type="pilot-type3">
<AAA:TokenValue>3923c7ecb979e7078ab8745191a7b25348cdc
b48</AAA:TokenValue>
   <AAA:Conditions NotBefore="2008-07-25T09:38:39.890Z"
        NotOnOrAfter="2008-07-26T09:38:39.890Z"/>
   <AAA:DomainsContext>
   <AAA:Domain      domainId="http://testbed.ist-
phosphorus.eu/viola">
            <AAA:AuthzToken   Issuer="http://testbed.ist-
phosphorus.eu/viola/aaa/TVS/token-pilot"
SessionId="b0b6202d7bd7fb7b591b5de29950d21fdb8bf375"
        TokenId="e7c88fad8cff42d7faaa961b96411ae6">
   <AAA:TokenValue>f09194bbddeef95bc4acb187f71b0bb20b2d
0b44</AAA:TokenValue>
<AAA:Conditions                         NotBefore="2008-07-
18T21:55:15.296Z"
          NotOnOrAfter="2008-07-18T21:55:15.296Z"/>
   </AAA:AuthzToken>
   <AAA:KeyInfo>http://testbed.ist-
phosphorus.eu/viola/_public_key_</AAA:KeyInfo>
     </AAA:Domain>
   </AAA:DomainsContext>
 </AAA:AuthzToken>
```

(b) Example XML token type 3 containing domain-related context that may include the pilot token and key information from the previous domain

Access tokens contain three mandatory elements: the SessionId attribute that holds the GRI, the TokenId attribute that holds a unique token ID attribute and is used for token identification and authentication and the TokenValue element. The optional elements include: the condition element that may contain two time validity attributes notBefore and notOnOrAfter, the decision element that holds two attributes ResourceId and result, and optional element obligations that may hold policy obligations returned by the PDP. Pilot tokens may contain another optional domains element that serves as a container for collecting and distributing domain-related security context.

For the purpose of authenticating token origin, the pilot token value is calculated from the concatenated strings "DomainId, GRI, TokenId". This approach provides a simple protection mechanism against pilot token duplication or replay during the same reservation/authorisation session. The following expressions are used to calculate the TokenValue for the access token and pilot token:

```
TokenValue   =   HMAC(concat(DomainId,   GRI,   TokenId),
TokenKey)
```

In the current implementation [40], the TokenKey is generated from the GRI and a common shared secret value among all trusted domains. It means that only these domains can generate valid tokens and correspondingly verify the authenticity of the received tokens. The shared secret can be distributed as a part of the DSA creation. It is also suggested that all participating resources and/or domains cache received tokens and check their uniqueness.

5.5 Security Token Service for Federated Access Control to Provisioned Cloud Infrastructure

Consistent access control to the provisioned cloud infrastructure services requires security mechanisms that should allow federated access control and identity management to potentially multi-domain and multi-provider cloud resources from the user organisational or residential domains. Such functionality is generically provided by the GEMBus security token service (STS) that complies with the related WS-Security standards such as WS-Trust and WS-Federation [30, 41]. The STS is a mechanism that conveys security context information between services that may reside in different security and administrative domains. STS can issue and validate security tokens and support service identity federation and federated identity delegation.

Figure 5.13 depicts an example of the messages exchanged when a user attempts to access a service using tokens to secure the connection. First, the service consumer initialises and sends an authentication request to STS. The STS then validates the consumer credentials and issues a security token to it. With the token, the consumer sends a request message including the token to the producer. The consumer sends the token to STS to check its validity. After running its validation process, the STS sends a response with the status of the token to the producer, which processes it and replies to the consumer.

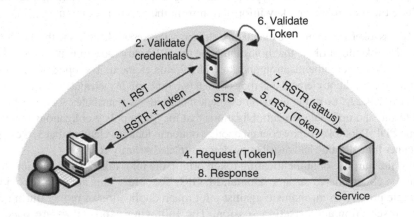

Fig. 5.13 STS operation in federated access control to multi-domain resources

Two different architectural elements are defined for token issuance and validation: the ticket translation service (TTS) is responsible for generating valid tokens according to the received credentials and for renewing and converting security tokens, and an authorisation service (AS) performs token validation and can retrieve additional attributes or policies from other sources to perform the validation.

The GEMBus STS can be used in both cases as part of the provider access control infrastructure or can be provisioned and deployed as part of the delivered cloud infrastructure that is managed by the user where GEMBus is used as a platform for on-demand services provisioning and management.

5.5.1   STS Functionality and Standard Compliance

Security mechanisms must comply with requirements that may conflict with security, privacy and simplicity of use. It is important that the security protocols deal with user attributes and related information in an appropriate manner, taking the conservative disclosure of attributes and abiding to user privacy policies whenever possible. It is also important that these directives are enforced by all entities, both in the infrastructure itself and in the participant services, dealing with user data in a consistent manner. From the point of view of services, it is very important to protect information by ensuring the identity of consumers who use the services. The most adequate manner to satisfy these requirements relies on the use of a token that allows the transfer of security data along the exchanged messages.

The mechanisms needed to provide secure communications within the GEMBus architecture base their operation on the STS. This service, described in WS-Trust, makes it possible to issue and validate security tokens. The GEMBus STS supports the WS-Trust interoperability profile defined by the EMI, and support for other profiles can be easily added.

Web Services Security (WS-Security) is a communication protocol that provides the means for applying security to Web Services. It is part of the WS-* family of Web service specifications published by OASIS. It is a flexible and feature-rich extension to SOAP to apply security to Web Services. The protocol specifies how integrity and confidentiality can be enforced on messages. It allows the communication of various security token formats, such as SAML [33], Kerberos [42] and X.509 [29], though the protocol is able to accommodate practically any kind of token format. Its main focus is the use of XML Signature [43] and XML Encryption [44] to provide end-to-end security. The protocol is officially called WSS and associated with other specifications like WS-Trust, WS-SecureConversation [45] and WS-Policy [46].

WS-Trust provides extensions to WS-Security, specifically dealing with issuing, renewing and validating security tokens, as well as how to establish, assess (the presence of) and broker trust relationships between participants in a secure message exchange. WS-Trust defines:

- The concept of a STS: A Web service that issues security tokens as defined in the WS-Security specification

- The formats of the messages used to request security tokens and the responses to those messages
- Mechanisms for key exchange

5.5.2 STS Operational Models

When establishing the identity of a requesting party, it is important to take into account that not only the identity of the entity performing the actual request must be established. Being able to identify the original requestor (the one on whose behalf the requesting party is acting) is crucial as well. In this respect, we can reduce the possible situations to two basic models: the star model and chain model, suggesting the possibility of a more complex combination of both (see Fig. 5.14).

In the star model (Fig. 5.14a), the final user is identified at a client endpoint, which acts as consumer of the requested services on the user's behalf by connecting to the appropriate service producer endpoints. Therefore, a single statement (or its translations into the required formats thereof) can be used to identify the consumer and the original requesting user. The figure illustrates this architecture, in the case of using SOAP for transport requests and a SAML token to express security statements.

In the chain model (Fig. 5.14b), the final user is identified at a consumer endpoint, which sends an initial request on behalf of the user requesting a service to a first service producer endpoint, which then forwards the request to a second producer endpoint, and this to a third one, and thus successively. Therefore, the initial statement (built by the original consumer endpoint) needs to be forwarded as requests are passed from one service endpoint to the next in the chain. The statement must contain information about the original user and the initial consumer endpoint and should contain information about the service endpoints through which the request has been forwarded.

The AS in Fig. 5.14(a) and (b) refers to a service taking care of validating the security statements received within a certain request. It relies on the use of security tokens along with requests to transfer relevant identity statements plus the availability of a service (provided by the infrastructure itself) able to verify the validity of the security tokens. If a common token format is used or, conversely, an available service is able to generate appropriate tokens by translating among equivalent ones, there are two distinct phases in securing service access:

1. Token request and generation undertaken by the local mechanism that the user decides to employ, as long as a minimal set of requirements on level of assurance (in several aspects: identity assessment, required credentials, strength of the link to the individual, etc.) is fulfilled
2. The validation of the token received by the requested service, probably using some of the statements inside the token to retrieve additional attributes from trusted sources and/or to request an access decision from a policy decision point

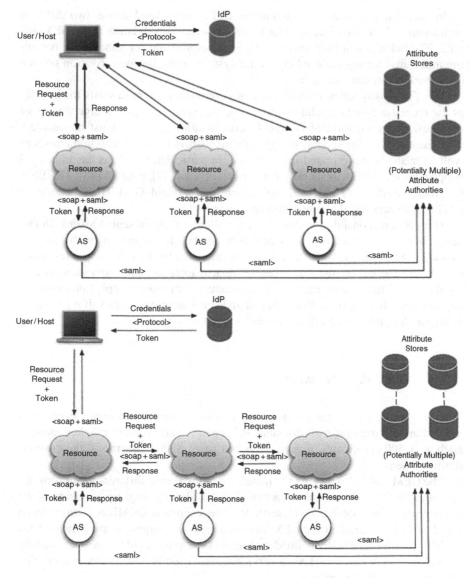

Fig. 5.14 STS operational models: (**a**) star; (**b**) chain

In conclusion, the GEMBus security architecture requires:

- A common token format to guarantee interoperability at the security level
- A service able to act as the source of such tokens and provide a way to translate other token formats into the common format
- A service able to validate security tokens and to provide authorisation decisions

In accordance with these requirements and as considered above, two different architectural elements are defined for token issuance and validation in the GEMBus STS. The ticket translation service (TTS) is responsible for generating, renewing and transforming valid tokens in the system, while the authorisation service (AS) performs token validation.

The TTS mostly relies on external identity providers that must verify the identity of the requester based on valid identification material. To support a large amount of services, the application of different authentication methods must be ensured. This must include the support of currently standardised authentication methods as well as methods incorporated in the future. In particular, GEMBus has imbedded support for the eduGAIN identity federation services [47], eduPKI [48], TERENA Certificate Service (TCS) [49] and other International Grid Trust Federation (IGTF) [50] accredited identity infrastructures.

The AS is responsible for checking the validity of the presented tokens. In this case, the requester is usually a service that has received a token along with a request message and needs to check the validity of the token before providing a response. Checks carried out on the token can be related to issue date, expiration date or signature(s). This process can also be associated with more complex processes of authorisation that imply attribute request and check security policies. If the token is valid, the AS provides an affirmative answer to the service.

5.5.3 STS Token Formats

The WS-Security specification allows a variety of signature formats, encryption algorithms and multiple trust domains. It is open to various security token models, such as X.509 certificates, user id/password pairs, SAML assertions and custom-defined tokens.

The GEMBus TTS supports the transformations among different token formats, according to service descriptions as stored in the GEMBus registry by means of the appropriate profile identifiers. Nevertheless, the canonical GEMBus security token (applicable by default in all GEMBus-supported exchanges) is the relayed-trust SAML assertion originally defined within the GN2 project [45] to provide identity information in scenarios where a service is acting on behalf of a user identified through an identity federation.

The SAML construct used in this case is able to convey information about the user accessing the producer. It fulfils two essential constraints:

- It is bound to the consumer by the original identity provider (IdP) that identified the requesting user, so it is possible to check that the information it contains about the user has been legally obtained.
- It is bound to the producer by the consumer, so a potentially malicious producer cannot use this information to further impersonate either the consumer or the user.

To comply with these two requirements, the token consists of an SAML assertion expressing data related to the user authentication with:

- A valid audience restricted to the producer(s) to which it is addressed, through a SAML condition element containing an identifier uniquely associated with them
- A statement expressing that this specific method of relayed trust must be used to evaluate the assertion, through a specific value in the SAML construct identifying the subject confirmation method
- The identity assertion(s) received from the IdP as evidence for this confirmation process, as part of the SAML element SubjectConfirmationData

A sample SAML assertion following the above procedures for a consumer with the identifier: urn:geant:edugain:component:perfsonarclient:Ne tflowClient10082 acting on behalf of a user identified at the IdP: urn:gean t:edugain:be:uninett:idp1 and connecting to a consumer identified by: urn:geant:edugain:component:perfsonarresource:netflow. uninett.no/data should have an SAML 2.0 content as the one displayed below (some line breaks and indentation are added to improve readability):

```
<?xml version="1.0" encoding="UTF-8"?>
<Assertion
 xmlns:xsi="http://www.w3.org/2001/XMLSchema-
instance"
 xsi:schemaLocation="urn:oasis:names:tc:SAML:2.0:asse
rtion"
 Version="2.0" ID="100001"
 IssueInstant="2006-12-03T10:00:00Z">
<Issuer>
urn:geant:gembus:security:sts:gemsts
</Issuer>

<!-- An audience restriction, that will restrict this
security token to be valid for one single resource only.
-->
 <Conditions>
  <AudienceRestriction>
   <Audience>
    urn:geant:edugain:component:perfsonarresource:
    netflow.uninett.no/data
   </Audience>
```

```
  </AudienceRestriction>
   </Conditions>

  <Subject>
   <NameID>aksjc7e736452829we8</NameID>
   <SubjectConfirmation
  Meth-od="urn:geant:edugain:reference:relayed-trust">
  <SubjectConfirmationData>
    <Assertion
     xmlns="urn:oasis:names:tc:SAML:2.0:assertion"
     xmlns:xsi="http://www.w3.org/2006/XMLSchema-
     instance"
     Version="2.0" ID="_200001"
     IssueInstant="2006-12-03T10:00:00Z">
     <Issuer>
     urn:geant:edugain:be:uninett:idp1
     </Issuer>

<!-- This inner assertion is limited to only be valid for
the client performing the WebSSO authentication. This
inner assertion cannot be reused or used at all by others
than the NetflowClient10082 instance. But NetflowClient10082
can use it as an evidence when used inside an assertion
issued by NetflowClient10082 using the relayed-trust
confirmationMethod. -->
     <Conditions>
      <AudienceRestriction>
       <Audience>
        urn:geant:edugain:component:perfsonarclient:
       NetflowClient10082
       </Audience>
      </AudienceRestriction>
     </Conditions>

<!-- This is the inner Subject and authNstatement prov-
ing the authentication itself.
  These elements and attributes must be identical in the
inner and outer assertion:
     - Assertion/Subject/NameID
     - Assertion/AuthnStatement@AuthenticationMethod
The inner assertion confirmation Method must be
     urn:oasis:names:tc:SAML:1.0:cm:bearer. -->
     <Subject>
```

```
      <NameID>aksjc7e736452829we8</NameID>
      <SubjectConfirmation Meth-
   od="urn:oasis:names:tc:SAML:2.0:cm:bearer"/>
      </Subject>
      <AuthnStatement AuthnInstant="2006-12-
   03T10:00:00Z">
         <AuthnContext>
          <AuthnContextClassRef>
   urn:oasis:names:tc:SAML:2.0:ac:classes:Password
          </AuthnContextClassRef>
         </AuthnContext>
      </AuthnStatement>
<!-- Enveloped Signature for SubjectConfirmation -->
<Signature>
   <!-- Signed by the IdP -->
   <SignedInfo>
   <CanonicalizationMethod Algorithm="…"/>
   <SignatureMethod Algorithm="…"/>
   <Reference>
    <DigestMethod Algorithm="…"/>
    <DigestValue/>
   </Reference>
   </SignedInfo>
   <SignatureValue/>
</Signature>
</Assertion>
</SubjectConfirmationData>
</SubjectConfirmation>
</Subject>

<Signature>
<!-- Signed by TTS -->
   <SignedInfo>
    <CanonicalizationMethod Algorithm="…"/>
    <SignatureMethod Algorithm="…"/>
    <Reference>
     <DigestMethod Algorithm=".."/>
     <DigestValue/>
    </Reference>
   </SignedInfo>
   <SignatureValue/>
   </Signature>
</Assertion>
```

5.5.4 TTS and AS

The ticket translation service (TTS) is responsible for issuing, renewing and converting security tokens, responding to consumer requests for issuing, renewing or converting security tokens for services that require it.

Each of these operations can only be done by the TTS, unlike token validation that can be offloaded in certain cases from the security service, the service itself or at the framework integration elements such as interceptors, message routers or binding components, especially when session tokens (as described below) are used to simplify interactions.

The main TTS operations are:

- Issuing: To obtain a security token from an identity credential (identity token)
- Renewing: To renew an issued security token
- Converting: To convert a security token type to another security token type

The TTS operation is as follows:

1. The consumer obtains an identity token (SAML assertion, grid proxy certificate token, etc.) from an identity infrastructure. Typically, the consumer requires users to send such a token in order to provide access.
2. The consumer sends a request for issuance, renewal or conversion to the TTS using either the identity token (issuance) or a security token (renewal or conversion).
3. The STS validates the consumer's token (using security policies) and sends a security token to the consumer.

The authorisation service (AS) is responsible for supporting the token validation functions, responding to requests for validating tokens of consumers and services that require it.

The token validation process can be performed by the AS itself or act as a proxy redirecting the validation process to the external service that generated it. For external validation, the authorisation service may query an external service or IdP and forward the response to the consumer. When the authorisation service itself performs validation, the process must verify the information contained in the token by checking the issuer, issue and expiration date, signatures, etc. In addition to the token, the authorisation service can perform a more complex authorisation process, retrieving attributes related to the token subject and consulting a policy decision point (PDP) for authorisation decisions.

As described in the previous section, the architecture proposed by GEMBus is based on message exchanges performed by different services that can be connected in many ways. Since the ESB is the main integration mechanism provided by GEMBus and it can also act as a container, it is possible to develop and deploy a service directly on the bus. But it is more interesting to exercise its integration capabilities, such as interceptors, message routers and binding components. Whether deployed inside the bus or running as an external service, the STS can be used in a service composition to transparently provide its capabilities, using the above-mentioned mechanisms.

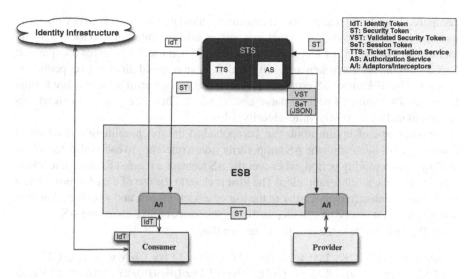

Fig. 5.15 STS extended operation with support of the session tokens

Figure 5.15 illustrates a scenario in which a security token service extended with support for session tokens is integrated in the GEMBus architecture. In this example, the consumer obtains an identity token (e.g. an SAML assertion) from an identity infrastructure. Then it sends an authentication request to the STS using the identity token. The STS validates the consumer identity token and issues a security token (ST) to the consumer. With the new token, the consumer sends a request message to the provider that is intercepted by an element that extracts the ST and sends a token validation request to the STS. The AS module validates the consumer token and issues a response with a validated security token with an optional session token (SeT). Finally, the interceptor passes the message to the provider. It processes the consumer request and sends the response message to the consumer.

5.5.5 Session Management

Session management is the process of keeping track of consumer activity across different levels of interaction with the producer.

Assuming that each message to a service is attached with a token that the service must validate at the authorisation service, this will very likely mean a high workload for the security services and additional delays in service provision. The objective of managing GEMBus sessions is to speed up the security system performance without compromising security goals.

There are several mechanisms to strengthen the validation of the tokens based on the idea of sessions: It is possible to include a new type of token called session token that is returned to the requester after successful validation in the AS. The main feature of this type of token is rapid validation at the expense of lower security features

compared to a normal token, though this can be alleviated (if not solved) by reducing
its lifetime. When the requester makes a new request for validation to the AS, it can
include the two tokens or just the session token. When the AS receives the query, it
first checks the session token and, if it is valid, it can respond directly to expedite the
process. The GEMBus STS employs a lightweight yet powerful session token format
based on JWT, much faster to parse and validate. There are plans to extend this
format to make them fully valid security tokens.

Another type of optimisation can be applied to the token validation mechanism
done by the AS by making the AS temporarily store a reference to each validated token.
Within a given validity period, whenever the AS receives a request for the same token,
it does not make a full revalidation. The idea is close to the use of a cache, providing a
performance enhancement similar to the use of session tokens, and with the additional
advantage of not involving changes in the requesters that make use of the AS.

A JWT session token example looks like this:

```
eyJ0eXAiOiJKV1QiLCJhbGciOiJSUzI1NiJ9.eyJhdWQiOiJ1c
m46Z2VhbnQ6ZWR1Z2Fpbjpjb21wb25lbnQ6cGVyZnNvbmFycmVzb3
VyY2U6bmV0Zmxvdy51bmluZXR0Lm5vXC9kYXRhIiwiaX_
NzIjoidXJuOmdlYW50OmVkdWdhaW46Y29tcG9uZW50OnBlcmZzb
25hcmNsaWVudDpOZXRmbG93Q2xpZW50MTAwODIiLCJpYXQiOjEzM-
jA0MDQ0MDk2MzAsImF0dHIiOnt9LCJleHAiOjEzMjA0MDgw
MDk3MTR9.UG1_PoSyd45QqY7m4IoQj9rDdIt3IvXfHRYSa27I1
JbKacI6bDTLewn_0JUuUjeKJoEwQ0MX9KmnT2M1ZD11RhFGPFhhXm
5MyHNPSC7v9ruzXqk89M8MWbJwpo9elIh8aG4gPGcpGIIuHJ2VLHHDI
IstnX4Z83XfTjg4RHzLkWCRzwzbb4hkIvx6vAPNcGhcC5CfERa
opI6qiDJzpNE_StaU_BI0POUa_3BZU0mVoV4gc_fV_gJipCHXER0z
8rrRBqDuS1Alw2hxBmM2adMTQz9Zk0FlW_74WLMVVHysjltk7Vn4oEc
phXN154wg1A8sKk6uaIZaH6oI1-f_oDtfA
```

This token is divided in three parts (header, claims and signature), all of them
base64 encoded. The header and claims contain the following information:

```
<?xml version="1.0" encoding="UTF-8"?>
//JWT Header
  {
   "typ": "JWT",
   "alg": "RS256"
  }
  //JWT Claims
  {
   "aud":
"urn:geant:edugain:component:perfsonarresource:netflow.unine
tt.no\/data",
   "iss": "urn:geant:gembus:security:sts:gemsts",
   "iat": 1320404409630,
   "attr": {},
   "exp": 1320408009714
  } </Issuer>
```

where

typ – type of token, normally JWT

alg – algorithm used to sign and verify, in this case, RSA with SHA256

aud – represents the audience restriction

iss – token issuer

iat – issue instant

exp – expiration time

attr – attributes contained in the token.

The token can contain more claims such as nbf (not before condition) and custom claims. The signature represents the base64-encoded header and claims parts concatenated by a dot.

5.6   Future Research Directions

This chapter presents ongoing research on developing the architecture and framework for dynamically provisioned security services as part of the provisioned on-demand infrastructure services. The presented results provide a good basis for further research in a few important directions that should lead to the problem solution including architecture, information models, required security services, mechanisms and protocols and implementation platform.

Consistent security services implementation and operation require well-defined general infrastructure definition and design, which is considered by the authors as a necessary part of the further research on cloud security architecture. Currently existing cloud architecture frameworks are primarily oriented toward business-oriented applications and service delivery from the cloud provider to the user. Internal cloud implementation by cloud providers remains behind the "cloud curtain" that also imposes limitations on the quality of service control and security of the provisioned cloud environment. Virtualisation technologies used in clouds bring services design and related security problems to a new level and actually allow decoupling of the functional services infrastructure from the physical infrastructure and platform. To achieve the same level of security assurance in virtual infrastructures as in physical infrastructures, many currently adopted security models need to be revisited and re-factored to support new requirements originating from the distributed virtualised environment in clouds.

The following main topics are identified as further research topics related to both general cloud architecture and cloud security architecture:

- Defining new relational models in the provisioning of cloud-based infrastructure services that should reflect different ownership, administration and use relations between main actors in the current cloud services provisioning process such as provider, operator, broker, carrier, customer (enterprise) and user
- Extending the composable services architecture to reflect different virtualisation techniques for compute, storage and network components of the provisioned virtualised infrastructure, defining CSA control and management functionality

- Extending the GEMBus middleware platform to support full functionality of the cloud PaaS model for SOA-based services, in particular, creation of the dynamically configured infrastructure security services that can be used by user applications in the provisioned on-demand services
- Extending the infrastructure services modelling framework to include security-related attributes within the services composition and management information base
- Extending dynamic access control infrastructure, currently defined for infrastructure level access control, to integrate it with user access control using federated user campus or enterprise identities and accounts
- Further definition and development of the DACI trust management model and virtual infrastructure bootstrapping protocol

5.7 Conclusion

The primary focus of this chapter is the security infrastructure for cloud-based infrastructure services provisioned on demand that in fact should be a part of the overall cloud infrastructure provisioned on demand. The proposed solutions should allow moving current enterprise security infrastructure – that currently requires large amounts of manual configuration and setup – to a fully functional virtualised infrastructure service.

To provide the background for defining security infrastructure, the authors provide an overview and short description of the proposed architectural framework for on-demand provisioned cloud-based infrastructure services that includes such components as the infrastructure services modelling framework (ISMF), the composable services architecture (CSA) and the service delivery framework (SDF).

This chapter discusses conceptual issues, basic requirements and practical suggestions for provisioning dynamically configured security infrastructure services. This chapter describes the proposed dynamically provisioned access control infrastructure (DACI) architecture and defines the necessary security mechanisms to ensure consistent security services operation in the provisioned virtual infrastructure. Practical implementation of DACI reveals a wide spectrum of problems related to the distributed access control, policy, trust management and related security context management. In particular, this chapter discusses the use of the security token service for federated inter-domain access control and identity management, as well as authorisation tokens for security context exchange during provisioning sessions in multi-domain and multi-provider environments.

Consistent security services design, deployment and operations require continuous security context management during the whole security services lifecycle, which must be aligned to the main provisioned services lifecycle. The proposed security services lifecycle management (SSLM) model addresses security problems specific for on-demand infrastructure service provisioning that can be solved by introducing special security mechanisms to allow security services synchronisation and their binding to the virtualisation platform and run-time environment. This chapter discusses how these security mechanisms can be implemented by using the TCG Architecture and functionality of Trusted Platform Module that are currently available in almost all computer platforms and supported by most VM management platforms. This chapter also describes the proposed security infrastructure bootstrapping protocol that uses TPM functionality and can be integrated with DACI.

The proposed DACI and its component functionalities are currently being developed and implemented within the framework of the two EU projects GEYSERS and GEANT3.

Acknowledgement This work is supported by the FP7 EU-funded project GEANT3 (FP7-ICT-238875) and the FP7 EU-funded integrated project the Generalised Architecture for Dynamic Infrastructure Services (GEYSERS, FP7-ICT-248657).

References

1. NIST SP 800-145: The NIST definition of cloud computing. http://csrc.nist.gov/publications/nistpubs/800-145/SP800-145.pdf. Accessed 29 Jan 2012
2. NIST SP 500-292: Cloud computing reference architecture, v1.0. http://collaborate.nist.gov/twiki-cloud-computing/pub/CloudComputing/ReferenceArchitectureTaxonomy/NIST_SP_500-292_-_090611.pdf. Accessed 29 Jan 2012
3. Demchenko, Y., Mavrin, A., de Laat, C.: Defining generic architecture for cloud infrastructure as a service provisioning model. In: Proceedings CLOSER2011 Conference, Nordwijk, Netherlands, 7–9 May 2011. SciTePress (2011). ISBN 978-989-8425-52-2
4. Demchenko, Y., van der Ham, J., Ghijsen, M., Cristea. M., Yakovenko, V., de Laat, C.: On-demand provisioning of cloud and grid based infrastructure services for collaborative projects and groups. In: Proceedings of the 2011 International Conference on Collaboration Technologies and Systems (CTS 2011), Philadelphia, PA, USA, 23–27 May 2011
5. Demchenko, Y., de Laat, C., Lopez, D.R., Garcia-Espin, J.A.: Security services lifecycle management in on-demand infrastructure services provisioning. In: Proceedings of the IEEE Second International Conference on Cloud Computing Technology and Science, Indianapolis, IN, USA, pp. 644–650 (2010)
6. Demchenko, Y., Ngo, C., de Laat, C., Wlodarczyk, T., Rong, C., Ziegler, W.: Security infrastructure for on-demand provisioned cloud infrastructure services. In: Proceedings of the 3rd IEEE Conference on Cloud Computing Technologies and Science (CloudCom2011), Athens, Greece, 29 Nov–1 Dec 2011 (2011). ISBN 978-0-7695-4622-3
7. Ngo, C., Membrey, P., Demchenko, Y., de Laat, C.: Security framework for virtualised infrastructure services provisioned on-demand. In: Proceedings of the 3rd IEEE Conference on Cloud Computing Technologies and Science (CloudCom2011), Athens, Greece, 29 Nov–1 Dec 2011 (2011). ISBN 978-0-7695-4622-3
8. European Grid Infrastructure (EGI). https://www.egi.eu/. Accessed 9 Nov 2011
9. NIST-SP 500-291: NIST cloud computing standards roadmap. http://www.nist.gov/customcf/get_pdf.cfm?pub_id=909024. Accessed 29 Jan 2012
10. OASIS reference architecture foundation for service oriented architecture 1.0, Committee Draft 2, 14 Oct 2009. http://docs.oasis-open.org/soa-rm/soa-ra/v1.0/soa-ra-cd-02.pdf (2009). Accessed 9 Nov 2011
11. Pautasso, C., Zimmermann, O., Leymann, F.: RESTful Web Services vs. Big Web Services: Making the Right Architectural Decision, 17th International World Wide Web Conference (WWW2008), Beijing, China (2008)
12. Chappell, D.: Enterprise Service Bus. O'Reilly, Beijing/Cambridge (2004)

13. OSGi service platform release 4, version 4.2. http://www.osgi.org/Download/Release4V42. Accessed 9 Nov 2011
14. TMF service delivery framework. http://www.tmforum.org/servicedeliveryframework/4664/home.html. Accessed 9 Nov 2011
15. TMF software enabled services management solution. At http://www.tmforum.org/BestPracticesStandards/SoftwareEnabledServices/4664/Home.html. Accessed 9 Nov 2011
16. Generalised architecture for dynamic infrastructure services (GEYSERS Project). http://www.geysers.eu/. Accessed 9 Nov 2011
17. OWL 2 web ontology language. http://www.w3.org/TR/owl2-overview/. Accessed 9 Nov 2011
18. van der Ham, J., Dijkstra, F., Grosso, P., van der Pol, R., Toonk, A., de Laat, C.: A distributed topology information system for optical networks based on the semantic web. Elsevier J. Opt. Switch. Netw. 5(2–3), 85–93 (2008)
19. GEANT project. http://www.geant.net/pages/home.aspx. Accessed 9 Nov 2011
20. GEMBus architecture, GEANT3 project report deliverable DJ3.3.2, Jan 2011
21. Fuse ESB: OSGi based ESB. http://fusesource.com/products/enterpriseservicemix/#documentation. Accessed 9 Nov 2011
22. Apache ServiceMix an open source ESB. http://servicemix.apache.org/home.html. Accessed 9 Nov 2011
23. Spring security. Reference documentation. http://static.springsource.org/spring-security/site/docs/3.1.x/reference/springsecurity-single.html. Accessed 9 Nov 2011
24. Demchenko, Y., de Laat, C., Koeroo, O., Groep, D.: Re-thinking grid security architecture. In: Proceedings of the IEEE Fourth eScience 2008 Conference, Indianapolis, USA, 7–12 Dec 2008, pp. 79–86. IEEE Computer Society Publishing, Los Alamitos (2008). ISBN 978-0-7695-3535-7/ISBN 978-1-4244-3380-3
25. Foster, I., Kishimoto, H., Savva, A., Berry, D., Grimshaw, A., Horn, B., Maciel, F., Siebenlist, F., Subramaniam, R., Treadwell, J., Von Reich, J.: GFD.80 The Open Grid Services Architecture, Version 1.5. Open Grid Forum, 5 Sept 2006
26. NIST SP 800-14: Generally accepted principles and practices for securing information technology systems. National Institute of Standards and Technology. September 1996. http://csrc.nist.gov/publications/nistpubs/800-27/sp800-27.pdf (1996). Accessed 29 Jan 2012
27. TCG Infrastructure Working Group reference architecture for interoperability. Specification ver. 1.0. 16 June 2005. http://www.trustedcomputinggroup.org/specs/IWG/IWG_Architecture_v1_0_r1.pdf (2005). Accessed 9 Nov 2011
28. Demchenko, Y., Gommans, L., de Laat, C.: Extending user-controlled security domain with TPM/TCG in grid-based virtual collaborative environment. In: Proceedings of the International Symposium on Collaborative Technologies and Systems, Orlando, FL, USA, 2007, pp. 57–65
29. RFC5280 Internet X.509 public key infrastructure certificate and certificate revocation list (CRL) Profile. May 2008. http://www.ietf.org/rfc/rfc5280 (2008). Accessed 9 Nov 2011
30. Web services trust language (WS-Trust). ftp://www6.software.ibm.com/software/developer/library/ws-trust.pdf. Accessed 9 Nov 2011
31. Li, H., Singhal, M.: Trust management in distributed systems. Computer 40(2), 45–53 (2007)
32. Abdul-Rahman, A., Hailes, S.: A distributed trust model. In: Proceedings of the 1997 Workshop on New Security Paradigms – NSPW'97, Langdale, Cumbria, UK, pp. 48–60 (1997)
33. Assertions and protocols for the OASIS security assertion markup language (SAML) V2.0, OASIS Standard, 15 March 2005. http://docs.oasis-open.org/security/saml/v2.0/saml-core-2.0-os.pdf (2005). Accessed 9 Nov 2011
34. Fisher, D., McCune, J.M., Andrews, A.D.: Trust and Trusted Computing Platforms. Software Engineering Institute, Carnegie Mellon University, Pittsburgh, PA (2011)
35. Intel hardware technologies to secure clouds. http://www.intel.com/content/www/us/en/enterprise-security/processors-with-built-in-cloud-security.html. Accessed 9 Nov 2011
36. Intel cloud builders guide for enhancing server platform security with VMWare. http://www.intel.com/Assets/PDF/general/icb_ra_cloud_computing_VMware_TCP.pdf. Accessed 9 Nov 2011

37. Brickell, E., Camenisch, J., Chen, L.: Direct anonymous attestation. In: Proceedings of the 11th ACM Conference on Computer and Communications Security – CCS'04, Washington DC, p. 132 (2004)
38. Parno, B.: The Trusted Platform Module (TPM) and Sealed Storage. RSA Laboratories' Technical Notes, 21 June 2007. http://www.rsa.com/rsalabs/technotes/tpm/sealedstorage.pdf. Accessed 9 Nov 2011
39. Demchenko, Y., Wan, A., Cristea, M., de Laat, C.: Authorisation infrastructure for on-demand network resource provisioning. In: Proceedings of the 9th IEEE/ACM International Conference on Grid Computing (Grid 2008), Tsukuba, Japan, 29 Sept–1 Oct 2008, pp. 95–103 (2008). ISBN 978-1-4244-2579-2
40. GAAA Toolkit pluggable components and XACML policy profile for ONRP. Phosphorus Project Deliverable D4.3.1, 30 September 2008. http://www.ist-phosphorus.eu/files/deliverables/Phosphorus-deliverable-D4.3.1.pdf. Accessed 9 Nov 2011
41. Web services federation language (WS-Federation), version 1.0, 8 July 2003. http://msdn. microsoft.com/ws/2003/07/ws-federation/ (2003). Accessed 9 Nov 2011
42. RFC4120 The Kerberos network authentication service (V5). http://www.ietf.org/rfc/rfc4120. txt. Accessed 9 Nov 2011
43. XML-signature syntax and processing. W3C recommendation, 10 June 2008. http://www. w3.org/TR/xmldsig-core/. Accessed 9 Nov 2011
44. XML encryption XML encryption syntax and processing. W3C recommendation, 10 December 2002. http://www.w3.org/TR/xmlenc-core/ (2002). Accessed 9 Nov 2011
45. Web services secure conversation language (WS-SecureConversation). http://msdn.microsoft. com/library/en-us/dnglobspec/html/ws-secureconversation.asp. Accessed 9 Nov 2011
46. Web services policy framework (WSPolicy), version 1.2, March 2006. http://specs.xmlsoap. org/ws/2004/09/policy/ws-policy.pdf. Accessed 9 Nov 2011
47. eduGAIN – GEANT federated authentication and authorisation infrastructure. http://www. geant.net/service/edugain/pages/home.aspx. Accessed 9 Nov 2011
48. EduPKI GEANT PKI service. https://www.edupki.org/. Accessed 9 Nov 2011
49. TERENA Certificate Service (TCS). http://www.terena.org/activities/tcs/. Accessed 9 Nov 2011
50. The International Grid Trust Federation. http://www.igtf.net/. Accessed 9 Nov 2011

Recommended Reading

For interested readers, it is recommended to become familiar with general background information related to both cloud technologies and basic security models and standards. In particular, the following additional literature can be recommended.

First of all, it is recommended to read NIST standards on cloud computing and virtualisation technologies for which an up-to-date list is available at the NIST Cloud Program webpage (http://www.nist.gov/itl/cloud/):

- NIST SP 800-145, "A NIST definition of cloud computing". http://csrc.nist.gov/publications/nistpubs/800-145/SP800-145.pdf
- NIST SP 500-292, Cloud Computing Reference Architecture, v1.0. http://collaborate.nist.gov/twiki-cloud-computing/pub/CloudComputing/ReferenceArchitectureTaxonomy/NIST_SP_500-292_-_090611.pdf
- DRAFT NIST SP 800-146, Cloud Computing Synopsis and Recommendations. http://csrc.nist.gov/publications/drafts/800-146/Draft-NIST-SP800-146.pdf

- Draft SP 800-144 Guidelines on Security and Privacy in Public Cloud Computing. http://csrc.nist.gov/publications/nistpubs/800-144/SP800-144.pdf
- DRAFT NIST SP 800-293, US Government Cloud Computing Technology Roadmap, Volume I, Release 1.0. http://www.nist.gov/itl/cloud/upload/SP_500_293_volumeI-2.pdf
- NIST SP500-291 NIST Cloud Computing Standards Roadmap. http://collaborate. nist.gov/twiki-cloud-computing/pub/CloudComputing/StandardsRoadmap/NIST_SP_500-291_Jul5A.pdf
- SP 800-125 Guide to Security for Full Virtualisation Technologies.
- http://csrc.nist.gov/publications/nistpubs/800-125/SP800-125-final.pdf

For background security, read the following literature:
These RFCs on the generic AAA Authorisation framework provide a general context for developing authorisation infrastructure for on-demand provisioned services and access control infrastructure:

- RFC2903 Generic AAA Architecture Experimental RFC 2903, Internet Engineering Task Force, August 2000. ftp://ftp.isi.edu/in-notes/rfc2903.txt
- RFC 2904 AAA Authorization Framework. Internet Engineering Task Force, August 2000.ftp://ftp.isi.edu/in-notes/rfc2904.txt

Cloud computing technologies with their distributed virtualised computing environments motivate revisiting foundational security concepts and models and rethinking existing security models and solutions. The following foundation publications on computer security (proposed for the mainframe-based computing model) can be recommended:

- Anderson, J.: Computer Security Technology Planning Study. ESD-TR-73-51, ESD/AFSC, Hanscom AFB, Bedford, MA 01731 (Oct. 1972) [NTIS AD-758 206]. http://csrc.nist.gov/publications/history/ande72.pdf
- Bell. DE., La Padula, L.: Secure Computer System: Unified Exposition and Multics Interpretation. ESD-TR-75-306, ESD/AFSC, Hanscom AFB, Bedford, MA 01731 (1975) [DTIC AD-A023588]. http://csrc.nist.gov/publications/history/bell76.pdf
- Biba K.J.: Integrity Considerations for Secure Computer Systems. MTR-3153, The Mitre Corporation, Apr 1977
- Anderson, R., Stajano, F., Lee, J:. Security Policies. http://www.cl.cam.ac.uk/~rja14/Papers/security-policies.pdf

Chapter 6
Modeling the Runtime Integrity of Cloud Servers: A Scoped Invariant Perspective

Jinpeng Wei, Calton Pu, Carlos V. Rozas, Anand Rajan, and Feng Zhu

Abstract One of the underpinnings of cloud computing security is the trustworthiness of individual cloud servers. Due to the ongoing discovery of runtime software vulnerabilities like buffer overflows, it is critical to be able to guage the trustworthiness of a cloud server as it operates. The purpose of this chapter is to discuss trust-enhancing technologies in cloud computing, specifically remote attestation of cloud servers. We will discuss how remote attestation can provide higher assurance that cloud providers can be trusted to properly handle a customer's computation and/or data. Then we will focus on the modeling of the runtime integrity of a cloud server, which determines the level of assurance that remote attestation can offer. Specifically, we propose *scoped invariants* as a primitive for analyzing the software system for its integrity properties. We report our experience with the modeling and detection of scoped invariants for the Xen virtual machine manager.

Keywords Assurance • Cloud computing • Integrity • Scoped invariants • Trusted computing

J. Wei (✉) • F. Zhu
School of Computing and Information Sciences, Florida International University,
Miami, FL, USA
e-mail: weijp@cs.fiu.edu; fzhu001@fiu.edu

C. Pu
College of Computing, Georgia Institute of Technology, Atlanta, GA, USA
e-mail: calton@cc.gatech.edu

C.V. Rozas • A. Rajan
Corporate Technology Group, Intel Corporation, Hillsboro, OR, USA
e-mail: carlos.v.rozas@intel.com; anand.rajan@intel.com

S. Pearson and G. Yee (eds.), *Privacy and Security for Cloud Computing*,   211
Computer Communications and Networks, DOI 10.1007/978-1-4471-4189-1_6,
© Springer-Verlag London 2013

6.1   Introduction

According to IDC's 2008 cloud services user survey [1] of IT executives, security is the number one concern in adopting cloud computing. Part of the reason is that the operating systems supporting the cloud are just the conventional ones used today, which means that they can be compromised and be infected with malware. Not surprisingly, a prospective cloud user is concerned about delegating his data and computation to a cloud server that can be compromised at runtime, even if the server starts in a known-good condition and the cloud provider is trusted.

In other words, a trusted cloud server is not necessarily trustworthy, due to the inherent difficulty of eliminating software vulnerabilities and other operational errors (e.g., configuration mistakes). Therefore, technologies that can enhance the trust of cloud servers are highly demanded.

One way that can enhance the trust of cloud servers and relieve the concern of a potential cloud user is remote attestation [2], which enables the cloud user or a trusted third party to measure the "healthiness" (or integrity) of a cloud server at runtime, so that the compromise (or degraded integrity) can be detected in a timely manner.

There has been a long line of research in software integrity [2–13] because malware like rootkits [9] must modify the victim software in some way, thus violating its integrity. In general, the integrity of a system can be approximated by a set of properties that must be satisfied by a "healthy" software system. For example, many rootkits modify the system call table, so a property evaluated by many integrity monitors is whether the system call table has known-good values. It is through such properties that an integrity monitor differentiates a "healthy" system from a corrupted one.

Identifying integrity properties is critical to the effectiveness of any integrity measurement *mechanism*, because without a good set of integrity properties, the use of such mechanisms can be severely limited. For example, if the integrity properties only cover the system call table, a new rootkit can manipulate other function pointers (such as those found in device driver jump tables) to achieve its goal and remain undetected.

Therefore, in this chapter, we study the problem of systematically identifying integrity properties given the target software, which can then be used as input to an integrity measurement mechanism. Specifically, we make the following contributions:

We propose *scoped invariants* as an important class of integrity properties. Scoped invariants are code or data that has a constant value under some context (called their scope). An example scoped invariant is the Interrupt Descriptor Table (IDT) entry for page fault, which contains a constant function pointer once the system finishes its initialization. Scoped invariants are building blocks of more general integrity properties and are amenable to integrity checking.

Our second contribution is a dynamic analysis tool that detects scoped invariants. Our tool runs the target program in a machine emulator and monitors memory writes and events generated by the target program. Memory writes monitoring supports or rejects the hypothesis that a variable is an invariant, while event monitoring helps decide the scopes in which hypotheses about invariants apply.

Our third contribution is a scoped invariants case study of the Xen virtual machine manager [14], which is the foundational software of many cloud providers. Our tool identifies 271 scoped invariants essential to Xen's runtime integrity. One such invariant property, that the addressable memory limit of a guest OS must not include Xen's code and data, is indispensable for Xen's *guest isolation* mechanism. The violation of this property demonstrates that the attacker only needs to modify a single byte in the Global Descriptor Table (GDT) to achieve his goal.

The rest of the chapter is organized as follows. Section 6.2 gives background information about remote attestation and our security assumptions. Section 6.3 discusses our modeling of software integrity and proposes scoped invariants as an important class of integrity properties. Section 6.4 presents an automated scoped invariants detection scheme based on dynamic monitoring and statistical inference. Section 6.5 discusses our implementation of an automated tool for deriving scoped invariants. Section 6.6 evaluates our methodology and tool by studying scoped invariants of Xen. Section 6.7 discusses related work, and Sect. 6.8 concludes the chapter.

6.2 Background on Remote Attestation and Integrity Measurement

In this section, we introduce remote attestation as a useful trust enhancement technology for cloud computing; then we discuss the importance of integrity modeling in remote attestation and our security assumptions.

6.2.1 Remote Attestation as a Trust Enhancement Technology

A customer of a cloud server may want to determine that the cloud server is "healthy" (free of viruses, Trojan horses, worms, and so on), so it can be *trusted* to properly handle the customer's data and computation; he may also want to keep track of the cloud server's health status so that he can stop using the cloud server as soon as he suspects that the server is compromised, to minimize the damage or the delay for recovery. Trusted computing is a technology that can satisfy the needs of such a cloud customer.

A major goal in trusted computing is to provide reliable knowledge about a system to a user or a service provider. That knowledge is normally obtained by an evaluation of the identity and *integrity* of a system, and it serves as evidence that a target system will not engage in some class of misbehaviors, thus it can be trusted [15]. To this end, the Trusted Computing Group [16] has introduced the concept of *remote attestation*.

Remote attestation enables a computer system in a networked environment to decide whether a target computer has integrity, e.g., whether it has the appropriate configuration and hardware/software stack, so it can be trusted. The idea of remote attestation has been widely accepted. For example, the trusted platform module (TPM) [17] chip has become a standard component on modern computers.

An *integrity measurement system* (IMS) for remote attestation typically consists of three components: the target system, the measurement agent, and the decision maker [2]. The target system is a computer system whose "healthiness" is being evaluated (e.g., a cloud server); the measurement agent is a software or hardware entity that reads or *measures* the status (e.g., memory content) of the target system; and the decision maker is an entity (e.g., a cloud customer) that draws a conclusion about the integrity of the target system, given the measurements obtained by the measurement agent. Theoretically, a decision maker has some integrity model in mind, which determines the amount of measurements (or evidence) to be collected from the target system; and it is easy to understand that the integrity guarantee by an IMS is only as strong as the comprehensiveness of the integrity model.

6.2.2 Security Assumptions About the Integrity Measurement System

Our first assumption is that the measurement agent is isolated from and independent of the target system; therefore, it has a true view of the internal states (including code and data) of the target system. This is a realistic assumption due to the popularity of machine emulators such as QEMU [18], and it has also been shown that the measurement agent can run on dedicated hardware such as a PCI card [9]. Our second assumption is that measurement results are securely stored and transferred to the decision maker. This can be supported by hardware such as a trusted platform module (TPM) [17]. The third assumption is that the target system's states (e.g., code and data) may be compromised by a powerful adversary who can make arbitrary modifications; therefore, the decision maker can rely on very few assumptions about the trustworthiness of the target system.

Based on these assumptions, the decision maker is given a true view of the target system, and its task is to estimate the "healthiness" of the target system. The healthiness includes functional correctness (e.g., a function that is supposed to reduce the priority level of a task is not modified to actually increase the priority level) and nonfunctional correctness (e.g., the priority level can be modified by a privileged user instead of a normal user). In the following subsections, we model the healthiness as integrity properties.

Moreover, the healthiness of the target system may change over time because it may be under constant attacks. Therefore, the integrity of the target system may need to be periodically re-evaluated.

6.3 Formal Definition of Scoped Invariants

In this section, we introduce and formally define *scoped invariants* as a class of integrity property; we also define *dependencies* among scoped invariants.

6.3.1 Formalizing Integrity Properties

In theory, any software system can be modeled as an automaton with states and state transitions. For simplicity of presentation, we assume that the system can be in one of n possible states: $s_1, s_2, ..., s_n$. Example states are initialization, entering a function, returning from a function, system termination, and so on. Each state is characterized by a particular combination of values of the system's internal variables. Based on this general formalization, we can model runtime software integrity as a set of properties $\{P_1(s), P_2(s), ..., P_m(s)\}$. A runtime property $P_i(s)$ is a function on state s that evaluates to *true* or *false*. If a system state s satisfies all P_i's, we can say that s is a "healthy" state. Different runtime properties may have different structures, but each of them can be generalized to be a Boolean expression with the operators $\wedge$(and), $\vee$(or), and $\neg$(not). More complex properties can be constructed out of primitive properties using the operators mentioned above. A primitive property has the form $func(v_1(s), v_2(s), ..., v_l(s))$ which takes variables $v_1(s), v_2(s), ..., v_l(s)$ and returns *true* or *false* ($v(s)$ is the value of v in state s). *func* can have arithmetic operations inside as well as relationship operations like ==, <, and >.

6.3.2 Definition of Scoped Invariants

Scoped invariants are one special class of primitive property with the form $v(t) == k, t \in [s_1, s_2)$. For example, it stipulates that the value of variable v must be a specific value k when the system enters state s_1 and continue to be this value until the system enters another state s_2 (assuming that there is a sequence of state transitions from s_1 to s_2). We call such a primitive property a *scoped invariant*, and (s_1, s_2) is called its *scope*. An example scoped invariant is a global variable whose value does not change after initialization (e.g., once the system enters the *running* state). For example, the Interrupt Descriptor Table (IDT) entry for page fault is such a scoped invariant. Scoped invariants can be regarded as a simplified form of temporal logic.

Scoped invariants represent an important class of integrity properties. They may include critical internal control data of the system (e.g., function addresses) that are supposed to remain constant. Examples of such scoped invariants include the Interrupt Descriptor Table (IDT), whose importance to system integrity has been well understood. Another type of scoped invariant holds security policy data, and the violation of such invariants can directly defeat the corresponding security measures. For example, by tampering with the list of "bad" IP addresses, the attacker can defeat a blacklist-based IDS (Intrusion Detection System).

Note that the scopes of different invariants can vary significantly, depending on whether they are global variables, heap variables, or local variables. The scope of a global invariant can span as much as the entire execution of the program; the scope of a heap invariant must fall within the allocation and the freeing of the heap memory block; finally, the scope of an invariant that is a local variable in a function must be a subset of the interval between the entrance and the exit of the function.

In this chapter, we focus on estimating the target system's integrity from the measurement of scoped invariants. Other forms of integrity properties are subjects of future research.

6.3.3   Using Scoped Invariants for Integrity Measurement: Practical Issues

Scoped invariants fit conveniently into the software integrity measurement paradigm because they are amenable to runtime attestation. Given a scoped invariant $v(t) = k, t \in [s_1, s_2)$, the measurement agent can start to read the value of variable v once the system enters state s_1. Then the decision maker can verify if the measurements of v are "good" until the system enters state s_2. The verification of v is simple – just comparing the runtime measurements of v against some known-good value k. Note that k may be difficult to obtain if it depends on something external to the target program, e.g., configuration parameters. Here we assume that k has been determined somehow, e.g., using the dynamic detection technique discussed in Sect. 6.4.

Although theoretically the definition of the scope of a scoped invariant is simple – just identifying the two boundary states – in a real system, it is nontrivial, because typically we do not have an *explicit* and *direct* representation of program states. Instead, we can only *infer* program states from registers, main memory, or file system. For example, if the program is sequential, the program counter (PC) can tell us the progress that has been made by the program since it is started. However, if there are loops in the program, the PC *alone* may not be sufficient because the corresponding instruction may be part of a loop body and we do not know the number of iterations the program has gone through the loop body. In this case, we may need additional information such as the value of a *loop guard* variable to better infer the program state. Finally, when the program handles asynchronous events such as hardware interrupts, the program execution becomes nondeterministic, and it may be very hard to reliably infer the program states.

Another related issue is the granularity of the program states, which influence the cost of integrity measurement. At one end of the spectrum, the program can have very coarse-grained states (e.g., *initialization*, *running*, and *termination*). Here the *running* state covers most of the program's life span. At the other end of the spectrum, the program can have very fine-grained states (e.g., one state per instruction execution or even multiple states within one instruction). While the most fine-grained states enable the integrity measurement agent to have the closest thus the clearest view of the target system, it is the most expensive. On the other hand, the coarse-grained states may lead the decision maker to miss many important events (including integrity violations due to attacks), but it is cheaper for the decision maker to keep track of the program states. Therefore, there is a tradeoff between the granularity of program states and the effectiveness of integrity monitoring.

The third issue is the tracking of program states by the measurement agent. As we mentioned in Sect. 6.2.2, an attacker may change the target program in arbitrary ways, so we cannot rely on the target program to notify the measurement agent about its states. Instead, we can only let the agent actively *poll* the state from a different domain. Specifically, the agent can run in a more privileged domain from which it can intercept the target program's execution and inspect registers, memory, and files of the target program. As will be discussed in Sect. 6.4, a machine emulator is a good choice to run the measurement agent securely.

One related issue is performance overhead introduced by integrity measurement. As discussed above, a measurement agent needs to intercept the target program's execution, which causes delays in the target program. Obviously, the slowdown factor depends on the frequency (how often a measurement is taken) and duration (how long each measurement takes) of the measurements, and the duration depends on the number of invariants that need to be checked.

6.3.4   Composition of Scoped Invariants

Scoped invariants are building blocks of more general integrity properties. In this section, we discuss how we can evaluate more general integrity properties from the result of evaluating individual scoped invariants. The key observation is to look at the dependency relationship among integrity properties and build a hierarchy (represented in invariant dependency graphs or IDGs, defined shortly). We extend the definition of scoped invariant (see Sect. 6.3.2) so that the variable v can be an arbitrary object (e.g., a function, a code segment, or a data structure).

In a complex target system such as an operating system, the integrity of different functionality modules is often related. This is because a module may invoke functions provided by some external module (the *callouts*), and it may supply *callback* functions that are supposed to be called by an external module. If an external function (e.g., init_timer in Fig. 6.1) that is called by a module (e.g., the Xen scheduler) misbehaves, the control integrity of the calling module (e.g., the Xen scheduler) may be influenced. Similarly, if an external module (e.g., softIRQ) misbehaves by not invoking the callback function (e.g., schedule in Fig. 6.1) supplied by a module (e.g., the Xen scheduler calls open_softirq), that module may not get control as expected.

Correspondingly, different scoped invariants can be correlated. Below we formally define dependency between scoped invariants and a data structure (called invariant dependency graph) that can be used to express the structural dependency relationship among a set of scoped invariants.

Definition 1 (dependency between scoped invariants): a scoped invariant i_1 is said to depend on another scoped invariant i_2 if one of the following cases is true:

1. i_1 and i_2 are both codes and there is a callout from i_1 to i_2, or i_1 has a callback function supposed to be invoked by i_2.

```
DEFINE_PER_CPU (struct schedule_data, schedule_data);
static struct scheduler ops;
......
static void vcpu_periodic_timer_fn(void *d){......}
int sched_init_vcpu(struct vcpu *v,   unsigned int processor){
......
 init_timer(&v -> periodic_timer,  vcpu_periodic_timer_fn, v, v -> processor);
......
}
static void schedule(void){......}
void __init scheduler_init(void){
......
 open_softirq(SCHEDULE_SOFTIRQ, schedule);
......
}
```

Fig. 6.1 Code snippet of the Xen scheduler ($XEN/xen/common/schedule.c)

2. i_1 is code and i_2 is data, but whether control can go to i_1 depends on the value of i_2.
3. i_1 and i_2 are both data and the evaluation of i_1 depends on the evaluation of i_2.

Case 2 of definition 1 applies to the situation in which i_2 is a function pointer and i_1 is the function that i_2 points to.

Definition 2: An invariant dependency graph (IDG) is a directed acyclic graph $G = <V, E>$, where each member of V represents a scoped invariant, and if $i_1 \in V, i_2 \in V$, and i_1 depends on i_2, there is an edge $e = (i_1, i_2) \in E$.

An IDG thus is a convenient representation of scoped invariants and their relationship. An example IDG is shown in Fig. 6.1.

An IDG also provides useful guidance in terms of how to evaluate the integrity of a target system in a bottom-up way: for example, if an integrity property i depends on $i_1, i_2, \cdots,$ and i_m, then in order for i to be *true*, $i_1, i_2, \cdots,$ and i_m must all be *true*. Thus, a decision maker should evaluate $i_1, i_2, \cdots,$ and i_m before evaluating i.

6.4 Automated Detection of Scoped Invariants

In this section, we present a scoped invariants detection scheme based on dynamic profiling and statistical inference. We will discuss first the rationale (Sect. 6.4.1) and then two technical components: memory write monitoring (Sect. 6.4.2) and event monitoring (Sect. 6.4.3).

6.4.1   Overview

The inference of scoped invariants can be labor intensive and error-prone if performed manually. Therefore, tools are needed to automate this process.

By definition, a scoped invariant $v(t) == k, t \in [s_1, s_2)$ has a constant value k when the system state is between s_1 and s_2. Accordingly, the scoped invariant detection must answer the following questions for each scoped invariant: (1) What are the starting and end states that define the scope? (2) Which variable (v) is involved? and (3) What is the known-good value (k)?

Note that scoped invariants are defined as such with respect to their scopes, i.e., the same variable can be an invariant in a narrower scope but not in a broader scope if the broader scope includes an operation that changes the value of the variable. Therefore, we must first decide the scope and then decide whether a variable is an invariant within that scope.

Our invariant detection employs a dynamic profiling approach. Specifically, we run the target program in a machine emulator and monitor memory writes and events generated by the target program. Memory writes monitoring supports or rejects the hypothesis that a variable is an invariant, while event monitoring helps decide the scopes in which hypotheses about invariants apply. In the remainder of this section, we first discuss memory write monitoring and then discuss event monitoring.

6.4.2   Memory Writes Monitoring

By definition, a scoped invariant should not be modified other than at initialization. In other words, a variable that is modified multiple times is unlikely to be an invariant. Based on this reasoning, we can detect invariants by observing how the target software modifies its variables: if a variable is modified multiple times, it is unlikely to be an invariant; otherwise, it is an invariant.

Using dynamic profiling, we run the target software and collect its modifications to variables, which translate to memory writes. There are multiple ways to do this, including program instrumentation and emulation. Using emulation, we can run the target software in a machine emulator, which can intercept every memory write operation (e.g., a MOV instruction). With this capability, we can record the target memory address and the value written in each memory write operation. The result of dynamic profiling is a sequence of tuples: $w_1, w_2, \cdots, w_n$, where $w_i = (addr_i, v_i)$.

Given a sequence $w_1, w_2, \cdots, w_n$, we can compute the frequency c_i of updates to each unique address $addr_i$. Then, we can sort $addr_i$'s at the ascending order of c_i's, and the sorted list of $addr_i$'s is a list of potential invariants with the most likely at the beginning and the most unlikely at the end. Note that the computation here captures addresses that are updated at least once; addresses that are not updated in the sequence are automatically inserted at the beginning of the sorted list as the most likely invariants.

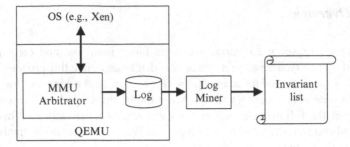

Fig. 6.2 Scoped invariant detection architecture [19]

6.4.3   Event Monitoring

In addition to memory writes, the machine emulator also intercepts other events that help define the scopes of the invariants. As discussed in Sect. 6.3.3, program states can be defined at various granularities, with different trade-offs between integrity measurement precision and cost. We choose to monitor two types of such events: function calls and function returns. The reason is that functions can give semantic meaning for creating (by initialization) or re-creating (by updating) an invariant. In other words, we can say that the scope of an invariant is between when it gets its value in some function and when it is assigned a different value in another function. Tracking the invocations and returns from functions is thus important for determining the scopes of invariants.

For example, the global variable `opt_noirqbalance` of Xen controls whether IRQ balance should be enabled, and Xen allows this configuration parameter to be modified by the hypercall `platform_op`. Obviously, this variable is an invariant between two consecutive `platform_op` hypercalls that modify it.

6.5   Implementation

We develop a prototype tool that can automatically derive invariants. As Fig. 6.2 shows, we first run the target software on top of QEMU [18], a CPU emulator, which enables us to log all memory write operations of the target software (by the MMU arbitrator). We also log important system events such as entering and exiting a function, which represent program states that define invariant scopes. Then the Log Miner performs an offline processing of the log – given the sequence of memory write operations between two system events, ranking the memory locations based on the number of modifications to them (with the least modified on the top) and mapping the memory locations to global variables (using symbol information).

The output of the Log Miner is a list of candidate invariants, ranked from the most likely to the least likely. If a variable is indeed an invariant, it will be ranked high in the candidate list – i.e., we will not miss the true invariants. However, some non-invariant variables may be ranked high because the condition that leads to their updates is not satisfied during the limited profiling. This is a typical limitation of dynamic analysis, which can be remediated by profiling the target program multiple times, each with a different set of input. We can also filter such non-invariant variables using static analysis of the source code, which is out of the scope of this chapter.

6.6 Evaluation

To test the applicability of scoped invariants, this section takes Xen as the target system to do several case studies. We first discuss the motivation of choosing Xen as the target system (Sect. 6.6.1); next, we discuss a scoped invariant with GDT that is critical to Xen's guest isolation mechanism (Sect. 6.6.2). In Sect. 6.6.3, we describe a scoped invariant dependency study of the Xen scheduler. Section 6.6.4 presents the result of an automated study of Xen's global invariants.

6.6.1 Choice of Xen as the Subject of Study

Virtualization is the foundational technology for cloud computing, and Xen [14] is one representative VMM (virtual machine manager) that allows multiple operating systems (called guest OSes or simply guests) to share the same physical machine. As the lowest layer in the cloud computing software stack, the runtime integrity of Xen is the root of trust for a cloud computing environment.

It is generally believed that Xen is more secure than commodity operating systems such as Windows and Linux because it is smaller and simpler. However, we cannot rule out the possibility of a malicious modification to Xen at runtime. For example, there could be vulnerabilities with Xen that can be exploited [20, 21]. Even if Xen is completely bug-free, there are environmental issues such as DMA and system management mode (SMM) [22] that can modify Xen at runtime. Therefore, we feel it useful to choose Xen as the target system to perform an integrity study. The particular Xen version studied in this chapter is a prerelease of Xen 3.0.4.

6.6.2 Study of the GDT Scoped Invariant

One essential security goal of Xen is guest isolation, e.g., a guest operating system should not have access to information about other guests on the same platform nor should a guest have access to Xen's internal state information.

This guest isolation goal is achieved by scoped invariants associated with some entries of the Global Descriptor Table (GDT) [23]. Specifically, to avoid unauthorized access to its internal state from guests, Xen leverages the standard IA-32 segmentation and protection rings architecture: a guest operating system runs in ring 1 and guest processes run in ring 3, and four special *guest segments* are defined for them. For example, the data segment for ring 3 has the selector 0xe033 in the GDT. The "limit" of these guest segments is intentionally made smaller than 4 GB such that Xen's code and data are excluded (Xen's code and data reside at the top of every address space).

Such a configuration is represented in the form of scoped invariants because information about these guest segments is stored in memory, in a data structure called gdt_table. Setting of the proper descriptor values for gdt_table is performed in the initialization phase of Xen, and after that, the "limit" fields of the relevant entries are not supposed to change; in other words, they are scoped invariants.

It is easy to understand that a runtime modification to the gdt_table entries (e.g., setting the "limit" field to 4 GB) could undo the effect of Xen's initialization and expose the complete 4 GB address space back to the guests. Then suddenly a guest can freely read Xen's data, violating the guest isolation security goal.

We have experimentally confirmed that modifying the "limit" field of the gdt_table entries at runtime enables a para-virtualized guest to read Xen's data and retrieve the list of domains on the platform by loading its **DS** register with 0xe033. This means that our hypothesis is valid. And it turns out that only one byte needs to be modified (from 0x67 to 0xFF). We should note that Xen virtualizes the GDT for each guest domain, which means that each guest domain has its own GDT. However, each guest GDT derives its entries for the guest segments from the same gdt_table. Therefore, a modification to the gdt_table applies to all guest domains.

The GDT example demonstrates how a particular scoped invariant can influence Xen's high level security goals – i.e., guest isolation. Therefore, this invariant must be checked by a decision maker.

6.6.3 Integrity Dependency Analysis of the Xen Scheduler

In this section, we perform an integrity dependency analysis of the Xen scheduler. We will demonstrate the dependencies among scoped invariants. We choose the scheduler because it is one of the most important functionalities of Xen, which allows multiple operating systems to share the physical CPU. The quality of this sharing is determined by the scheduler. Besides, if we can verify the integrity of the scheduler, we can trust it to run other security measures such as integrity monitors for the guest kernel.

The security goal that we choose is *complete mediation*. Under the context of scheduling, it means that no task should be able to use the CPU without the permission from the scheduler. In other words, the scheduler should always be able to control when and for how long a particular task can use the CPU.

Figure 6.4 shows the invariant dependency graph associated with the Xen scheduler. Below we will discuss the reasoning behind this graph.

In order to fulfill complete mediation, the scheduler needs two necessary conditions: (1) when running, the scheduler correctly implements a scheduling algorithm

Table 6.1 Scoped invariants associated with the Xen scheduler

1	$RC_{scheduler}$ [*initialization, termination*] $= KGC_{scheduler}$
2	RC_{timer} [*initialization, termination*] $= KGC_{timer}$
3	$RC_{do\_softirq}$ [*initialization, termination*] $= KGC_{do\_softirq}$
4	$RC_{inthandler}$ [*initialization, termination*] $= KGC_{inthandler}$
5	RD_{idt} [*initialization, termination*] $= KGD_{idt}$
6	RD_{gdt} [*initialization, termination*] $= KGD_{gdt}$
7	RD_{tss} [*initialization, termination*] $= KGD_{tss}$
8	$RD_{pgtable}$ [*initialization, termination*] $= KGD_{pgtable}$
9	$RD_{softirq\_handlers}$ [*initialization, termination*] $= KGD_{softirq\_handlers}$

RC means runtime code, *KGC* means known-good code, *RD* means runtime data, and *KGD* means known-good data

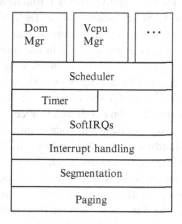

Fig. 6.3 Module structure related to the Xen scheduler

(e.g., the credit-based scheduling algorithm in Xen) and (2) the scheduler can have a chance to run when it needs to. Condition (1) can be satisfied by guaranteeing the integrity of the scheduler code. Satisfying condition (2) is challenging because from time to time the scheduler has to give up CPU so that the normal tasks can make progress, but it must be able to regain control of the CPU to do its job. If these two necessary conditions are not guaranteed, we say that the security goal of complete mediation for the scheduler is not achieved. Therefore, we have derived from the security goal two integrity properties: (1) the scheduler code is not compromised or, equivalently, the scheduler code is a scoped invariant (#1 in Table 6.1) and (2) the scheduler is able to get control when it should.

In order to achieve integrity property (2), Xen scheduler relies on the timer functionality (Fig. 6.3), which guarantees that control will go to a callback function supplied by the scheduler after some amount of time into the future. For example, when the scheduler decides to let a task run, it starts a timer which will expire after an interval equal to that task's time slice. The callback function (s_timer_fn) associated with this timer forces a decision to be made concerning which task runs next. This timer helps to avoid the situation where a task excessively occupies CPU and nobody can stop it.

Xen scheduler has to trust the timer facility mentioned above to work as expected (e.g., the timer should guarantee precision of some degree); otherwise, Xen scheduler cannot achieve its goals. Therefore, the timer is a scoped invariant (#2 in Table 6.1), and the integrity of Xen scheduler is dependent on the integrity of the timer facility.

The timer facility in turn relies on the soft IRQ mechanism of Xen (Fig. 6.3). Different from hard IRQs (hardware interrupts), which can interrupt the currently running task at almost any point, soft IRQs do not directly interrupt currently running task. Instead, they are piggybacked in the hardware interrupt handling procedure, e.g., after an interrupt has been served but before the interrupt handler returns. Specifically, the interrupt handler procedure calls do_softirq, which in turn checks the presence of soft IRQs and calls their respective handler functions. Therefore, the code of do_softirq should be a scoped invariant (#3 in Table 6.1).

For the soft IRQ mechanism to work, several preconditions must hold. One of them is that do_softirq must be invoked in the interrupt handling procedure. This is an issue because do_softirq is not invoked by hardware but the interrupt handling procedures which are code in the memory. Therefore, the integrity of interrupt handling code is a precondition for the integrity of Xen's soft IRQ mechanism. In other words, the interrupt handling code is a scoped invariant (#4 in Table 6.1).

However, even if the interrupt handling code is intact, they must be called when interrupts happen. The hardware provides the Interrupt Descriptor Table (IDT) for the software to register interrupt handlers. Each entry of this table has information about the address of the function to invoke when the corresponding interrupt happens. Therefore, the integrity of the IDT is a precondition for the integrity of interrupt handling of Xen and, one step further, the soft IRQ mechanism of Xen. So the relevant IDT entries are scoped invariants (#5 in Table 6.1).

In normal execution mode, an IDT entry refers to code in memory in terms of a segment selector and an offset. Each memory segment has a base address and a limit, and the information about the segments is stored in the Global Descriptor Table (GDT). When an interrupt happens, the handler function's segment selector and offset are fetched from the IDT. Then the segment selector is used to get the base address from the GDT, and the offset is added to the base address to form the linear address of the interrupt handling function. Therefore, the GDT entry must give the correct base address in order for the right interrupt handling function to be located. In other words, the relevant GDT entries are scoped invariants (#6 in Table 6.1) because they are used to evaluate (the linear address of) the interrupt handling code.

Furthermore, some interrupts are handled by task gates (e.g., double fault), whose details (such as handler function entry and stack pointer) are stored in task state segments (TSS). So according to our model, there is a dependency relationship from the IDT entry to the relevant TSS, so the TSS becomes a scoped invariant (#7 in Table 6.1).

Finally, there is another layer of indirection due to modern CPU's paging mechanism. Specifically, an interrupt handling function address derived from IDT, GDT,

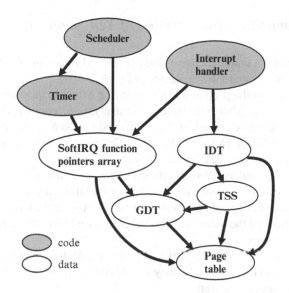

Fig. 6.4 Invariant dependency graph related to the Xen scheduler

and perhaps TSS is a linear address, and the paging mechanism of the underlying hardware maps this linear address to physical address in physical memory, where the handler code resides. But software can control the mapping by supplying page tables, and the page tables are again in memory which can be modified. Therefore, the integrity of page tables is essential to the interrupt handling process of Xen and, due to all the above description, the integrity of the Xen scheduler. So the relevant page table entries are also scoped invariants (#8 in Table 6.1).

In Fig. 6.4, the dependency edges from GDT, IDT, and TSS to page tables are due to the fact that in the Intel architecture, GDT, IDT, and TSS are known to the CPU in terms of linear addresses. In order to evaluate such data structures, the CPU needs to go through paging mechanism controlled by the page tables.

As mentioned above, in order for the soft IRQ mechanism to work, several preconditions must hold. We have described one of them: that do_softirq be invoked in the interrupt handling process. But we need one more precondition. Specifically, do_softirq consults a function pointer array (softirq_handlers) for the handler of a particular soft IRQ, so the content of this array must not be compromised. In other words, the relevant entries in the softirq_handlers array are scoped invariants (#9 in Table 6.1). For example, Xen scheduler registers a function schedule for soft IRQ 1, meaning that schedule will be called when soft IRQ 1 is raised (see Fig. 6.1). But if an attacker modifies the function pointer for soft IRQ 1, some other function instead of schedule will be called. Then Xen scheduler is essentially bypassed.

Another important soft IRQ is the timer soft IRQ, which implements the timer facility. We have mentioned that Xen scheduler relies on it. The timer facility registers timer_softirq_action as the call back function.

We can summarize the integrity analysis of Xen scheduler with the invariant dependency graph in Fig. 6.4.

6.6.4   A Comprehensive Detection of Xen Scoped Invariants

We have performed a comprehensive study of scoped invariants for Xen, using the QEMU-based profiler and the Log Miner in Fig. 6.2.

We first ran Xen in the profiler and used the Log Miner to generate the candidate scoped invariants list. Then we did a static analysis to confirm the real scoped invariants. Our static analysis scans the source code of Xen to locate all statements that write to a candidate invariant. We found that most of the candidate invariants have only one such statement (for initialization).

Our analysis suggests that most of the Xen global variables are scoped invariant at runtime. If we only consider the number of variables declared, 75% of them (271 out of 362) turn out to be invariants. If we also consider the size of the variables, then more than 90% of the memory locations corresponding to these global variables are invariant at runtime.

Table 6.2 shows some of the identified invariants. We have classified them based on an informal reasoning about why they should be invariants. Below we give details of some of these scoped invariants:

- `sched_sedf_def` is a data structure that stores the addresses of several functions that together implement the simple earliest deadline first (SEDF) algorithm of Xen. These functions are invoked when a virtual CPU is initialized, suspended, resumed, and so on. Obviously, they should be scoped invariants because otherwise an attacker can modify them to induce Xen's control flow to a malicious scheduling algorithm. Conceptually, `sched_sedf_def` is similar to the IDT. From Table 6.2 we can see that there are 27 more such scoped invariants in Xen.
- `opt_sched` holds the value of a boot-time parameter, which selects one of the built-in scheduling algorithms to be used by Xen. Since Xen does not support on-the-fly change of its scheduling algorithm, this variable should be a scoped invariant.

Table 6.3 gives more information about the invariants `idle_pg_table`, `idle_pg_table_12`, and `idt_table` identified in Table 6.2. First, since only part of such data structures (arrays) are invariants, Table 6.3 gives the range information. We have used macros (e.g., DIRECTMAP_VIRT_START) from Xen source code because their exact values depend on the harxdware configuration (e.g., whether Physical Address Extension [23] is enabled). Second, the column denoted "initialized by" shows the last function that sets the value of a particular scoped invariant. The goal of identifying functions in the "initialized by" column is to specify the start of the scope of a scoped invariant because since then the value of the scoped invariant is supposed to be constant.

6.5   Discussion

The degree to which a set of scoped invariants can approximate runtime integrity of a software system remains a research question. For example, the invariants that we identified are all necessary conditions, but they may not be sufficient. Assuming that

Table 6.2 Sample scoped invariants (global variables) identified for Xen

Type	Total number	Examples
Static variables that are definitely invariants	63	schedulers, large_digits, small_digits
Effectively static structures (e.g., contains important function pointers)	28	sched_bvt_def, sched_sedf_def, ioapic_level_type, ioapic_edge_type, amd_mtrr_ops, apic_es7000, hvm_mmio_handlers, exception_table, hypercall_table
Variables that are effectively invariant given a particular boot configuration	17	opt_badpage, opt_sched, opt_con-switch, opt_console, acpi_param, debug_stack_lines, lowmem_emergency_pool_pages, dom0_nrpages
Variables that are effectively invariant given a hardware configuration	102	new_bios, ioapic_i8259, mp_bus_id_to_pci_bus, boot_cpu_logical_apicid, es7000_plat, dmi_ident, hpet_address, vmcs_size, max_cpus, max_page, cpu_present_map, vector_irq, irq_vector
Variables that are effectively invariant given a software configuration	4	softirq_handlers, gdt_table, change_point_list, key_table
Arrays whose entries are mostly invariant	7	idle_pg_table, idle_pg_table_12, e820, e820_raw, irq_2_pin cpu_sibling_map, cpu_core_map, idt_table

a right set of scoped invariants is at hand, we can estimate the runtime integrity of the system by verifying them. If all of them are verified, we have more confidence about the system's integrity. But if some of them do not pass the verification, we know that the system has lost its integrity.

6.7 Related Work

In this section, we give a survey of existing research related to our work, grouped into different topic areas.

6.7.1 Invariants Detection

The Daikon invariant detector [24] generates likely invariants using program execution traces collected during sample runs. Daikon is the closest to our work in theory, but the two are different: Daikon instruments the program-source code to emit data traces at specific program points, while our tool transparently intercepts program execution from a machine emulator.

Table 6.3 More information of `idle_pg_table`, `idle_pg_table_12`, and `idt_table`

Table name	Start offset	Number of entries	Initialized by
idle_pg_table	0	4	xen/arch/x86/boot/x86_32.S
idle_pg_table_12	DIRECTMAP_VIRT_START/ (1<<L2_PAGETABLE_SHIFT)	DIRECTMAP_PHYS_END/ (1<<2_PAGETABLE_SHIFT)	__start in xen/arch/x86/boot/head.S
idle_pg_table_12	0	16 MB/(1<<L2_ PAGETABLE_SHIFT)	__start in xen/arch/x86/boot/head.S
idle_pg_table_12	FRAMETABLE_VIRT_START/ (1<<L2_PAGETABLE_SHIFT)	(FRAMETABLE_MBYTES<<20)/ (1<<L2_PAGETABLE_SHIFT)	init_frametable in xen/arch/x86/mm.c
idle_pg_table_12	RDWR_MPT_VIRT_START >>L2_PAGETABLE_SHIFT	(max_page * BYTES_PER_LONG) >>L2_PAGETABLE_SHIFT	paging_init in xen/arch/x86/x86_32/mm.c
idle_pg_table_12	RO_MPT_VIRT_START >>L2_ PAGETABLE_SHIFT	(max_page * BYTES_PER_LONG) >>L2_PAGETABLE_SHIFT	paging_init in xen/arch/x86/x86_32/mm.c
idle_pg_table_12	IOREMAP_VIRT_START >>L2_ PAGETABLE_SHIFT	IOREMAP_MBYTES >> (L2_PAGETABLE_SHIFT – 20)	paging_init in xen/arch/x86/x86_32/mm.c
idt_table	0 129	128 127	init_IRQ in xen/arch/x86/i8259.c, apic_intr_ init in xen/arch/x86/apic.c, trap_init in xen/arch/x86/traps.c, percpu_traps_init in xen/arch/ x86/x86_32/traps.c
idt_table	128	1	dom0 kernel

6.7.2 Integrity Measurement Mechanisms

There has been a long line of research on integrity measurement. Approaches such as IMA [12] use hashing or digital signatures to measure the software at load time. Recently, ReDAS [25] and DynIMA [5] advance the state of the art by supporting software integrity measurement at runtime. Other related work includes [2, 6, 9–11, 13]. These approaches generally focus on the mechanism for measurement but not the integrity properties.

Copilot [9] is a coprocessor-based integrity checker for the Linux kernel. The properties that the Copilot prototype checked were kernel code, module code, and jump tables of kernel function pointers. Although Copilot later provided a specification language [10], its focus was not on deriving integrity properties. We work out the properties from analyzing the target software itself.

Livewire [6] leverages a VMM (a modified version of VMware workstation) to implement a host-based intrusion detection system. It can inspect and monitor the states of a guest OS for detecting intrusions and interposes on certain events, such as interrupts and updates to device and memory state. Like Copilot, Livewire does not focus on the identification of integrity properties but only checks known properties.

LKIM [2] produces detailed records of the states of security relevant structures within the Linux kernel using the concept of contextual inspection. However, the identification of security relevant structures relies on domain knowledge. This chapter proposes an approach for systematically finding such structures.

6.7.3 Specialized Integrity Property Measurement

Some specialized integrity properties have been measured, such as control-flow integrity [3] and information-flow integrity [26]. [3] checks if the control transfer from one function to the next is consistent with a precomputed control-flow graph, so we can think of it as checking a sequence property of the target software. [26] checks the integrity of a system by reasoning about information flows, but it assumes that there is no direct memory modification attack, e.g., information flows are triggered by well-defined interfaces (function calls or file reads).

6.7.4 Rootkits Detection and Recovery

As we mentioned, there has been a lot of research on rootkits. A nice survey of rootkits and detection software is given in [9]. From [27], you can also find a list of popular rootkits. All the integrity measurement mechanisms (such as [6, 9, 11, 13]) mentioned above can be used for rootkit detection. Some work such as [7] and [8] attempts to detect rootkits and recover the software from known-good copies.

6.7.5   Trusted Computing

The Trusted Computing Group [16] has proposed several standards for measuring the integrity of a software system and storing the result in a TPM (trusted platform module) [17] whose state cannot be corrupted by a potentially malicious host system. Industry vendors such as Intel have embedded TPM in their hardware. Such standards and technologies have provided the root of trust for secure booting [28] and enabled remote attestation [15]. There has been a consistent effort in building a small trusted computing base (with hardware support such as TCG and application level techniques such as AppCore [29]). A small trusted computing base facilitates integrity analysis and monitoring.

6.8   Conclusion

In this chapter, we have discussed remote attestation as a critical and useful trust-enhancing technology for cloud computing. We studied one important aspect of remote attestation that is often ignored, the problem of systematically modeling the runtime integrity of a target system, e.g., a cloud server. We proposed scoped invariants as an important class of integrity properties, and we designed and implemented automated tools that can derive scoped invariants out of the target software.

To evaluate our methodology, we applied our tools to the Xen VMM and identified 271 scoped invariants that are critical to Xen's runtime integrity. We experimentally confirmed some of these invariants, including one that can be violated to defeat Xen's guest isolation mechanism.

References

1. IT Cloud Services User Survey, pt.2: Top Benefits & Challenges. http://blogs.idc.com/ie/?p=210. Accessed 16 Aug 2010
2. Loscocco, P.A., Wilson, P.W., Pendergrass, J.A., McDonell, C.D.: Linux kernel integrity measurement using contextual inspection. In: Proceedings of the 2007 ACM Workshop on Scalable Trusted Computing (STC). ACM, New York (2007)
3. Abadi, M., Budiu, M., Erlingsson, U., Ligatti, J.: Control-flow integrity. In: Proceedings of ACM Conference on Computer and Communications Security (CCS). ACM, New York (2005)
4. Baliga, A., Kamat, P., Iftode, L.: Lurking in the shadows: identifying systemic threats to kernel data. In: Proceedings of the 2007 IEEE Symposium on Security and Privacy, Oakland, CA (May 2007)
5. Davi, L., Sadeghi, A., Winandy, M.: Dynamic integrity measurement and attestation: towards defense against return-oriented programming attacks. In: Proceedings of the 2009 ACM Workshop on Scalable Trusted Computing (STC). ACM, New York (2009)
6. Garfinkel, T., Rosenblum, M.: A virtual machine introspection based architecture for intrusion detection. In: Proceedings of Network and Distributed Systems Security Symposium (NDSS), (Feb 2003)

7. Grizzard, J., Dodson, E., Conti, G., Levine, J., Owen, H.: Toward a trusted immutable kernel extension (TIKE) for self-healing systems: a virtual machine approach. In: Proceedings of 5th IEEE Information Assurance Workshop, West Point (2004)
8. Levine, J., Grizzard, J., Owen, H.: Re-establishing trust in compromised systems: recovering from rootkits that trojan the system call table. In: Proceedings of the 9th European Symposium on Research in Computer Security, Sophia Antipolis, France (2004)
9. Petroni, N., Jr., Fraser, T., Molina, J., Arbaugh, W.A.: Copilot—a coprocessor-based kernel runtime integrity monitor. In: Proceedings of the 13th USENIX Security Symposium. USENIX Association, Berkeley (2004)
10. Petroni, N., Jr., Fraser, T., Walters, A., Arbaugh, W.A.: An architecture for specification-based detection of semantic integrity violations in kernel dynamic data. In: Proceedings of the 15th USENIX Security Symposium. USENIX Association, Berkeley (2006)
11. Petroni, N. Jr., Hicks, M.: Automated detection of persistent kernel control-flow attacks. In: Proceedings of the 14th ACM Conference on Computer and Communications Security (CCS). ACM, New York (2007)
12. Sailer, R., Zhang, X., Jaeger, T., Doorn, L.V.: Design and implementation of a TCG-based integrity measurement architecture. In: Proceedings of the 13th USENIX Security Symposium, San Diego (2004)
13. Zhang, X., Doorn, L.V., Jaeger, T., Perez, R., Sailer, R.: Secure coprocessor-based intrusion detection. In: Proceedings of the Tenth ACM SIGOPS European Workshop, Saint-Emilion, France (2002)
14. Barham, P., Dragovic, B., Fraser, K., et al.: Xen and the art of virtualization. In: Proceedings of the ACM Symposium on Operating Systems Principles (SOSP), Bolton Landing, NY, (Oct 2003)
15. Sheehy, J., Coker, G., Guttman, J., et al.: Attestation: evidence and trust. http://www.mitre.org/work/tech_papers/tech_papers_07/07_0186/07_0186.pdf (2008). Accessed 16 Aug 2010
16. Trusted Computing Group: http://www.trustedcomputinggroup.org. Accessed 16 Aug 2010
17. Trusted Platform Modules: http://www.trustedcomputinggroup.org/developers/trusted_platform_module/specifications. Accessed 16 Aug 2010
18. Bellard, F.: QEMU, a fast and portable dynamic translator. In: Proceedings of the 2005 USENIX Annual Technical Conference. USENIX. Association, Berkeley (2005)
19. Wei, J., Pu, C., Rozas, C.V., Rajan, A., Zhu, F.: Modeling the runtime integrity of cloud servers: a scoped invariant perspective. In: International Workshop on Cloud Privacy, Security, Risk and Trust (CPSRT 2010), in conjunction with the 2nd IEEE International Conference on Cloud Computing Technology and Science (CloudCom 2010), Nov. 30 – Dec. 3, Indianapolis, IN (2010)
20. Xen local security-bypass vulnerability. http://www.securityfocus.com/bid/26954/discuss. Accessed 16 Aug 2010
21. Xen "move-to-rr" RID local security bypass vulnerability. http://www.securityfocus.com/bid/26716/discuss. Aaccessed 16 Aug 2010
22. Intel 64 and IA-32 Architectures Software Developer's Manual, Vol. 3B: System Programming Guide, Part 2.
23. Intel 64 and IA-32 Architectures Software Developer's Manual, Vol. 3A: System Programming Guide, Part 1.
24. Ernst, M.D., Perkins, J.H., Guo, P.J., McCamant, S., Pacheco, C., Tschantz, M.S., Xiao, C.: The Daikon system for dynamic detection of likely invariants. Sci. Comput. Program. 69(1–3), 35–45 (2007)
25. Kil, C., Sezer, E., Azab, A., Ning, P., Zhang, X.: Remote attestation to dynamic system properties: towards providing complete system integrity evidence. In: Proceedings of the 39th Annual IEEE/IFIP International Conference on Dependable Systems and Networks (DSN'09), Lisbon, Portugal (2009)
26. Jaeger, T., Sailer, R., Shankar, U.: PRIMA: policy-reduced integrity measurement architecture. In: Proceedings of the 11th ACM Symposium on Access Control Models and Technologies (SACMAT 2006), Lake Tahoe (2006).

27. Chkrootkit. http://www.chkrootkit.org/. Accessed 28 Jan 2012
28. Arbaugh, W.A., Farber, D.J., Smith, J.M.: A secure and reliable bootstrap architecture. In: Proceedings of the 1997 IEEE Symposium on Security and Privacy. IEEE Computer Society, Washington, DC (1997)
29. Singaravelu, L., Pu, C., Haertig, H., Helmuth, C.: Reducing TCB complexity for security-sensitive applications: three case studies. In: Proceedings of the 1st ACM SIGOPS/EuroSys European Conference on Computer Systems, Leuven, Belgium (2006)

Recommended Reading

- Armbrust M, Fox A, Griffith R, Joseph AD, and et al. (2009) Above the clouds: A Berkeley view of cloud computing. Technical Report UCB/EECS-2009–28, 2009. Available at http://www.eecs.berkeley.edu/Pubs/TechRpts/2009/EECS-2009–28.html
- Brown A and Chase J (2011) Trusted Platform-as-a-Service: A Foundation for Trustworthy Cloud-Hosted Applications. ACM Cloud Computing Security Workshop, October 2011.
- Haeberlen A (2010) A case for the accountable cloud. ACM SIGOPS Operating Systems Review, Volume 44 Issue 2, April 2010.
- Hoglund G, Butler J (2005) Rootkits: subverting the Windows kernel. Addison-Wesley Professional, Boston, Massachusetts, 2005.

Part IV
Risk Considerations

Chapter 7
Inadequacies of Current Risk Controls for the Cloud

Sadie Creese, Michael Goldsmith, and Paul Hopkins

Abstract In this chapter, we describe where current best practice in information security risk controls is likely to be inadequate for use in the cloud. In particular, we focus on public cloud ecosystems where cloud users will need to be mobile within the marketplace in order to achieve maximum benefits, as we believe these environments to be particularly challenging to the security control model. Our analysis is with reference to those risk controls defined by the ISO27001/27002 standards and the NIST Recommended Security Controls for Federal Information Systems and Organizations Special Publication 800–53 Revision 3. We highlight here only those we consider not to easily scale into such cloud environments, and by implication those not referred to, we believe, will transfer with relative ease.

Keywords Access control • Cloud computing • Encryption • Risk control • Security

7.1 Introduction

Cloud computing is a global hot topic and represents a significant opportunity to the enterprise to realise the benefits envisaged either for a user or for a provider of cloud services and applications. However, users will need to be

S. Creese (✉) • M. Goldsmith
Cyber Security Centre, Department of Computer Science,
University of Oxford, Oxford, UK
e-mail: sadie.creese@cs.ox.ac.uk

P. Hopkins
Security and Identity Management Department, Logica, Reading, UK

S. Pearson and G. Yee (eds.), *Privacy and Security for Cloud Computing*, 235
Computer Communications and Networks, DOI 10.1007/978-1-4471-4189-1_7,
© Springer-Verlag London 2013

convinced that cloud environments are a secure space within which to operate and that their enterprise functions will not be exposed to unnecessary or unacceptable risks as a consequence. Methods for predicting and understanding sources of vulnerability within a cloud environment are currently only addressed via isolated deep investigations, and consequently we (as a community) lack a broad understanding of where vulnerability is likely to occur. There has also been only limited consideration of threat motivators and, due to the relative immaturity of the business model, only limited (but increasing) evidence of attack.

This means that pragmatically the approach to planning information risk management strategies must be rooted in the current understanding of best-practice development prior to the cloud concept. Unsurprisingly, the general approach being adopted is one of extending existing controls (developed by such internationally recognised bodies as ISO and NIST and the Cloud Security Alliance), particularly those focused towards use of outsourcing and trusted third parties. Anecdotally, many organisations that would be considered part of critical national infrastructures, and so potentially exposed to higher levels of risk than most, have declared their cloud interests to be limited to private cloud environments, in order to avoid concerns relating to data assets being resident in environments outside their direct control.

Conversely, many within the security community are claiming that, for some users, particularly SME organisations and individuals, cloud offers considerably better security than they already enjoy. Certainly, it is true that for many (perhaps the majority of) SMEs, information and network security risks are not high on the agenda, and so the practice is relatively immature or non-existent. The issue to be addressed in assessing such claims is really that of risk exposure. For example, at the current time, many SMEs will not be the subject of targeted attacks on their data assets from external entities, but rather their key concerns are likely to surround their exposure to malware and the impact that viral infection might have on their day-to-day business. A move into the cloud could conceivably expose them to new risks as they become part of a large group of users whose assets on aggregate could be of interest to malicious entities. Consequently, a move to the cloud might mean that SMEs do need to develop a more mature information security capability in order that they can become more intelligent customers of the cloud service in this regard.

Our research seeks to understand where current best practice in information security risk controls is likely to be inadequate for use in the cloud. This has an impact on both cloud service providers and users, as the responsibility and ability to provide such controls will necessarily be divided between both. In particular, we focus on public cloud ecosystems where cloud users will need to be mobile within the marketplace in order to achieve maximum benefits. We believe these environments to be particularly challenging to the security control model. We present here an analysis of the adequacy of current risk controls, as defined by the

ISO27001/27002 standards [1, 2] and in the NIST Recommended Security Controls for Federal Information Systems and Organizations Special Publication 800–53 Revision 3 [3].

7.2 Definitions

There are many definitions of cloud computing and services. For the purposes of the current study, we adopt the US National Institute for Standards and Technology definition:

> A model for enabling convenient, on-demand network access to a shared pool of configurable computing resources (e.g., networks, servers, storage, applications, and services) that can be rapidly provisioned and released with minimal management effort or service provider interaction. [4]

The commonality between all cloud definitions is the underlying utility-computing concept. The vision for mature adoption of cloud technology is a future service ecosystem where users (enterprise or individual) consume resources on demand, their investment is closely coupled to their use and they are mobile in the market, readily adopting new cloud services and just as easily switching cloud suppliers in order to optimise cost and access the services which best meet their changing needs. This necessitates a shared resource infrastructure, rapid provisioning of services, an upstream supply chain in order to handle peaks in capacity demand and agile and responsive providers of enhanced services specific to the cloud.

There are currently three different categories of service for cloud computing, although it is an evolving domain and so these may change over time: Software-as-a-Service (SaaS) where applications are hosted and delivered online via a web browser offering traditional desktop functionality such as in the case of Google Docs, Gmail or MySap; Platform-as-a-Service (PaaS) where the cloud provides the software platform that user-provided software runs on, such as the Google Apps engine; and Infrastructure-as-a-Service (IaaS) where a set of computing resources, such as storage and computing capacity, are hosted in the cloud via virtualisation, on which customers deploy their own software stacks to run services, as with Amazon EC2, Amazon S3 and SimpleDB.

Clouds can be classified as private or public or as some hybrid combination of the two. From a security perspective, private clouds have the advantage of lying 'within' at least the logical enterprise boundary and as such can exploit existing security mechanisms, but they do not offer the benefits associated with mobility in the marketplace and may extend services across public networks. We concern ourselves here primarily with public and hybrid clouds, where potentially valuable assets are being placed fully outside the enterprise boundary, since this is where we expect particularly hard security challenges to exist.

7.3   Known Vulnerabilities

In a recent article [5], Grobauer, Walloschek and Stöcker discuss vulnerabilities in cloud computing and to what extent they can fairly be said to be vulnerabilities specifically due to the cloud rather than general vulnerabilities manifesting in it. They identify four main categories of cloud vulnerability proper:

1. Those intrinsic to or prevalent in core cloud technologies

    (a) Web applications and services
    (b) Virtualisation
    (c) Cryptography

2. Those whose root cause lies in essential characteristics of the cloud (according to the NIST definition [see Sect. 7.2])

    (a) On-demand self-service
    (b) Ubiquitous network access (over standard protocols)
    (c) Resource pooling [so co-tenancy and potential data remanence, discussed in later sections]
    (d) Rapid elasticity [one of the main aggravators to the next class]
    (e) Measured service

3. Those where cloud innovations render established controls difficult or impossible [which is the main subject of this chapter]
4. Those prevalent in state-of-the-art offerings [i.e. where the market-leading offerings contain flaws, even if these are not a problem inherent in the cloud concept]

To which we can add:

5. Those where the de-perimeterisation inherent in the cloud model actually expands the potential attack surface, in that data is no longer held within an organisation's security perimeter, nor necessarily that of a bounded set of carefully vetted and trusted outsourced providers

Cloud services are inherently vulnerable to all of the existing classes of web-enabled infrastructure attacks, which include attacks against the authentication and authorisation functions. Any mistakes made have all of their potential weaknesses and negative consequences magnified when designing for a massively distributed infrastructure, as demonstrated when a flaw in Google's cut-down version of the OASIS SAML architecture allowed any rogue service provider to masquerade as their user to any other service [6]. Careless use of cryptography coupled with URI-based parameter specification prevalent in web services can lead to serious flaws, as when Amazon EC2's AWS Version 1 signature scheme allowed a wide range of chosen-plaintext collisions, including adding more or less arbitrary key-value pairs wrongly authenticated under the signature of a related query [7].

Since most clouds are accessed via existing tools such as browsers, attacks against browsers, including malicious helper objects or extensions, are more important than before, again simply because of the scale of data they allow access to. The management and provisioning interface for cloud services is also typically web-based and thus presents a whole new potential attack surface. Human error can also have greatly magnified effects in the cloud, as when Google accidentally shared rather more of its eponymous Docs than their authors intended [8]; one may be reassured by the fact that the isolated incident affected 'less than 0.05% of all documents'.

Attacks against the transport layer (TLS/SSL) can also be levied against clouds, so recent concerns about rogue CAs [9], stripping SSL before it is presented to the user [10], and the SSL renegotiation attack [11] may all impact on cloud security.

Published attacks range from the social (choice of bad passwords, such as those by the Twitter administrators [12]) to the deeply technical, such as research done by Rutkowska and others on hypervisor weaknesses in memory segregation and controls on the virtual machines that underpin modern clouds [13–16]. There has even been research on cloud cartography, an attempt to map a cloud and then determine where a target server is being hosted, and gaining access to a virtual machine on the same physical hardware [17].

Maintaining strict API access controls to sprawling databases, such as those of Facebook, is difficult and can allow information leakage which can then be used to launch further attacks. The magnitude of clouds again plays a part with regard to sites that must deliver large quantities of content whilst still attempting to provide protection and security against intruders. Facebook, for example, assumed that people's photographs were safe when mirrored on their content delivery network (CDN) because they were identified by a 'random' number. Unfortunately, the CDN's resilience strategy allowed a brute force of the possibilities in a relatively small time by distributing the guesses against all the mirrors.

Measured service provides new scope for financial attacks, analogous to the well-established click-through fraud, although we are not aware of any large-scale incident yet. Many cloud-storage offerings include download bandwidth in their pricing structure; a blogger reports on how unexpected popularity of some uploads brought a larger than expected bill [18]. This is on a trivial domestic scale, but it suggests how mischief or worse might be achieved; one could even imagine an unscrupulous storage provider arranging with a friendly cloud to download his customers' largest files with distressing frequency.

For clouds can indeed be used maliciously. So-called acid clouds can be used to harvest virtual-machine content passed to them as part of a provisioning chain or to launch attacks in a very distributed manner. For example, operating similarly to other PaaS offerings, the Zeus botnet offers Fraud-as-a-Service to clients [19], who receive a centralised command and control server for managing the vast array of compromised machines, much as a cloud would be managed. These clouds can then be used for tasks from password cracking to distributed denial-of-service attacks. They could simply be used to host malicious content, such that the forensic trail would be extremely difficult to follow, or to allow attackers to dynamically reallocate their payloads as and when the authorities shut down one offending host. Legitimate clouds, too, can become the source of attacks, either from malicious customers or from compromised virtual machines (researchers from the Center for Advanced Security Research Darmstadt estimated – based on a sample of 1,100 Amazon Machine Images tested – that in June 2011 some 30% of customer-deployed VMs were vulnerable [20]). There is quite strong anecdotal evidence that Session Initiation Protocol (SIP) brute-force attacks increasingly originate from within legitimate clouds, and these, if directed inwards, naturally bypass any perimeter controls that the cloud may deploy and enjoy excellent bandwidth. Even clouds are not immune to DDoS attacks, as the 2009 Bitbucket incident [21] illustrates.

7.4   Adequacy of Risk Controls

Over recent years, a number of practice guides [22] and standards [1–3] have emerged from workshops and standards committees so as to provide a relatively uniform set of suggested security controls for enterprises' security-management function. The security community is engaged in a number of initiatives to address security risks associated with the cloud, as for example the Cloud Security Alliance [23], which has recently launched a certification programme for professionals wishing to demonstrate cloud-security knowledge, and the ENISA Cloud Computing Information Assurance Framework [24]. In general, the community is adopting the practical strategy of seeking to extend existing best practice into the cloud. However, we believe that this is unlikely to be sufficient for all cloud implementations and, in particular, for the highly dynamic and flexible business models envisaged in a mature cloud environment. We outline our rationale below. Using ISO27001/27002 [1, 2] and the NIST Recommended Security Controls for Federal Information Systems and Organizations [3], we have identified those areas where there are potential issues with the suitability of controls for deployment within the cloud environment, and hence these are unlikely to directly address the associated vulnerabilities.

7.4.1   Physical Controls

Physical protection and regulated access are important controls for an organisation in restricting access to both software and hardware, thus gaining assurance as to the integrity of the machine and the data and software upon it. Within clouds, the inability of user organisations to implement this control is of considerable concern, with applications and data stored on potentially untrusted and multi-tenanted machines. Even if the cloud service provider is prepared to make warranties regarding physical controls and air gaps, the user still has to be content with the cloud essentially delivering the control (as it is their environment). Previous best-practice guidelines for outsourcing call for physical audits and for the presence of certifications (e.g. SAS 70 Type II) to seek assurance that the physical control is adequate. But if a cloud user wishes to be mobile in the cloud marketplace and to benefit from the competition within the market, the cloud service provision will be likely to rely on multiple suppliers drawn from a dynamic environment, where relationships between cloud users and providers may be extremely short lived. This situation could be further aggravated as the cloud ecosystem matures and suppliers are themselves driven to outsource in order to cater for the variability in customer demand. The ability to establish relationships and assess adequacy of physical security measures through current audit practices is not practical in such a dynamic environment. Indeed, audits are in essence single-point events with no continuous monitoring of the environment taking place, a process often integrated with the facilities security-management function.

But the securing of physical premises for cloud sites is not very different to current practice for any data-hosting centre; the one key inadequacy is the inability to verify rapidly and practically the physical controls of multiple cloud service providers.

This particular control could perhaps be delivered through some kind of proxy body which performs third-party audits on behalf of cloud user communities. To be effective as a control, however, the cloud user must have the ability to respond to unsatisfactory deployment of the control, which would mean either being able to force the supplier to change behaviour or to be willing to switch to a supplier who does deliver the control appropriately.

7.4.2 Application Development and Maintenance

Cloud systems offer the potential for development to take place using the APIs and SDKs at varying levels of abstraction within the cloud (e.g. IaaS, PaaS). Whilst they are currently well-documented and 'open' APIs, they are essentially proprietary in nature, and often the underlying implementation is closed source, as, for example, with Google Apps and Microsoft Azure SDK [25]. This means that there is essentially no direct way for users to gain confidence in the integrity of the code and whether it might be vulnerable to attack. Whilst the risks of closed-source execution are nothing new, they are conventionally typically mitigated by monitoring controls (such as intrusion detection systems) and the ability to test and examine the behaviour of the closed-source software (i.e., security test and evaluation). We examine later the inability to simply translate current monitoring-control practice into the cloud and here focus on the control of software integrity.

The proprietary nature of closed-source library functions and the variation in service abstraction levels together reduce the ability of applications to be ported between cloud implementations. Some standardisation of APIs, however, is being pursued by projects, such as the Cloud Interoperability Forum initiative [26], which seek to provide a metadata description of the APIs as they develop rather than try to standardise on a particular vendor's API. There appears to be very little evidence in the literature to date on standardising the security APIs. This means that cloud service providers will be forced to assess each one using bespoke rationales, a process which could be costly and error prone, should they decide that software integrity is of concern.

However, this latter point remains open to debate. There is a significant chance that cloud suppliers will simply transfer the risk to users via terms which effectively absolve them of any responsibility for the integrity of software being delivered, offering guarantees only in terms of patch implementation regimes and the like. Arguably, this is not unlike the situation for users outside of the cloud, with the added benefit that patching is performed on their behalf. But the cloud environment might itself become part of the attack surface, and thus become very attractive to attackers, since it offers a potentially much greater reward due to the volume of data assets stored there and the larger catchment of users who might be subjected to denial-of-service attacks and related revenue-earning attacks.

A number of service providers also provide development environments within the cloud [27, 28], and thus, given the closed nature of the environment, it is not clear how the integrity of codebase and intellectual property will be protected. It is true that the lack of controls relating to intellectual property is not an entirely new issue, given the proliferation of collaborative open-source projects, but it does almost certainly exclude the use of the cloud to provide either critical software or code with inherently valuable intellectual property (to the authoring organisation) since the code immediately sits outside of the physical control of the organisation within a multiple-user third-party environment. Indeed, anecdotal evidence within the gaming community points to the delivery of online games being considered an appropriate use of cloud, whilst it is entirely inappropriate to the development of new game concepts.

Many of the critical controls for assuring code development, such as change control and the separation of test environments, are likely to be straightforward to implement within a cloud environment. However, they will be heavily dependent on effective account management, access controls and logging (that is protected) to counter the threat from external parties. As with the physical controls discussed above, this could mean that these controls will not perform well in highly dynamic cloud environments.

7.4.3 Vulnerability Management

Identifying and managing vulnerabilities is a well-understood security control, extending across many operational aspects of an organisation, from testing to fixing and patching systems. In particular, meeting the need for an enterprise to control its patch deployment to a service-based system and regression testing with other organisations' applications is likely to prove complex. One patch or configuration change in the service or API could disable an organisation's cloud-deployed code; but hesitation may essentially mean that an application is vulnerable, with a compromised function or call available on that organisation, until the service provider decides to fix the issue. Whilst not an inherent vulnerability of the cloud per se, it means that the ability of an organisation to close a vulnerability gap in its system, once it becomes aware of it, is indeterminate, as it is essentially reliant upon the cloud service provider to implement it. (Where the solution is a full SaaS shrink-wrapped solution, such as Salesforce.com, the responsibility and vulnerability window is less likely to occur, but remediation remains at the sole discretion of the service provider.)

Where a cloud user is operating multiple machines (which itself he may not know), there may be added complexity: it may not be the case that all machines are patched simultaneously, and so for a period of time, some subset may be protected whilst others are not. In terms of situational awareness, this introduces uncertainty, and without real-time data on the patching operations, it could introduce significant uncertainty with respect to the current level of exposure to risk. In particular, this means that a cloud user may be more exposed for some business processes than others. When managing vulnerability within an organisation, it would be possible to prioritise patch activity to ensure that the technology supporting key business processes, and in particular specific tasks deemed to be most critical at that point in time, is dealt with first. Enabling such prioritisation within a cloud model would require the ability for enterprise users to express prioritisation policy in a manner which the cloud service could quickly respond to. At this time, we are not aware of any functionality that caters for this. (It should be noted that this is not a common functionality supported in non-cloud environments, however, but it is particularly pertinent for the cloud, as the user here is likely to have a much more uncertain view of their current status with respect to patching and vulnerability exposure.)

This issue exists for all service levels in the cloud – how, for instance, would a provider need to react in the circumstances where it found that all of its 'gold standard' operating system builds used pervasively across the client base have vulnerabilities within them? How can a cloud provider manage its vulnerability management resource best when the many users of its services are likely to have varying priorities in terms of the criticality of the various functions they receive?

7.4.4 Monitoring

It is not clear how monitoring within cloud environments is successfully to be achieved, as different cloud service levels will have different monitoring requirements and provision. Azure [25] proposes an environment in which applications have a dedicated API for formatting and logging. However, the provision of an API is not in itself sufficient. There are many services and interfaces which can generate logging information. Currently, monitoring is used to generate audit trails for compliance as well as to detect unauthorised attempts to access or penetrate systems. Whilst the two are not always combined, the general trend has been to do precisely that and to aggregate the information. This facilitates the profiling of the information or activity flows in order to refine understanding of the events (e.g. to aggregate application events and network level events into security information and event management (SIEM) devices) [29].

In the cloud environment, the same controls could be applied, so applications can be coded to generate logging information for their user and sensors could be used to monitor for unauthorised traffic, but predominately at the host layer. At the network level, the visibility of the network traffic is very much the domain of the cloud service provider; enterprises are constrained to the placement of sensors on their virtual machines (if operating at the IaaS level), or alternatively the sensor placement and information are simply not available.

But even if the cloud service provider is willing to provide such a monitoring service, the problem is not trivial, with current practice dictating that the sensors are tuned according to their environment to reduce the perennial problem of false positives. In a dynamic environment, where machines are moved between hosts and the applications are tailored, such an approach could become problematic as it will require a certain level of dynamism in sensor architecture; host and network layer sensors will need to be reconfigured as machines are mobilised.

As cloud users wish to move between cloud service providers, they are likely to face different monitoring regimes with differing reporting standards. This could make compliance monitoring for the user challenging, as they cannot simply rely on a common approach. Without a common monitoring approach, users may not be able to directly compare the data that they are provided, making it difficult to understand the relative maturity of their security controls or the relative level of risk exposure that they may face when using multiple cloud service providers.

The recent trend towards use of anomaly detection also seems to be contraindicated in this scenario since the range of non-anomalous behaviour will vary widely between applications and so will require tailored sensors, potentially at the granularity of individual users. This may not prove practical or cost- effective, even if it should be technically viable, in contrast to more constrained domains such as the financial services sector. Should the customer be willing to pay the premium, then they will undoubtedly expect rapid re-provisioning which in turn will require equally speedy learning algorithms in order to establish what normal behaviour is and to provide a monitoring service without excessive 'noise' arising from false warnings. Whilst the challenges of delivering anomaly detection are similar for cloud and for non-cloud environments, since false positives and false negatives are of concern for both, the cloud does potentially add an extra level of complexity when machines are mobile within it since in these circumstances the likely variance of environmental factors must be larger, not only because the hardware infrastructure changes with time but also because the cohabitants of the hardware will be changing their behaviours (in a largely unpredictable fashion). Since the operational environment will probably change what constitutes 'normal', this will make anomaly detection increasingly complex, as the learning algorithms will have to factor in deviations due to local operating environment, which in itself may be deviating due to other third-party users.

Questioning the validity of monitoring is restricted not only to that of network (IP-layer) traffic but also to what is often termed layer-7 or application traffic. Web application firewalls attempt to filter out malicious traffic and therefore come with a set of predefined signatures but again must be tuned to the applications they protect. Whilst these applications are likely to be less dynamic in their construction, their tuning and operation are just as problematic as for IDS sensors. The number of sensors can be potentially large, with sensors having to be placed not just within network segments but intra-VM. Normally, many of these IDS/IPS devices are configured as hardened security appliances, thus reducing their attack surface to the minimum possible and so creating few additional vulnerabilities within the system deployment. Whilst these can readily be deployed within the various network segments, they must also occupy the virtual machine form as well. Traditional enterprise controls use strong 'certified' appliances to also store encryption keys and provide encryption termination points prior to inspection by the devices. Soft VMs emulating these devices would not be able to rely on that physical separation from other applications and tenants. With the monitoring controls essentially embedded into the cloud service provider or built into company applications within the cloud, it is hard to determine how security monitoring and log generation could be protected against malicious cloud providers potentially with full access to the software generating the events, clock synchronisation and also any encryption-key material used to protect them.

For the majority of cloud service providers, availability of the hosted services is critical to revenue streams, and thus they are unlikely to not have monitoring controls on the performance of key systems and on communications usage [30]. However, two questions remain unanswered: firstly, whether the cloud service provider adequately monitors the internal infrastructure for attacks within the cloud and: secondly, whether the extent of the monitoring within the cloud environment of the customer's behaviour for malicious activity is targeted at the cloud providers or other consumers. Our current assumption is that it is unlikely that current controls extend past abnormal performance or bandwidth usage. Indeed, it may transpire that in certain jurisdictions the disincentives to carry out what amounts to attack activity within and from a cloud are simply not strong enough and that it is not in the interests of the cloud providers to concern themselves too much with what could validly be interpreted as acceptable cloud use. Of course, should monitoring mechanisms develop which do make practical the differentiation of malicious and benign cloud use, then it will become more difficult for them to claim ignorance as a defence against having allowed resources to be utilised in malicious activity. This situation is analogous to that currently faced by Internet service providers.

7.4.5 Identification and Authentication

The identification and authentication of users is exceptionally important in ensuring that organisations and users are both authorised to access the correct service and information but also billable for the services they use from the provider's perspective. (Hence, the importance of some cloud services' authentication mechanisms will depend on the business model adopted, e.g. ad-based or billable based on CPU/ bandwidth/data metrics). For the organisation, the identification and authentication of the service to the users and organisation is as important as the user's ability to access the service. Where previously in-house services were protected by encapsulation within a private domain – authenticity of the services was assumed. The inadequacy of this control is nothing new to consumers, and potential solutions do exist. However, their users wish to be particularly mobile within the cloud marketplace, they will find themselves partially limited by the ability to provide the users of cloud services with agile authentication of service to user. It is likely that in reality periods of overlap will exist in order to ensure that the day-to-day enterprise processes do not get compromised due to a user's inability to access the service.

Similarly, the ability of users to authenticate themselves to multiple services to use multiple clouds (or for clouds to authenticate themselves across multiple services!) is a well-known issue and the derivation of a number of federated ID management schemes. For such solutions, trust between schemes is essential to facilitate the attesting to identity and sharing these across multiple providers. Due to the inherent lack of trust between domains, it is highly likely that certain single providers will become ID brokers; however, they are likely to have significant scalability and interoperability concerns if true identify is to be verified. The ability to port identity and authentication schemes and credentials between cloud service providers should certainly be an enabler for mobility within the marketplace. Unfortunately, this may become a driver for not prioritising interoperability across identity frameworks as cloud suppliers seek to hold on to their customers.

7.4.6   Access Control

Many applications and cloud services can readily be built to include strong access controls. However, their adequacy will be affected by three issues within a cloud environment.

We note that, for performance reasons, a number of cloud service providers (e.g. SNS) offload their large data files to content delivery networks (CDNs). Due to their generic nature and to replication issues, these have no effective access controls or significant authentication mechanisms to protect the information. Whilst this architecture is adopted for performance and some cloud services may simply not have the facility to protect their data, others may prefer to make provision for this. The ability of a cloud user to control how exposed their data may be in this context will depend upon whether they are able to negotiate the terms of use of CDNs by their suppliers. Unfortunately, such negotiations can only be done on a case-by-case basis and so will introduce latency into the processes associated with establishing service provision.

Whilst access controls can still to some extent be created, set and revoked within a cloud application, the platform is essentially in a separate administrative domain. In a SaaS or PaaS service model, the provider designs, produces and controls the application or API, whilst in an IaaS model they control the underlying operating system or virtual hardware. As such, the provider always controls the lowest levels of their provision, and the access control integrity cannot be guaranteed in this environment. Further, the cloud user may not be provided with any reporting in terms of the access controls relating to cloud service administration, meaning that they cannot be aware of any potential sources of integrity issues in this regard.

There are a number of different models for access control to resources. In a federated environment, it will be very difficult to translate those controls across multiple cloud applications without a common understanding and agreement. This is not an uncommon problem in the enterprise environment, with multiple access controls implemented on differing applications and operating systems. With clouds currently typically presenting proprietary offerings, interoperability of access controls across applications and environments is something which is not immediately on the horizon. This could either be a cause of vulnerability or result in lock-in.

7.4.7 Encryption

Encryption is a key control in protecting the confidentiality and integrity of data within and communicated with the cloud. Communications to and from the cloud are typically provided by an HTTPS-protocol connection to a web service and so benefit from Secure Sockets Layer (SSL) protection of the data whilst in transit. This protocol has proved a reliable method of providing cryptographically secure communication for 10 years, although, as is often the case with encryption, the manner of use of the protocol, key management and performance may all undermine its effectiveness. The protection of the data whilst processing or whilst stored is however of considerable concern [23]. Current uses of the cloud recommends either storage only of non-critical data [31], or that it be encrypted prior to storage [23] and only decrypted when it is back at consumer premises. Essentially, this is required as the organisation has no ability to impose strong logical or physical controls within the cloud, as discussed earlier. Whether the data is transmitted or stored in encrypted form, processing is necessarily carried out on plain text by the provider, and encryption provides no real protection against misbehaviour of the provider nor against an attacker successful in penetrating the service-provider controls. This is of course also true for conventional outsourcing solutions, but if cloud resources become more commoditised, the data may be in the hands of third, fourth or more remote parties, where it is unlikely to be possible to ensure sufficiently close commercial relationships and the dedication of adequate logical, physical and commercial controls [32].

Ideally, what is required is the ability to process data whilst in an encrypted form. Gentry's fully homomorphic scheme (supporting both multiplication and addition of unknown plaintexts) based on an encryption using ideal lattices [33] was a significant advance in this context and has inspired a number of further research projects. However, whilst promising, the scheme remains impractical for immediate deployment; with the current focus on data processing tasks, this will also need to be extended to complicated collaborative tasks such as the word-processing of documents whilst under strong encryption.

Just as the case in non-cloud environments, the key-management aspects are critical to ensuring the success of any encryption scheme. Current commercial solutions, such as the use of hardware security modules (HSMs) to stored organisational keys, and associated distribution, revocation and recovery mechanisms will not necessarily adapt well to a distributed cloud environment currently.

7.4.8 Continuity and Incident Management

Current cloud services are intended to be highly scalable and resilient in their service delivery, with availability of systems being a key driver. Thus as a technical control, there are many particular options that can be explored in order to develop the continuity of information systems, either under electronic attack or due to disaster scenarios. However, the adequacy of this control has to be examined in the context of its remote provision by one or more cloud service providers; to achieve continuity when depending upon a cloud, supply chain will require both technical solutions to maintain state across multiple servers and various contractual flow-downs to ensure that the supply chain provides adequate performance guarantees.

7.4.8.1 Accountability

Current cloud service contracts have a distinctly 'take it or leave it' approach to the service on offer. This approach is understandable given that economic, and possible regulatory, considerations involved with generating special terms and conditions for every customer make this simply neither feasible nor scalable. At the time of writing, very limited choice is offered in terms of security-related service guarantees or reporting as standard.

This creates two problems. Firstly, it creates an operational barrier, with any service-performance guarantees limited purely to those deemed important by the provider. The organisation's ability to decide and take actions is consequently limited, making them reliant on the service provider, whose interests may diverge (e.g. repeated attacks against a single organisation may result in the termination of service to that organisation in order to protect the provider's other customers). The normal consultative framework for decision making simply does not exist, as it can do in outsourcing. Thus, creating a meaningful incident response and continuity process is likely to prove difficult unless cloud users lock themselves into a (single or possibly limited multiple) trusted cloud supplier, so adopting current best practice in outsourcing. Of course, this will mean giving up mobility within the market and will have the usual cost ramifications of single-source provision. It may be that this particular control needs close attention and ultimately involves a trade-off between mobility and exposure to risk. Secondly, as we identified in the earlier sections, establishing accountability is not necessarily trivial. The integrity and availability of reliable identifiers for processes, applications and users are not guaranteed nor is the access to audit trails.

7.4.8.2   Liability

As many organisations seek to use commercial contractual means as a standard control, to define ownership, responsibilities and liability within third parties, the current cloud environments are likely to be responsive (given the size of the business opportunity). However, with tighter integration with other service providers, the nesting and depth of these arrangements are likely to exacerbate the problems. A number of providers [34–36] have been researching and experimenting with mechanisms for embedding support for contractual terms (service level agreements) into the infrastructure itself and thereby potentially enabling automatic negotiations. However, this work is far from complete in establishing which parameters can acceptably be negotiated within the legal framework on behalf of either a user or another service provider. Moreover, orchestrating and developing an agreement across multiple layers of technology and suppliers (except in the case of the simplest of provisioning examples) will require an agreed framework supporting planning, negotiation and orchestration [37].

7.4.8.3   Forensic Investigation

The ability to conduct an investigation in order to determine liability and regulatory compliance or to improve service provision is hampered by a number of the previously mentioned issues, particularly the potential lack of access (and guarantee of integrity) to systems and data. Geographic boundaries create cross-jurisdictional issues, which can make discovery and recovery of data difficult, even with the same provider, let alone if the service provision is hosted amongst multiple cloud suppliers. Should future cloud users be able to negotiate a service which is configured to quickly provide the evidence required in support of investigations (often referred to as forensic readiness), the effectiveness of such an approach will depend critically upon the function being pervasive within the cloud supplier environment including up the supply chain.

7.4.9   Compliance

Compliance of a business with the appropriate regulatory and legal constraints is key to ensuring that the business minimises its exposure to legal challenge and gives its customers confidence that their business transactions and data are handled appropriately. Both 27001 and NIST SP800–53 require appropriate controls to be implemented so as to meet regulatory constraints. However, such controls are dependent upon a number of factors: the business function being carried out in the cloud (regulatory domain), the customer-supplier relationship (business-to-business, business-to-consumer, government-to-citizen, etc.), and the applicable jurisdiction and laws. Compliance with data protection and privacy laws and norms is considered amongst the most challenging issues. Key concepts, such as when cloud providers are considered to be data controllers versus data processors [38], often require clarification. Studies conducted within the EU, such as [38], have outlined both best-practice advice and issues to be resolved if this aspect of risk controls is to be scaled. For the immediate future, most businesses will rely on clarifying legal and regulatory conditions (and accountability) through terms and conditions of service. The time and resource that it can take to establish such terms will inevitably limit their mobility within the cloud marketplace as well as limit the choice of suppliers.

7.4.10   People (Security Team)

The composition of any security team is organisation- and business-specific. However, just as there are particular skill sets and roles in developing, architecting and deploying systems, there is also an in-service or maintenance team for the IT and security infrastructure. With the majority of the infrastructure being run by the cloud service provider, it is the provider who is most likely to deploy multiple security controls such as firewalls and IDS/IPS sensors to protect their customers; the consequence of which is that the technical skills to monitor, interpret and react to IDS/IPS alerts, to interpret and patch infrastructure vulnerabilities and to perform firewall administration must necessarily reside at least with the cloud provider, who understands and hosts the infrastructure. (It is less clear whether this would be the case for the monitoring of the customers' applications, given that this will usually require an in-depth understanding of the customers' business, and this is likely to become unsustainable given the variety and number of potential business applications without significant automation currently beyond the state-of-the-art). The consequence of this is that the investigative function, again where it focuses on the impact on the infrastructure, is likely to be provided by the cloud service provider, unless the cloud user maintains the capability and is provided with the relevant data in a timely manner.

Given their access to sensitive systems and information, the core security team for most organisations are vetted, recruited and managed carefully. The scale and access required for the technical alerting and response functions within the cloud environment will mean that this is outside of the organisation's influence. Thus, for most resource-sensitive enterprise users, the security team's skill set is likely to be focused on due diligence, on the appropriateness of controls and on relationship management and less about the IDS and platform vulnerabilities. Technical skills will need to be focused on the organisational private stack and its interface with the cloud services and on protection within the cloud to endpoint domain.

7.4.11   People (Business Function)

Training and general awareness material is used to educate users within an organisation as to the risks of using various enterprise services. The effectiveness of this control has never been established and depends greatly upon the organisational business and culture; however, it is a well-established control. For a cloud environment, the potential attack surface against the user has been increased, with many previously internal controls preventing users releasing data or interacting with third-party services now in the control of the cloud service provider. And yet, particular dangers are just as likely to arise in the same areas as today, for instance, around collaboration (where third parties access/populate data and applications) and privacy of personal data. Usage of the cloud may make risk less tangible, as pushing data outside the enterprise boundary becomes more commonplace, and this could encourage apathy since the cloud user appears to have nothing within his control. Such trends could ultimately result in increased vulnerability, but it will be many years before enough data is available to assess these issues properly (even assuming that such data should be made accessible).

As usage of the cloud becomes strategic and commonplace within enterprise environments, organisations may find it necessary to develop cloud-usage policies in support of security (where such policies might vary across role, business unit, data and application type, etc.). This may be a complex security environment for staff and will likely result in accidental violations of policy. Organisations will need to decide whether to prioritise security and operate a restrictive strategy or to prioritise business need and be more permissive (allowing staff to override usage policy if necessary to get the job done).

7.4.12   Security Testing

Security testing is used to verify that any application or system has minimal actual weaknesses and vulnerabilities (appropriate with the business risk appetite). Hence, it is a core control used as part of any information security management system. Ownership of the 'cloud service' (at the varying levels) creates problems in conducting security tests since these should be aimed at assessing the whole security of the solution and not just verifying that security claims or a particular application is correct. Testing designed to imitate malicious attackers can appear aggressive to service owners, resulting in their seeking assurances that no other services will be disrupted as a result of the testing, and they may restrict it to the application alone. This has always been a recurring problem with security testing and is not one that can be easily mitigated. Even if the provider wishes to enable testing and not to constrain the scope too specifically, for most service providers the potential volume of tests, given the number of independent clients requiring assurance, could prove prohibitive for a cloud service. Such restrictive measures around actual security testing may require the use of static code analysis for flaws to take on an increased importance. It has been noted that just as the use of virtualisation enables monitoring of code execution and therefore potentially reduces the protection afforded to organisations and users running code in the cloud, so it also enables dynamic behaviour of the code to be monitored. The challenge remains in establishing the model of the allowable desired behaviour of the application against which it can be compared and checked. Any such protection mechanisms will need to ensure that standard maintenance practices, such as patching (which in itself might become a source of vulnerability), can be allowed for.

7.4.13 Accredited Components

The use of products or appliances evaluated against Common Criteria, CTAS and CCTM [39] does not appear appropriate for cloud-based services, except insofar as they focus on the core technology-level components such as the hypervisor (for selected virtual-machine builds). The configuration and provisioning of services above that layer (i.e. IaaS, PaaS and SaaS) are likely to be so dynamic that their deployment in the evaluated configurations is unlikely and unverifiable in a cost-effective manner, especially where services are transient. Indeed, as the assurance sought from a device increases, so the evidence and detail required increases, something many cloud providers would find difficult to service with individual requests, except for the most default of configurations. Thus, the use of accredited components would seem a particularly moot control in clouds since they would have to exist within an environment for which no guarantees can be made about the precise network and application configuration.

7.4.14 Data Remanence

Residual data or applications that remain after they are no longer required pose a risk to an organisation. Normally, data is removed and a secure disposal method employed to remove all electronic traces from the physical equipment before they are scrapped or obsoleted. The cloud business model is one where hardware is of necessity, reused and re-provisioned, making these normal methods for mitigating data remanence risks unusable. Questions remain as to whether it is possible to access previous customers' data based upon the cloud service offered. At the IaaS level, the basic construct of most hypervisors is to offer memory that has no trace of previous disc remnants. However, the methods used by distributed file systems in order to store potentially large data sets efficiently require fast access to many areas of the file systems directly. Thus, programmatic access to these without any constraints, for example, reading beyond what has been reallocated to the current customer, may enable that data to be accessed even if it has originally been freed.

7.4.15 Asset Management

The replacement of servers or storage devices that become faulty or are at the end of their service life is no different to the current practice for the disposal of servers. More interestingly is the question of how uniquely configured virtual machines and data stores should be accounted for within the asset management system of any organisation, as in this instance we are dealing with virtual assets that can be quickly replicated and replaced or tampered with as they are provisioned or de-provisioned. Traditionally, asset management has focused on the tracking of physical equipment and its characteristics. Such processes will need to be updated in order to facilitate tracking of virtual assets' location and state.

7.5 Conclusions

This chapter is a complete analysis with respect to ISO27001/27002 and the NIST recommendations [1–3]. It is clear that there are many areas of control that need to be evolved or even innovated in order to provide appropriate protection for hybrid and public cloud usage. Certainly, it is not currently possible for a public cloud user to fully achieve compliance with standards such as ISO27001 whilst remaining mobile in the marketplace; the technology to implement some of the controls is simply not available, whilst for others the access and resources required would necessitate long-term relationships severely limiting the ability of the user to be agile in his supplier selection.

Issues surrounding jurisdiction cannot be ignored, and it may be that clouds 'hover' over single nations, or those which have some joint policing agreements, in order to avoid legal issues surrounding export of personal data and to support digital-forensics investigations.

It is likely that for the immediate future, any organisation considering its assets to be particularly valuable or sensitive will not use public clouds and instead will focus on private (or virtual private) clouds. In this way, they hope to maintain their ability to deploy current risk controls, trading mobility in the marketplace for security. Certainly, this will limit their ability fully to exploit the paradigm and, for many, will actually mean just the adoption of service-orientated architectures, as opposed to fully embracing the cloud business model.

Acknowledgements We would like to recognise the significant contribution that Mike Auty made in the original research upon which this chapter is based. We also thank Lockheed Martin Corporation who partially supported this work as part of their internal research and development programme.

References

1. British Standards Institute: Security techniques – information security management requirements. BS ISO/IEC 27001:2005 (2007)
2. British Standards Institute: Security techniques – code of practice for information security management. BS ISO/IEC 27002:2005 (2007)
3. Ross, R., Johnson, A.: Recommended security controls for federal information systems. National Institute of Standards and Technology, Special Publication 800–53–3 (2009)
4. Mell, P., Grance, T.: NIST Definition of cloud computing v15. National Institute for Standards and Technology. http://www.nist.gov/itl/upload/cloud-def-v15.pdf (2009). Accessed Oct 2011.
5. Grobauer, B., Walloschek, T., Stöcker, E.: Understanding cloud computing vulnerabilities. IEEE Secur. Priv. Mag. **9**(5), 50–57 (2011)
6. Armando, A., Carbone, R., Compagna, L., Cuellar, J., Tobarra, M.L.: Formal analysis of SAML 2.0 web browser single sign-on: breaking the SAML-based single sign-on for Google Apps. In: Proceedings of 6th ACM Workshop on Formal Methods in Security Engineering. ACM Press, New York (2008)
7. Percival, C.: AWS signature version 1 is insecure. Demonic Dispatches blog. http://www.daemonology.net/blog/2008–12–18-AWS-signature-version-1-is-insecure.html (2008). Accessed Oct 2011
8. Kincaid, J.: Careless in the cloud: Google accidentally shares some docs. Seeking Alpha. http://seekingalpha.com/article/124761-careless-in-the-cloud-google-accidentally-shares-some-docs?source=feed (2009). Accessed Oct 2011
9. Sotirov, A.: Creating a rogue CA certificate. http://www.phreedom.org/research/rogue-ca/ (2008). Accessed Oct 2011
10. Marlinspike, M.: SSLstrip. Thoughtcrime Labs. http://www.thoughtcrime.org/software/sslstrip/ (2009). Accessed Oct 2011
11. Ray, M., Dispensa, S.: SSL/TLS Authentication Gap (SSL Gap). http://www.phonefactor.com/sslgapdocs/Renegotiating_TLS.pdf (2009). Accessed Oct 2011
12. Technology Expert: Twitter's celebrity account hack: a study in weak passwords. http://technologyexpert.blogspot.com/2009/01/twitters-celebrity-account-hack-study.html (2009). Accessed Oct 2011
13. Higgins, K.J.: Hacking tool lets a VM break out and attack its host. Darkreading. http://www.darkreading.com/securityservices/security/app-security/showArticle.jhtml?articleID=217701908 (2009). Accessed Oct 2011
14. Rutkowska, J.: Security challenges in virtualized environments. Invisible Things Labs. http://invisiblethings.org/papers/Security%20Challenges%20in%20Virtualized%20Enviroments.pdf (2007). Accessed Oct 2011
15. King, S.T., Chen, P.M., Wang, Y.-M., Verbowski, C., Wang, H.J., Lorch, J.R.: SubVirt: implementing malware with virtual machines. In: Proceedings of the 2006 IEEE Symposium on Security and Privacy, Berkeley (2006)
16. Sharif, M., Lee, W., Cui, W., Lanzi, A.: Secure in-VM monitoring using hardware virtualization. In: Proceedings of the ACM Conference on Computer and Communications Security (CCS), Chicago (2009)
17. Ristenpart, T., Tromer, E., Shacham, H., Savage, S.: Hey, you, get off of my cloud! Exploring information leakage in third-party compute clouds. In: Proceedings of the ACM Conference on Computer and Communications Security (CCS). ACM, New York (2009)
18. Heuer, T.: When Blobs attack – understanding cloud storage bursts and viewing logs. Method ~ of ~ failed. http://timheuer.com/blog/archive/2010/02/08/tracking-cloud-storage-usage-with-s3stat-amazon-s3-azure.aspx (2010). Accessed Oct 2011
19. Electric Alchemy: Cracking passwords in the cloud: insights on password policies. http://news.electricalchemy.net/2009/10/password-cracking-in-cloud-part-5.html (2009). Accessed Oct 2011
20. CASED: Careless behaviour of cloud users leads to crucial security threats. http://www.cased.de/upload/1308567676-press_____Cloud_en.pdf (2011). Accessed Oct 2011

21. Metz, C.: DDoS attack rains down on Amazon cloud – code haven tumbles from sky. The Register. http://www.theregister.co.uk/2009/10/05/amazon_bitbucket_outage/ (2009). Accessed Oct 2011
22. Information Security Forum: Standard of good practice for information security (2005)
23. Cloud Security Alliance: Security guidance for critical areas of focus in cloud computing V2.1. http://www.cloudsecurityalliance.org/csaguide.pdf (2009). Accessed Oct 2011
24. ENISA: Cloud computing information assurance framework. http://www.enisa.europa.eu (2009). Accessed Oct 2011
25. Microsoft: Windows Azure Platform. http://www.microsoft.com/windowsazure/ (2010). Accessed Oct 2011
26. Cohen, R: Cloud computing interoperability forum. http://www.cloudforum.org/ (2010). Accessed Oct 2011
27. Salesforce.com: Developerforce. http://developer.force.com/ (2009). Accessed Oct 2011
28. Mozilla Labs: Skywriter. http://mozillalabs.com/skywriter/, now http://ace.ajax.org/ (2010). Accessed Oct 2011
29. Chuvakin, A., Peterson, G.: Logging in the age of web services. In: Proceedings of the 2009 IEEE Symposium on Security and Privacy, Oakland (2009)
30. Killourhy, K.S., Maxion, R.A., Tan, K.M.C.: A defense-centric taxonomy based on attack manifestations. In: Proceedings of the International Conference on Dependable Systems and Networks, Florence (2004)
31. Mather, T., Kumaraswamy, S., Latif, S.: Cloud Security and Privacy: An Enterprise Perspective on Risks and Compliance. O'Reilly, Sebastopol, CA (2009)
32. Chow, R., Golle, P., Jakobsson, M., Shi, E., Staddon, J., Masuoka, R., Molina, J.: Controlling data in the cloud: outsourcing computation without outsourcing control. In: Proceedings of the ACM Workshop on Cloud Computing Security. ACM, New York (2009)
33. Gentry, C.: Fully homomorphic encryption using ideal lattices. In: Proceedings of the ACM Symposium on Theory of Computing. ACM, New York (2009)
34. SLA@SOI EU Framework 7 project. http://sla-at-soi.eu/. Accessed Mar 2012
35. Automated SLA Monitoring for Web Services, Akhil Sahai, Vijay Machiraju, Mehmet Sayal, Aad van Moorsel, Fabio Casati, Technical Report, HP Laboratories, http://www.hpl.hp.com/techreports/2002/HPL-2002–191.html. Accessed Mar 2012
36. Chau, T., Muthusamy, V., Jacobsen, H.-A., Litani, E., Chan, A., Coulthard, P.: Automating SLA modeling. In: Chechik, M., Vigder, M., Stewart, D. (eds.) Proceedings of the 2008 Conference of the Center for Advanced Studies on Collaborative Research: Meeting of Minds (CASCON '08). ACM, New York. http://doi.acm.org/10.1145/1463788.1463802 (2008). Accessed Mar 2012
37. Theilmann, W., Happe, J., Kotsokalis, C., Edmonds, A., Kearney, K., Lambea, J.: A reference architecture for multi-level SLA management. J. Internet Eng. 4(1), 289–298 (2010)
38. Robinson, N., Valeri, L., Cave, J., Starkey, T., Graux, H., Creese, S., Hopkins, P.: The cloud: understanding the privacy, security and trust challenges. RAND Technical Report 933 (2011)
39. CESG: Products and Services. http://www.cesg.gov.uk/products_services/index.shtml. Accessed Oct 2011

Recommended Reading

The key background reading for this chapter are the ISO/IEC and NIST Standards documents [1–3]. Amongst the other works cited, the Cloud Security Alliance *Security Guidance for Critical Areas of Focus in Cloud Computing* [23], the ENISA *Cloud Computing Information Assurance Framework* [24] and Grobauer, Walloschek and Stöcker's *Understanding Cloud Computing Vulnerabilities* [5] discuss the additional issues specifically arising within cloud computing from a complementary variety of angles.

Chapter 8
Enterprise Information Risk Management: Dealing with Cloud Computing

Adrian Baldwin, David Pym, and Simon Shiu

Abstract Managing information risk is a complex task that must continually adapt to business and technology changes. We argue that cloud computing presents a more significant step change and so implies a bigger change for the enterprise risk and security management lifecycle. Specifically, the economies of scale that large providers can achieve are creating an ecosystem of service providers in which the marketplace (rather than consuming enterprises) determines security standards and properties. Moreover, the ability to consume high-level services from different environments is changing the nature of one-size-fits-all security policies. At HP Labs, we are doing research on developing trusted infrastructure that will exploit and improve security management in the emerging cloud architectures. We are developing and using economic and mathematical modelling techniques to help cloud stakeholders make better risk decisions, and we are pulling these strands together to establish principles and mechanisms that will improve and enable federated assurance for the cloud.

Keywords Assurance • Cloud computing • Modelling • Risk management • Trusted infrastructure

8.1 Introduction

Managing IT risks remains a significant challenge for most companies, yet most companies are ever more reliant on IT. A typical company will have a vast number of activities, policies, and processes that help manage and mitigate digital risks.

A. Baldwin (✉) • S. Shiu
HP Labs, Bristol, UK
e-mail: Simon.Shiu@hp.com

D. Pym
University of Aberdeen, Aberdeen, UK

S. Pearson and G. Yee (eds.), *Privacy and Security for Cloud Computing*,
Computer Communications and Networks, DOI 10.1007/978-1-4471-4189-1_8,
© Springer-Verlag London 2013

Ideally, these would be viewed as part of a coherent strategy wrapped around a security or risk management lifecycle. The complexity of the IT stack from network through to application and users means, however, that tasks tend to be carried out in isolation. The typical risk management lifecycle involves risk assessment, setting policies to mitigate these risks, implementing controls and running systems in accordance with these controls, and monitoring and audit to ensure risks are mitigated. The monitoring of risks can provide better information to understand the emerging risk situation. Moreover, having an integrated view of risk across the lifecycle and technology stack should improve risk management so that risk assessment can adequately assess technical controls and human behaviour, and the technical controls can be designed to be responsive to the changing risk landscape.

Cloud computing is not just another technology evolution to which this lifecycle must react. Rather, it brings a fundamental shift in how IT services are procured and provided. In this chapter, we argue that the use of cloud moves a company from a position in which it is largely in control of how it manages IT risks to one in which it is reliant on others as stewards of its information, charged not only with caring for its basic security information security—confidentiality, integrity, and availability (CIA)—issues but also with respect to its objectives and ethics. We believe that cloud computing will become far more than a scalable computing platform and that an ecosystem of business-level cloud services will emerge [9, 45, 46]. As this ecosystem grows, it will enable companies to adapt their business models based on innovation in the business services ecosystem. This will only be possible if companies are assured that cloud service providers will act as good stewards of their data and regulators ensure that the overall ecosystem is sustainable and resilient to shocks [9, 45, 46].

Many companies have outsourced parts of their IT operations and even their IT and risk governance functions. This has the effect of breaking up the lifecycle, with each service provider taking responsibility for different aspects. Contractually, however, the company remains in control. Cloud is different. Each cloud service provider must scale its operations to run services for many companies. Indeed, this is how we expect cost benefits to be gained and has the implication that cloud services will be standardized, with terms and conditions defined by the service provider rather than negotiated between a company and an outsourcing service provider. From the perspective of engagement with a services ecosystem, there is a change in the procurement model. No longer do we see an IT stack that operates under a set of security policies; instead, we procure business IT services with appropriate terms and conditions. This enables smaller service providers to participate, running their services based on cloud platforms provided by the large IT service providers. This already creates a service supply chain which can become more complex as services are bundled. For example, a complete financial operations service could be offered by combining the offerings of smaller service providers running accounts payable, accounts receivable, and general ledger services. Complex supply chains complicate the stewardship concerns [9, 45, 46].

In this chapter, we consider how enterprises currently manage their IT risks and how this will need to change as cloud computing emerges and is adopted. Cloud adds complexity to the information risk lifecycle. Companies no longer control all the security activities, or even have visibility of them, and when a company uses an array of cloud services, each will have its own sets of policies and procedures and be based on different underlying technologies. We must therefore develop richer ways of assessing and managing information risk. We see three significant areas that must be addressed:

1. *Understanding risk:* Moving to cloud will remove control and flexibility from the users of services, meaning better risk planning must be achieved prior to contract negotiation and service initiation. From an enterprise perspective, we have been using ideas from economics, mathematical modelling, and simulation techniques to gain a better understanding of risk [47]. We provide a case study that uses these techniques showing how they help security decision-making and discuss the approach [13]. As the cloud develops, businesses will rely on a complex set of interrelated services, and as such, when managing risk, we need to understand the resilience of the overall ecosystem [22]. We will discuss how we are extending our current modelling approach to help these new kinds of risk analysis and decision [9, 55].

2. *Need for monitoring and assurance:* Security may well be improved in the cloud, particularly for companies who lack a mature security management methodology, provided companies understand that their risks are being adequately managed. As IT functions are spread across the cloud, companies will need not only event monitoring systems that cross the cloud boundaries but also assurance systems that demonstrate that each service provider is maintaining their required security policies and that the combination adequately manages risk. Here we may see a movement to automated audit and the sharing of audit information [4, 5, 7] rather than the expensive manual audit process.

3. *Better Infrastructure:* It is hard to get an accurate picture of what is happening through monitoring and assurance. An alternative approach is to have an infrastructure layer that enforces policies and provides attestation. Here we look at how developments in trusted infrastructure (TI) will change the rules for risk within the cloud. We will draw from previous work on TI (see [43]), where virtualization and TCG [44, 52] are combined to provide mechanisms to attest to system properties, draw boundaries around services, and allow policies to control data flow. We have recently started a 'Trust Domains' project[1] to build on these ideas, further exploring the required technologies and linking it to the previously mentioned modelling and simulation. These technologies could be used to create trust domains, with predictable expected behaviour, that span multiple service providers and so help re-establish a company's control of its risk lifecycle.

---

[1] 'Trust Domains' is a collaborative project funded by the UK's Technology Strategy Board and EPSRC. It is led by HP Labs and includes the Universities of Aberdeen, Birmingham, and Oxford, and Perpetuity Group.

Section 8.2 starts with a general overview of typical enterprise architecture and operations and uses this to frame and discuss the risk and security lifecycle. We then focus on risk analysis and decision-making, covering standards and state of the art and leading on to case studies we have done using techniques from economic and mathematical modelling. The main contribution of the chapter is in Sect. 8.3. We start with a discussion of how cloud changes the kinds of risk analyses and decisions that must be made. Section 8.3.2 provides a significant description of information stewardship and why we think it is an important expansion of information security. In Sect. 8.3.3 we provide an example where we have used a real options switching model to help enterprises frame the problem they have when they consider using cloud services. Much of the value of this model is that it frames the uncertainty that business and IT managers must handle—which we relate back to stewardship. In Sect. 8.3.4, we review our early work, looking at how to model the ecosystem and how this will facilitate decision-making for all cloud stakeholders. Section 8.3.5 considers architecture and shows the impact that trusted infrastructure will have on security and risk analyses. The new layers of relationship and technology will mean providing assurance will be both harder and more important. Section 8.3.6 relates both the stewardship and architecture research to challenges and solutions for assurance. Finally, 8.3.7 ties all these points back to the risk lifecycle we see for cloud computing. Section 8.4 describes our future directions, which largely tie in with our ongoing collaborations in the Cloud Stewardship Economics and Trust Domains projects, both funded by the UK Technology Strategy Board.

8.2 Background

Within this chapter we argue that cloud will fundamentally change the way in which enterprises consume IT, radically changing aspects of their current security lifecycle and security decision-making. We start by looking at current enterprise IT architecture and how this will change as business services emerge in the cloud. We then review the current best practice for enterprise security management along with research aimed at improving the security decision-making.

8.2.1 Enterprise Architecture and Cloud

Before looking at risks and the way the security management lifecycle must change, it is useful to consider the current enterprise IT stack and the transformations of it that may happen with cloud. Most large companies will have built up a complex mixture of legacy data centres, infrastructure, and applications. Many will have gone through centralization and consolidation efforts, which will have produced rationalized and documented enterprise architectures [3, 49]. Even if not, the IT layers and management controls described here are fairly typical and indicative of the architecture. Our point is that, more so than previous technology and service trends, cloud computing is radically changing this architecture.

A typical company will have a set of IT services supporting their business processes such as finance, supply chain, and order management processes. These may be standard applications although they will often have undergone considerable customization to fit with the company's business processes. That is, new applications will be rolled out to support new or changing business processes, the number of interfaces between applications will grow, and different applications and components will often be administered by different IT teams.

Many of these enterprise applications sit on middleware platforms that provide a variety of services such as identity management, messaging, and databases. These services are often critical to the security of the enterprise and can be difficult to manage effectively. For example, frameworks such as COBIT [36] commonly identified access management as a risk, but since most enterprises have a complex mix of centralized provisioning and single sign-on, with distributed application and component access control lists, it is often difficult to provide sufficient assurance [4].

Below the middleware sit the datacentres that provide compute power and storage. The datacentre administrators will often run the back-end operating systems, manage the physical hardware and its security, as well as run some pieces of middleware, such as databases. A large company will have a number of geographically dispersed datacentres to enhance resilience. Companies will typically have a separate IT team running each of the network and the client systems (laptops) and another managing their operating systems.

There are standards that help companies manage their IT stack. ITIL [41] sets out a number of strategic planning and operational processes that should be followed to ensure the smooth running of an enterprise IT system. The security team will set policies across all these IT layers to ensure that risks are mitigated. They will often work with standards such as COBIT and ISO27000 [35] to help them design a comprehensive security management system. In addition to considering all these layers and teams, the setting of a security policy is a negotiation between the business, the operational staff, and the security team. Many enterprises have risk committees to review decisions and provide a way to informally discuss trade-offs between the different needs of a business.

We can see the structure of cloud computing emerging in a similar way; see Fig. 8.1. Looking at the NIST definitions [42], we have infrastructure-as-a-service (IaaS) providing the basic datacentre capabilities, that is, the compute power and storage. As we move up the stack, we have platform-as-a-service (PaaS), that is, where the service provider runs middleware on top of the infrastructure. Then we have the software-as-a-service (SaaS) layer providing the applications to run the business processes. Some would argue that we should talk of process-as-a-service which allows a number of applications to be combined to support a business process or even of humans-as-a-service where services are augmented with people's skills.

Traditionally, many companies have struggled with running their own IT systems—or do not see it as their core competence—and this has led many to follow IT out-

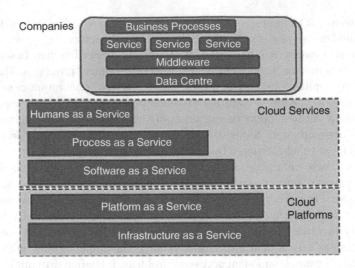

Fig. 8.1 The structural components of enterprise IT and cloud computing

sourcing strategies. That is, they hire a company to take on their IT systems and deliver them as a service. Typically, this will involve a big deal and bespoke contracts will be drawn up, setting out terms and conditions that meet the customer's needs [21]. When needs change, these terms and conditions can be changed, albeit at a cost.

Cloud provides a very different model of control. Cloud providers aim to provide scalable services at low cost—much lower than through outsourcing—and this can only be achieved by offering the same application and terms and conditions to many customers. Thus a cloud service provider may offer a small menu of choices rather than designing and running bespoke services. The result is a customer can no longer control the terms and conditions, including security policies, used in running a service. Control over this has switched from the customer to the service provider, and customers must rely on service providers to be good stewards of their data.

Companies seeking to move their IT operations to the cloud could consider just moving their applications onto an infrastructure- or platform-as-a-service provider's systems. This would relieve them of the need to buy hardware and help them scale their compute and storage needs. One of the current models for enterprises using the cloud is to offload compute-intensive tasks. In these cases, security (i.e. confidentiality and integrity) and availability (cf. sensitivity and criticality) are not normally critical. An alternative usage model is where a company will seek to get some of its enterprise applications from the cloud, for example, looking to salesforce.com to provide a customer relationship management system.

Rather than going to the basic platform providers, a company could directly procure its business services. This would relieve companies of many of their IT functions although they would still need to perform network and client management. As this happens, the ability to provide robust messaging and identity services across a range of different business-level services becomes critical.

Considering how cloud systems have been emerging, and in the interests of conceptual clarity, we have chosen to work with a simplified three-layer model as a basis for our discussion (see Fig. 8.1). Here we combine the infrastructure- and platform-as-a-service into a cloud-platform-provider layer. We believe there will be a limited number of companies offering such services due to the massive investment costs needed to build datacentres. The presence of such cloud platforms will allow a large number of small software developers to offer their products as services in a cost-effective manner. The third layer of our cloud model is companies that consume services[2] or platforms. We develop this model further both in [9] and later in this chapter.

8.2.2   Pre-cloud Enterprise Risk Analysis and Decision-Making

Even without the cloud, year on year enterprises see more failures and attacks, meaning they are compelled to spend more on information security. However since resources are limited, organizations need principles and guidance for how much and where to spend on security. The common answer is that it should be based on risk—that is, focus resources on highest impact and likelihood events.

Ideally, an organization would drive all security investment and operations from a risk perspective, but a challenge to this is that there are many other stakeholders, incentives, and processes with which risk choices have to live. That is, in theory (and to some extent practice), an organization will follow a lifecycle such as that in Fig. 8.2, whereby business-driven risk assessments set the context and priorities for

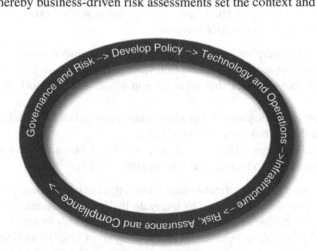

Fig. 8.2 The typical enterprise risk management lifecycle

---

[2] Throughout this chapter, we are concerned with how companies use the cloud and ignore consumer cloud services.

security controls, policies, and investments, which in turn guide infrastructure procurement and operations, and the monitoring and audits of the IT environments test whether the controls are effective and mitigating risks, thus closing the loop. There are many standards and frameworks to help govern and apply best practice through the lifecycle, such as:

- The ISO27000 [35] series of standards for information security that provide a framework for referencing known security best practices and organizing them in a coherent governance framework.
- COBIT [36] that sets out control objectives for IT from a business perspective and complements the slightly more technical focus of ISO27000.

Complementing these, there are several methodologies [51] that aim to help organizations perform systematic evaluations of their IT risks. Typical steps include:

- A scoping phase to determine the nature of the risk, that is, assets, components, and boundaries. For digital information and services that depend on many layers of abstraction and distributed interdependent systems, this can be a difficult and subjective task.
- A threat analysis, where the attacks, motivations, opportunities, and vulnerabilities are considered.
- An analysis of the likelihood and impact of any of the threats occurring, which in turn guides prioritization and choices as to whether to accept, mitigate, or transfer risks.

The standards and frameworks are extremely useful and relevant. In practice, however, there are still many challenges applying the described principles in specific complex environments, primarily because:

- The teams procuring and running infrastructure are under pressure to improve and maintain service levels which often work against the risk priorities.
- Performing risk analyses that take account of all the trade-offs is inherently difficult.
- The enterprise architecture and processes are always changing, making assumptions made during risk analysis out of date.
- Many complex IT environments rely very heavily on human behaviour—and we lack rigorous ways to incorporate this into risk models.

There is a great deal of current research looking at many of these problems. See [1] for examples of work seeking to integrate insights from human behaviour or psychology. [11, 29] are specific examples of recent research on how better to integrate knowledge of human behaviour into the analysis of risk. There is also research on the economics of information security, ranging from showing how to apply standard (business understood) return on investment cases for security investment [31] to the application of sophisticated utility functions [34].

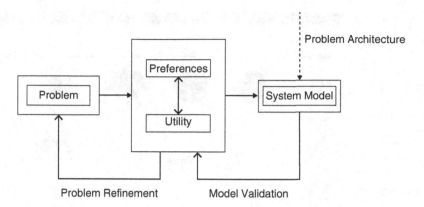

Fig. 8.3 A framework for using economic and system models to support organizational decision-making

HP Labs has developed the idea of combining economic and system models to help organizations with risk assessment, security analysis, and decision-making[3]; see [47]. Economic models, represented as utility functions, are used to help stakeholders think about and share their preferences and priorities for different business outcomes. We then use structural models to help stakeholders think about and share their assumptions for how different investment and policy choices will affect the outcome. Finally, we use a discrete process simulation tool [25, 26] that allows stakeholders to explore and predict consequences of their different assumptions. Figure 8.3 provides a schematic of this methodology.

HP Labs has also conducted a series of customer case studies [8, 50] to develop and refine this process. An early example was to help a large enterprise decide between a range of policies and investments to manage risks from software vulnerabilities, see [13].

Most large organizations have evolved a complex set of processes and technologies to deal with software vulnerabilities. These include testing and deploying patches over multiple environments and regions, deploying and updating antivirus signatures, reliance on gateway and network boundaries and protections, intrusion-prevention systems, processes to accelerate patching processes, and so on. The risk question was whether to spend more resources to improve the effectiveness of all these controls and, if so, where. More specifically, should the organization invest in some new host-based intrusion-prevention technology, invest to improve the patching process, or spend the money on other (perhaps non-security) projects.

---

[3] Much of this work was based on the UK Technology Strategy Board-funded Trust Economics project, with partners from University of Newcastle, University of Bath, University College London, Merrill Lynch, and National Grid.

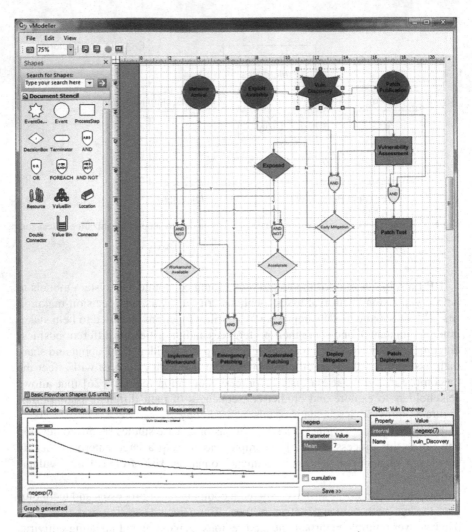

Fig. 8.4 Structural components of a typical vulnerability management environment

The first task is to find some components and abstractions to help the stakeholders think about the complex system. In the given study, it was decided that it would be useful to model how long (typically) it takes to mitigate risks from a known vulnerability. The team separated aspects that were under the control (or influence) of the organization (how fast they patch, when signatures would be deployed) from external factors (when vulnerabilities are publicly disclosed, when vendors release patches, when malware starts spreading). They then separated out concurrent processes that affect risk mitigation (i.e. testing, patching, signature updates) and discuss how architecture and decisions (typically) affect their progress. The result was something like that which is represented in Fig. 8.4.

The structural models already help ensure shared understanding between stakeholders, so they can discuss, say, whether scheduling is significantly delaying patch testing or when and how often the assessment team accelerate patch processes. However, with such a complex system of interdependent concurrent processes and actions, it can be very difficult to see or reason about the cause and effects. To address this (using best available assumptions and empirical data), we use Gnosis [23–26] to create an executable mathematical model of the system.[4] Using Gnosis we can run Monte Carlo-style simulations to explore the interactions and their effect on time to mitigate risks. By varying parameters, stakeholders can see the (model) predicted effect of different investment choices. Results are typically shared as histograms showing, say, the difference in time taken to mitigate risk for different investment choices. For example, the results show quantitatively how an investment in HIPS should increase the number of early mitigations, whereas similar investment in patching will reduce the long tail of vulnerabilities that take a long time to mitigate. This would be a simplistic initial result, and further experiments can explore the effect based on different assumptions about the threat environment or differentiate on different types of mitigation.

So far, this example has only discussed the effect on risk mitigation. Most security decisions involve multiple trade-offs between mitigating different kinds of risks, maintaining services, and minimizing costs. To formulate this, we encourage stakeholders to define a utility function expressing their preferences between the multiple outcomes, building on the approaches to decisions with multiple objectives developed by Keeney and Raiffa [38]. We have developed some simple tools for preference elicitation and then use the system models to explore the effect of different security choices on these other outcomes, see [15].

Our experience is that focusing, via system models, on the utility (of outcomes) provides a constructive way to engage multiple stakeholders (with different knowledge and incentives) in the complex process of risk assessment and choosing security investment and policy. Providing evidence for this is difficult as organizations, people, and problems vary so much. We have done some preliminary studies that suggest our methodology affects the justifications security professionals might use, which fits with why it might be useful for multi-stakeholder decision-making, see [48]. We are currently looking at further cognitive studies to generate more precise hypotheses for how and why economic and system modelling affect security decisions.

Part of the problem is that many security problems (like patching components and network security) are about mitigating risks on infrastructure that many applications rely on. Business stakeholders find it easier to reason about motivations and impacts of application failures rather than on the complex dependency of many

---

[4] Gnosis is a discrete process modelling language that (partially) captures a discipline of mathematical system modelling based on mathematical models of the concepts of location, resource, and process (all modelled using algebraic/logical tools) and environment (modelled stochastically) [23–26].

applications on shared infrastructure. One helpful outcome (from a risk perspective) of the shift to cloud computing is the ability to consume software-as-a-service from multiple environments. Although there will still be complex interdependencies between applications, it is helpful for a business to analyse discretely the risks for different applications or, conversely, to be able to look at the impact of infrastructure failures in the context of the only/few applications running on it. We shall return to this point when we discuss trusted infrastructure, which also allows us to decouple risk analyses at different layers, so simplifying the whole problem.

This section has described some of the challenges enterprises face in aligning security policies and investments to business priorities. We have argued that, in some cases, the shift to cloud computing may disaggregate typically complex enterprise architectures (and so simplify risk analysis). Conversely, however, in the current lifecycle (even when outsourcing), the organization at least maintains control of all the components and services. The emerging problem with cloud computing is that organizations will lose this control and will rely on a number of firms making different choices about how the applications and infrastructure holding their data and executing their transactions will be defended. It will be a bigger challenge to help businesses create effective risk and security strategies whilst tapping into the flexibility and cost structures of cloud computing.

8.3   Risk and Security Management in the Cloud

Moving to the cloud does nothing to reduce dependence on IT; instead, it means that a company is dependent on service providers to do the right thing and act as good information stewards. That is, enterprises must rely on others to manage their information and the processes that create, maintain, and use the information. The shift of control over policy, operational, architectural, and assurance options from the customer to the cloud service provider means that the customer must employ careful risk planning to choose the service that offers the best trade-off between the service provided, the level of risk, and the cost.

Instead of running one security management lifecycle, an enterprise now must rely on a multitude of service providers, each running their own security lifecycle (see Fig. 8.5). An enterprise is then faced with two issues: firstly, to decide on whom to trust for what service and how much information they need about that company's lifecycle, and, secondly, how to gain a coherent overview of its risks. These issues are at the heart of the transformation of the security lifecycle as enterprises move to cloud. Here we argue that as the lifecycle breaks up and changes, companies need better risk planning methodologies (Sects. 8.3.1, 8.3.2, 8.3.3, and 8.3.4), better architectural support (Sect. 8.3.5), and better assurance (Sect. 8.3.6). That is, each of the individual elements of the security management lifecycle needs improving in such a way that allows a company to understand the risks to which each service is subject and hence get this joined up risk view. Here we look at each of these three areas separately before bringing the discussion back to the overall lifecycle.

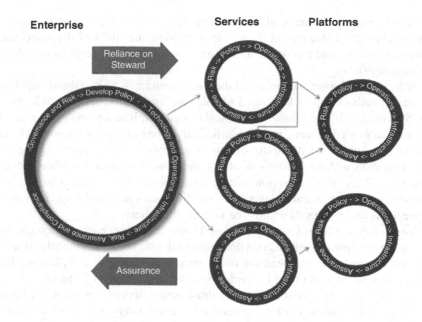

Fig. 8.5 Security lifecycles where an enterprise must rely on other services to be stewards who must run a good security management lifecycle; these in turn may depend on a service supply chain; assurance information should flow back

8.3.1 Decision-Making About Risk in the Cloud

Although companies will often have some form of IT risk planning, security is often reactive to events. This may be inevitable both due to the 'arms race nature' of security and the fast pace of technology innovation and change. A company's ability to adapt its security to circumstances relies on the ability to control security policies and infrastructure. As cloud services are used, this ability to react is very much reduced. As one of many customers of a service, it can be hard to influence service offerings and switching between services can be expensive (especially if there are no standardized data formats). That is, there is a danger that customers get locked into a particular provider or *de facto* standard service models—hence the need for good initial risk planning.

Part of this risk planning must take account of the opacity of the service and what assurance information is available to the customer to ensure that the promised levels of service are maintained.[5] In performing this risk planning, companies and their security officers need a much richer concept of stewardship. They must consider more factors than just the confidentiality, integrity, and availability of services that

---

[5] This is particularly important for security processes, where failures may not be obvious, or not obvious until a serious incident has occurred.

they would manage to internally. In particular, we would argue that they must consider about the objectives of the service provision, the ethics of the associated business decisions, and the sustainability and resilience of the services on which they depend [9].

Earlier in this chapter, we discussed the current enterprise IT stack with separate services all built on top of horizontal middleware, datacentre, and network offerings. Security has become hard in this world (arguably, it always was [2]) since a security policy in a datacentre must be sufficiently strong to provide the sought level of protection, but not too disruptive of enterprise applications. Communicating the technology risks and the business needs up and down this stack has often proved challenging. This interconnection and dependency has made it hard to take an economic approach to security because of the difficulties in articulating changes in service levels and risk levels within one-size-fits-all policies.

Cloud offers a different way to procure IT services. Now each service can be thought of as a separate entity. Cloud does entail a degree of loss of control and ability to react, and hence the need for more upfront planning, so complicating the decision-making aspects of the lifecycle. However, the ability to focus on a single service and drop the one-size-fits-all infrastructure security policies typically simplifies each decision. Looking at each service separately means we can get a much clearer understanding of the trade-offs between risk, service level, and cost. Thinking of services in this way provides a more modular way to think of security, hence simplifying decision-making. However, much of the complexity is hidden in the way the service is delivered.

As businesses start to use the cloud for critical business functions, we believe that an ecosystem of service and platform providers will start to emerge. A company may just worry about the way service providers they use manage risk, but they should also worry about the overall resilience within the ecosystem. A simple example of this need arises in the construction of service supply chains, where one service provider uses others to provide parts services and platforms to deliver the underlying IT infrastructure. Risks may emanate from failures of any of these services, even though such failures may be unknown to the end-user. Other risks can occur because of interdependencies between service providers and the resources (e.g. investment capital and skilled staff) upon which they rely. As with enterprise IT, where risks occur because of the complexity of the infrastructures, we believe modelling decisions in the cloud ecosystem can help us gain an understanding of these risks.

The emergence of a cloud ecosystem will represent a major shift in the way in which enterprises purchase IT provision. This means that the surrounding environment will change and, in doing so, it will cause shocks to the ecosystem. Criminals will start to see concentrated value in certain services and may invest considerable resources in attacks. Regulators will be concerned about the stability of companies and their ability to deliver services, and so, rules, regulations, and laws will eventually catch up with the emergence of cloud. In turn, enterprises thinking about the risks of procuring from the cloud will also be taking into account implicit assumptions about the sustainability and resilience of this ecosystem.

In the next section, we explore each of these themes and consider the use of models to help understand assumptions, risks, and decisions.

8.3.2 Information Stewardship

Typically, when thinking about security, people think of confidentiality, integrity, and availability (CIA) as a distinct and complete set of declarative properties [12] that, to varying degrees, system managers will seek to maintain. Pym et al. [32–34] introduce the idea that these elements can be combined along with cost to form a utility function for security decision-making that characterizes the relative extent and form of the managers' preferences between the various properties. When we start to think about how risks are managed around cloud, it is still useful to think about the CIA concepts, but we need a wider conceptual framework to understand the implications of stewardship. Information stewardship for a cloud service needs to include additional concepts around management and duty of service (i.e. the appropriate achievement of the agreed objectives), the supervision of values and respect for ethics, along with the long-term sustainability of services and their resilience to rare-event shocks.

In choosing a service, a company must think about whether the service provider will act as a good information steward or, more accurately, a good-enough steward for the required service and at the given cost. In doing this, the risks associated with the service must be considered. A customer may place few stewardship requirements on a service storing encrypted data whereas the requirements for a service running their financial processes will be much greater. Some aspects such as the ethics of the service provider may have a wider consequence than just the service being used. A manufacturing company's reputation could be hugely damaged by the use of child labour for even a small part of one of its products. In the same way, the use of a service provider who appears unethical could cause damage to the wider ecosystem rather than just to the service in question. As a first stage in looking at stewardship of the service, the service provider's identity needs to be checked. Are they whom we expect them to be, is the company financially solid, are they owned by our competitors? In establishing their identity, we must also establish the jurisdiction under which they operate. Some of these basic checks must be done before looking more deeply into the stewardship concepts.

The information steward is responsible for maintaining the usual CIA properties, along with maintaining data privacy. As such, we would expect that he would run the normal information security processes; for example, vulnerability management processes, ensuring access to information is controlled, and ensuring software and hardware is of sufficient quality. The effort put into each security process must be traded off against the cost, the service provided, the value of the data, and risks when things go wrong. As well as trying to maintain these basic security properties, the steward must communicate how much effort he will make in achieving this trade-off. Models such as the one described in Sect. 8.2.2 could help form the basis of this communication.

Establishing the boundaries of stewardship is also important. For what, exactly, is the steward taking responsibility? For an enterprise service being moved into the cloud, the service provider will be acting as an information steward both for the basic information and for the way in which the transactions are handled, but the enterprise will probably still remain responsible for managing the identities and rights of its staff access when they access the service. Care should be taken that the stewardship boundaries and hence responsibilities are clear.

Even with the best technologies, management, and risk planning, there will still be security incidents. The information steward will have responsibilities around managing such incidents and keeping the service users informed. However, the use of a steward will not reduce the accountability that the enterprise has for ensuring their data (e.g. PII that they hold) is secured. In looking at stewardship, we need to look at what happens when things go wrong and how incidents can be jointly managed to reduce loss and damage to reputations. Incidents that happen to one customer using a service provider may cause reputational damage to others using the same service—so it is the duty of the information steward to maintain their reputation. Disclosure may become an important aspect of stewardship, forcing those acting as information stewards to disclose incidents publically. This has become the case in the USA [54] for personally identifiable information where disclosure policies support a loose regulatory environment.

Businesses need services to run constantly or continuously over time and to remain fit for purpose. This means that they can be relying on services for long periods of time. In looking at the information stewardship offered by a service, a customer should think about these long-term requirements:

- Will the service respond appropriately to changes in the threat environment?
- Will the service respond appropriately to regulatory changes?
- Will the service itself change as needs change? For example, we would expect an accountancy service to change its rules as accountancy standards evolve.
- Are there good (cheap, efficient) exit routes if things go wrong or other changes are needed?
- What measures can be taken when things go wrong (arbitration, law)?
- What happens if the service provider is taken over or spun out as a separate company?

In addition to thinking about stewardship at the level of an individual service, we also need to consider the overall stewardship of the cloud ecosystem. Here we must consider the properties of sustainability and resilience [20] provided by the overall system. The influence needed for this level of stewardship will be beyond the individual participants, except perhaps the large platform providers. However, regulators, or clubs of service providers or users, may form in order to set rules and ensure appropriate overall stewardship of parts of the ecosystem.

8.3.3 Migrating to Cloud

As business-level cloud services start to emerge, a business will be faced with a decision—do they keep using their current IT systems or do they switch to using cloud services, and assuming so, which cloud services do they use. The decision may be to move all IT to the cloud, but a more likely and recurring decision will be whether to keep an internal application running or to replace it with a cloud service. This decision will often be triggered by a business need to upgrade an application. Clearly information stewardship should be part of that decision, but a company needs a framework for thinking through the decision.

In Sect. 8.3.2, we discussed the need to frame security decisions with a utility function [32–34] that allows stakeholders to trade off different aspects of security, such as confidentiality and availability, as well as considering cost. In Sect. 8.2, we discussed how security policies tend to apply across the board, so that one decision will affect many parts of the business. If cloud decisions relate to single services, then security decisions can become more modular, and so simpler. That is, when a security decision affects many different aspects of a business, it can be hard to estimate the cost and productivity effects. Isolating these factors to a single service can help focus the decision. Conversely, moving a single service to the cloud may still have wider impacts on the wider enterprise IT. For example, moving many applications out from a company's datacentre will reduce the economies of scale, increasing costs for those that remain. In other ways, the cloud decision is more complex in that the decision to move encompasses factors representing business decisions, as well as cost and information stewardship factors.

Formalizing preferences in a utility function provides a framework for comparing the different values that a company would get between different cloud services options or the internal IT option. It allows an enterprise to express how it wishes to value a gain in one factor, such as business value, against a loss in a stewardship factor. It can then use this function to look at the different service options' terms and conditions.

This still leaves the question as to the optimal time to switch to a cloud service, assuming it offers better utility. That is, even if the cloud service offers better immediate utility, there may be greater longer-term utility in using the option to wait (until company finances are better or until uncertainty relating to the value is reduced). A cloud switching model, using real option theory [53], has been developed in [55] to explore this question. The problem of whether to use a cloud service is expressed as a choice between staying with internal IT, switching to a cloud service, or opting to wait (and monitor).

An advantage of this framing is that much of the financial economics relating to discount rates and the time value of money can easily be reused. That is, most real option models take account of the fact that decision-makers will have different cash flow, levels of capital, risk appetite, and patience for a return on investments made. This makes it natural to show, for example, how a large oil and gas firm with huge reserves, used to long cycles of investment, will feel quite differently about utility than, say, a start-up having little capital and worried about whether it will be in business in 12 months' time.

Clearly, there is uncertainty over security and stewardship, and the switching model [55] allows these issues to be framed as affecting uncertainty over the value the business can achieve with each decision option. For example, an enterprise will have some (but not complete) confidence in internal IT's ability to keep up with regulations and the threat environment. They will likely be more uncertain about whether using the cloud service will enable them to maintain security and compliance. Moreover they will implicitly be concerned about all the information stewardship points discussed in Sect. 8.3.2.

Finally, there is clearly potential value in having an option to wait to decide. As time passes it will become clearer whether early adopters are having success, whether security incidents are more common and whether it seems resilient and sustainable. For some firms the value will be high enough to warrant early adoption, for others it will be a clear no, and for others a wait-and-see approach will be appropriate.

It is not that the model provides accurate predictions about the outcomes but rather that it frames the assumptions, so that stakeholders can debate the options and trade-offs appropriately. Moreover, it is also not that decision-makers are unaware of all these aspects to their decision options but, as discussed in [48], there is significant value in bringing all the issues together in an appropriate way.

In discussing this model with cloud stakeholders, many raised the question of being able to explore the issues of lock-in (being tied to a particular cloud provider) and the ability (ease) of switching back to previous states. These can be treated as uncertainties within the current framework, but it is also natural to consider the economic models that explore precisely this situation, see [39]. As discussed in the 'Future Directions' section, below, our current work in this area is focused on testing and refining this type of model stakeholders, and as part of this we are looking at these iterative migration models.

As cloud services start to emerge, a company will need a framework for thinking about when it should start to use a cloud service and which service is the most suitable for it. Taking a utility theory approach forces the company to think about the different outcomes of the decision and how they may trade off against each other. The framing provided by the 'cloud switching' model [55] provides a way to think about the costs of moving service as well as uncertainties associated with the utility. Much of this uncertainty may come from the loss of control and the need to rely on others to be good information stewards.

8.3.4   The Cloud Ecosystem

A company can try to choose a cloud provider that best meets its needs, including one that it believes will be resilient to failures. Each service, however, sits within an ecosystem of other services, service customers, and cloud platforms, and their

Cloud as an Ecosystem

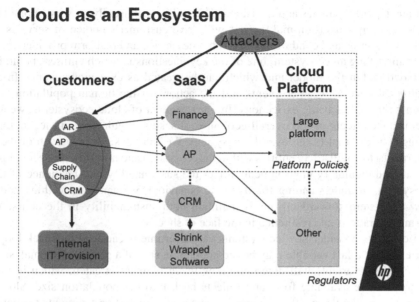

Fig. 8.6 A three-layered cloud ecosystem

success and resilience may well be affected by the success and resilience of other services. Within the ecosystem, there will be limited sets of available resources, for which each service provider must compete if it is to be successful, and each service provider will work hard to develop its own reputation. However, news of incidents— and the overall reputation of the cloud ecosystem—may swamp their branding. Finally, there will often be a service supply chain within which a service provider relies on other services and cloud platforms to allow it to deliver the contracted service. These factors mean that as a rich cloud ecosystem emerges, the success, sustainability, and resilience of an individual service will be dependent on those properties of others in the ecosystem.

In our analysis of this ecosystem [9], we draw quite significantly on research carried out on ecological ecosystems [20]. The ecological ecosystem consists of various organisms that exist in a habitat or a series of linked habitats. The ecosystem will be affected by the way the organisms interact (due to their biology) as well as due to external influences such as the weather, fires, or pollution. In studying an ecosystem and its dynamic behaviours, we can start to see how resilient the ecosystem is to different shocks and hence start to manage it in a sustainable way. Analysing from an ecosystem perspective helps us develop good stewardship properties.

Instead of organisms in various habitats, we have an ecosystem consisting of customers consuming cloud services, cloud service providers offering the services, and cloud platforms providing the basic infrastructure for these services (see Fig. 8.6). Instead of the interaction between these entities being driven from their biology, it is driven by their need to maximize (or at least satisfy) their utility, so influencing their policies and decisions. This utility will usually be very implicit in each company's decision-making but will drive customer's choice of services as well as the terms and conditions offered by the service and platform providers.

In modelling an ecosystem, one of the key questions is which entities should be included within the model and which can be treated as exogenous events. In an ecological system, weather events and the actions of the human population will often be treated as being exogenous. In our treatment of cloud ecosystems, we are keeping the effects of the overall economy, attackers, regulators, and technology changes as external to the overall ecosystem. We can consider how each of these external factors will affect entities within the ecosystem and how different economic, threat, and regulatory environments affect the sustainability and resilience of the ecosystem. In understanding the dynamic behaviour, we can start to think about how ecosystem stewardship helps maintain both sustainability in the course of normal operations and resilience in the face of shocks.

Ecologists consider how ecosystems vary overtime because of feedback loops. For example, a fast variable may be the population size of a particular animal, such as deer. This variable will determine how much biomass is eaten, which in turn determines the available food and reflects back into the population size. Slower variables may be things like changes in the capacity of soil or sediments to supply water or nutrients or changes in types of plants and animals in the ecosystem. Exogenous controls may be changes in the regional climate. Ecologists then consider two different factors as being responsible for these changes: the ecological factors and the societal factors (i.e. mankind's effect on the ecosystem). Within our view of cloud ecosystems, we can draw out similar feedback loops—see Fig. 8.7—drawing out the business or economic environment and technological environment rather than, though analogously to, the societal and ecological factors described by ecologists.

Here, in Fig. 8.7, we can see the fast variables being linked with the regular IT decisions that enterprises make around their IT needs. Here they may make a decision to continue to run their own IT or to move to the cloud. In making their decisions, they will seek to maximize (but, in practice, typically satisfy) their utility as discussed above. These decisions will be based on their needs as well as the state of the ecosystem. For example, their decisions will be based on the different costs, the different services available in the cloud, the terms and conditions offered, and their beliefs in how good an information steward a service provider will be. Their decisions will of course affect the state of the ecosystem. For example, if a company decides to use a cloud service rather than its internal IT, it will release, or not require, resources such as IT staff and investment capital. On the other hand, additional network bandwidth may well be required.

In an equilibrium state, the resources moved by each of these decisions will cancel each other out. However, we can get reinforcing feedback loops that will help move the ecosystem to a different equilibrium state. For example, as a service provider starts to get more business, it will be able to scale better and hence offer better or cheaper services. This will attract more customers as well as making it easier for them to get resources, such as skilled IT staff and investment capital.

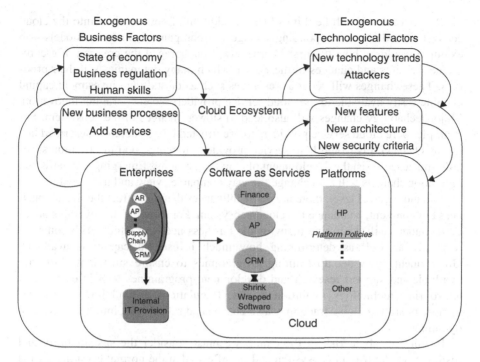

Fig. 8.7 Dynamics of the cloud ecosystem

This reinforcement feedback will lead to a movement of IT from company's internal provision and into the cloud.

There are, of course, other feedback loops at this fast-variable scale. Some cloud services will fail either because they get insufficient business or because of stewardship failures (e.g. security incidents, failures to maintain services, failures in meeting the reputational needs of customers). Such incidents may lead to customers pulling services back from the cloud into their own datacentres. Other feedbacks will be caused by technology changes—for example, as the availability of new software features encourages companies to upgrade their systems. Where companies invest in creating new features in the cloud, or in shrink-wrapped software, this will help determine the cloud adoption rates.

One critical factor associated with how fast feedback loops work within the ecosystem will be the costs associated with changing provider or moving back to internal IT. When a company chooses a particular service provider, it may be hard or costly to get its data out of that service and into the correct form for a different service, or there may be costs associated with integrating a new service into its business processes. High movement costs may mean that service providers have less incentive to update features and act as good stewards. It will also lead to a slowdown in the speed of these feedback loops.

Slower variables will be things like the addition of new services into the cloud ecosystem and the corresponding changes to companies' business models—an example would be how the first Internet wave encouraged the creation of e-commerce websites and changes in the way in which many companies sell their products. These changes will occur as resources such as IT staff and investment capital become easily available to the cloud service providers, so encouraging innovation. Major technology changes will also lead to slower changes in the ecosystem. For example, were cloud service providers to use 'trusted infrastructure' (described late in this chapter) this would help service providers in being good information stewards and hence assist the development of cloud ecosystems. Emerging standards and regulation changes will also change the way companies view and use cloud.

At a more global level, there are many influences that will affect the overall business environment, and hence the cloud ecosystem. For example, the overall state of the economy will determine many of the business needs to which each company responds, as well as determining how much investment capital is available. Governments may set up training programmes to ensure sufficient skills are available and support research and development programmes to help ensure that appropriate technology evolution occurs. Regulations around how businesses operate or around global trade may also change and reflect back into the ecosystem dynamics.

In thinking about risk in the cloud, we must consider the sustainability and resilience of the overall ecosystem and the effects that the normal evolution of the ecosystem and rare-event shocks may have on a given enterprise. A clear conceptual model of cloud ecosystems and their dynamics is a necessary prerequisite for allowing us to think through these effects. We can start to extend the system modelling approach [25] used to help us understand security decisions in the enterprise to understand the dynamics of the overall ecosystem, the effects of shocks, and different ecosystem stewardship approaches. Pym et al. [9] describe such an approach to modelling based on a location, resource, and process calculus [23, 24] that has previously been used for system modelling and security decision-making.

8.3.5   Trusted Infrastructure and Cloud

In much of this chapter, we have concentrated on the risk side of the security management lifecycle and how this is affected as business operations move into cloud. Having good system architecture helps to reduce risk and can make reporting and assurance easier. Following our previous argument, as an enterprise moves from running its own applications to using cloud services, it loses control not only of the people, policy, and process parts of some aspects of its operations but also of the technical architecture and the application code base.

We have hypothesized a world in which there will be a relatively few cloud platform providers that provide the basic compute and storage platforms, along with much of the middleware, and service providers who will write software, run it on the platforms, and use it to offer business-level services. These services would be provided to many customers using common management processes and contracts. There are two natural technical architectures to support such multi-tenanted services: the first is to write the software to support multiple customers at the same time (application virtualization); the second is to run many instances of the software each within its own container (infrastructure virtualization).

The two different styles of virtualization that can be used to produce a multi-tenanted service carry very different risk profiles. Although in both cases many of the risks will be due to two factors:

1. The complexity of the trusted computing base—that is, the parts of the software stack that must be trusted to maintain separation and information security.
2. The complexities of managing the service and infrastructure—ideally, we will have services that can be designed around the principle of least privilege and ensure there are separations of duty between different administrative roles, along with strong audit. Traditionally, in the enterprise, separations between application, database, and system administrators have been viewed as very important, as have separations between developers and those running production systems. These are seen as risk-reduction measures aimed at limiting what each individual can do and know along with making it hard for a rogue employee to cover his tracks.

If we move to a world in which each application provider must code its application to support multiple customers, this has two effects on the trusted computing base. Firstly, the code complexity will increase as multiple customers need supporting and, secondly, much of this code will be bespoke (this may be improved with supporting libraries and coding patterns). With this style of service provision, we are thus very dependent on the skills of a given service provider and, since code will be proprietary, it will be very hard to validate the trustworthiness of the application. Third-party code reviews and code verification techniques may help in producing certifications to enhance trust.

The administrative model with application virtualization is also somewhat unpredictable as it will be a consequence of the software design. A rogue administrator or a hacker who can gain administrative privileges will easily be able to gain access to the details of many customers. This concentration of data may encourage attackers, as the value may make the investment of time and effort in sophisticated attacks worthwhile. This was perhaps demonstrated in attacks on email service providers reported early in 2011, where sophisticated attacks were carried out on email advertising distribution services, allowing spammers to get mailing lists for multiple customers as well as use the services to send out spam [40].

The alternative to creating multi-tenanted applications is to run each customer's instance of an application within a separate container. This has the advantage of keeping the application code simple, so reducing bugs and vulnerabilities, reducing the impact of a breach, and, where trust can be gained in containment technologies, enhancing trust in the service. Many of the business applications offered in the cloud will be complex and need to scale, supporting many transactions and requiring

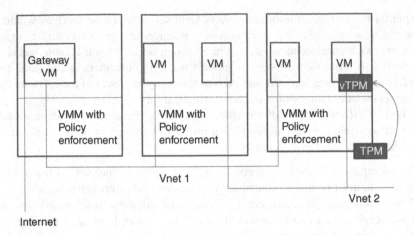

Fig. 8.8 Virtual infrastructure can be created with a mixture of virtual machines, virtual networks, and virtual storage with attestation provided by TPMs

each instance of the application to run on multiple servers connected by networks. This makes it hard to use simple sandboxing technologies, such as those available in Java.

Virtualization of servers [10], networks [37], and storage can be combined to allow us to build complex boundaries around applications. Each part or service within the application can be run within a different virtual machine, each with its own virtual storage, and the whole lot connected with one or more virtual networks (Fig. 8.8), along with a gateway connecting them to the Internet to receive/process transactions and management requests. This whole system can effectively replicate what would run within an individual company's data. This architecture can support flexing in that more virtual machine instances can be added into the network to match the required transaction rates. This way of running services could have an additional management burden in setting up the application for each customer and hence relies heavily on having automated configuration systems [30] that support deployment and flexing [28].

Trusted computing technologies, as defined by the Trusted Computing Group [44, 52], can help in building trust in to some of our basic infrastructure, and these ideas have been extended to support virtualization. The trusted computing module provides a hardware root of trust upon which other trust functions can be built. In particular, three principle functions are provided:

1. A cryptographic identity for a device
2. Attestation of the software stack that is running and that has been used to boot a system
3. Safe storage for cryptographic keys that can be linked to attestation

These three functions allow us to know that we are connecting and relying on the computer systems we expect to and that they are in the form that we expect. In terms of basic virtualization, we can use TCG-based mechanisms to identify servers and check that the base system software is the virtualization layer. As we move up the stack, we can measure and attest to the various management components, such as the management domain and any separate driver domains. The idea of a virtual TPM [16] has also been introduced so that the integrity of a particular virtual machine can be tested and reported. As we build up the attestation in our virtualized infrastructure, we can also use the TCG mechanisms to help manage cryptographic keys necessary to secure network and storage virtualization [6].

We are concerned that cloud services be deployed in a secure and trustable manner, so having a simple containment strategy is not sufficient unless the container has the correct security and trust properties. Here we look to a number of principles for improving infrastructure that can be built using virtualization and trusted computing:

- *Reduced trusted computing base.* Complex code will always be subject to bugs that lead to vulnerabilities, and hence, as a principle, it is important to reduce the code base that is being trusted. For trusted infrastructure, this means ensuring that the software maintaining separations and managing critical system components and policies is kept to a minimum. For example, if we look at the Xen virtualization layer, not only must we keep the code within the hypervisor to a minimum, but we must also remove all the supporting functions from the management domain (dom0). This means we must work out a minimal set of services that are needed to support virtual machine management and remove the rest of the management stack into other virtual machines that are not part of the trusted computing base. As we construct larger systems, we still need to keep mindful of minimizing the trusted computing base. For example, critical application components can be kept small and run in separate virtual machines running a minimal operating system. Where we need protected storage and communications, the supporting keys can be linked to the attestations of this minimal image. In constructing cloud applications within containers, one particularly sensitive function is the gateways that expose the application to the Internet; again, this can be built on a minimal code base.

- *Separate management components.* Defence in depth has long been a principle deployed in enterprise computing, so that a breach on the perimeter does not allow the hacker entry to all of the enterprise systems. The same principle must be applied to the infrastructure supporting cloud. Even as we minimize the trusted computing base, we can keep components separate, so that a break in, say, a network driver does not allow easy access to storage drivers or cryptographic keys.

- *Separation of policy enforcement from application space.* As we build an infrastructure using trusted virtualization, we create containers within which applications can run. We can also control the nature of the container by setting policies within the infrastructure controlling the containment. This means that the containers can be created with properties that are not under the control of those running the application software or anyone who has subverted the application. These policies can also be communicated as part of the TCG attestation measurements, thus giving others confidence that certain policies are enforced. For example, networking policies can be enforced so that messages to or from a container, or systems within a container, can only be sent to certain IP addresses.

- *Separate audit from application space.* Aside from policy enforcement being separated from the application environment, we can run audit functions outside of the normal application space. Keeping audit out of the application space means that audit records can be protected from tampering.
- *Attestation to communicate trust in the system.* As well as building more secure systems with a minimal trusted computing base, trusted virtualization allows the configuration and code base to be communicated and attested to though TCG mechanisms. Those relying on systems can therefore gain confidence that the systems are in a trustworthy state.

As we develop infrastructures [17, 27, 37] that support each of these principles, we can build up trustable containment architectures. Considering the cloud ecosystem as described in Sect. 8.3.4, it seems that the use of trusted virtualization by cloud platform providers will aid each of the service providers in producing more secure services. Trusted virtualization provides a better architectural basis for systems— rather than increasingly more complex security processes and procedures, intended to compete in an arms race—suggesting that the security objectives as expressed by our utility functions may be achievable without big cost increases. From an ecosystem perspective, if such technologies become widely adopted, this should help increase the overall level of both trust and security, so improving the overall reputation of the cloud ecosystem and encouraging the move to cloud.

From an enterprise lifecycle perspective, the use of trusted virtualization has a number of advantages. A company can get information and assurance as to the properties of the infrastructure on which its cloud services are running. This can help both in the initial risk planning to ensure that appropriate levels of security are achievable and in ensuring that both companies and service providers know that systems are being operated properly.

8.3.6 Assurance

Assurance is about providing confidence to stakeholders that the qualities of service and stewardship with which they are concerned are being managed and maintained appropriately. Cloud computing implies many stakeholders relying on many parties, so that efficient and effective assurance will be both complex and fundamental to a sustainable cloud ecosystem. There is considerable research and discussion on assurance (often driven by regulation) relating to cloud [5, 18, 19]. In this discussion, we start from some basic principles about assurance in federated environments. We discuss their implications and the associated opportunities in the context of the stewardship and trusted infrastructure research described in this chapter.

The principles of assurance are to decide what risks you are concerned about, to understand how these risks are (in theory) mitigated, and then to seek evidence that these mitigations are effective. For example, when the Sarbanes-Oxley Act forced companies to demonstrate the integrity of their financial accounts, it was clear there were risks associated with how financial processes and reports depended on IT applications and infrastructure. This led to significant scrutiny of how people are able to change and access the IT infrastructure, which in turn meant many audits on identity management controls.

Analogously, information stewardship implies reliance (and obligations) on many parties to demonstrate how they are controlling risks. Access and identity management will be a part of this, and stakeholders will need different levels and types of assurance associated with all the controls in federated identity management. To expand, multiple parties are involved in registration of people and users, provisioning of credentials, revocation of credentials, creating authorization policy, authentication (of credentials), and enforcement of authorization policy. In turn, each stakeholder will care differently about each of these steps and so will want different visibility into them. Moreover, we advocate the need for standard publicly reported metrics and data and the ability for customers occasionally to be able to demand deeper views on specific data relating to their service. The nature of public versus private information for assurance and an expanded discussion of identity assurance are given in [5].

In general, cloud providers will not be able to offer cost-effective services if they must satisfy different audit and assurance requirements for each of their customers. Therefore, from an efficiency perspective, standardized approaches to assurance will be necessary. This is the same argument for standardized sets of terms and conditions—a cloud service provider cannot scale their business if they have to accept auditors checking different aspects from each of their many customers. Moreover, we expect similar analyses of risks and their federated mitigations will be needed to develop these standards.

In addition to assurance from individual providers, each stakeholder will (perhaps implicitly) be concerned about the stewardship of the whole ecosystem. For this reason, we expect there will be a role for metrics that hint at the sustainability and resilience of the whole ecosystem. Initially, they will likely emerge as requirements from clusters of stakeholders—for example, these could be vertical industries such as healthcare and financial services but also disparate groups with common concerns and views on, say, privacy or law enforcement. It is too early to suggest what these metrics might be, but the conceptual and modelling work described here and in [9, 45, 46] are about exploring this question.

The work on trusted infrastructure also has direct links to assurance. From an efficiency perspective, it is hugely beneficial if application developers and providers exploit trusted separation in the infrastructure, as opposed to controlling and allowing sharing within the application. The former allows common assurance patterns to be established for when and how to trust infrastructure environments and should significantly reduce the number of assurance patterns that need to be considered for applications. For example, if cloud platforms routinely run separate service instances in separate and contained trusted infrastructure domains, then service consumers need only seek assurance about a standard set of concerns how the infrastructure controls and maintains its boundaries.

Assurance in most enterprise environments is still a complex mix of automated monitoring and physical audits. Since the amount of assurance activity needs to rise, there will be a need for much more reliance on automation. There are many immediate benefits from trusted infrastructure for this, including being able to trust the information, and attestation of components.

8.3.7   The Lifecycle Under Cloud

Companies are already struggling with managing IT risks and maintaining an explicit security management lifecycle. Many rely on standards such as ISO27000 [35] as a way of maintaining discipline and, in the background section, we argue that better methodologies are needed to help understand security decisions. Cloud fundamentally changes the way that companies consume IT, as they give up control and rely on others to act as good information stewards. The use of cloud also means that companies have to think of IT in terms of the services rather than the technology components. This has long been the aim of system management through standards such as ITIL, but cloud forces this change in thinking. This means we need to reassess the way in which we think about the security lifecycle.

Each individual service has its own security management lifecycle with the service provider being responsible maintaining its smooth running. It may achieve this by running its own IT systems and operating a traditional security management lifecycle or may itself be a service consumer relying on the security lifecycles that others maintain.

A service consumer will need to maintain an overview on risk and hence needs an aggregated security management lifecycle. This still maintains the risk and governance aspects that are now associated with choosing the right stewardship characteristics for a service. The assurance elements then must be seen in this light: Are the chosen stewardship characteristics being maintained and is risk therefore managed appropriately? Cloud services will not remove all IT from a company and hence the company must still maintain the appropriate policy setting and operational control for the systems that it does run (e.g. clients for end customers or datacentres for the cloud platform providers).

Having a coherent lifecycle for each individual service becomes more important as organizations' ability to react to surprises is reduced. Hence, as we think about risks and how each potential steward will manage them, we must also consider what attestations and assurance metrics are necessary. As services are spread over multiple providers, or as business processes use multiple providers, we need to ensure a consistency between the cycles of each of the constituent services. In the past, this was achieved by having one set of policies, but now we need more careful planning between the various lifecycles; otherwise there will be weak points and potential threats.

We have argued that, for a single enterprise, modelling can help in gaining a better understanding of risk and the trade-offs associated with different policy options. Here, we argue that understanding risk, and the different stewardship options, is even more critical. Consequently, model-based risk methodologies will become increasingly important: system models can be used to explain risks and how they are mitigated.

Consider the VTM (vulnerability and threat management) model discussed in Sect. 8.2. The model sets out assumptions about the threat environment as well as different controls within the enterprise. Having a model forces us to specify each mechanism coherently. Simply discussing these assumptions and controls can help in gaining common understanding between various stakeholders, but executing the model, to explore a range of system and policy design choices, allows the consequence of these assumptions controls to be explored and provides evidence as to the likely outcome of employing different mechanisms. In this way, security management moves on from a world in which experts give their opinions to one in which assumptions and abstract mechanisms are clearly specified and their interactions can be explored. Further examinations of the model can help to explore how changes or failures in different processes and technologies can lead to different security failings, so providing a basis for deciding which assurance metrics are important [14].

As the move to the cloud-based services continues, it is not just security teams, or indeed the wider risk committee, who are trying to understand the different policy options and risks. Now both the service provider and the consumer, or those higher in the service supply chain, must adopt a view on risk and be satisfied that appropriate controls are being used. System models can help communicate the risks and mitigations, so allowing customers and service providers to explore different options. In this way, models may become a vital communication point in joining up the risk elements of the lifecycle. Modelling also helps in understanding which assurance metrics are important and hence linking all the pieces of the lifecycle.

No service is an island: in looking at risk, we cannot just look at the performance of the individual pieces on which we rely. We see cloud as an ecosystem in which resource movements or failures in unconnected pieces will affect our IT provision: these factors must be included the lifecycle. As well as selecting and monitoring the cloud services we use, we must consider other factors that may affect their function and, in looking at the security management lifecycle, we need to understand which ecosystem changes may cause changes in the risk profile. These changes may represent changes to exogenous variables within a system model of a particular service. As we reassess the way the lifecycle works, we must also consider the individual pieces of the lifecycle. In particular, we need to ensure that there are appropriate ways of thinking about the risks of handing over data and what architectural and assurance controls will help mitigate these risks. Pre-cloud, our research agenda needed to be based around improving risk decision-making methodologies, better infrastructure, and assurance. As cloud emerges, these needs do not disappear, but methodologies must take account of this breakup of the lifecycle and be informed by the need for good information stewardship.

8.4   Future Research Directions

The work described here is a rich mix of:

- Empirical work with stakeholders and professional experts to understand the real dynamics and problems faced by risk and security teams.
- Conceptual work with computer scientists, economists, logicians, mathematicians, and psychologists to develop rigorous and clear analyses and approaches.
- Design and engineering by technologists to develop alternative architectures to suit different lifecycles of security management.

Cloud and enterprise computing are continually changing and producing security challenges, and so we see the need to continue and integrate each of these activities. To that end, we will continue to use the partnerships in the TSB-funded Cloud Stewardship Economics and Trust Domains projects to help us to do this.

Thus far the Cloud Stewardship Economics project has involved both empirical and conceptual work. We have done workshops, surveys, and structured interviews with various stakeholders [22], built a series of economic models [33, 34, 55], and iteratively developed a conceptual framework for analysing information steward-ship [9]. These will all continue, but in addition, we will begin to engage stakehold-ers in using the models to make better decisions. Our vision is to use models to enable structured war-gaming and scenario planning between stakeholders. This involves even tighter integration between the economists, security researchers, cloud/enterprise IT experts, and security professionals.

The Trust Domains [54] project is less mature but has a larger ambition to inte-grate and affect architecture and technology. The focus is less about governance and policy and more about achieving operational assurance when multiple stakeholders must share infrastructure. These can be dynamic situations—such as a cross-border civil emergency, where multiple non-trusting groups with infrastructure and appli-cations must suddenly share information and resources—or pre-planned situations, such as long-term (controlled) sharing of resources and information between non-trusting groups. What expectations do such stakeholders have, how explicitly can they describe sharing policy and requirements, and how would they be assured that their information and concerns are suitably managed?

The main focus at the moment is on empirical studies (structured interviews) with a range of potential stakeholders (typically enterprises). From these, we are developing and refining our view on expectations for how information should be managed and how assurance should be provided in shared environments. This in turn will drive both requirements for trusted infrastructure to realize trust domains (containers with relevant properties) and how to use models to more rigorously describe and communicate requirements and real-time operations.

Both these projects directly address the transformed lifecycle of enterprise risk and security management. Clearly, they will not solve all the problems. For exam-ple, even if we design strong and appropriate trust domains and robust information stewardship strategies, there may well be many regulation and commercial drivers that strongly influence risk and security outcomes. Moreover, the nature of technology generally, and cloud specifically, is that they will bring many unforeseen changes. Nevertheless, by working closely with industry and customers, we expect to influence positively the context for cloud associated risk management.

8.5   Conclusions

The development of cloud computing may lead to significant changes in the way companies consume IT, moving from them managing large technology stacks to purchasing business-level services. As this happens, companies will lose control of the way in which their services are run, needing instead to choose between the terms and conditions offered by different service providers. This switch in control may increase the difficulties faced by companies responding to specific security events or failures. This observation emphasizes the need to have a better understanding of risk and how it is mitigated. To achieve this, we need better methodologies, based on rigorous conceptual and mathematical modelling of systems, of human behaviour, and of the wider environment.

As users employ cloud services, they rely on others not only to provide those services, but also to protect their information and appropriately control its interactions and evolution. To understand how this should work, we must widen our view of the declarative goals of information security from confidentiality, integrity, and availability (CIA) to include ideas of duty of service (to ensure that the desired objectives are addressed) and respect for values and ethics. Moreover, the sustainability and resilience of the ecosystem itself must be managed. We describe this broader concept as information stewardship.

This shift of perspective from security to stewardship implies a change in how security (now stewardship) is managed and, we contend, this will be best approached by considering the security management lifecycle, as already operated by many companies. Each IT service will have its own security management lifecycle, possibly dependent on the security management lifecycles of other services and platforms further down the service supply chain. We contend that these interdependent security management lifecycles must be viewed from the perspective of information stewardship. As the flexibility of management is reduced, so we can expect greater coherence between the different elements—such as risk analysis, policy-making, operations, and assurance—of the lifecycle. We must also draw together the various service lifecycles to give consistent pictures of risk, policy-making, operations, and assurance. We see mathematical modelling as playing a huge role in delivering the methodologies that must be developed to achieve all this in the form of practical tools.

Lastly, we consider the stewardship of the ecosystem itself. In the cloud, IT operations will be purchased from highly connected ecosystems of services, consumers, and platform providers. Changes in one part of the ecosystem can affect many other parts in complex ways that will, typically, be difficult to conceptualize.

We contend that modelling, of the kind we have sketched in this chapter, can help decision-makers to understand these complex relationships and dependencies. From the perspective of managing the security lifecycle, managers must use this information to understand how different events in different components of the ecosystem may affect the systems for which they are responsible. From the wider perspective of the stewardship of the ecosystem itself, we must ensure that the ecosystem is managed to be sustainable and resilient. These features of the ecosystem are public goods, and we contend that there is a clear role for regulators in their stewardship.

Acknowledgments This chapter draws on the work of and conversations with all of the security research team in HP Labs. Specifically, we thank Boris Balacheff and Chris Dalton for their advice about all areas relating to trusted infrastructure, Yolanta Beres and Jonathan Griffin for their work on process modelling of vulnerability management, Chew Yean Yam and Christos Ioannidis (University of Bath) for work on the switching (real options) model, Matthew Collinson (University of Aberdeen) and Brian Monahan for work on foundations and process modelling across all the projects, Marco Casassa Mont for work on identity assurance, and Martin Sadler for overall vision. We would also like to thank and acknowledge all our partners in the Cloud Stewardship Economics and Trust Domains projects and the UK Technology Strategy Board for its funding of these projects.

References

1. Acquisti, A., Anderson, R., Schneier, B.: 4th Security and Human Behavior Workshop, Carnegie Mellon University. http://www.heinz.cmu.edu/~acquisti/SHB/ (2011). Accessed 1 Jan 2012
2. Anderson, R.: Why information security is hard: an economic perspective. In: Proceedings of the 17th Annual Computer Security Applications Conference (ACSAC), pp. 358–365. IEEE Computer Society Press (2001)
3. Armour, F.J., Kaisler, S.H., Liu, S.I.: Building an enterprise architecture step by step. IT Prof. **1**(4), 31–39 (1999). doi:10.1109/6294.781623
4. Baldwin, A., Beres, Y., Shiu, S.: Using assurance models to aid the risk and governance life cycle. BT Technol. J. **25**, 128–140 (2007). doi:10.1007/s10550-007-0015-7
5. Baldwin, A., Beres, Y., Shiu, S.: Using assurance models in IT audit engagements, HP Labs Technical Report HPL-2006–148 (2006)
6. Baldwin, A., Dalton, C.I., Shiu, S., Kostienk, K., Rajpoot, Q.: Providing secure services for a virtual infrastructure. SIGOPS Oper. Syst. Rev. **43**(1), 44–51 (2009). doi:10.1145/1496909.1496919
7. Baldwin, A., Mont, M.C., Beres, Y., Shiu, S.: Assurance for federated identity management. J. Comput. Secur. **18**(4), 541–572 (2010)
8. Baldwin, A., Mont, M.C., Shiu, S.: Using modelling and simulation for policy decision support in identity management. Policy **2009**, 17–24 (2009)
9. Baldwin, A., Pym, D., Sadler M., Shiu, S.: Information stewardship in cloud ecosystems: towards models, economics and delivery. In: Cloud Computing Technology and Science (CloudCom), 2011 IEEE Third International Conference on, Athens (2011)
10. Barham, P., Dragovic, B., Fraser, K., Hand, S., Harris, T., Ho, A., Neugebauer, R., Pratt, I., Warfield, A.: Xen and the art of virtualization. In: Proceedings of the Nineteenth ACM Symposium on Operating Systems Principles, Bolton Landing, NY, 19–22 Oct 2003. doi:10.1145/945445.945462

11. Beautement, A., Coles, R., Griffin, J., Ioannidis, C., Monahan, B., Pym, D., Sasse A., Wonham, M.,: Modelling the Human and Technological Costs and Benefits of USB Memory Stick Security, in Managing Information Risk and the Economics of Security, Springer, New York (2009)

12. Beautement, A., Pym, D.: Structured systems economics for security management. In: Proceedings of the WEIS 2010, Harvard University. http://weis2010.econinfosec.org/papers/session6/weis2010_beautement.pdf (2010)

13. Beres, Y., Griffin, J., Shiu, S., Heitman, M., Markle, D., Ventura, P.: Analysing the performance of security solutions to reduce vulnerability exposure windows. In: Proceedings of the Annual Computer Security Applications Conference (ACSAC), pp. 33–42. IEEE, Anaheim (2008)

14. Beres, Y., Mont, M.C., Griffin, J., Shiu, S.: Using security metrics coupled with predictive modeling and simulation to assess security processes. Empir. Softw. Eng. Meas. **2009**, 564–573 (2009)

15. Beres, Y., Pym, D., Shiu, S.: Decision support for systems security investment. In: Proceedings of the Business-driven IT Management (BDIM), IEEE Xplore (2010)

16. Berger, S., Cáceres, R., Goldman, K.A., Perez, R., Sailer, R., van Doorn, L.: vTPM: virtualizing the trusted platform module. In: Proceedings of the 15th Conference on USENIX Security Symposium, Vancouver, 31 July–4 Aug 2006

17. Cabuk, S., Dalton, C.I., Eriksson, K., Kuhlmann, D., Ramasamy, H.V., Ramunno, G., Sadeghi, A., Schunter, M., Stüble, C.: Towards automated security policy enforcement in multi-tenant virtual data centers. J. Comput. Secur. **18**(1), 89–121 (2010)

18. CAMM (Common Assurance Maturity Model Guiding Principles): http://common-assurance.com/resources/Common-Assurance-Maturity-Model-vision.pdf (2010)

19. Catteddu, D., Hogben, G.: Cloud computing information assurance framework, ENISA Report. http://www.enisa.europa.eu/act/rm/files/deliverables/cloud-computing-information-assurance-framework/ (2009). Accessed 1 Jan 2012

20. Chapin III, F.S., Kofinas, G.P., Folke, C. (eds.): Principles of Ecosystem Stewardship: Resilience-Based Natural Resource Management in a Changing World. Springer, New York (2009)

21. Chen, Y., Bharadwaj, A.: An empirical analysis of contract structures in IT outsourcing. Info. Syst. Res. **20**, 484–506 (2009)

22. Cloud Stewardship Economics: http://www.hpl.hp.com/bristol/cloud_stewardship.htm (2012)

23. Collinson, M., Monahan, B., Pym, D.: A logical and computational theory of located resource. J. Log. Comput. **19**(6), 1207–1244 (2009). doi:10.1093/logcom/exp021

24. Collinson, M., Monahan, B., Pym, D.: A discipline of mathematical systems modelling. Forthcoming monograph. College Publications (2012)

25. Collinson, M., Monahan, B., Pym, D.: Semantics for structured systems modelling and simulation. In: Proceedings of the Simutools 2010, ACM Digital Library and EU Digital Library. ISBN: 978–963–9799–87–5 (2010)

26. Core Gnosis: http://www.hpl.hp.com/research/systems_security/gnosis.html (2012). Accessed 1 Jan 2012

27. Dalton, C., Plaquin, D., Weidner, W., Kuhlmann, D., Balacheff, B., Brown, R.: Trusted virtual platforms: a key enabler for converged client devices. SIGOPS Oper. Syst. Rev. **43**(1), 36–43 (2009). doi:10.1145/1496909.1496918

28. Degabriele, J.P., Pym, D.: Economic aspects or a utility computing service HP Labs technical report, HPL-2007–101 (2007)

29. Eskins, D., Sanders, W.H.: The multiple-asymmetric-utility system model: a framework for modeling cyber-human systems. In: Proceedings of the 8th International Conference on Quantitative Evaluation of Systems (QEST), Aachen (2011)

30. Goldsack, P., Guijarro, J., Loughran, S., Coles, A., Farrell, A., Lain, A., Murray, P., Toft, P.: The SmartFrog configuration management framework. SIGOPS Oper. Syst. Rev. **43**(1), 16–25 (2009). doi:10.1145/1496909.1496915

31. Gordon, L.A., Loeb, M.P.: Managing Cybersecurity Resources: A Cost-Benefit Analysis. McGraw Hill, New York (2006)
32. Ioannidis, C., Pym, D., Williams, J.: Information security trade-offs and optimal patching policies. Eur. J. Oper. Res. **216**(2), 434–444 (2012). doi:10.1016/j.ejor.2011.05.050
33. Ioannidis, C., Pym, D., Williams, J.: Fixed costs, investment rigidities, and risk aversion in information security: a utility-theoretic approach. In: Schneier, B. (ed.) Proceedings of the Workshop on Economics of Information Security (WEIS 2011). Springer (in press)
34. Ioannidis, C., Pym, D., Williams, J.: Investments and trade-offs in the economics of information security. In: Dingledine, R. and Golle, P., eds. *Financial Cryptography and Data Security: Proceedings of the 13th International Conference on Financial Cryptography and Data Security.* Berlin, Heidelberg: Springer, pp. 148–166 (2009)
35. ISO.: ISO 27000 Series of Standards (Supersedes ISO 17799). http://www.27000.org (2007). Accessed 1 Jan 2012
36. ITGI: Control Objectives for Information and Related Technologies (COBIT), 4th edn (2005)
37. Kallahalla, M., Uysal, M., Swaminathan, R., Lowell, D.E., Wray, M., Christian, T., Edwards, N., Dalton, C.I., Gittler, F.: SoftUDC: a software-based data center for utility computing. Computer **37**(11), 38–46 (2004). doi:10.1109/MC.2004.221
38. Keeney, R.L., Raiffa, H.: Decisions with Multiple Objectives: Preferences and Value Tradeoffs. Wiley, New York [Reprinted, Cambridge University Press, New York (1993)] (1976)
39. Khwaja, T.: Should I stay or should I go? Migration under uncertainty: a real option approach, Public Policy Discussion Papers 002–10. Economics and Finance Section, School of Social Sciences, Brunel University (2002)
40. Krebs, B.: Epsilon breach raises specter of spear phishing. http://krebsonsecurity.com/2011/04/epsilon-breach-raises-specter-of-spear-phishing/ (2011). Accessed 1 Jan 2012
41. Lloyd, V.: Planning to implement service management (IT Infrastructure Library). The Stationery Office Books. http://www.itil.co.uk/publications.htm (2011). Accessed 1 Jan 2012
42. Mell, P., Grance, T.: The NIST Definition of Cloud Computing (Draft). Technical report, National Institute of Standards and Technology, US Department of Commerce, 2011. Special Publication 800–145 (Draft) (2011)
43. Open Trusted Computing: http://www.opentc.net/ (2012). Accessed 1 Jan 2012
44. Pearson, S., Balacheff, B., Chen, L., Plaquin, D., Proudler, G.: Trusted Computing Platforms: TCPA in Context. HP Books, Prentice Hall (2003)
45. Pym, D., Sadler, M.: Information Stewardship in cloud computing. Int. J. Serv. Manage. Eng. Technol. **1**(1), 50–67 (2010)
46. Pym, D., Sadler, M., Shiu, S., Mont, M.C.: Information stewardship in the cloud: a model-based approach. In: Proceedings of the CloudComp 2010. Lecture Notes of the Institute for Computer Sciences, Social Informatics and Telecommunications Engineering (LNICST). Springer (To appear, 2010)
47. Pym, D., Shiu, S., Coles, R., van Moorsel, A., Sasse, M.A., Johnson, H.: Trust economics: a systematic approach to information security decision making. Final Report for the UK Technology Strategy Board 'Trust Economics' project. http://www.hpl.hp.com/news/2011/oct-dec/Final_Report_collated.pdf (2011). Accessed 1 Jan 2012
48. Shiu, S., Baldwin A., Beres, Y., Casassa Mont, M, Duggan, G., Johnson, H., Middup, C.: Economic methods and decision making by security professionals. Schneier, B. (ed.) Proceedings of the Workshop on Economics of Information Security (WEIS 2011). Springer (in press)
49. Spewak, S.H., Hill, S.C.: Enterprise Architecture Planning: Developing a Blueprint for Data, Applications and Technology. QED Information Sciences, Inc., Wellesley (1993)
50. Squicciarini, A.C., Rajasekaran, S.D., Mont, M.C.: Using modeling and simulation to evaluate enterprises' risk exposure to social networks. IEEE Comput. **44**(1), 66–73 (2011)
51. Stoneburner, G., Goguen, A., Feringa, A.: Risk Management Guide for Information Technology Systems Technical Report, National Institute of Standards and Technology, U.S. Department of Commerce, NIST Special Publication 800–30. http://csrc.nist.gov/publications/nistpubs/800–30/sp800–30.pdf (2002)

52. The Trusted Computing Group: http://www.trustedcomputinggroup.org/. Accessed 1 Jan 2012
53. Trigeorgis, L.: Real options: an overview. In: Schwartz, E.S., Trigeorgis, L. (eds.) Real Options and Investment Under Uncertainty: Classical Readings and Recent Contribution. MIT Press, Cambridge (2001)
54. US Congress. S. 3742: Data Security and Breach Notification Act of 2010. http://www.govtrack.us/congress/bill.xpd?bill=s111–3742 Accessed 1 Jan 2012
55. Yam, C-Y., Baldwin, A., Ioannidis, C., Shiu, S.: Migration to Cloud as Real Option: Investment decision under uncertainty. In: Proceedings of the Trust, Security and Privacy in Computing and Communications (TrustCom), IEEE (2011)

Glossary

A6 A project that provides an interface and namespace for automated audit, assertion, assessment, and assurance of cloud infrastructures.

Communications data Data generated by the use of a communication technology, whether for voice or data communications.

Community cloud A cloud infrastructure shared by several organisations with shared concerns.

Confidentiality The property whereby information is not made available or disclosed to unauthorised individuals, entities, or processes.

Cloud Familiar term that refers to cloud computing.

Cloud bursting A technique used by hybrid clouds to provide additional resources to private clouds on an as-needed basis. If the private cloud has the processing power to handle its workloads, the hybrid cloud is not used. When workloads exceed the private cloud's capacity, the hybrid cloud automatically allocates additional resources to the private cloud.

Cloud computing A commonly accepted definition is provided by NIST: "Cloud computing is a model for enabling ubiquitous, convenient, on-demand network access to a shared pool of configurable computing resources (e.g. networks, servers, storage, applications, and services) that can be rapidly provisioned and released with minimal management effort or service provider interaction." The cloud model promotes availability and is composed of five essential characteristics (on-demand self-service, broad network access, resource pooling, rapid elasticity, measured service), three service models (Infrastructure as a Service (IaaS), Platform as a Service (PaaS), and Software as a Service (SaaS)), and four deployment models.

Cloud Security Alliance (CSA) A non-profit organisation that promotes research into best practices for securing cloud computing.

Cloud Service Provider (CSP) A provider of cloud services.

Composable Services Architecture (CSA) This provides an architectural framework for creating and managing composable services that can be created on demand and using general virtualisation techniques.

S. Pearson and G. Yee (eds.), *Privacy and Security for Cloud Computing*,
Computer Communications and Networks, DOI 10.1007/978-1-4471-4189-1,
© Springer-Verlag London 2013

Data controller An entity which alone, jointly, or in common with others determines the purposes for which and the manner in which any item of personal information is processed.

Data processor An entity which processes personal information on behalf and upon instructions of the data controller.

Data protection A legal regime that governs the processing of personal data, i.e. personal information or data that identifies an individual data subject either directly or indirectly.

Data subject An identified or identifiable individual to whom personal information relates, whether such identification is direct or indirect.

Direct Anonymous Attestation (DAA) A cryptographic protocol that allows a user to convince a verifier in a privacy-friendly way that he or she uses a trusted platform (i.e. one that has embedded within it a certified hardware module: the Trusted Platform Module or TPM).

Dynamic Access Control Infrastructure (DACI) This is created as a part of the general infrastructure created on demand and allows dynamic configuration and reconfiguration during operation. DACI includes necessary security services and mechanism to support security context management during the whole dynamically provisioned security services. Special DACI mechanisms such as bootstrapping allow binding of the virtualised security infrastructure and virtualisation platform.

Dynamic Security Association (DSA) These are created during the provisioning of the virtual infrastructure as a part of the DACI creation.

Emulation The act of using hardware and/or software to duplicate the functions of a first computer system in a different second computer system, so that the behaviour of the second system closely resembles the behaviour of the first system.

Enterprise Service Bus (ESB) An industry adopted software architecture model and platform for designing and implementing the SOA-based services, applications, and infrastructures. ESB is primarily a Web Services-based platform using SOAP messaging, but recently ESB includes also support of the REST protocol.

Evidence Material placed before a tribunal of fact, either a judge or jury, to support or counter an assertion.

Forensics The gathering of material as potential evidence in legal proceedings.

GEANT Multidomain Bus (GEMBus) The ESB-based middleware platform for composable services that allows creation and management of the multidomain composable services. Initially, GEMBus has been developed by the GEANT3 project to support the Composable Services Architecture (CSA).

Hybrid cloud A composition of two or more clouds that remain separate but between which there can be data and application portability. Under this model, users typically outsource non-business critical information and processing to the public cloud while keeping business critical services and data within their control.

Infrastructure as a Service (IaaS) The delivery of computing resources as a service, including virtual machines and other abstracted hardware and operating systems; a model where a virtual IT infrastructure is rented by a user from a provider as a service.

Infrastructure service A generic IT infrastructure definition includes the total set of foundation components and non-functional attributes that enable applications to function and are shared by many applications. Foundation infrastructure components include servers, datacentres, network, peripheral devices, OS, virtualisation platforms, and end user devices. The cloud infrastructure may be multi-layer, including internal cloud provider infrastructure whose virtualised instances are provided as services, and also external or inter-cloud infrastructure that can be provided by either cloud operators/brokers or network services providers.

Infrastructure Services Modelling Framework (ISMF) This provides a basis for virtualisation and management of infrastructure resources, including description, discovery, modelling, composition, and monitoring.

Integrity Trustworthiness of data or resources, usually phrased in terms of preventing improper or unauthorised change.

Integrity modelling The process of specifying the expected properties of a system in order to detect improper change.

Interception The recording or monitoring of the content of a communication in the course of its transmission.

Invariant dependency graph A graph that concisely represents the dependency relationships among scoped invariants.

Invariants detection The process of deriving scoped invariant specifications from a programme.

ISO 27001 An information security management system standard published by the International Organisation for Standardisation (ISO) and the International Electrotechnical Commission (IEC).

Information Technology Infrastructure Library (ITIL) A set of practices for IT service management (ITSM), for example a set of policies concerned with information security management as defined by ISO/IEC 27001 standards.

Jurisdiction The authority of a body to act in a certain manner; the applicability of a law to certain persons, or the boundaries of a regulated field.

Law enforcement agency Any public body given statutory powers to investigate and prosecute criminal conduct.

Multi-tenancy An architecture in which a single instance of an application serves multiple customers who have the ability to change some parts such as the interface, but not the code.

Mutual legal assistance Bilateral or multilateral agreements between nation states under which a requesting state may request the formal assistance of the requested state for the provision of evidence, generally involving judicial processes.

Partner cloud Cloud services offered by a provider to a limited and well-defined number of parties.

Personally identifiable information (PII) Any information that could be used to identify or locate an individual (e.g. name, address) or information that can be correlated with other information to identify an individual (e.g. credit card number, postal code, Internet Protocol (IP) address).

Personal information or data Facts, communications,, or opinions which relate to the individual and which it would be reasonable to expect him or her to regard as intimate or sensitive and therefore want to restrict their collection, use, or sharing; alternatively data that identifies an individual data subject either directly or indirectly.

Platform as a Service (PaaS) The delivery of a solution stack for software development including a runtime environment and lifecycle management software, thereby allowing customers to develop new applications using APIs deployed and configurable remotely.

Privacy The fundamental right of an individual to have control over the processing of his or her personal information as well as to protect his or her intimate sphere.

Privacy impact assessment A process that helps organisations to anticipate and address the likely privacy impacts of new initiatives, foresee problems, and negotiate solutions to ensure data protection compliance.

Private cloud A cloud infrastructure operated solely for an organisation, being accessible only within a private network and being managed by the organisation or a third party (potentially even off-premise).

Processing Any operation or set of operations performed upon personal data, which includes obtaining and recording data; retrieval, consultation, or use of data; and the disclosure of data or making it available via other means.

Public cloud A publicly accessible cloud infrastructure.

Rapid elasticity The ability to scale resources both up and down as needed. To the consumer, the cloud appears to be infinite, and the consumer can purchase as much or as little computing power as they need.

Remote attestation A trusted computing technique that enables a computer system in a networked environment to decide whether a target computer has integrity, e.g. whether it has the appropriate configuration and hardware/software stack, so it can be trusted.

Risk control Mechanism deployed to mitigate a risk to an acceptable level.

Scoped invariant The property that a certain object has a known good value between two system events.

Secure Token Service (STS) A mechanism that conveys security context information between services that may reside in different security and administrative domains. STS can issue and validate security tokens, support service identity federation, and federated identity delegation.

Security Protection of information, especially via preservation of confidentiality, integrity, and availability.

Security Audit as a Service (SAaaS) An infrastructure to support IT security audits of cloud computing infrastructures.

Sensitive data Data related to an individual that is granted some measure of special treatment. Examples include information on religion or race, health, sexual orientation, and union membership.

Service Delivery Framework (SDF) This defines the services provisioning stages, which define the services lifecycle and may be organised as a service provisioning workflow, and supporting infrastructure components that typically include services lifecycle management system.

Service/resource lifecycle In the context of resources and services virtualisation, the services or resources lifecycle includes a number of the following stages: request, creation/composition, deployment, operation, and decommissioning, generally defined by a lifecycle management model. A virtualised or provisioned on-demand resources or services lifecycle is typically managed by a special lifecycle management system.

Software as a Service (SaaS) The delivery of applications as a service, available on demand and paid for on a per-use basis; a model of software deployment where users rent an application from a provider and use it as a service.

Static Security Association (SSA) These exist between physical infrastructure components or are established before starting virtual infrastructure provisioning; in particular, SSA can be established based on the signed SLA for virtual infrastructure creation.

Trusted computing Technologies and proposals for resolving computer security problems through hardware enhancements (such as Trusted Platform Modules) and associated software modifications.

Trusted Computing Group (TCG) Architecture A set of standards created by the industry Trusted Computing Group. The TCG Architecture defines abstract models, protocols, and functional components that allow the creation of trusted computing environments bound either to providers or user security domains.

Trusted Platform Module (TPM) A key hardware component of the TCG Architecture that supports hardware-based cryptographic functions and is used for hardware authentication.

Ubiquitous network access A scenario where a cloud provider's capabilities are available over the network and can be accessed through standard mechanisms via both thick and thin clients.

Virtual infrastructure Virtual infrastructure is created based on physical infrastructure, individual computer/IT components, and network infrastructure using special virtualisation software that allows creation of virtualised instances of the physical resources that may be a combination or partition of the latter. Physical resources can run multiple instances of the virtual resources, and it is the function of the virtualisation software to provide virtual resource isolation and load balancing.

Virtualisation This refers to the abstraction of compute resources (i.e. central processing unit (CPU), storage, network, memory, application stack, and databases) from applications and end users consuming the service. The abstraction of infrastructure yields the notion of resource democratisation (whether infrastructure, applications, or information) and provides the capability for pooled resources to be made available and accessible to anyone or anything authorised to utilise them via standardised methods.

Index

A

AAI. *See* Authentication and authorisation
    infrastructure (AAI)
Abuse, 22
Abuse and nefarious use, cloud resources, 132
Access, 23–24
    control, 246–247
    tokens, 191
Accountability, 11, 34, 117, 248–249
Accountancy, 272
Accredited components, 252
Acid clouds, 239
Adequate protection, 18
Amplified cloud security problems
    (amplified CSP), 129
Anomaly detection, 160
Anonymization, 34
Application
    development, 241–242
    security audit, 140
    tenancy, 88
    virtualization, 279
Architecture, 260–263
Article 29 Working Party, 63
AS. *See* Authorisation service (AS)
Asset management, 253
Assurance, 26–28, 259, 282
Attack surface, 238
Attestation, 281
Audits, 28–29, 125, 258
    analysis, 142
    as-a-Service, 142
    from the cloud, 145
    report, 146
    system, 135
    types, 137–140

Authentication, 245–246
Authentication and authorisation infrastructure
    (AAI), 186
Authorisation service (AS), 195, 202
Authorisation token (AuthzToken), 191
AuthzToken. *See* Authorisation token
    (AuthzToken)
'Autonomic' technologies, 7, 8
Availability, 128

B

Backup, 25
Barriers to cloud, 32
Beginning of development, 112
Best fit, 105
Better cloud monitoring and audit, 158–159
Better overview, 148
Botnet incident, 127
Brand image, 13
Business process flows, 151
Business services ecosystem, 258

C

Changing infrastructure, 150
CIA. *See* Confidentiality, integrity,
    and availability (CIA)
Cloud, 4, 127
    audits, 136–150
    characteristics, 151
    computing, 4, 74, 126, 258
    computing and services, 237
    computing contracts, 129
    controls matrix, 143
    ecosystem, 5, 274–278

S. Pearson and G. Yee (eds.), *Privacy and Security for Cloud Computing*,
Computer Communications and Networks, DOI 10.1007/978-1-4471-4189-1,
© Springer-Verlag London 2013